SCANDINAVIA IN
THE FIRST WORLD WAR

Scandinavia in the First World War

Studies in the War Experience
of the Northern Neutrals

Edited by
Claes Ahlund

NORDIC ACADEMIC PRESS

Nordic Academic Press
P.O. Box 1206
S-221 05 Lund
Sweden
www.nordicacademicpress.com

© Nordic Academic Press and the Authors 2012
Typesetting: Karin Österlund
Jacket design: Maria Jörgel Andersson
Jacket illustration: Caricature in the Danish magazine
Hver 8. Dag, 20 November 1916
Printed by ScandBook, Falun 2012
ISBN 978-91-87121-57-9

Contents

Preface

This book is about the impact of the First World War on the neutral Scandinavian countries, Denmark, Norway, and Sweden. It offers a series of original analyses in a research field that is well established internationally, but seriously underdeveloped in Scandinavian historiography.

The introduction offers a systematic, comparative view of the history of the Scandinavian countries during the war, along with the general background for the more detailed case studies. The subsequent chapters represent a number of different approaches in history, media studies, and literary studies. Some of them explore how intellectuals tackled the issues raised by the war, or aspects of the military and economic consequences of the war, and a third group deal with the immediate war experience of Scandinavian nurses, seamen, and soldiers—volunteers in the Australian Imperial Force as well as Schleswig Danes mobilized in the German armed forces.

Scandinavia in the First World War is the first major result so far of the international and interdisciplinary 'Network for the study of neutral Scandinavia in the First World War', which I initiated in 2009 and have since then coordinated. Three network seminars have been arranged: in Uppsala in 2009, in Lund in 2010, and in Uppsala again in 2011, the results of which can be studied in the present volume. Financially, the network has benefited from the generous support of Riksbankens Jubileumsfond and a most welcome publication grant from Sven och Dagmar Saléns stiftelse.

Finally, I would like to express my gratitude to Svante Nordin, Karen Gram-Skjoldager, Michael Jonas, and Louise Nilsson, all of whom are members of the network but for various reasons are not among the authors of this book, and who have formulated highly valuable ideas and suggestions in the discussions of the work in progress during the network seminars.

Claes Ahlund

Scandinavia in the First World War

Rolf Hobson, Tom Kristiansen,
Nils Arne Sørensen & Gunnar Åselius

In December 1914, the kings of Denmark, Norway, and Sweden met in the city of Malmö on the south coast of Sweden to demonstrate Scandinavian unity and a common determination to remain neutral in the ongoing war. At that point, the fighting had not taken a decisive turn on the battlefield. In an indirect strategy, an adjunct to the conventional fighting, the belligerents embarked on trade war and blockade to besiege their enemies' economy and society at large. This profoundly changed the character of the war. It also subjected the Scandinavian countries to relentless pressure.

When the war ended four years later, all three countries had indeed succeeded in staying out of the conflict. From that perspective, the 'Meeting of the Three Kings in Malmö' in 1914 and the follow-up meeting in the Norwegian capital Kristiania (present-day Oslo) in November 1917 would appear to have been important events. They were certainly perceived as such by contemporaries. In 1914, the Swedish weekly *Hvar 8 dag* commented on the Malmö meeting that at a time when the great European races—Slavs, Romans, and Teutons of Germanic and Anglo-Saxon descent—had engaged in a fierce struggle to protect their interests, the fact that some eleven million 'Northern Teutons' had formed a mighty block of their own must be attributed some importance.[1]

However, the interests of the three Scandinavian countries were not as uniform, nor was their unity as strong, as their governments wanted the world to believe. Throughout the war, this lack of common interest was carefully concealed. The kings' meeting was in lieu of a closer military and diplomatic cooperation that would have undermined the neutrality of each Scandinavian country. The main objective for all the governments was to remain non-belligerent at almost any cost. This necessitated a policy of response and adjustment that time and again placed them in an awkward legal position, and on occasion left them neutral by the skin of their teeth.

Scandinavia 1914

The importance of the northern periphery

From the sixteenth century onwards, Scandinavia and the Baltic Sea area had played an important role in Europe as a source of strategic raw materials for the navies of the Western powers. With the coming of steam ships in the nineteenth century, the region gradually lost this role. Moreover, the Napoleonic Wars reduced Denmark and Sweden to minor European powers. Denmark's military defeat by the German states in 1864, compounded by the inability of Sweden–Norway to come to Denmark's assistance, further confirmed that image. In the period after 1871, this was generally acknowledged, and the great powers demonstrated a common interest in preserving Scandinavia as a low-tension region in Europe.

In 1905, when Sweden and Norway broke up from the loose political union that had united them since the Napoleonic Wars, Britain, Germany, and Russia resolutely intervened to secure a peaceful divorce. Afterwards, they took great pains to integrate independent Norway and its two Scandinavian neighbours into the European security system, first by negotiating the so-called Integrity Treaty with Norway in 1907, and then by laboriously negotiating the Baltic and North Sea treaties of 1908, in which all the great powers recognized the territorial status quo around the Baltic and the North Sea together with the bordering states.[2] Norway was not invited to take part in the negotiations for the status quo treaties even though it was clearly a North Sea state.[3]

With a total population of around eleven million, the Scandinavian countries had few demographic resources to offer from a strategic perspective. The economic resources of the region were, nonetheless, substantial. All three countries were open economies, highly dependent on foreign trade. For all three the main trading partners were Britain and Germany, a fact that was to test Scandinavian diplomacy to the utmost during the war. Scandinavian exports were dominated by (processed) raw materials: meat and dairy products, fish, forestry products, and iron and other minerals. By 1914, the Scandinavian economy was still dominated by agriculture, but industrialization was in full swing, and some industries—such as Swedish engineering and the Norwegian chemical industries based on the tamed energy of the mountain rivers—were to a high degree export-oriented.

From an international perspective, another key Scandinavian resource was its merchant navies. Norway could boast the fourth largest in the world, but the Danish and Swedish merchant navies were also impressive. The Scandinavian merchant marines to a large extent served the trade regime that encompassed the British Empire. The political implications of this were especially profound in Norway due to the pivotal role played by the merchant navy in the Norwegian economy. The overall objective for the belligerents once they had embarked on the trade war was to gain control over Scandinavian economic assets, or deny the enemy free access to their export and shipping industry. In course of the war Denmark would lose some 249 ships (253,622 tonnes), Sweden 260 (272,577 tonnes), and Norway 831 (1,535,275 tonnes).

Although Sweden had been linked to the German commercial treaty system through bilateral agreements in 1906 and 1911, for Sweden Germany's main economic importance was as an exporter to Sweden, whereas Britain was the dominant importer of Swedish products, and France stood for investment capital. Against this background, Swedish neutrality was difficult to avoid in 1914. Although there were strong pro-German sympathies among the Swedish royal family and in government, Knut Agathon Wallenberg, head of the country's leading financial family, had been appointed foreign minister. This ensured that trade interests would always weigh heavily in Swedish diplomacy. Likewise, Norway and Denmark were dependent on trade with both Britain and Germany and were consequently subject to unrelenting pressure from both. While the Germans grudgingly accepted that Denmark would continue its large agricultural exports to Britain after the outbreak of war, it took all the diplomatic skills of the Danish foreign minister, Eric Scavenius, to convince the British to allow imports to Denmark notwithstanding the naval blockade. Norway faced a similar situation. However, the merchant marine made it far more vulnerable to the Entente Powers' coercive measures than either Denmark or Sweden, since it to a large extent served the British. Moreover, the British controlled the sea lanes in the North Sea along with the supply of fuel, which both the Norwegian merchant and fishing fleets were totally dependent on.

Even if the great-power diplomats were interested in status quo and détente in Scandinavia in the years preceding the war, the military elites viewed the region somewhat differently. The reason was, of course, Scandinavia's geographical position, with Denmark and Sweden controlling the Baltic approaches and Norway flanking the debouches to the North Atlantic. According to international law on neutrality, the Scandinavian countries were under an obligation to muster naval and military forces to survey and intercept in cases of infringement. In the event of war, the Royal Navy planned to enter the Baltic Sea to support their Russian allies, either by attacking German naval bases or by landing troops on the coast of Pomerania. Regardless of the fact that the increased size of battleships and the evolution of weapons such as mines and torpedoes had made the thought of sending a British fleet into the Baltic risky, such offensive plans gained increased weight when Winston Churchill became First Lord of the Admiralty in 1911. Both in London and Berlin, naval planners therefore had to include scenarios for war in Scandinavia in their preparations. To operate in the Baltic Sea, the British would benefit from bases in Norway, Denmark, or even the south-west coast of Sweden, while the Germans in order to prevent them would need to control these areas before the British arrived. In addition, Russian military planners had to take into account the strong pro-German and Russophobic tendencies among Sweden's elites and prepare for the possibility of it entering the war on Germany's side.[4]

What matters here is that the Scandinavian countries escaped war with a much narrower margin than was generally realized in the immediate aftermath of 1918. This ensured that their former security policies would continue into the interwar period without much discussion. When Europe went to war again some twenty years later, plans and strategic calculations from last time—which for decision-makers in Berlin and London seemed only like yesterday—were taken out of the drawer and finally put to use. In retrospect, it seems clear that both Danish and Norwegian neutrality had been at considerable risk in 1917–18 as a consequence of the German submarine offensive and proposed British counter-measures. When a similar situation arose in the spring of 1940, Denmark and Norway were less lucky.[5]

All in all, in spite of their economic dependence on the belligerents, geography placed the Scandinavian countries in different positions: Denmark powerless in relation to neighbouring Germany; Norway in danger of being forced into a non-neutral status if its neutrality and territorial waters were subject to violations; and Sweden in a relatively easier position as the Scandinavian central power, not bordering the great powers. For a number of self-serving reasons, the great powers were not interested in dragging the Scandinavian countries into the war.

Scandinavian politics

Since Scandinavia is often regarded as being in the vanguard of democratic development, it is fair to ask in what way or to what extent domestic politics in the region influenced its ability to endure the burdens of war and to remain neutral. We will argue that the relative equilibrium and low tension that stemmed from the general democratization process of the nineteenth century left the Scandinavian countries both robust and resilient in the face of the strains of war. True, political instability, extreme radicalization, and social unrest buffeted these countries towards the end of the war as a result of the harsh living conditions suffered by ordinary people and the widespread disgust at war profiteering and the conspicuous consumption of the nouveaux riches. The most important question to ask, then, is why did the Scandinavian countries remain democratic and liberal in spite of the tremendous pressure they were under?

Norway gained full independence only in 1905. Nonetheless, the country came to serve as the Scandinavian role model in democratic politics. The Eidsvoll Constitution of 1814 was the first passed in Scandinavia to be based on liberal principles (the division of power and national sovereignty). Norway was, moreover, the first country to introduce what amounted to parliamentarianism in 1884, following a protracted and intense struggle between the Storting (the parliament) and the monarch. The full male franchise was introduced in 1898, thus doubling the size of the electorate overnight, and in 1913 Norwegian women were given the right to vote. Parliamentary politics were dominated by parties founded in the 1880s: first Høire (the Conservatives) and Venstre (the Liberal Party)—which by 1914 had a clear social–liberal profile—were the dominant parties up to the outbreak of war. The Labour Party, founded in 1887, was still struggling to establish itself as a national party. The breakthrough came when its first member of parliament was elected in 1912. Venstre was the leading party, having gained a clear majority in the Storting in the 1912 elections, and the party leader Gunnar Knudsen (1848–1928) was in a strong position as head of government when the war broke out.

Norway had gone through a period of relatively extensive rearmament in the decade preceding the dissolution of the union with Sweden. After 1905, however, the armed forces slipped down the list of political priorities. Only with the new army organization that was passed by the Storting in 1909 and the new building programme for the navy from 1912 were steps taken to prepare the armed forces for neutrality assignments and war. At the outbreak of war, the armed forces were well prepared for neutrality duties, but far less so for armed conflict.

In Denmark things were more complicated. Here politics had been dominated by a constitutional struggle for almost fifty years. After defeat in the Schleswig War of 1864, the Danish Constitution of 1849 had been revised in order to secure a privileged position for the elites. The liberals and their social-democratic allies originally fought for a return to the more democratic

1849 Constitution, but later added the introduction of universal suffrage for both men and women to their agenda. The constitutional struggle had its ebbs and flows. In the mid 1880s, it brought Denmark to the brink of civil war, while the 1890s and 1900s were characterized by compromises between conservatives and moderate liberals. One of the key dividing issues in Danish politics in the late nineteenth and early twentieth centuries was defence policy. The conservatives wanted to base Danish neutrality on a strong defence, while the radical wing of the liberals fundamentally questioned the value of anything beyond merely symbolic military forces. In 1909 the issue was settled in a compromise backed by Conservatives and Moderate Liberals but opposed by the radicals who in 1905 had broken away from the Liberal Party and established the new Radikale Venstre (Social Liberal Party). When this party was asked to form government under the leadership of Carl Th. Zahle in 1913, the King explicitly demanded that the new government should accept the defence policy of the 1909 compromise. The Social Liberals accepted this, as their key goal was to secure the passing of a new constitution that had been negotiated for several years by the main parties. In 1914, Danish politics was characterized by deeply entrenched divisions, but at the same time the more or less continuous negotiations on constitutional reform since 1909 also meant the key players knew one another very well. This might be part of the explanation why an informal *Burgfrieden* was easily established when war broke out.[6]

In Sweden, the issue of defence played a key role in the constitutional struggle between Left and Right during the years before the war. Things had come to a head in February 1914, when the Liberal government of Karl Staaff was forced to resign after King Gustav V had publicly sided with a protest march of 30,000 Conservative farmers demonstrating against the government's defence policy. The Staaff government was prepared to spend money on armaments, but the central issue was not so much the level of defence spending as the question of parliamentary control over the military. Staaff had appointed civilian politicians as ministers of the army and navy and had appointed parliamentary defence committees to review both the costs and the organizational structure in a long-term perspective. The military were reduced from answering directly to the monarch to a role as expert advisers to democratically elected politicians. With the benefit of hindsight, these reforms signalled an important step towards Sweden's political modernization, but was seen at the time by the Right as an assault on traditional practice, according to which the King was 'Supreme War Lord' and the only rightful authority for the officer corps. However, work in the 'Staaff defence committees' progressed surprisingly smoothly and led to increased mutual understanding between Left and Right, as well as between the political and military elites who quickly accepted their new respective roles. In the heated atmosphere of the times, however, those changes went quite unnoticed.[7]

For the Right, the fact that the issue was linked to defence and the nation's survival assisted popular mass mobilization. Some historians have portrayed the famous Farmers' March in February 1914 as a reactionary setback on Sweden's road to modern democracy. It could be argued, however, that the opposite was closer to the truth: the fact that the Swedish Right took to the streets and organized a large-scale popular demonstration in the nation's capital showed that it had finally embraced the symbols and rituals of mass democracy.

Although universal male suffrage for Andra kammaren (the Lower House) of the Riksdag (Parliament)—with exception for draft-dodgers, welfare recipients, tax evaders and other 'disorderly people'—had been introduced in 1909, women still lacked the vote. Moreover, Första kammaren (the Upper House) was still elected by plutocratic municipal assemblies where major tax-payers could cast up to 40 votes. Therefore, Liberals and Social Democrats were still demanding the democratization of the Upper House, votes for women, and the firm establishment of parliamentary rule with the monarch reduced to a purely symbolic figurehead. In Sweden, as in many other European countries, the First World War would finally secure these reforms.

To solve the defence issue and rule the country until ordinary elections had been held, a caretaker government under the governor of the county of Uppsala, Hjalmar Hammarskjöld, was appointed after Staaff's resignation. Hjalmar Hammarskjöld's cabinet consisted of conservative high officials and businessmen who lacked political experience and parliamentary skills. Although the government had intended to resign after the elections, it was forced by the outbreak of war to stay on. All political parties rallied round Hammarskjöld and the policy of neutrality, and Social Democrats and Liberals accepted without protest the heavy increase in spending that the Hammarskjöld defence Bill entailed. Soon, however, politicians on both Right and Left came to see the Prime Minister as a tactless and arrogant man. That the Constitution of 1809 deprived the Riksdag of all control over foreign policy increased their distrust, especially since Hammarskjöld—who had had a distinguished career as an expert in international law—regarded himself as solely competent in the field and saw no reason to ask the Riksdag for advice. This did not strengthen his position as the nation's leader in a time of crisis. The strong parliamentary opposition against the government weakened Sweden's position in its dealings with the belligerents.[8]

All in all, the decision of the Scandinavian countries to declare themselves neutral was entirely uncontroversial throughout the war. Moreover, the domestic political climate in all three countries was such that other controversies were easily put aside in face of external threats. This situation prevailed until the cost of living rose dramatically. The ensuing social deterioration and the example of the Russian Revolution in 1917 led to a radicalization of the labour movement that was regarded as profoundly destabilizing.

Scandinavian foreign policies

Although the Scandinavian countries' neutral status was not guaranteed by international treaties as was Belgium's, Luxembourg's, and Switzerland's, the cornerstone of the security policy of all three Scandinavian countries was non-alignment in peace and neutrality in war. This is easily explained not only by their status as small states with minimal international clout, but also by the fact they were open economies with innumerable links to both the Entente Powers and the Triple Alliance. Moreover, they had all been active in promoting the development of international neutrality law in the period preceding the war, and they had a long-standing tradition of neutrality stretching back to the eighteenth century. It is, however, more meaningful to write about Scandinavian neutralities in the plural, since the policies of the three countries hinged on both specific geopolitical interests and historical experience. In Denmark and Sweden, security policies were to a high degree dictated by the fear of their great-power neighbours, Germany and Russia, while Norway was under the impression—rightly or wrongly—that it enjoyed effortless security in the shadow of the Royal Navy and its sheer remoteness from the continental theatre of war.

Swedish security policy had depended on France and Britain as counterweights to allegedly expansionist Russia since the Crimean War. This was laid down in the November Treaty of 1855 to which the Scandinavian dual monarchy, Britain, and France were signatories. In the decades after 1871, Sweden came to rely heavily on newly unified Germany instead. This tendency was reinforced by Sweden's cultural orientation and dynastic ties (the Swedish Queen Victoria was the first cousin of Germany's Emperor Wilhelm). Secret conversations between the Swedish and German Chiefs of Staff in Berlin in November 1910 marked a symbolic high-water mark. Discussions focused on Russia, but did not go very far, and no agreement was reached. Rather, fears grew among the Swedish security elite that Germany could drag Sweden into a great-power war. It was generally believed that British protection against Russia would come with fewer strings attached. Internationally, however, Sweden was perceived as ardently anti-Russian and therefore pro-German.[9]

Danish security policy was completely dominated by the German question. Only a few years after the devastating defeat against Germany in 1864, the Franco-Prussian War and the establishment of the German Empire in 1871 made it clear that Denmark could not hope to win back Schleswig. German unification and the steady rise of Germany as a great power convinced successive Danish governments that neutrality was the only option left to the country. True, there was a widespread perception that Germany was the hereditary enemy and Danish national identity continued to be centred on a core of anti-German notions, yet the inescapable fact remained that political and strategic realities dictated that Danish security policy had to be pro-German—or at least the government had to avoid provoking their mighty neighbour south of the border.[10]

The military importance of Denmark in a Europe-wide war would turn on the fact that access to the Baltic Sea could be controlled from Danish territory. As a declared neutral, Denmark, of course, was bound by the provisions of the Second Hague Convention of 1907. Naturally, this was acknowledged by both the military establishment and the government; and in the 1912 Royal Decree on Danish Neutrality, although belligerent warships were allowed innocent passage through Danish waters, they were forbidden the use of ports and territorial waters as bases. As the German navy would have no use for Danish bases, this was clearly directed against Britain. In actual fact, Denmark did very little to prepare the defence of Danish waters against such an infringement of neutrality, and Danish defence plans focused almost exclusively on Copenhagen.[11]

Norway was a newcomer on the international scene, and from the outset sought guarantees from the great powers for its independence. After relatively swift diplomatic recognition in the wake of the dissolution of the union with Sweden, a guarantee of its territorial integrity was given by the British, French, Germans, and Russians in the treaty of November 1907. The country immediately embarked on non-alignment and neutrality. It has been said that neutrality was an unwritten part of the Norwegian constitution. At the same time, Norwegian security policy was biased and not at all as virtuous as the pious official rhetoric would have it. The basic position was neutrality in war, but if the country were to be attacked there was a firm belief that Britain—from self-interest— would come to its assistance. There was a widespread notion that the country and its economic assets were well within the British sphere of influence and that it was therefore covered by an 'implicit guarantee'.[12] That is why defence issues did not loom large on the political agenda and why neutrality measures were regarded as far more important than preparations for war.

Scandinavianism – the unwelcome factor

Political Scandinavianism—the dream of a united Scandinavia that had been widespread, at least among the educated elites, from the 1840s—suffered an abrupt demise in the wake of the Danish–German war of 1864. Norwegian and Swedish promises (and Danish expectations) of support came to nothing, and rang hollow to those who supported Scandinavian assistance. This fact has tended to overshadow the fact that on a cultural level Scandinavianism lived on among groups and individuals who strove to promote the many links and similarities between the Scandinavian peoples and cultures. Scandinavianism even experienced an Indian summer from the late 1890s, when a number of Scandinavian or Nordic societies and associations were founded and a host of meetings, conferences, and exhibitions were arranged in order to develop Scandinavian co-operation in a variety of ways, but it was superseded by a long and deep Nordic winter after the dissolution of the Swedish–Norwegian Union in 1905.[13] This was the case for civil society and government alike. Until at least 1911, the Norwegian government—and in particular the army—tended to regard Sweden as a likely military threat, although there were some signs of a reassessment among strategists. The winter chill of Swedish revanchism and haughtiness were clearly felt up to the outbreak of war in 1914. Consequently, there was little tradition of political cooperation between the three countries, with the notable exception of neutrality issues.

In diplomacy, foreign affairs, and defence, there was no such thing as altruistic Scandinavianism. Since neutrality in war was undisputed in all three countries, the governments simply had to take into account the fact that international law barred cooperative aspirations in this respect, or at least made them very unlikely. Denmark, Norway, and Sweden had gone as far as they could when they harmonized their neutrality regulations before they were communicated in December 1912, albeit in strict accordance with Section 13 of the Second Hague Convention concerning the 'Rights and Duties of Neutral Powers in Naval War'. The Convention, of course, recognized no neutral blocs. The Scandinavian countries also agreed not to make any changes to the rules without consulting one another.[14] When push came to shove, once war had broken out the lack of idealistic Scandinavianism became glaringly obvious except for the posturing of the kings and ministers in Malmö in December 1914. It strikes us that the Scandinavians, to borrow a phrase, were three nations separated by an almost common language. Merely raising the question of Scandinavian security cooperation was for obvious reasons exceedingly unwelcome when seen from the vantage point of government: it could jeopardize their legal status as neutrals. Even the suspicion of the great powers would be shattering.

The Norwegian government had learned a harsh lesson during the recent negotiations over the treaty signed in 1907 and the concomitant abrogation of the November Treaty of 1855. The first Norwegian objective in this drawn-out process was to secure a great-power guarantee of its permanent neutrality. The Storting had actually voted in favour of negotiating permanent neutrality status as early as 1902. This was definitely achievable, but in order to promote Scandinavian unity in times of war and mitigate Swedish reactions in the wake of the 1905 upheaval, the government wanted an escape clause written into the treaty—namely that it would be exempt from the neutrality regulations if one its Scandinavian neighbours were to be attacked. Both lack of diplomatic experience and a residual notion of Scandinavianism led the Norwegian government to put forward propositions that astonished the other parties by their lack of realism. The result was a treaty that guaranteed territorial integrity but not neutrality.

All in all, the question of Scandinavianism did not fall within the remit of the governments as long as they were bound by their status as neutrals. Nonetheless, the issue resurfaced time and again during and immediately after war, and to an even greater extent as the 1930s wore on and the neighbouring great powers turned into totalitarian systems.

Thinking about war and peace

Every state—that is the harsh lesson of history—must be prepared for the test that war can pose to its power and ability to survive. When war stalks the land with its destructive, but also in many ways creative and regenerating, power, right yields to might.[15]

This quote is taken from the Norwegian army strategy textbook and indicates that the world view of Scandinavian officers was not much different from that of their Continental counterparts. Similar expressions of militarism and social Darwinism emanated from relatively small groups of radical nationalists. Apart from these sections of the population, it is safe to say that Scandinavian statesmen and public opinion shared a world view which differed significantly from the bellicism that was so prevalent in European societies before the First World War. There was a strong belief in the efficacy of international law as a force for moderation and conflict resolution. A close-knit elite of politicians, diplomats, international jurists, and other academics was convinced that international law was so well established as to ensure that neutrality would remain a viable option for their countries even in the event of a major war between the alliance blocs of Europe.

Towards the end of the nineteenth century, the liberal peace movement grew increasingly influential in the Scandinavian countries. Its most important contribution was to interpret neutrality as a morally superior position to that of military alliances and to promote the claim that neutrality furthered peace in international relations.[16] Idealism and national interests dovetailed neatly in this interpretation, which has remained a distinctive feature of Scandinavian political culture to this day. There was widespread parliamentary support for the arbitration movement and the Inter-Parliamentary Union, and the Nobel Peace Prize provided a pulpit from which the Scandinavian view of the world could be expounded.

The labour movement did in fact provide an effective example of what could be achieved when socialist internationalism remained true to its principles. It argued forcefully for a peaceful dissolution of the union of Norway and Sweden and threatened a general strike to back up its demands. Norway became one of very few examples of a nation-state not born in war. The socialist peace movement was also voluble in its criticism of arms expenditure and nationalist militarism, but this only found a wider echo when the war demonstrated their terrible consequences.

The most important result of this understanding of international politics was an unshakeable commitment to neutrality that was so widespread as to go unquestioned, and a firm belief among the political class that neutrality was a viable option. Even when total war had demonstrated that this was not the case, the belief remained that Scandinavia should and could stay aloof from great-power conflicts.

Scandinavian war experiences

Responses to the outbreak of war

By declaring themselves neutral in accordance with international law on 3–4 August, and by mobilizing the armed forces to protect their legal status, the Scandinavian governments demonstrated that they firmly believed that they could remain detached from the evolving conflict. Only an insignificant minority of public opinion was outspokenly in favour of siding with one or other of the belligerents. The declarations of neutrality were issued almost as a matter of course and remained by and large undisputed throughout the war. This position, however easy to reach, proved to be all but plain sailing when the governments were forced to handle a myriad of day-to-day issues that threatened their status. After all, the neutrality declarations were prepared and issued in the firm conviction that none of the three had a stake in the conflicts of interest that precipitated hostilities. Moreover, none of the Scandinavian countries was at that point prepared for the vulnerability of their foreign trade and the protracted and troublesome interruption of supplies that the war was to bring. At the outset, belligerents and neutrals alike believed that the war would last no more than a few months.

The Danish answer to the *Augusterlebnis*—the supposedly popular jubilation in Germany at the outbreak of war—was primarily one of nervousness: according to contemporary reports, many were worried that the hostilities would spill over into Denmark. For the government, the immediate task in the final days of July was twofold: it was imperative to mobilize the armed forces for neutrality duties, while they had to convince Germany that Denmark had no ambitions to join Germany's enemies. Although the Social Liberal government was highly sceptical of the utility of an armed neutrality guard (the secretary of defence, Peter Munch, was even

close to being an outright anti-militarist), the government followed the advice of the military leaders and started mobilization
on 1 August. Danish diplomats worked to assure the Germans of
Denmark's ability to shore up its neutrality, but verbal assurances
did not suffice. On 5 August Germany demanded that Denmark
lay minefields in the Belts in order to establish strict control over
traffic to the Baltic Sea. This was clearly directed against Britain,
and, furthermore, in 1912 Denmark had promised the British not
to take such a measure. However, after lengthy discussions that included the leaders of the opposition parties, the armed forces and
the King, the government gave in to German demands.[17]

In Sweden the navy, the wartime garrison of certain fortresses,
and older reservists in the local defence forces along the north-
eastern border and in coastal areas were mobilized on 2–3 August.
Also, the yearly call-up of reservists for refresher training was issued
a few weeks earlier than scheduled. Certain statements that had
been made by the German Emperor to the Swedish King in 1913
gave reason to fear a German ultimatum at the outbreak of a general European war, demanding that Sweden join the Central Powers.
The Swedish declaration of neutrality on 3 August was therefore
followed by a joint declaration of Swedish–Norwegian neutrality,
issued in Christiania on 8 August. In spite of this, rumours that
Sweden intended to enter the war were still rife the next day and
led the commander of the Russian Baltic Fleet, Admiral Nicolai
Essen, to prepare to sail for the island of Gotland to demand that
the Swedish naval forces he expected to find there should stay in
port for the duration of the war. Only at the last moment was
Essen's operation called off.[18]

Essen's suspicions were in part aroused by the fact that Swedish
public opinion distinguished itself among the European neutrals
by frequent displays of strongly pro-German sentiments. Since
German social democracy was a model for the Swedish labour
movement, German sympathizers could be found on the political Left as well as the Right. In 1915, three leading members of
the Social Democratic Party were expelled for having advocated
Sweden's entry into the war on Germany's side together with a
group of Conservative Germanophiles.[19]

Apart from traditional Russophobia, dynastic bonds, and Sweden's long-standing cultural and commercial ties, the strong pro-German bias had to do with how the leading international news agencies had carved up the world market between them around 1870. Scandinavia had been allotted to the German-based agency Wolff, and during the first weeks of the war the Swedish press came to rely heavily on German news reports. Through informal, friendly talks, the Swedish foreign ministry did what it could to influence the press towards a more neutral stance. In comparison with the Second World War, when no fewer than thirty-five newspapers were convicted in court cases connected to Sweden's relations with foreign powers, communication between the government and the press during the First World War was more relaxed. In 1914–18, there were only six such libel convictions, most of which concerned propaganda pamphlets produced by the belligerents and not domestic newspapers.[20]

Norway found itself on the horns of a dilemma in the summer of 1914. By and large, the country was politically and militarily wholly unprepared for war. The armed forces had not been to war or fired a shot in anger since 1814. Neither the defence leadership nor the political authorities had any experience of dealing with international crises. However, they firmly believed that international law and institutions provided them with the tools and framework to stay out of the conflict and to allow international shipping and vital foreign trade to continue unhindered. Historical precedent gave some reason for such an assumption. But it was to prove unfounded as the war progressed.

Geography and economic ties put Norway close to the line of fire from the outset of the war, and made up the inescapable and unwelcoming circumstances under which the government was forced to operate. As early as 8 August some thirty ships of the Royal Navy steamed into Norwegian territorial waters off Stad on the west coast. They were searching for German naval vessels and were undoubtedly in breach of international law.[21] The Norwegian navy intercepted immediately, and the government was left to handle the incident diplomatically. The first lesson learned by the government was simple and brutal: to invoke the full letter of international law could actually cause tensions to escalate and work against national interests; at worst, Norway might become engaged in an armed conflict with Britain. The government therefore decided that the infringements should be regarded as incidental and not as a pretext for constant pressure on Norwegian neutrality. The handling of the incident established a pattern for the rest of the war, namely that every infringement was to be treated as *sui generis*. In this respect the situation was different in Denmark and Sweden. On the one hand, all three countries could benefit from uninterrupted trade with the belligerents in accordance with international neutrality law, albeit more easily in Denmark and Sweden. On the other, their stance could be construed as a hypocritical cover for blatant profiteering, in a war in which majority opinion became progressively more sympathetic to the cause of Britain and France.

From 1916 onwards, the three Scandinavian foreign ministries even coordinated their efforts to impose censorship, suppressing news telegrams that threatened to undermine the neutrality of any Scandinavian country or contained sensitive information about their military measures or ship movements in their territorial waters.[22] New laws to that effect were passed by the parliaments. All in all, none of the Scandinavian governments at any time wavered in their determination to stay out of the war and to muddle through each passing crisis as best they could.

Neutrality and the role of the armed forces

According to the Hague Convention, there was no doubt whatsoever that countries claiming neutral status were obliged to keep their territorial waters under surveillance so that they could intercept in cases of violation. If not, they would put their neutral rights at risk. Consequently, all the Scandinavian countries mobilized their neutrality guards, albeit to varying degrees. This was not overly controversial. However, the extent of the neutrality guard and whether it should involve a substantial part of all the services and also be prepared for escalation to war were much more contentious issues. The reason was that the costs of keeping up a protracted military engagement with the capacity to counter deliberate violations would become exceedingly burdensome when added to the deteriorating economic and social conditions caused by the war.

The Danish navy was heavily engaged in mining the Belts from August 1914. For the rest of the war, laying, maintaining, and guarding the minefields was the navy's most important assignment. It was also engaged in clearing drifting mines in order to protect ship movements, the fisheries, and coastal communities. Altogether the navy destroyed some 10,000 mines during the war. The Danish army had a much less eventful time. In 1914, 47,000 men were mobilized to guard Danish neutrality. The bulk of them were positioned close to Copenhagen since it was realized that it would be impossible to defend most of Denmark from attack by a major military power.

As time passed and the danger of Denmark being involved in the war seemed increasingly unlikely, a power struggle between the military leadership and the secretary of defence followed. Whereas the officers wanted to maintain the mobilized force, Peter Munch found it both useless and too expensive to continue with the force level from the early phase of the war. Furthermore, discipline in the units was a growing problem as many of the conscripts found the task of defending the capital against a seemingly non-existent enemy pointless. In the end, the number of conscripts was reduced by about half. For the military leaders this bitter pill was sweetened by the construction of a series of fortifications on the perimeter of Copenhagen.[23]

In Sweden, the Army Bill which the Hammarskjöld government put forward in 1914 meant that the army doubled its organization from six to twelve divisions. However, there was not enough equipment for such a large force and many of the more than 200,000 conscripts who had been listed in the mobilization tables would have lacked basic equipment if they had been called up. Moreover, as there were few visible threats to the country, the Swedish army never kept more than 13,000 men under arms at any one time during the war (conscripts in basic training are excluded from that number). This can be compared with the Second World War, when there was an almost constant fear of invasion. During that conflict, the number of mobilized conscripts never sank below 25,000, and at times even rose above 300,000. In the summer of 1918, as the fighting culminated on the Western Front in France, the Swedish army kept fewer than 2,000 men in preparedness.[24]

Instead, the main burden of defending Swedish integrity fell on the navy. The navy also played an instrumental role during the Civil War in Finland in early 1918, evacuating Swedish citizens from the town of Pori (Björneborg) on the west coast of Finland and civilians from the Swedish-speaking Åland Islands (in all, some 2,785 people were evacuated to Swedish territory). Finally, the navy transported the Swedish expeditionary force that in February temporarily occupied the Åland Islands.[25]

In Norway, the government believed that the country was in a somewhat more vulnerable position than its neighbours. The navy was put on alert a few days before the outbreak of war. At that time, fortunately, a substantial part of the armed forces were on summer manoeuvres and new recruits were going through their basic training period. The navy was then ordered on 29 July to be prepared for neutrality duties, and on 2 August the order was issued by the government. On 5 August the bulk of the mobilization plan was carried through. In addition to a number of hired civilian patrol boats and an elaborate surveillance and warning system that used civilian telecommunications facilities and information gathered by lighthouse keepers, the customs service, local police, harbour authorities, and pilots, the navy proper was mustered along vulnerable sections of the coast. The maritime system was on full alert for the duration of the war while the army and coastal artillery were far less prepared.

At first glance a total Norwegian naval mobilization might appear somewhat drastic. However, it was a reflection of the dominant threat perception among politicians and the defence leadership at the time, and was regarded as an inescapable commitment under international law. The territorial waters of the south-west coast were widely assumed to present a challenge in a war between the leading sea power, Britain, and the leading land power, Germany. Moreover, Norwegian authorities rightly assumed that the great powers had a common interest in keeping the country neutral, although the government dreaded that the belligerents might infringe on Norwegian neutral rights if they suspected that the adversary was not respecting its neutrality. That called for the presence of a vigilant neutrality guard.

The government regarded it as paramount to mobilize the neutrality guard to its full extent at the outbreak of war. That would signal its intentions, will, and capacity to any violator of its neutrality. Hopefully it would also have a deterrent effect. It was regarded as more expedient to reduce the neutrality guard eventually rather than to step it up in the course of a crisis. The crux of the set-up was to combine naval and an array of civilian resources for surveillance, information gathering, and interception. The neutrality guard was not only made up of sailors. A substantial part of the coastal artillery (defending the major towns) and army units tasked with protecting the forts from land-based assaults were also mobilized. The laying of controlled minefields at the inlets and in the inner leads was also a vital part of the defensive measures. By and large, the neutrality guard proved to be surprisingly effective throughout the war. In addition to intercepting a vast number of infringements by the belligerents, it was also engaged in convoying, escorting, salvage operations, and mine clearing. It was nonetheless the Ministry of Foreign Affairs and the diplomats who had to tackle the abundance of delicate neutrality issues and thus stood in the line of fire.

There seems to have been a certain discrepancy among the Scandinavian countries as to the imperative of mustering the armed neutrality guard. That was probably due to the differences in the assumed vulnerability and exposure of the countries. In Norway, the armed neutrality guard appears to have been most highly valued, while in Denmark and Sweden the armed forces' state of preparedness was far more controversial since wide swathes of public opinion did not regard it as necessary.

The interventionist state

The First World War led to a tremendous increase in the expenditure of the governments of both belligerent and non-belligerent countries. This in turn necessitated strict governmental controls over both domestic economies and foreign trade in order to prevent grave imbalances in the economy. New economic and planning models and institutions were developed, as were alternatives to classical laissez-faire economics and dogmatic free trade. The outbreak of the war thus signalled potentially overwhelming challenges. Initially, no one knew whether the major powers would submit the Scandinavian countries to the relentless logic of economic warfare, or whether they would accept that the Scandinavian countries could continue their pre-war trade patterns roughly within the limits of neutrality law. In the autumn of 1914, Sweden found its two main export commodities—iron ore and timber—listed as contraband by the British and the Germans respectively. However, the fact that both belligerents wanted to continue their own imports from Sweden made them tolerate the fact that Sweden traded with the enemy as well.

In order to escape sanctions and involvement in the trade war, the Danish Rigsdag (Parliament) authorized the government to ban the export of essential commodities immediately after the outbreak of war. It was imperative to secure supplies for the population, but also to signal that Denmark would not become an entrepôt through which imports from, say, Britain could be re-exported to Germany. Although trade agreements with the warring powers were negotiated by business representatives who had to issue guarantees against re-exports to enemy countries, these guarantees were from the beginning underpinned by Danish legislation and thus the government. This strategy succeeded, and Denmark was able to keep up its trade with both Britain and Germany for the first three years of the war, although the pressure from the great powers demonstrated repeatedly that this trade regime would only continue as long as the great powers felt that it was in their own best interests.[26]

In Norway, the problems of foreign trade were solved through a series of agreements between business organizations and Norway's trading partners. These agreements were from the start negotiated with the full understanding of the authorities, and in reality were underwritten by the government. This came into the open in 1916, when the prohibition of re-exports, which were a crucial part of these agreements, was written into law.

For all three Scandinavian countries the situation deteriorated dramatically when the US launched a trade embargo against neutral powers in the summer of 1917, an initiative that was soon copied by Great Britain. An important response to this challenge was a much stronger focus on intra-Scandinavian trade: thus the Scandinavian share of Danish imports rose from 6 to 30 per cent from 1916 to 1918, and the rise in the share of exports was even more dramatic—from 6 to 39 per cent.[27] Denmark and Sweden were able to alleviate the worst consequences of the Allied embargo by expanding trade with Germany, but the strain on the economy was massive. In the course of 1917, Swedish imports fell to less than 50 per cent of pre-war levels while food prices rose some 40 per cent. For Norway the situation was even more precarious as the country was dependent on imported food, primarily grain. After difficult negotiations, the US in April 1918 reopened for exports to Norway on the condition that Norway limit its exports to the Central Powers. Sweden and Denmark reached similar agreements with the US in May and September 1918. The agreements clearly demonstrated that it was virtually impossible for small countries such as the Scandinavian ones to uphold an unbiased neutrality. The logics of geography and the asymmetry in the power bases of Britain (and its allies) and Norway inevitably left Norway in the position of a 'neutral ally', to quote the title of Olav Riste's 1965 study of Norwegian relations with the belligerent powers.[28] Denmark's neutrality for the same reasons had to be pro-German, and same went for Sweden, although, as will be enlarged on later, geopolitical necessity was far from the only factor pushing Swedish neutrality in a decidedly pro-German direction.

It was not only in foreign trade that the hand of the state became very visible during the war. A few days after the outbreak of war, the Danish Rigsdag passed emergency legislation that gave government the power to regulate prices and more generally intervene in the market to ensure the supply of food and other essential goods for the population. The government quickly set up a regulatory system, assisted by an 'Extraordinary Commission' with representatives of key political and economic interests. During the war this commission mushroomed into about forty sub-commissions and boards, not to mention local commissions in all local authorities that oversaw the development of a thoroughly regulated economy, controlled by the state in close collaboration with the major economic interest organizations. Within this framework, maximum prices of essential goods were introduced, the distribution of raw materials regulated, housing rents controlled, and the state also became a buyer of key imports such as wheat. Norway and Sweden saw a similar development, with laws passed that gave the government the right to deal more or less freely with certain kinds of privately owned goods and commodities, as well a growing number of government commissions and boards, incorporating representatives from the most important political and economic interest groups, that regulated the allocation of resources and controlled prices.[29]

All in all, notwithstanding their non-belligerent status, the vulnerability of neutrality, and the economic strains put on Scandinavia, the war saw the breakthrough of strong central government with broad responsibilities for economic planning and welfare for its citizens.

Social relations in wartime

In spite of increasing state regulation and the relative prosperity of certain sectors, broad sections of society suffered a decline in living standards. Inflation and the shortage of consumer goods—in combination with the conspicuous consumption of the nouveaux riches—caused widespread poverty and political unrest. The radicalization of the labour movement was especially pronounced in Norway, but Denmark and Sweden also saw a schism between reformist and revolutionary factions. In hindsight, these were probably the salient features of wartime Scandinavia, and they anticipated the political controversies in all three countries in the interwar years. The profound social divisions had a long-term impact that was only overcome after the Second World War.

Government regulation could neither prevent shortages nor inflation. Prices rose steadily throughout the war. In Denmark the cost of living almost doubled from 1914 to 1918. In Norway and Sweden the situation was even worse, and prices rose by up to 140 per cent and 250 per cent respectively. Black markets flourished and as the war wore on basic foodstuffs became not only expensive but also scarce. Government regulations and the shortage of fodder made it irresistibly tempting for many farmers to slaughter their livestock and sell the meat illegally rather than to accept the official maximum prices. In response, the governments imposed rationing of essential foods: in Denmark, first bread, then sugar and pork from the beginning of 1917; in Sweden, sugar in 1916, bread, flour, meat and milk in 1917, and even potatoes in 1918. The Norwegian government followed suit from January 1918 after massive demonstrations against the 'dear times'. The demonstrations were organized by the trade unions, whose members not only suffered from shortages but also witnessed the growing social divide at close quarters. 'The sailors are drowning, the people are starving, capital reaps the profits' was one of the slogans at a Kristiania (Oslo) demonstration in the summer of 1917.[30]

The slogan dramatized reality, but for workers and large sections of the middle class the war represented at best a period of austerity, whereas agriculture, fisheries, industry, mining, and shipping were well placed to profit from the unlimited demands of the conflict. Farmers routinely complained about government regulations and fixed prices. At the same time many of them made huge profits, not at least on the black market. In Norway, the war is also to a large extent remembered for the reckless speculation, profiteering, and lavish lifestyles in a boom era of jobbery. Contemporary sources such as newspapers, fiction, and satirical magazines carry numerous tales of the conspicuous consumption of the upper classes, especially the nouveaux riches.[31] The Danish word for war profiteer was 'goulash baron', a play on the fortunes made out of low-quality processed food sold to the Central Powers. However, the goose that really laid golden eggs during the war years was shipping. Shipping rates soared, as did profits and company values on the stock exchange.

Since the social and economic history of wartime Scandinavia is still under-researched, it is difficult to go beyond impressionistic pictures. Nonetheless, the overall social trend is underpinned by some sombre statistics. The Danish case is illustrative. While real income either stagnated or fell by 10–12 per cent for pensioners, and white- and blue-collar workers, it rose by 39 per cent for the self-employed. The trend is even more striking if we look more closely at the statistics: real income for bankers rose by 62 per cent, for industrialists by 67 per cent and for self-employed in the transportation sector—that is, primarily in shipping—by 79 per cent.[32]

It is easy to document that the authorities were well aware of the social problems and the potential political repercussions of the widening gap between rich and poor. This was the background for social policies aimed at alleviating the rising cost of living for the working classes as well as the often precarious job situation. In part, such policies were financed by increased taxes, especially for the well-off—for example, through taxes on 'extraordinary incomes' such as war profits. Denmark was the first country to introduce such taxation in 1915.[33] By means of such measures the Danish government was successful in defusing most left-wing criticism. In Norway, the government acted more slowly and hesitantly, and clearly under pressure from protests and demonstrations, thus helping to create the conditions for the radicalization of large parts of the labour movement from 1918.

In Sweden, social and political protests to a high degree fused during 1917, leading to victory for the Social Democrats and the Liberals in the general election and to important democratic political reforms in 1918. The Conservative Swartz government also had to handle growing domestic unrest as the Allied blockade caused food riots in several Swedish cities. Nervousness grew as soldiers protested against insufficient rations in the barracks. In addition, the political Left organized demonstrations demanding a democratization of municipal suffrage which would change the composition of the Riksdag's upper house. In May 1917, the Social Democratic Party split into a reformist and a revolutionary wing; the latter would develop into the Swedish Communist Party after the Bolsheviks had seized power in Russia that same autumn.[34]

A similar party split, less dramatic but historically equally important, took place at the other end of the political spectrum in 1917, when an independent Farmer's Party (eventually to develop into the centrist-liberal Swedish Centre Party) broke away from the Swedish Right. The new party was formed from the rank and file of the Swedish conservative movement (who in 1914 had participated in the Farmer's March against the Staaff government), in opposition to those urban, bourgeois industrialists and aristocratic officials who had dominated the Swedish Conservative Party since its foundation in 1904. Clearly, the tensions between town and country fomented by the war contributed to this divide, which during the rest of the twentieth century would weaken the alternative to social democracy in Swedish politics.[35]

In the historiography of the First World War, gender relations have been a central issue since the 1970s. While it is clear that gender roles underwent great changes during the war, when millions of men went to war whilst women had to take up new responsibilities within the family and on the labour market, the degree to which these developments had a long-term impact is more open to question. Did the war further female political rights and emancipation in a broader sense, as Arthur Marwick provocatively argued in a series of books from the late 1960s onwards? Or did war actually cement traditional gender roles and patriarchy, as many feminist historians have argued? As only relatively few men were mobilized during the war in Scandinavia, the impact of the war years on gender relations was relatively slight. In Sweden, preparations were made to include women in the mobilization for total war through voluntary women's organizations for military medical and veterinary services (see, for example, Anne Hedén's contribution to this volume). The government commissions for Unemployment and National Economizing also identified roles for women as replacement workers for men who had been called up, or sewing uniforms for local defence forces. However, it has been argued, in the plans for national mobilization women were assigned tasks that would not threaten the established gender division of labour.[36]

The Nordic countries were at the forefront of equal rights for women before the outbreak of war. Women had been enfranchised in municipal elections in the Scandinavian countries long before the war. Finland adopted universal female suffrage in 1906 (the first country to do so) and Norway followed suit in 1913. Danish women were given the right to vote in 1915, while universal suffrage was introduced in Sweden only in 1919. While the timing of the democratic reforms in Sweden from 1917 was clearly linked to the pressure of the war on Swedish society, the link between female suffrage and wartime in Denmark was purely accidental. That female suffrage would be part of a constitutional reform was clear before August 1914, and the outbreak of war delayed the vote for women by a few years as the new Danish constitution of 1915 was put on hold until the end of hostilities.

Most interpretations of social change during the war have approached the subject from the perspective of the (inexorable) 'rise of the labour movement'. However, focusing on the political protests of organized labour makes it difficult to evaluate the overall economic and social impact of the war. Industrial workers no doubt felt the pressure of inflation, but their trade unions could also force employers to concede compensatory wage rises. Pensioners, public employees, and others on fixed incomes were not so lucky, but the *déclassement* of the lower middle class has not received much attention from historians.

It is also difficult to evaluate the overall economic impact of the war. Disruptions to supplies and international trade had a serious impact on open economies dependent on exporting goods and services, and certain sectors were obviously depressed. But on the other hand, the belligerents' insatiable demand for raw materials, foodstuffs, and shipping opened up extremely profitable opportunities which shipowners, mining companies, industry, and agriculture were quick to exploit. Norsk Hydro had no qualms about exporting explosive components to the munitions industries on both sides; Allied pressure soon cut off the German market, but almost one-third of France's consumption of nitrates throughout the war was imported from Norway.[37] That greed overruled concern for the national interest was also evident in the Danish courts, which had to deal with hundreds of cases where individuals and firms tried to circumvent the ban on re-exports to Germany.[38]

Given the present state of research, it is only possible to indicate general conclusions about the social impact of the war. The bulk of the income generated in sectors that profited from the war seems to have found its way into the pockets of the owners—

with the probable exceptions of agriculture, forestry, and fisheries. Workers in these sectors benefited to a certain extent, but one group—seamen—bore the heaviest burden of any profession as a result of German submarine warfare and Allied mines (some 2,000 Norwegian, 700 Swedish, and 650 Danish sailors were lost at sea). Workers in many industries suffered a decline in purchasing power, but also benefited from the economic stimulus of vastly increased government spending. Many groups dependent on fixed incomes were impoverished. The net result was a widening social divide—the very visible presence of a few rich and many poor—which goes a long way in explaining the bitter political divisions of the interwar years.

Diverging neutralities

Given the different economies and foreign relations of the Scandinavian countries, it is unsurprising that they embarked on different practices to uphold their neutrality in spite of the official facade of close cooperation. They were in a situation without much room for manoeuvre or to demonstrate pious ideals. The international law on neutrality was not so rigid as to escape interpretation. None of the Scandinavian countries intended to invoke the full letter of the law, but rather set out to employ it to serve their commercial, diplomatic, and political interests all at the same time. Consequently, there was no such thing as a common Scandinavian war policy. This put the foreign ministries on the front line throughout the war.

Rhetorically, Sweden under Hjalmar Hammarskjöld had the highest profile among the European neutrals. When the three Scandinavian countries in November 1914 protested to Britain, France, and Germany over disturbances in their trade caused by the war, Hammarskjöld drafted the text, according to which the great powers should be grateful to the Scandinavian neutrals who had struggled to preserve international law and unselfishly defended the principles of civilization in the hour of darkness.[39]

Like Denmark, Norway often came under heavy pressure in trade negotiations, especially from Britain, which could cut the country off from global markets. In January 1917, the British threatened to stop coal exports to Norway and thus left the Norwegian government with no other alternative than to comply with British wishes.[40]

In spite of governmental grandstanding, Swedish foreign policy was far from neutral. In August 1914, the foreign minister, Wallenberg, had secretly promised the government in Berlin that Swedish neutrality would observe a 'benevolent' attitude towards Germany, possibly driven by fears of an ultimatum to join the war on Germany's side. This benevolence included the black out of Swedish lighthouses and the laying of mines in the Sound (directed against British submarines in the Baltic Sea), a transit ban on military equipment across Swedish territory (directed against French and British exports to Russia), as well as the secret transmission of diplomatic cables to German missions overseas through the Swedish consular service. In addition, Swedish diplomats tried to convince Italy and Romania not to enter the war on the side of Germany's enemies. None of these measures was probably very important to the German war effort as a whole, but later they would become a burden on Sweden's relations with the victors.

Swedish meat exports saw a ninefold increase in the autumn of 1914, especially to Germany. The Germans also imported large quantities of horses from Sweden for their army, and in 1915 secretly agreed to tolerate continued Swedish timber exports to Britain provided the Swedish government guaranteed that the horse trade would continue. During 1916, however, the food shortages began to be felt in Sweden due to the British blockade. Britain refused to let goods through without guarantees that they would not be re-exported from Sweden to Germany. Hammarskjöld refused as this would mean Sweden committing an un-neutral act by participating in British economic warfare. In response, the British prevented Swedish ships from leaving their home ports. However, Sweden had an advantage in its geographic location, which meant that the country was also the quickest link between the Western powers and their Russian ally. Hammarskjöld therefore countered British punitive measures with punitive measures against Allied transports to Russia on Swedish railways.[41]

Hammarskjöld's handling of the conflict with Britain created tensions within the government, especially between the prime minister and the more pragmatic foreign minister Wallenberg. In early 1917, when the Riksdag had turned down a government plea for more money for the armed forces, the Hammarskjöld government finally resigned. Hammarskjöld's successor as prime minister, Carl Swartz, belonged to the moderate Conservatives and could not pretend to be an unpartisan official.

America's entry into the war in the spring of 1917 weakened the position of all neutral countries, including the Scandinavians. All of a sudden, neutral rights and the neutral zone no longer had a great-power defender. What finally doomed the Conservative Swartz government was US foreign minister Edward Lansing's revelation of the so-called Luxburg telegram in September 1917. Although Lansing's main intention was to embarrass Germany, Sweden was likewise mortified when it was revealed that the Luxburg telegram and thousands of other German diplomatic cables had been transmitted with the help of the formally neutral Swedish Foreign Ministry. Swartz suffered a shattering defeat in the ongoing general election and had to resign.

The new Liberal–Social Democratic government under Nils Edén began negotiating with the Allies. The first trade agreement in May 1917 merely provided a temporary relief. The second treaty, which was concluded in May 1918, saw Sweden finally agree to offer guarantees against re-exports to Germany and put Swedish shipping abroad at the disposal of the Western powers. The major problem in Sweden's relations with the Allies had then been removed. In spite of the trade treaty with the Allies in May 1918, Sweden's pro-German orientation remained—at least in a regional Baltic context. The Liberal–Social Democrat government silently blessed Germany's intervention in the Finnish Civil War and signed a secret treaty with Berlin after the Red defeat, according to which Germany would demolish the Russian fortifications in the Åland Islands provided Sweden would accept Germany's position as the dominant power in the Baltic region in future.[42]

As already mentioned, Norway's position towards Britain was similar to Sweden's relations with Germany. There was almost no leeway, since geography and trade dependence left the Norwegian government with no possibility of sanctions against Britain. On the contrary, a British blockade or stop in exports of coal and oil would have had an immediate and devastating effect on the Norwegian economy. Norway constituted a special case since it became de facto part of the Allied war effort; first when it allowed Western weapons transits to Russia in the far north from 1916, and then in 1918 in the wake of the laying of the American–British mine barrage across the North Sea. In order to deny Germany innocent passage in protected Norwegian territorial waters (as was offered by international law) the Norwegian government continued the mine barrage in the inner leads and thus became part of the Allied blockade of Germany. But at that time Germany was so occupied by events in other operational theatres that little attention was given to this issue.

Finally, it should be noted that the diverging neutralities of the Scandinavian countries did not leave them at odds with one another in any real sense; instead, it was their relations with the belligerents that differed.

The Scandinavian front

Except for the émigrés in many parts of the world, Scandinavian participation in the war was essentially an issue limited to Denmark and Sweden. In Sweden there was widespread sympathy for the Finns, and many signed up to form the Swedish Finland Brigade to support Finnish independence and the Whites against the Reds in the civil war that broke out in January 1918. The Norwegian government did what it could to prevent its citizens from signing up for service in other countries, thus underscoring the sense of detachment from the Baltic region that permeated Norwegian foreign policy at the time, even though there was widespread public sympathy for the Finns.

In Denmark many people felt that the war was very close to home, since some 26,000 men from the Danish-German minority in Schleswig were mobilized in the German armed forces. The Schleswigers were mostly of peasant stock, and the majority were enrolled in the army in locally recruited regiments which fought on all the major fronts during the war. Public interest in their war experiences was great in Denmark. Both during and after the war numerous collections of letters, memoirs, and novels were published, often explicitly framing their war experience as especially meaningless since they were not fighting for their own country. However, it is not this nationally framed experience that is the dominant feature of this body of literature; instead, it is striking how closely the war experience of the Danish-oriented Schleswigers resembles what we encounter in the narratives left us by for instance British, French, and German soldiers.

A few Danes also chose to join up as volunteers, primarily in the armed forces of the Entente Powers. While we do not have comprehensive data on the volunteers, it is telling that one historian has managed to find only 147 Danes serving in France, of whom only 93 served in combat units while the rest served as nurses and doctors and the like. Even though the Danes serving on the Entente side were few and far between, their experiences generated interest in Denmark in the form of published letters and memoirs. Thus the only well-known Danish memoir of the war is by Thomas Dinesen (the brother of Karen Blixen) who served in the Canadian army—and enjoyed himself thoroughly. During 1918–19, a number of Danish volunteers joined the fight against the Bolsheviks in the Baltic. The largest group to be organized was the Dansk-Baltisk Auxiliær Corps, which went on to fight in Latvia, Estonia, and Russia. The number of volunteers was about 200—a far cry from the 2,000 that the organizers had hoped for—and their exploits evoked no lasting response in Danish collective memory.[43]

Few Swedes had any direct experience of the large-scale, industrial attrition that was the warfare waged in 1914–18. One notable exception was Elow Nilson, who served with the French Foreign Legion and was killed at Verdun in 1916, and whose letters from the front were published posthumously. Otherwise, most Swedish war volunteers served on the German side (on the Eastern Front against Russia, like the famous cavalry officer Count Gilbert Hamilton), and above all on the White side in the Finnish Civil War. Some of the approximately 1,000 Swedes who volunteered to fight with the Whites against the Reds in Finland in the spring of 1918 served as staff officers in General Mannerheim's headquarters. The overwhelming majority, however, served in the so-called Swedish Brigade.[44]

The participation of Norwegian citizens was almost negligible— that is, if the numerous sailors in the merchant marine are exempted. True, some officers volunteered for the Western powers such as the retired colonel and jingoist Henrik Angell in France and Major Tryggve Gran in the Royal Flying Corps. The bulk of those who took part in the fighting were emigrants of Norwegian extraction from America or sailors dwelling in belligerent countries such as Australia and New Zealand. Officially, the Norwegian government did not allow officers, NCOs, or privates enrolled in the armed forces to seek foreign service. The vast majority of personnel in the Norwegian army and navy were conscripts and reservists aged 18 to 44 years, and even though they only served for short periods during their initial training and subsequent exercises, or when they attended military schools and academies, nonetheless they were in the mobilization lists for the army or the navy and were thus barred from service in other countries until they were dismissed.

Notwithstanding the extensive losses of sailors and tonnage, and far smaller losses on land, the Scandinavian countries emerged from the war with exceedingly small human and material costs compared to the belligerents. Nonetheless, the war had a profound impact on Scandinavian societies and their post-war development—more or less along the lines of other European countries. In some ways the war became an avenue of continued internationalization.

The long-term consequences of the War in Scandinavia

Scandinavia and the peace settlements

The pressing question for the Scandinavian countries during the peace negotiations was their future relations with the victors and the nascent League of Nations, which all three eventually joined in 1920. Moreover, the long-standing questions of Denmark's border with Germany in Schleswig, Sweden's position on the status of the contested Åland Islands, and the Norwegian quest for sovereignty over the Spitsbergen Archipelago in the Arctic were also a part of the wider peace settlement. Finally, all countries were to some extent still engaged in the ongoing crisis in the recently independent Baltic States and Finland. For obvious reasons, the Scandinavians were not invited when peace talks opened in Paris on 18 January 1919. However, in March President Woodrow Wilson summoned fourteen neutral states—among them Denmark, Norway, and Sweden—to take part in an informal conference in preparation for the establishment of the League of Nations.[45]

In some quarters of Norwegian politics there was a determination to benefit from the peace settlement, prompted by claims for reparations for the excessive war losses of the merchant marine. After floating such quixotic ideas as taking over territories in north-western Russia or possibly a German African colony as compensation, the Norwegian government settled on the far more trivial questions of membership of the League and of gaining sovereignty over the Spitsbergen Archipelago, which at the time was still *terra nullius*. Norway's cordial relations with Britain and the valuable services it had offered the Entente Powers made the negotiating climate favourable, and the gambit of claiming Spitsbergen turned out to be successful: a treaty to that effect was signed in 1920, and after a drawn-out ratification process it went into effect from 1925. True, the Treaty gave all the signatories equal rights to exploit the archipelago's resources, but it was nonetheless for nationalistic reasons regarded as a diplomatic triumph in Norway.[46] The process leading up to membership of the League of Nations, meanwhile, was more chaotic by far.

Influential circles in the Storting wished to combine membership of the League of Nations with neutrality in war as a fallback position.[47] That turned out to be unattainable since the League's draft Covenant was based on collective security which, in turn, was incompatible with neutrality. The former neutrals were invited to present their opinion of the proposed arrangement in March 1919, but they had no real influence on the formation of the League of Nations. Wilson insisted that the Covenant should be a part of the peace treaties that were negotiated in Paris, and its formulations were therefore determined by the talks between the Allies and associated powers. Neither the neutrals nor the defeated took part in these talks. The Covenant was communicated to them on 28 April 1919, and there was no doubt that the League still recognized war as a legal measure, albeit within the limits laid down in international law.

Article 8 of the Covenant recognized 'that the maintenance of peace requires the reduction of national armaments to the lowest point consistent with national safety and the enforcement by common action of international obligations'. This was broadly uncontroversial in Scandinavia, even though there would be a debate over what the 'lowest point consistent' meant in real terms.[48] The military leadership was clearly the most reluctant in Norway because in their view the country would lose the freedom to choose its own enemies, and, moreover, the structure of the army and the navy would have to be adjusted to new assignments. Both politicians and officers dreaded the prospect of being dragged into conflicts in which the country had no stake. Nonetheless, the Storting passed the Bill on membership of the League with a comfortable majority. True, the country did not join enthusiastically, but there was no viable, neutral alternative. In passing the Bill, 100 MPs voted in favour and 20 against. The only party that was categorically against membership was Labour, with its 16 MPs. They held that the League was a victors' cabal that would embark on an anti-socialist policy to overthrow the Soviet regime. In their view only socialism would secure the peace. In Denmark, the socialist members of the Rigsdag voiced no similar criticism and voted in favour of Danish membership of the League. The parliamentary vote in January 1920 was unanimous, but behind this common front lurked a scepticism about the League that nearly matched the Norwegians'.[49]

Norwegian politics was also characterized by severe friction between the socialist and non-socialist blocs throughout the interwar years. The socialist parties were steadily gathering strength after 1918. After a passing flirtation with the Comintern, the Labour Party left it in 1923. The Norwegian labour movement was split into a revolutionary and a reformist faction. The revolutionary faction became the Communist Party and never exercised any real influence except within the labour movement. The reformists, however, strengthened their position in the Storting and formed a government (based on an agreement with the Agrarian Party) in March 1935, thus inaugurating the heyday of social democracy that was only to come to an end in the 1960s.

Sweden's involvement in the peace settlement after the war turned on its dispute with Finland over the Swedish-speaking Åland Islands, situated closer to Stockholm than to the Finnish mainland and therefore deemed strategically important. In February 1918, after the outbreak of civil war in newly independent Finland, some 7,000 Ålanders presented an address to King Gustav V, asking to become a part of Sweden again. Shortly afterwards, Swedish warships arrived and landed troops on the islands to prevent the civil war in mainland Finland from spreading. Swedish troops negotiated an armistice between the Whites, the Reds, and the Russian garrison in the islands, and started to disarm them. Only after a month, when a German expeditionary force had landed, did the Swedish troops evacuate. The Swedish intervention had been dictated by the honest wish to protect the civilian population, but there had also been more opportunistic motives. If the Åland Islands could be annexed in a coming peace settlement, the strategic situation of the Swedish capital would be considerably improved.

Edén's Liberal–Social Democratic coalition government took Sweden into the League of Nations in January 1920. The Conservatives and Leftist Socialists protested, as they considered the League to be a tool to force the Treaty of Versailles upon Germany and Soviet Russia. The Liberals and Social Democrats were firm believers in the Wilsonian world order, but also saw the League as an ally in securing Åland for Sweden, especially since the Ålanders had organized a referendum in which 96 per cent of voters supported the idea of joining Sweden. However, in May 1921 the League found in favour of Finland, although a few months later the demilitarization and political and cultural autonomy of the islands were secured through an international treaty.[50]

In the case of Denmark, it can be argued that the most important consequence of the war was that it paved the way for the unification of Northern Schleswig with Denmark and thus allowed the

Danish-oriented population to 'return home', to use the language of the time. Although the Rigsdag in October 1918 had decided that it only wanted a border revision based strictly on the criteria of nationality, the results of the 1920 plebiscites, which demonstrated a strong German majority in Central Schleswig (including the main city of Flensburg), were a disappointment to many Danish nationalists, and hopes for an alternative, more southerly border was one of the main factors that led King Christian X to sack the Zahle government in the spring of 1920. However, the dominant feeling was one of jubilation, and in the following years the 'Reunification' (as the process is normally called in Denmark) came to be seen as a key event that represented the final fulfilment of a Danish nation-state. It soon completely overshadowed the much more complex experience of the war years in the imagined community of the Danes.[51]

To a high degree Danish historiography has followed suit. Interest in the war years has been limited, and interpretations of Danish history in a longer perspective have tended to see the war as a parenthesis that was soon overcome. It is also true that the most striking features of the war years were soon rolled back. The neutrality guard was dismantled as early as in March 1919; in 1919–20 the vast majority of the economic regulations that had been introduced were dropped; and in January 1921, the key regulatory body, the Extraordinary Commission, was dissolved; and while the harsh restrictions on exports to Germany set down in the Danish trade agreement with the US in September 1918 remained in place, trade with the Allied countries was liberalized in April 1919. Yet this picture of the war years as a parenthesis must be nuanced. As a consequence of the regulated economy, interest groups gained a stronger say. The membership of trade unions almost trebled—an essential precondition for the victories they secured for their members in the wake of the war (in the shape of substantial wage increases and the introduction of the eight-hour working day), although fear of the radicalization of the working classes inspired by revolutionary upheavals elsewhere probably also explains why the employers chose to give in to many of the demands.[52] The key roles played by industrialists, shipowners, and the wholesale traders' organization secured them a much stronger position within their trades, and consequently a stronger position vis-à-vis other interests. It is telling that agricultural interests who strongly felt that they had to bear an unfairly large part of the regulatory burden, in 1919 finally managed to join forces in Landsbrugsrådet, the Agricultural Council that quickly grew into one of the strongest interest groups in the country, and remained so for the rest of the twentieth century.[53]

In politics, Denmark's Social Liberal government became the target of ever-growing criticism soon after the armistice. Liberals felt the winding up of regulations was proceeding too slowly and complained about 'state socialism', while Conservatives (and quite a few Liberals as well) were highly critical of the government's policy on the Schleswig question. The fall of the government in 1920 led to a brief constitutional crisis, but the ensuing elections demonstrated that the Social Liberals had lost almost half of their popular support, and the party never regained its pre-war strength. However, the politics of wartime left an important legacy in cementing a strong alliance between the Social Liberals and the Social Democrats. This alliance was to dominate Danish politics until the early 1960s and its main achievement was the construction of the Danish welfare state. The combination of regulation, control, and social policy initiatives launched during the war can be seen, in a longer historical perspective, as crucial groundwork for this political project.

Scandinavian internationalism and imminent isolationism

The membership of the League of Nations can very well be termed 'internationalism', but it was nonetheless only a part of Scandinavian liaison with the outside world, and it came to an end in the latter part of the 1930s as a result of the deterioration in international relations. Since the nineteenth century, internationalism was commonly understood as a movement that encouraged arms control, and political and economic cooperation between countries. Its advocates maintained that this would prevent armed conflict and promote growth in a variety of ways. At the outbreak of the First

World War, internationalism could look back on a fairly successful history. Some 450 international organizations had come into being, ranging from practical bodies such as the Telegraphic Union (1865) and the Universal Postal Union (1874) to the Institute of International Law (1873) and the International Red Cross (1863). The most important political organization was probably the Inter-Parliamentary Union (1886), of which the Norwegian Christian Lange was the secretary general from 1909 to 1933. The interwar years produced a number of international arms control agreements for the first time. In different ways, all these organizations encouraged multilateralism and cooperation in areas not covered by traditional diplomacy.

The dominant position of the League in the 1920s was a result of the lack of a power balance between the traditional great powers. When Germany and the Soviet Union regained their strength and set out to challenge the states system the League gradually lost its authority and became increasingly marginalized. In the words of Mark Mazower, 'diplomacy flowed around Geneva rather than through it, and a rival ideological vision of a European order emerged in Berlin.'[54] The five years leading up to Hitler's *Machtübernahme* witnessed a few French efforts to stabilize Europe through the League. First, the useless Briand–Kellogg Pact (1928) which set out to forbid war. Then came Briand's grandiose proposals for European unity (1929 and 1930)—equally futile. Finally, there was the failure of the disarmament conference in Geneva in 1932. After that, internationalism at its most lofty was clearly in decline. When Germany marched out of the League in 1933, the whole idea of liberal universalism came under savage attack and left the League increasingly paralysed.[55]

In 1937, E. H. Carr remarked that if 'European democracy binds its living body to the putrefying corps of the 1919 settlement then it will merely be committing a particularly unpleasant form of suicide.'[56] At that time the 'Oslo states', as the Northern neutrals were known in the 1930s, must have reasoned along the same lines.[57] The Italian attack on Abyssinia in 1935 and the German remilitarization of the Rhineland in 1936 brought about a fundamental shift in their focus from economic to national security issues. The coordinated efforts to slacken the League's sanctions regime was regarded as crucial by all the governments, since it would be almost impossible to do this on an individual, national basis. The Oslo states wanted to see a revival of the pre-League stance of non-alignment and neutrality. The question was discussed for the first time in Copenhagen in April 1936. There was a follow-up conference in Geneva in June that resulted in a joint declaration on 1 July, which stated that since the initial preconditions for their membership in the League no longer existed, they would not regard themselves as unreservedly bound by the Covenant. This was declared officially in a communiqué in 1938 and marked a definite break with the idea of collective security under the League. France and Great Britain ardently opposed this policy, which they considered to be pusillanimous.

Seen from outside the region, therefore, the Scandinavian countries looked to be floundering. On the one hand they were in the forefront in propagating internationalism, arbitration treaties, and disarmament. They had been widely regarded as a neutral bloc during the war. Moreover, for other peoples they came across as a relatively homogenous cultural entity, in overall agreement on important domestic and foreign policy issues. In retrospect, people outside Scandinavia were likely to ask why this did not translate into a closer cooperation in foreign policy and defence? Given that they shared liberal values and had similar views on international affairs, why were they unable to promote their interests jointly in order to increase their clout?

The consequences of war provoked abhorrence in both society and in politics. The establishment of an international order and institutions to hinder a new war, and not to prepare for another, became the salient issue. The Scandinavian countries can be said to have drawn selective lessons from their experience of the war— surprisingly similar ones, despite the fact that their policies had diverged. Perhaps most difficult to explain is the widespread refusal to recognize that neutrality had effectively collapsed in a total war. The difficulties Scandinavian diplomacy faced from the outset in getting the British to respect their rights as neutrals should have made this obvious, and it became an undeniable fact in 1917, when Germany declared unrestricted U-boat warfare and the US entered the war. One explanation for why the Scandinavian countries resolutely ignored the obvious is that they all remained formally neutral throughout the war.

Collective security, reinforced by fiscal constraints and economic depression, resulted in a reduction in military spending compared with both the pre-war arms build-up and the neutrality guard that had been maintained during the war. This was the case in all the Scandinavian countries, while newly independent Finland, with its troubled relations with Russia, was bent on establishing the armed forces necessary to defend the country. The Norwegian armed forces were gradually reduced in size and preparedness: conscription was retained, but at 72 days for the infantry it provided the shortest period of military training in Europe. Naval construction came to a halt in 1929. From then until 1936 the Navy only commissioned three coastguard vessels and an ocean-going minelayer. Moreover, except for coastguard and constabulary duties, no ships were kept ready for active service in the winter months until 1937. Exercises for all services, except for recruits' elementary training in summer, almost ground to a halt in the early 1920s and were not revived until the late 1930s. In Sweden, the unstable parliamentary situation allowed the military to fight a protracted delaying action until 1925, when the army's fighting strength was reduced from 12 to 4 divisions, the service time for conscripts radically shortened to 150 days, and a large portion of each year's intake automatically exempted from basic training. The cumulative effect of underfunding made it more difficult for the Scandinavian countries to muster the military means to maintain a protracted state of neutrality when they sought to return to it in the late 1930s.

Sweden's traumatic experience of domestic strife at a time of international crisis led to constitutional reform after the war, which institutionalized the Riksdag's control of foreign policy, with the creation in 1919 of Utrikesnämnden, the permanent committee on foreign relations. Moreover, when the Second World War broke out in 1939, a broad, four-party coalition government was formed, which in spite of much internal tension kept up an unwavering front of national unity throughout the conflict. This time, Sweden also demonstrated a more pragmatic attitude towards international law in its dealings with the belligerents than in 1914–17. Moreover, the demands for public consensus on foreign and security policy were to live on throughout the Cold War. Thus, it could be argued, Hjalmar Hammarskjöld's government would cast its shadow over Swedish politics for the rest of the twentieth century.

In the eyes of the Danish political establishment, the war represented a successful exercise in Danish diplomatic skills. The Social Liberal Peter Munch, the dominant voice in foreign policy debates (and Minister of Foreign Affairs, 1929–1940), was a keen internationalist; however, Danish security policy in the interwar years followed the path Munch had outlined before 1914, with a combination of neutrality and limited military expenditure with a strong domestic commitment to democratic institutions. By the late 1930s, his Social Democratic coalition partners, led by the prime minister, Thorvald Stauning, grew increasingly worried by the threat posed by Nazi Germany, but the Munch security policy regime was not seriously challenged before 1940.

In the Norwegian case, the lack of interest, or competence, in national security among politicians up to the late 1930s contributed to the ignorance of the broader population. Foreign policy and defence were the preserve of a handful of politicians, diplomats, and military leaders. Few politicians took a keen interest in the military dimensions of security policy or the military obligations laid down in international neutrality law. These obligations were to a large extent dismissed, or at least downplayed, by many politicians and intellectuals; widely discussed in the press, such matters completely eluded the tiny foreign policy elite. It should also be added that the debate was not overly subtle, since it was basically about the size of the defence budget. The overall result was that a number of unspoken assumptions were seldom challenged. It was taken for granted that Norway, and perhaps also Scandinavia, could remain aloof from future great-power conflicts as long as they complied with international neutrality law. The corollary—that a neutral stance had to be backed up by sufficient military means to make it effective and to comply with the Hague rules—was seldom presented as a stark choice, and the changes brought about in international politics by totalitarian ideologies, rearmament, and technology did not seem to alter threat perceptions much. Put bluntly, public opinion trusted in collective security to deter aggression; when that failed it trusted in traditional neutrality as a fallback that would not necessarily require increased defence spending; and if all else failed, it trusted that the Royal Navy's command of the sea and Britain's self-interest would prevent any other powers from attacking Norway.

Notwithstanding the obvious virtues of the League of Nations, there is at least one aspect of it that has escaped a thorough debate in Scandinavian historiography, namely the fact that the League in the 1920s served British and French imperial interests. The Wilsonian principle of national self-determination was actually restricted to Europe, with the notable exception of Germany. Otherwise, the French and British empires expanded to informally comprise huge swathes of the earlier Ottoman Empire, thus reaching their fullest extensions.[58] At the point when the League had become politically somewhat obsolete, sections of the Scandinavian body politic were embracing it wholeheartedly as a pious and altruistic institution unconstrained by national interests. This came to an end in 1938, when the Oslo states declared that they no longer regarded themselves bound by the Covenant's sanctions regime and that they intended to return to neutrality. Internationalism was definitely abandoned as a new war drew closer.

Notes

1 *Hvar 8 dag*, 1915/14 (3 January 1915).

2 Olav Riste, *Norway's Foreign Relations: A History* (Oslo: Universitetsforlaget, 2001).

3 Tom Kristiansen, *Mellom landmakter og sjømakter. Norges plass i britisk forsvars- og utenrikspolitikk 1905–1914* (diss.; University of Oslo, 1988); Folke Lindberg, *Scandinavia in Great Power Politics, 1905–1908* (Stockholm: Almquist & Wiksell, 1958); Pertti Luntinen, *The Baltic Question 1903–1908* (Helsinki: Suomalainen Tiedeaakatemia, 1975).

4 Patrick Salmon, *Scandinavia and the Great Powers, 1890–1940* (Cambridge: CUP, 1997).

5 Michael H. Clemmesen, *Den lange vej mod 9. April. Historien om de fyrre*

år før den tyske operation mod Norge og Danmark i 1940 (Odense: Syddansk Universitetsforlag, 2010).

6 For an overview of Danish history in the years leading up to 1914, see, for example, Bo Lidegaard, *A Short History of Denmark in the Twentieth Century* (Copenhagen: Gyldendal, 2009), 28–63.

7 Kent Zetterberg, *Militärer och politiker: en studie i militär professionalisering, innovationsspridning och internationellt inflytande* på de *svenska försvarsberedningarna 1911–1914* (Stockholm: Militärhistoriska förlaget, 1988).

8 The standard work on the Hammarskjöld government is Wilhelm M. Carlgren, *Ministären Hammarskjöld: Tillkomst—Söndring—Fall. Studier i svensk politik 1914–1917* (Uppsala: Almquist & Wiksell, 1967).

9 Gunnar Åselius, 'Storbritannien, Tyskland och den svenska neutraliteten 1880–1914: en omvärdering', *Historisk Tidskrift*, vol. 114 (1994), 228–66.

10 See Claus Bjørn & Carsten Due-Nielsen, *Fra helstat til nationalstat. Dansk udenrigspolitisk historie 1814–1914* (Copenhagen: Danmarks Nationalleksikon, 2003).

11 Michael Clemmesen, *The Danish Armed Forces 1909–1918* (Copenhagen: Royal Danish Defence College, 2007).

12 Riste 2001.

13 Cf. Ruth Hemstad, *Fra Indian Summer til nordisk vinter. Skandinavisk samarbeid, skandinavisme og unionsoppløsningen* (Oslo: Akademisk Forlag, 2008).

14 Rolf Hobson & Tom Kristiansen, *Norsk forsvarshistorie*, iii: *Total krig, nøytralitet og politisk splittelse, 1905–1940* (Bergen: Eide forlag, 2001), 60.

15 Gudmund Schnitler, *Strategi* (Kristiania: Grøndahl, 1914), 321, authors' translation.

16 Ove Bring, *Neutralitetens uppgång och fall—eller den gemensamma säkerhetens historia* (Stockholm: Atlantis, 2008), 141–53.

17 Cf. Bjørn & Due-Nielsen 2003, 496–501.

18 Torsten Gihl, *Den svenska utrikespolitikens historia*, iv: *1914–1919* (Stockholm: Norstedts, 1951) remains the standard work on Swedish foreign policy during the First World War.

19 Inger Schubert, *Schweden und das Deutsche Reich im Ersten Weltkrieg. Die Aktivistenbewegung 1914–1918* (Bonner Historische Forschungen; Bonn: Röhrscheid, 1981).

20 Nils Funcke, *Tryckfriheten under tryck. Ordets män och statsmakterna* (Stockholm: Carlssons, 1996), 37–38, 66.

21 Hobson & Kristiansen 2001, 113–114.

22 Svenbjörn Kilander, *Censur och propaganda: svensk informationspolitik under 1900-talets första decennier* (Uppsala: Almqvist & Wiksell, 1981), 95–100, 116–120.

23 Jens Ole Christensen, Michael H. Clemmesen & Ole L. Frantzen, *Københavns Befæstning—til fædrelandets forsvar* (Copenhagen: Gads forlag, 2012).

24 Arvid Cronenberg, 'Första världskrigets lantmilitära beredskap', in Johan Engström & Lars Ericson (eds.), *Mellan björnen och örnen. Sverige och Östersjön under det första världskriget 1914–1918* (Acta Visbyensia, 9; Visby: Gotlands fornsal, 1994), 87–116.

25 Lars Wedin, 'Kustflottan under första världskriget', in Gustaf von Hofsten & Frank Rosenius (eds.), *Kustflottan. De svenska sjöstridskrafterna under 1900-talet* (Stockholm: Kungliga Örlogsmannasällskapet & Marinlitteraturföreningen, 2009).

26 See Tage Kaarsted, *Great Britain and Denmark 1914–1920* (Odense: Odense University Press, 1979), 99–122; Kasper Elmquist Jørgensen, *Studier i samspillet mellem stat og erhvervsliv i Danmark under 1. Verdenskrig* (Frederiksberg: Samfundslitteratur, 2005), 192–213.

27 *Statistisk Aarbog* 1920.

28 Olav Riste, *The Neutral Ally. Norway's Relations with the Belligerent Powers in the First World War* (Oslo: Universitetsforlaget, 1965); Roald Berg, *Norsk utenrikspolitikks historie, ii: Norge på egen hand, 1905–1920* (Oslo: Universitetsforlaget, 1995).

29 The best general work on the impact of the war in Scandinavia is still Eli F. Heckscher, Kurt Bergendal, Wilhelm Keilhau, Einar Cohn, and Thorsteinn Thorsteinsson, (eds.), *Sweden, Norway, Denmark and Iceland in the World War* (Oxford: OUP, 1930).

30 The slogan can be seen in a photograph from the demonstration, reproduced in Christian A. R. Christensen, *Fra verdenskrig til verdenskrig* (Oslo: Aschehoug, 1961), 100.

31 See Bjarne Søndergaard Bendtsen, *Mellem fronterne* (Ph.D. thesis; Odense: University of Southern Denmark, 2011), 126–178.

32 See Jakob Lindberg, 'Indtægtsforskydningen i Danmark 1908–1920', *Nationaløkonomisk Tidsskrift* 59 (1921), 289–319.

33 Hans Christian Johansen, *Dansk skattehistorie*, vi: *Indkomstskatter og offentlig vækst 1903–2005* (Copenhagen: Dansk Told- og Skatehistorisk Selskab, 2007), 31–38.

34 Carl Göran Andræ, *Revolt eller reform: Sverige inför revolutionerna i Europa 1917–1918* (Stockholm: Carlssons, 1988).

35 Fredrik L. Eriksson, 'Bondeförbundet och liberalism 1914–1935', in Tomas Nilson & Martin Åberg (eds.), *Parti eller rörelse: perspektiv på liberala organisationsstrategier 1880–1940* (Lund: Sekel, 2010), 91–121.

36 Madelene Lidestad, *Uppbåd, uppgifter, undantag: Om genusarbetsdelning i Sverige under första världskriget* (diss.; Stockholm: Acta Universitatis Stockholmiensis, 2005).

37 Ketil Gjølme Andersen, *Flaggskip i fremmed eie. Hydro 1905–1945* (Oslo: Pax, 2005), 164–75.

38 See Lindberg 1958.

39 Wilhelm M. Carlgren, 'Svensk neutralitet 1914–1918 och 1939–1945', *Historisk tidskrift* [Sweden] (1979), 381.

40 Tom Kristiansen, *Sjøforsvaret i Krig og Fred. Langs kysten og på havet gjennom 200 år, ii: 1905–1960: Selvstendig og alliert i krig og fred* (Bergen: Fagbokforlaget, 2010), 239.

41 Wilhelm Carlgren, *Neutraliät oder Allianz? Deutschlands Beziehungen zu Schweden in den Anfangsjahren des Ersten Weltkrieges* (Stockholm: Almquist & Wiksell, 1962) is still a central work on the foreign policy of the Hammarskjöld government.

42 The standard work on Swedish foreign policy during the latter part of the First World War is Steven Koblik, *Sweden: the neutral victor Sweden and the Western powers 1917–1918: a study of Anglo-American–Swedish relations* (Lund: Läromedelsförlagen, 1972); on the Åland question, see Göran Rystad, 'Die deutsche Monroedoktrin der Ostsee: die Alandsfrage und die Entstehung des deutsch-schwedischen Geheimabkommens vom Mai 1918', in Göran Rystad et al. (eds.), *Probleme deutscher Zeitgeschichte* (Lund Studies in International History: Lund: Läromedelsförlagen, 1971).

43 See Claus Bundgaard Christensen, *Danskere på Vestfronten 1914–1918* (Copenhagen: Gyldendal, 2009); Bendtsen 2011; Niels Jensen, *For Dannebrogs ære. Danske frivillige i Estland og Letlands frihedskampe 1919* (Odense: Odense Universitetsforlag, 1998).

44 Elow Nilson, *Svenska hjältar vid fronten: ur en stupads dagbok* (Stockholm: Åhlén & Åkerlund, 1917); Lars Ericson [Wolke], *Svenska frivilliga: militära uppdrag i utlandet under 1800- och 1900-talen* (Lund: Historiska Media, 1996), 54–90, 184–190 covers Swedish volunteers in the East, including Finland, Estonia, and Russia in 1918–1920.

45 St.prp. [Storting Proposition, or parliamentary Bill] nr.33 1920, 'Om Norges tilslutning til Folkenes Forbund'.

46 For a detailed account, see Roald Berg 1995.

47 Odd-Bjørn Fure, *Mellomkrigstid. 1920–1940. Norsk utenrikspolitikks historie*, iii (Oslo: Universitetsforlaget, 1995).

48 For a more detailed account of Norwegian policy in 1919–20, see Hobson & Kristiansen 2001.

49 Karen Gram-Skjoldager, *Fred og folkerett. Dansk internasjonalistisk udenrigspolitik 1889–1939* (Copenhagen: Museum Tusculaneum, 2012), 117–174.

50 Göran Rystad, 'The Åland question and the balance of power in the Baltic during the First World War', in Göran Rystad, Klaus-Richard Böhme & Wilhelm M. Carlgren (eds.), *In Quest of Trade and Security. The Baltic in Power Politics 1500–1990*, ii: *1890–1990* (Stockholm: Probus, 1995), 50–105.

51 On the Schleswig question and its repercussions for Danish politics, see Troels Fink, *Da Sønderjylland blev delt, 1918–20*, 3 vols. (Aabenraa: Institut for Grænseregionsforskning, 1978–9).

52 Svend Aage Hansen & Inge Henriksen, *Socialebrydninger. Dansk socialhistorie 1914–39* (2nd edn., Copenhagen: Gyldendal, 1984), 92–103.

53 See Torben Hansgaard, *Landbrugsrådets tilblivelse* (Copenhagen: Landbohistorisk Selskab, 1976).

54 Mark Mazower, *Dark Continent. Europe's Twentieth Century* (London: Penguin, 1999), 65.

55 Ibid. 69.

56 Ibid.

57 The Oslo Agreement of 1930 between Belgium, the Netherlands, Luxembourg, Denmark, Sweden, and Norway was intended to alleviate the effects of the Great Depression; Finland joined the group in 1933. Until 1936, economic issues dominated proceedings. After that the coordination of their security policies was given priority. For a survey of the Oslo states, see Ger van Roon, *Small states in Years of Depression: the Oslo Alliance 1930–1940* (Assen/Maastricht: Van Gorchum, 1989).

58 Mark Mazower, *No Enchanted Palace. The End of Empire and the Ideological Origins of the United Nations* (Princeton: PUP, 2009), 23.

CHAPTER I

An album of war

The visual mediation of the First World War in Danish magazines and daily newspapers

Ulrik Lehrmann

> The press of countries at war loses its capacity to reflect a nation's life, the soul of a people. … What it omits saying, or has to omit saying, remains just as difficult for the future writer of history to uncover as it is difficult for him to find a thread in what is being said. But even so he must get a strong impression of the power and importance of the press from the press telegrams of the war.[1]

From a media perspective, the First World War was a crucial turning point for the modernization process of the Scandinavian press that was already underway. 'The First World War has been called the last great newspaper war—on the other hand, it changed the newspapers more than any previous war had done,' according to the latest Swedish history of the press.[2] The increase in the circulation of the daily and magazine press continued during the war, during which there was a great demand for the latest news. When it came to supplying news, the First World War was a large-scale testing ground for a Western European, and ultimately global, news network—something for which the spread of the telegraph network and the international telegram agencies' communications work and market sharing had laid the foundation in the latter half of the nineteenth century. In relation to the typological shift of the Scandinavian daily press from party newspaper to omnibus newspaper—which had not been introduced until the first decade

57

of the twentieth century and was far from complete—the war's stream of telegrams accentuated the journalistic focus on news. At the same time, the war coverage meant a modernization of newspaper layouts: front pages were cleared of advertising material; headlines spanned more than one column; war material was edited thematically as a separate topic; and—as will be examined more closely in this chapter—visual mediation through the use of photographic material intensified, especially in the daily press (the magazine press having already gone over to the almost exclusive use of reproduced photographs). The Norwegian media historian Tor Are Johansen also views the 1910s as the 'definitive breakthrough' for photographs in Norwegian newspapers—although he does not mention the importance of the war in this connection.[3] The photographic mediation of the war was not, however, an internal media concern but also, to an even greater extent, part of the propaganda war being waged by the powers involved. The First World War, thought of as photograph album, therefore marks a coming together of journalistic priorities and propaganda interests.

Photojournalism and image reproduction techniques

The visual representation of the First World War in the Scandinavian media was determined by the development of photojournalism, the network of sources, and the state of reproduction technology, as well as the various forms of state censorship of news media.

Photojournalism only started to develop seriously in the interwar years, but the publication of war photographs was known from the mid nineteenth century onwards (notably from the Crimean War and the American Civil War).[4] Media coverage of the First World War, however, produced a veritable flood of images, which is why coverage of this particular war marks a crucial turning point in relation to both photojournalism and film reproductions of war.[5] Not without reason has the First World War been characterized as the first mediated war in history on a number of counts, because those involved no longer stood opposite one another, face to face, but had media interposed between them, both in the form of such war technology as long-distance weaponry and by virtue of the fact that warfare was dependent on information conveyed by visual media, including aerial photography: 'the urgent need that developed for ever more accurate sighting, ever greater magnification, for *filming the war* and photographically reconstructing the battlefield'.[6] The visual media were not only of tactical importance in the war, but also part of the soldiers' understanding of it:

> The presence of photographers and cameramen changed the situation on the battlefield. The soldiers now all started to pose for the photographers and take part in mock battles in front of the cameras. Out of this developed a specific representational aesthetics of war, in which the reality of the action was staged on the basis of its communication by the media.[7]

Visual representations themselves became a war zone, and at the same time the visual mediation of the war was assessed as a fundamental change in the 'visual mechanisms of observation'[8] and an objectifying 'industrialization of the capacity for observation'.[9] The army leaders on both sides admittedly tried to control the flow of images as best they could, but in the long run this was difficult since not only official photographers but also common soldiers took photographs. British newspapers even organized competitions among the soldiers for the best war pictures.[10]

The motifs of the photographs that were published can be seen at a general level as presentations of national myths, with stereotypical conceptions of patriotism, heroism, and national solidarity as the crucial selection criteria for the photographs that found their way into the daily and weekly press, while the horror of war was underplayed.[11] As sheer propaganda, the war photographs at the start of the war presented a fairly stereotypical iconographic pattern, with motifs consisting of troop parades, cheerful soldiers marching past enthusiastic crowds, and military vehicles setting off for war.[12] The visualization of war as an imaginary reality without much contact with actual conditions was particularly maintained in the images in the German press, while the British press changed course after the Battle of the Somme, when it began to depict the horror of war. In the French press the brutality of war was also less glossed over than in the German press.[13]

The state of reproduction technology during the war was very unusual, particularly as far as the daily press was concerned, because it was in the middle of a transitional phase from drawings and xylography (printing from detailed engravings on wood) to photographic images, and because telegraphed pictures were still only a technical possibility. Since the 1860s, experiments had been carried out with picture transmission by telegraph,[14] and in 1908 an event was organized in connection with the launch of a Berlin–Copenhagen–Stockholm picture telegraph connection, over which the Danish newspaper *Politiken* and the Swedish *Dagens Nyheter* had the right of disposal for Scandinavia.[15] It was not until the 1920s, however, that the use of phototelegraphy really came into its own, which is why the 1920s are thought of in terms of the media and photojournalism as 'the decade of the flood of images'.[16] In 1921, the American telegraph company Western Union transmitted its first halftone photograph, followed by the American Telephone and Telegraph Company (AT&T) in 1924, and the radio organization RCA's 'radiophoto' in 1926. At the same time, international telegram agencies such as Associated Press started to set up actual picture services, whereas the German telegram agencies such as Wolffschen Telegraphen Büro and Telegraphen-Union took longer in developing the picture side of their activities.[17] But since the 1890s, even before the international picture agencies began to dominate the market, picture agencies had been springing up at the major illustrated weeklies and independent stereotyping and electrotyping establishments, offering a diverse stock of plates for xylography, drawings from photographs, and halftone reproductions of photographs.[18] These picture agencies, in Western Europe at least, had developed an exchange network of sorts.

There is not much to suggest that the Scandinavian press had actually made use of the technical potential for telegraphic picture transmission that opened up in 1908. There is, on the contrary, certain evidence to suggest that the use of news photographs, particularly in the daily press, had yet to oust the use of drawings.

Da Paris hjemsøgtes af tyske Aëroplaner.

Episode fra Bombeeksplosionen i Rue Vinaigriers.

Ovenstaaende Billede viser en Episode fra de Dage, da Paris hjemsøgtes af tyske Aëroplaner, der slyngede Bomber ned over Gader og Bygninger. En Bombe — udkastet fra en Flyvemaskine, der svævede højt til Vejrs — faldt ned paa Hjørnet af Rue Vinaigriers og moles'erede en Bagerbutik og en Vinhandlerforretning. Billedet gengiver et Fotografi, taget umiddelbart efter Bombeeksplosionen, og før man havde haft Tid til at fjerne Murbrokker og det i Stumper og Stykker sprængte Butiksinventar. Som man ser, anrettede Bomben ikke ringe Skade, men heldigvis blev ingen Mennesker dræbt eller saaret.

FIGURE 1: Drawing based on a photograph. 'The picture reproduces a photograph taken immediately after the explosion of the bomb.' Note the signature in the bottom right-hand corner. (*Politiken,* 2 October 1914) (Statens Avissamling, Statsbiblioteket Aarhus)

Even so, it is evident that newspapers and weekly magazines not only included what were definitely drawings from foreign press material showing the war, but that some of the illustrations in the newspapers were drawings based on photographs. Although it had been technically possible since the 1890s to reproduce photographs as halftone pictures, twenty years passed before newspaper photographs really gained a foothold, whereas the magazine press exploited the possibility of reproducing photographs much earlier.[19]

In the initial phase of the war, *Politiken* featured a number of drawings based on photographs. This may have been due to the fact that they were based not on photographs (positives) of sufficient quality to permit reproduction, but on foreign newspaper and magazine illustrations of such poor quality that they could only be made use of if they were converted into line drawings.[20] 'The picture is taken from a German magazine and is undoubtedly genuine', or 'The above picture is based on a photograph' are typical explanations for heavily touched-up photographs, which could just as well have been reproduced as drawings.[21] Quite apart from the issue of the technical quality of the reproduction, it should be borne in mind that line drawings (black-line or white-line cuts) were both quicker and cheaper as illustrations than autotype (halftone or greytone). Nor should it be underestimated that in 1914 there was still great prestige attached to illustrating. When *Politiken* moved to its present building on City Hall Square in Copenhagen in 1912, the newspaper had no fewer than five illustrators on the payroll—and only one press photographer.

There is another dimension to the question of newspaper illustrations, however: certain newspapers used very few of any kind. In certain circles, the use of photographs in newspapers still met with certain resistance, as they regarded the use of pictures rather than the information density of the printed word as the end of civilization as they knew it. So it was not until 1913 that the paper of the Conservative upper middle class, *Berlingske Tidende*, carried any form of illustration (and that was a drawing), nor until precisely 1913–14 that its first photographs appeared.[22] This attitude was typical of the time, with illustrations in newspapers being associated with the yellow press, whose readers were perceived as being virtually illiterate. As Walter Lippmann (1889–1974) put it, in his reflections on the propaganda efforts of the media during the war, this was an attitude that verged on a principle in emphasizing the immediate realism of the photograph and its effortless accessibility:

> Photographs have the kind of authority over imagination to-day, which the printed word had yesterday, and the spoken word before that. They seem utterly real. They come, we imagine, directly to us, without human meddling, and they are the most effortless food for the mind conceivable. … on the screen the whole process of observing, describing, repeating and then imagining has been accomplished for you.[23]

The transitional forms of reproduction in the visual mediation of the First World War also indicate that the photograph possibly does not mark the definitive breakthrough at all for media visualization—that it should be looked for far earlier, when it became possible to include illustrations printed from woodcuts. Especially when it came to the illustrated weeklies, this change took place in the latter half of the nineteenth century, and photographic reproduction by comparison was merely a technical innovation, not the decisive step we tend to consider it today, because we are easily tempted to ascribe a different truth value (the reality effect) to a photograph than to drawings and xylography. During the war, there was a certain amount of drawn material in *Illustreret Familie-Journal*, while *Illustreret Tidende* and *Hver 8. Dag*, as news magazines, were more oriented towards the use of photographic material. There are signs that the transition from drawings to photographs was still fluid in 1914, that the media had not yet come down decisively in favour of photographs, and that when it came to the development of a printed visual media culture, xylographic news pictures in the weekly press and drawings in the daily press were probably just as decisive as turning points in media history as was photographic reproduction.[24]

The flow of information and press legislation

With the outbreak of the war, the existing order in communications collapsed. As regards telegraphy, Germany was isolated by the Allies, since the underwater telegraph cables were destroyed. All telegraph traffic was therefore diverted round Germany and sent through neighbouring countries, with Denmark and Sweden included among the intermediate stations. In all the Scandinavian countries, the war was the cause of an enormous increase in telegraph traffic, and in each country there lay a hub of the European telegraphic network—there were in fact two such locations in Denmark (in Fredericia and Copenhagen).[25]

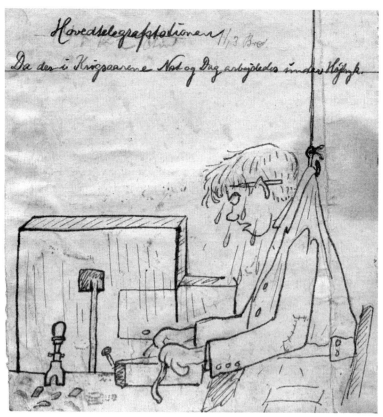

FIGURE 2: 'Main telegraph station. Where, during the war, work continues at full speed both day and night.' (c. 1918, Post & Tele Museum, Copenhagen).

Apart from the reciprocal telegraph connections between the Scandinavian countries, Denmark as the southernmost country was directly linked to Germany, Britain, France, and Russia (via the Baltic island of Bornholm)—thanks largely to the cable route of Store Nordiske Telegrafselskab. The cable route to Germany (Gedser–Warnemünde) was severed on 4 August 1914, and in November 1914 two direct cables to Russia were shut down. Two further cables between Denmark and France were shut down in September 1917, and later one of the two cables to Britain was also shut down. The connection to Russia was re-established by routing telegraph traffic through Sweden.

Postal connections were also affected by the war. Transit mail through Germany stopped, although direct mail between Germany and Denmark was maintained. This meant that all mail from Britain, France, the Netherlands, Belgium, and so on—including photographic prints and newspapers and magazines—reached Denmark by boat (and was thus exposed to unrestricted submarine warfare from 1917).

With regard to censorship, Britain had good reason to control trade with Denmark, so that Germany could not in this way acquire special resources, for example, horses from Iceland, or rubber from the US.[26] The key censorship measures, however, were directed against telegraphic information about the war itself, which for the warring parties stemmed from the wish to control information and propaganda alike. It was, however, not only at the sending but also the receiving end that censorship was imposed in the Scandinavian countries. At the main telegraph station in Copenhagen, all telegrams from both foreign agencies and the newspapers' own correspondents were subject to censorship, and conferences were held (in Gothenburg on 17–18 December 1917 and in Stockholm on 11 September 1918) where the Scandinavian countries attempted to arrive at common measures for telegram censorship. For both telegraph communications and the printed press it was the questions of military information, trade information, and explicit expressions of opinion about the countries waging war, which constituted the battleground for state and press on the boundaries of freedom of speech on issues that involved foreign powers.[27] As avowedly neutral countries, it was important for the Scandinavian governments that the media did not come down on the side of any of the combatants, which in certain quarters was itself regarded as a blow against freedom of speech.

In Denmark, the daily press came to an informal agreement with the government in August 1914 not to mention troop movements and not to adopt a partial attitude toward the belligerents. A few newspapers, however, did not stick to the agreement, and in 1915 the government found it necessary to introduce proper legislation in the form of a temporary Press Act which made it punishable either to cast doubt on the neutral attitude of the state authorities in relation to commercial initiatives or 'to incite the population against a nation at war'.[28] Similarly, the Swedish foreign office sent out a communiqué to the press the day before war broke out which stated that the newspapers should strive to ensure that 'announcements and statements about events in the war were formulated completely objectively and without taking the side of any of the warring factions, and to avoid any offensive remarks about them'.[29] In the Scandinavian countries, then, there was press legislation that mainly focused on regulating public access to possibly critical treatments of each state's balancing act between commercial policies and neutrality, where the foreign flow of information concerning the progress of the war attracted attention to the extent that publication in the newspapers of special pleading on the part of one of the warring parties could be perceived as a breach of what was in principle a neutral attitude.

Censorship also applied in principle to photographs and drawings, but the media in the neutral, Scandinavian countries found themselves in a situation where they received nothing but visual material that had already been approved by belligerents' censorship authorities. At the beginning of the war, the army leaders of the respective countries refused to give press photographers access to the fronts, but gradually they too came to realize the importance of being able to control the visual mediation of the war, which led them to employ their own war photographers. However, the photographers' limited freedom to operate is less interesting in the present context, where the focus is on the nature of the images that found their way into the Danish daily and weekly press, and so contributed to constructing the First World War as a visual reality. In that perspective, it is also worth noting that the flow of pictures and range of motifs was not only limited by censorship; photographic techniques, and in particular the picture conventions and genres that the illustrated weeklies and sentimental genre painting had cultivated in the latter half of the nineteenth century, also influenced the visual construction of the war and barred the development of photographic realism in press photography.[30]

Pictures of the war

During the first years of the war, the coverage was so massive that the media primarily passed on information on the course of the war, while other material was deemed less important. Week after week, month after month, the front pages of the newspapers were full of telegram material from the warring factions. In the Swedish newspaper *Dagens Nyheter*, the amount of foreign material increased fivefold during the autumn of 1914, making up 30 per cent of the editorial copy in November.[31] A survey of one Copenhagen newspaper (*Politiken*) and three local newspapers in the city of Odense (*Fyens Stiftstidende, Fyns Tidende*, and *Fyns Social-Demokrat*) shows, however, that war coverage shrank from 40–50 per cent of the editorial copy in the autumn of 1914 to about 20 per cent in the autumn of 1916 (see Table 1.2). Approximately 60 per cent of the war coverage comprised telegram material, and throughout the war the official communiqués of the respective army leaders and governments reigned virtually supreme when it came to telegram material, something that *Dagens Nyheter* was quick to spot early on:

> Where does the world press get the news from that it now dishes up, and that is repeated in one newspaper after another almost verbatim? It must now mainly be the task of the major telegram agencies to procure it, which in other words means that it is the respective army leaders—the general staff—that dispatch it, naturally well-laced with their own interests. So it is not 'the newspapers that are lying' when one telegram reports a defeat and the other reports a victory.[32]

So there was not very much independent journalism to be found in the newspapers; more a collage of telegrams that voiced the warring parties' differing versions of events.[33] Even though the percentage of editorial copy given over to the war decreased as the war became routine, it is worth noting that the share of illustrations in the coverage increased from 8 per cent in 1914 to 14 per cent in 1916 (see Table 1.3). At the same time, the nature of the illustrations also changed. While the illustrations in certain parts of the daily press in 1914 mainly comprised drawings from photographs, the illustrations in 1916 were almost exclusively direct reproductions of photographs. Seen with modern eyes, one can say that the war became visually more present—although it is far from certain that it was perceived as such at the time. The illustrations in the weekly magazines, meanwhile, mainly comprised photographs throughout the war.

Gerhard Paul, in his presentation of the universe of war pictures, points out that because of the technological advances, it was possible for the first time to freeze motion in a photograph, and that the down-to-earth reproduction of war's industrial technologies of destruction was a new photographic motif. On the other hand, war photographs were also more conventional in a mode reminiscent of genre painting and the landscape pictures seen from a tourist angle, only now in a more ravaged version.[34] Taking these ideas as my point of departure, I have undertaken a quantitative survey of the mediation of the war in the newspapers *Politiken* and *Social-Demokraten* for the space of one week in September 1914 and again in October 1916, and in the magazines *Illustreret Tidende*, *Hver 8. Dag*, and *Illustreret Familie-Journal*, October 1914 and 1916. In categorizing the survey data, I have distinguished between pictures that reproduce an action or the result of an action (for example, a bombed house) and therefore contain a narrative, situational element, and pictures that reproduce their motif in its objective nature in a broad sense (for example, a view of a town, portraits, or pictures of materiel). The categorization further involved a division into four recurring groups of motifs: urban pictures, landscapes, people (civil and military respectively), and materiel. In this way it has been possible to distinguish three main genres of pictures: the tableauesque picture, which at times also makes a strong appeal to the emotions, and is a narrative scene which includes actions or the result of actions for all groups of motifs; panoramic images of towns and landscapes as objects; (technically) documented images of materiel and individuals or groups of people as objects (discussed in the next section).

The number of illustrations dropped by half between 1914 and 1916. The news value of the war diminished as time passed. Comprehensive illustrative material must have circulated, however, for neither in 1914 nor in 1916 has it been confirmed more than once or twice that the same illustration was printed in several media. The strongest recurring motif in the war coverage in both 1914 and 1916 is scenes with soldiers.[35] In 1914, these scenes are flanked by urban panoramas, which as far as the newspapers were concerned largely consisted of pre-war pictures of the towns where the action was taking place (for example Antwerp or Reims). Indeed, the Swedish weekly *Hvar 8 dag* actually claimed in a controversy in the autumn of 1914 that when it came to pictures of soldiers, the other weeklies were printing 'lots of old pictures of manoeuvres'.[36] Apart from the touristy prospect pictures, the magazine press also printed many pictures of the physical destruction that resulted from bombing. In 1916, the scenes of soldiers are flanked by numerous portraits of leading military figures as well as pictures of materiel, with the number of urban pictures decreasing once the fighting had moved on from the towns of Belgium and Northern France.

The many scenes with soldiers only depict actual hostilities to a very limited extent, and where they do it is in drawings that elaborate on the scene of battle in a detailed battle painting style. Because of the strict censorship, the photographers did not have direct access to the front, and so there was nothing like the modern war photographs of actual hostilities and the immediate war zone, only pictures of the life for the soldiers behind the front. However, overly idyllic, touristy, and heroic portrayals are absent from most of the pictures of the soldiers' lives.[37] On the basis of a comprehensive survey of the coverage of the war in the Swedish weekly press, Lina Sturfelt proposes four basic narratives of the war: fatalism, heroism, fun and idyll, and the death factory. This categorization can only with difficulty be transferred to the visual representation of the war, however, partly because fatalism and heroism are very little represented in the visual material, and partly because few pictures of the soldiers' lives behind the front can automatically be categorized under fun and idyll (see below).

The pictures that were published in the Danish media mostly came from the presses of the Entente Powers (see Table 1.6), and this became even more marked as the war progressed. Yet the prioritizing of sources in the individual papers differed considerably. In 1914, *Illustreret Tidende* and *Social-Demokraten*, unlike the others, had almost twice as many illustrations with German motif angle than with an Entente motif angle,[38] which to a certain extent blurs the overall predominance of the Entente motif angle. In 1916, *Illustreret Tidende* had fallen into line with the rest of the magazine press, while both *Politiken* and *Social-Demokraten* had a fairly equal spread of sources.

Picture genres – prospects, tableaux, and instructions

The picture genres used to mediate the war were an extension of the picture formats developed during the breakthrough of visual media culture in the latter half of the nineteenth century. As did xylographs and, later, photographs, key genres such as landscapes and urban prospects, scenic narrative pictures, and technical drawings contributed to the dimensioning and spread of a visual space of knowledge and experience.

Because of the historical genres embedded in the visual construction of the war by the daily and magazine press, it adhered to special appeal structures in the form of preferred outlooks (optics) from which the flow of pictures gave (most) meaning. The landscape and the urban prospect appeal to a tourist gaze, characterized by a predominantly aesthetic attitude to the visual space. The instructional drawing or the technical illustration, known from illustrations of nineteenth-century inventions, speaks to analytical dissection and documentation, for it is intended to serve as a form of visual manual. The aim of the instructional drawing and, in a

TABLE 1.1 Motif groupings, picture genres, and predominant views

Motifs	Visual tradition	Reproduction technology and media	Optic
Urban and landscape	Prospect (LANDSCAPE PAINTING)	Xylography and photography —Postcard	Tourist view (visual aesthetic space)
Groups and portraits of military personnel and materiel	Instruction/ instructional drawing (TECHNICAL ILLUSTRATION)	Photograph/ Drawing —Illustrated weeklies —Technically informative books and magazines	Documentary view (knowledge space)
Evidence of war (ruins, battlefields), military and civilian actions	Tableau (NARRATIVE GENRE PAINTING)		Theatre view (emotional space)

broader sense, photographs of materiel, grouped soldiers, and general portraits is to convey knowledge about a given subject. Finally, there is the narrative genre painting as a framework for conveying evidence of war that contains a narrative subject: civilians with buckets in ruined houses, soldiers shooting at aircraft. This optic often seeks to elicit a strong emotional identification from the reader, and it therefore seems obvious to characterize it as a theatrical look—to emphasize a kinship between that visual tradition and the prevalent, melodramatic tendency of late nineteenth-century popular culture, especially the popular theatre, and the silent films of the early twentieth century.

In the visual representation of the war by the media, it was particularly in the initial phase of hostilities, when Germany invaded neutral Belgium, that urban prospects flourished. In the daily press this mainly took the form of urban scenes from before the war of the localities where the fighting was taking place, while the magazine press had a more even distribution of urban pictures from before and after German bombardments. The panoramic optic of the

Billeder fra Verdun.

Et Parti af Verdun før Krigen.

Det samme Parti fotograferet under Krigen.

Hver 8. Dag, 22 October 1916

DET UNDE

Den tyske Undervandsbaad U 9

Torpedoen ført ind i Udskydningsre

Torpedoen pustes med komprimet Luft
Ovenvande-Udskydningsrør

Illustreret Tidende,
4 October 1914

FIGURE 3: Prospects, instructions, and tableaux.
(Left) The same urban prospect as a tourist postcard and a war ruin respectively;

urban prospects set up a sounding board for the visual mediation of the war, which via a tourist view holds up for inspection, in an aestheticized state, an entire world from before the war. The pictures are not in themselves violently dramatic, but because of constant repetition and the contrast with houses reduced to rubble by shelling, the before–now pictures published particularly in the magazine press help to place the destructiveness of war in stark relief.

ARTILLERI

Verðenskrigen.

Torpedoen er i Vandet

n dykker ned i Vandet og fortsætter med sagen Maskine og Styring sin Bane

Paa Valpladsen i Belgien. Slaget er endt! — Belgiske Flygtninge paa Vej til Bryssel, hver søger at redde deres kæreste Ejendele. — Belgisk Artilleri, der holder Hvil udenfor Namur før Bombardementet.

Hver 8. Dag, 4 October 1914

(centre) a visual orientation on how submarine torpedoes work; and (right) scenes of the war showing fleeing civilians and soldiers. (Statens Avissamling, Statsbiblioteket Aarhus)

As a visual media phenomenon, the war to a great extent also comprised mute, massive materiel. Archive pictures of military materiel (cannons, ships) and pictures that show soldiers as objects *en masse* (typically marching) made up between a quarter and a third of the visual material. Images of materiel in particular tend to the technically instructive, which, combined with the explanatory captions, serves to impart knowledge about the war,

73

documenting it within its technical, industrial framework. This documentation view can also be read from the way the pictures have an analytically dissecting function in conveying, for example, submarine torpedoes, where a picture of the submarine serves as a frame for a detailed visual explanation of the torpedo itself (see Figure 3).

The largest category throughout the war was pictures of soldiers in scenes with a narrative element, albeit one often restricted to a limited situation. Captions such as 'The picture, which was taken at night, shows a British officers' mess kitchen at work', 'From the Saloniki Front—Scots on guard', 'At a field post', 'Belgian ambush of a railway station', and 'German army bakery' indicate that we are dealing with tableauesque motifs that are static and therefore easier to photograph, and that we seldom find ourselves at the front line. In *Politiken*, the difficulty of the situation was openly admitted: 'Among the multitude of war pictures that the film companies, the major illustration agencies, and the illustrated magazines sent out into the world there are also pictures of clashes and battles, but these are always before or after. If there is a real battle, one can be sure that it will not be a photograph but a drawn picture.'[39] In *Pressens Magasin*, readers were also openly warned against believing the photographs of battle scenes:

> This picture has got past the Austrian censors. On the back it says that it was photographed during the Russian offensive on the Austrian Front. It admittedly shows some Russian soldiers in the middle of a barbed wire fence. But these are certain to be prisoners who have acted in a film for a plug of tobacco the Austrian photographer has promised them.[40]

Pictures of soldiers were not, however, entirely devoted to scenes of everyday routine or preparations for battle. Corresponding to the urban prospects of shattered houses, there were also pictures of wounded soldiers and men fallen in battle, and these emphasized the brutality of war. The tableauesque scenes with a narrative element were indebted in genre terms to the narrative painting (genre painting) of the nineteenth century, and naturally enough there

Morgen efter Slaget ved Marne.

FIGURE 4: *Social-Demokraten*, 14 October 1914, front page. (Statens Avis-samling, Statsbiblioteket Aarhus)

were also strongly melodramatic illustrations—dead soldiers, dying horses—that most of all seem to be arranged photographs, or drawings based on genre paintings.[41]

On the whole, the visual mediation of the war by the daily and magazine press helped to bring the war close in a neutral country such as Denmark; as to media history, the war pictures marked a turning point in the use of photographically reproduced illustrative material by the newspapers. The largely urban prospects filled in the background of pre-war life. On the basis of this, the period saw a developing, technical mediation of the war in all its material massiveness—the technology itself and the substantial volume of pictures of materiel and objectified soldiers *en masse*—as well as a narrative angling of the war with its focus on the soldiers. The narrative dimension spanned several scenarios: the destructiveness and brutality of war was emphasized in pictures of shattered towns and bodies on the battlefield; at the same time, scenes with soldiers were also used to give an impression of how mundane life at war became 'mundanity' in the shadow of the war. In my opinion, there was no real tendency to portray the war as an idyll in these war pictures, as is sometimes claimed—rather a visual insistence on the necessary routinization of everyday life at the front. We know very little about what people at the time made of this flood of war pictures, but there is at least one thought-provoking statement that points to the interaction of the various media, while indicating the both forbidden and titillating aspects of conjuring up fantasy images of war and then leafing through them, booklike, at leisure:

> From time to time, among the hundreds of war accounts to which our eyes have gradually accustomed themselves, we suddenly stop at some episode or other that seizes us with dramatic force. Deep down inside us—as a thought of which we are almost ashamed—we feel a desire—without any form of risk involved—to be able actually to experience, to witness something similar. With all our dread and detestation of the war, we cannot even so ... protect ourselves from having a certain audience-like urge to hold onto its *images*. And then the strange thing happens, that the next time we open an illustrated magazine or enter a cinema, we find precisely the 'picture' that we saw in our imagination when we read our newspaper.[42]

The First World War as visual culture

Seen from a point of view of the history of cultural and consciousness, the First World War is more than diplomatic negotiations and acts of war. It was also a mental horizon that supplied the material with which people thought their everyday lives. The visual representation of the war by the daily and magazine press was only part of a more extensive visualization of the war, translated into everyday life. Danish advertising in 1914 and 1916 is an example of this: in advertisements for everyday items such as Stomatol toothpaste, confirmation robes, and the ersatz coffee Kafa, military technology and uniforms have become natural points of reference. Not only that; one can find war motifs in several advertisements that include competitions for readers in the form of puzzles, mazes, and general knowledge quizzes.[43] One can talk of the banalization and, in a longer perspective, the trivialization of the war experience.[44]

Berlingske Tidende, 6 September 1916

Pressens Magasin, 1916/1)

Politiken, 24 October 1914

FIGURE 5: The iconography of war as advertisement. (Statens Avissamling, Stats-biblioteket Aarhus)

77

What further contributed to fixing the war as a visual phenomenon in people's consciousness was the general release of silent films
with war-related motifs. The Boer War was the first war of which
there exist moving pictures, and by the time of the Russo-Japanese
War of 1904–1905 there were examples of travelling companies in
the Danish provinces showing films with motifs from the war.[45]
However, what we are dealing with here are scattered initiatives
and a delay of at least half a year between filming and release. In
the autumn of 1914, the situation was completely different. In
October alone, five Copenhagen cinemas (Palads-Teatret, Biograf-
Teatret, Metropolteatret, Kinografen, and Vesterbros Teater) ad-
vertised, extra-repertoire, 'The latest war films'—early newsreels
produced for propaganda purposes. One such advertisement indicates the piecemeal, episodic nature of the films, and, in this
case, its German origin: 'Latest war film: The Germans entering
Brussels—Tired troops taking a break—The losses are counted.
Red Cross wagons to transport the wounded—The Germans' first
action in Brussels'.[46] There must have been a number of films in circulation, for apart from the wide range of cinemas offering them,
there was also a relatively rapid turnover of films.[47] At Palads-
Teatret, for example, the war film repertoire changed four times
during October 1914, prefiguring the twenty-four hour news cycle
favoured today. The advertisements also emphasized the authenticity and topicality of the news reports: 'Unique Express News
Item'.[48] Alongside the cinemas, the round Panoptikon building for
three-dimensional panorama shows in Copenhagen was also able
to supply war experiences in the form of 'The great war panorama.
A night in the trenches'. The First World War was thus a telling
presence in media culture, stretching far beyond the photographs
and drawings mediated by the daily and magazine press; a media
culture that not only constructed the image of the war, but also
contributed to making it part of everyday life.

TABLE 1.2 One week's war coverage in three Odense papers and *Politiken* in 1914 and 1916

	War coverage as percentage of all editorial copy		Telegram material as percentage of war coverage		Military information as percentage of telegram material		Official sources as percentage of telegram material	
	1914	1916	1914	1916	1914	1916	1914	1916
Fyns Tidende	42%	21%	68%	62%	70%	88%	70%	94%
Fyens Stiftstidende	50%	23%	66%	58%	83%	94%	48%	99%
Fyns Social-Demokrat	37%	17%	65%	64%	82%	96%	84%	100%
Politiken	41%	15%	60%	56%	72%	67%	50%	82%

Survey periods: 7–13 September 1914 and 2–8 October 1916.

TABLE 1.3 One week's war coverage in *Politiken* in 1914 and 1916

Percentage	Telegram material	Overview, summary	Background, comments	Reports	Geographical maps	Illustrations	Other
1914	60	2	21	4	2	8	3
1916	56	–	29	–	1	14	–

Survey periods: 7–13 September 1914 and 2–8 October 1916.
War coverage 1914: 64,680 colmm. War coverage 1916: 23,660 colmm.

TABLE 1.4 Motifs used in *Politiken*'s and *Social-Demokraten*'s visual mediation of the war

Motifs	Action dimension				Subject matter			
	1914		1916		1914		1916	
Urban prospects	4	7%	2	8%	16	29%	2	8%
Landscapes			1	4%	1	2%	–	
Civilians	7	13%	2	8%	–		–	
Military personnel	15	27%	5	21%	5	9%	3	13%
Materiel	1	2%	2	8%	6	11%	5	21%
Other	–		2	8%	–		–	
Total (pictures)	27		14		28		10	

TABLE 1.5 Motifs in the magazines' visual mediation

Motifs	Action dimension				Subject matter			
	1914		1916		1914		1916	
Urban prospects	25	12%	7	7%	23	11%	7	7%
Landscapes	4	2%	5	5%	1		–	
Civilians	14	7%	8	8%	1		–	
Military personnel	76	37%	47	44%	23	11%	19	18%
Materiel	13	6%	7	7%	24	12%	6	6%
Other	2	1%	–		–		–	
Total pictures	134		74		72		32	

TABLE 1.6 Motif angles in newspapers and magazines

	1914		1916	
	Newspapers	Magazines	Newspapers	Magazines
German	35%	33%	42%	16%
Entente	44%	55%	42%	74%
Other	11%	14%	16%	10%

Notes

1 'The Press and War', *Journalisten* (1918), 2–3, 16.
2 Karl Erik Gustafsson & Per Rydén (eds.), *Den svenska pressens historia*, iii (Stockholm: Ekerlids Förlag, 2001), 146.
3 Tor Are Johansen, 'Illustrasjoner i dagspressen', in Hans Fredrik Dahl et al. (eds.), *Norsk presses historie*, ii (Oslo 2010), 138.
4 Tim N. Gidal, *Modern Photojournalism. Origin and Evolution, 1910–1933* (New York: Macmillan, 1973), 6–8, 15–19.
5 For the comprehensive account of the transition to photography and film, see Gerhard Paul, *Bilder der Krieges. Krieg der Bilder. Die Visualisierung des modernen Krieges* (Munich: Wilhelm Fink, 2004).
6 Paul Virilio, *War and Cinema* (London: Verso, 1989), 70; see also John Taylor, *War Photography. Realism in the British Press* (London: Routledge, 1991), 20–3.
7 Paul 2004, 106, 'Die Anwesenheit von Fotografen und Kameramännern veränderte die Situation auf den Schlachtfeldern. Soldaten begannen nun massenhaft für die Fotografen zu posieren und an Schaukämpfen vor den Kameras teilzunehmen. Ansätze einer spezifischen Repräsentationsästhetik des Krieges bildeten sich heraus, in der die Realität des Kampfgeschehens auf ihre mediale Vermittlung hin inszeniert wurde.'
8 Alain Sayag, '"Wir sagten Adieu einer ganzen Epoche". Französische Kriegsphotographie', in Rainer Rother (ed.), *Die Letzten Tage der Menschheit* (Deutsches Historisches Museum; Berlin: Ars Nicolai, 1994), 188, 'Wahrnehmungsmechanisme'.
9 Paul 2004, 108; cf. Frank Hischer, 'Der Erste Weltkrieg. Langzeitwirkung des ersten Bilderkrieges', in Claudia Gunz & Thomas F. Schneider (eds.), *Wahrheitsmaschinen* (Göttingen: V&R unipress, 2010), 217–32, who sees the iconography in the photographs from the First World War as a prototype for later visual representations of war in the twentieth century.
10 Taylor 1991, 46.
11 Ibid. 42–46.
12 Gidal 1973, 11–12; Kenneth Kobré, *Photojournalism* (Oxford: Focal Press, 2008), 426.
13 Paul 2004, 123–4.
14 'Casellis Pantelegraph', *Illustreret Tidende* 9/4 1865.
15 See the mention of 'Professor Korn's Picture Telegraphy' in *Politiken*, 10 August 1908; see also Karl Erik Gustafsson & Per Rydén (eds.), *Den svenska pressens historia*, iii (Stockholm: Ekerlids Förlag, 2001), 110. Korn's project and those of other picture telegraph pioneers is described in Gerhard Fuchs, *Die Bildtelegraphie* (Berlin: Verlag von Georg Siemens, 1926).

16 Elke Grittmann et al. (eds.), *Global, lokal, digital – Fotojournalismus heute* (Cologne: Herbert von Halem Verlag, 2008), 8–9.
17 Jürgen Wilke, 'Nachrichtenagenturen als Bildanbieter', in Grittmann et al. 2008, 62.
18 Gerry Beegan, *The Mass Image. A Social History of Photomechanical Reproduction in Victorian London* (London: Palgrave Macmillan), 2008, 163–6.
19 Thomas Hård af Segerstad, *Dagspressens bildbruk. En funktionsanalys av bildutbudet i svenska dagstidningar 1900–1970* (Acta Universitatis Upsaliensis, Ars Suetica 3; Uppsala: Textgruppen, 1974), 20; see also Stig Hjarvard, '"Det nyetste Nyt i Tekst og Billeder". Om fotografiets rolle i skabelsen af den moderne danske avis 1900–1940', *Sekvens*, 97 (1997), 155–85, which notes the co-existence of drawings and photographs in the 1910s. However, neither Segerstad nor Hjarvard deal with the special technological problems involved in printing photographs in newspapers.
20 *Politiken* established its own reproduction unit in 1912, which made photocopying, stereotyping, and electrotyping possible at the newspaper house, while *Berlingske Tidende* acquired its own stereotyping and elecrotyping unit as late as 1923. Generally speaking, the Scandinavian presses began to set up in-house units in around 1910 (Are Johansen 2010, 131, 137; Gustafsson & Rydén 2001, 110). The use of drawings based on photographs was not limited to wartime as far as *Politiken* was concerned. In the years leading up to the war there were many drawings that, just like the war drawings based on photographs, were marked with an 'A', referring to one of the newspaper's five illustrators (three of whom used the initial A: Axel Nygaard, Valdemar Andersen, and Axel Andreasen).
21 *Social-Demokraten*, 5 October 1914 and 14 October 1914. According to Gustafsson & Rydén 2001, 110 it was normal practice to use drawings if plates or photography produced pictures that were too muddy.
22 In Norway, one of the major Oslo newspapers, *Dagbladet*, did not begin to use photographs until the early 1930s (Are Johansen 2010, 131).
23 Walter Lippmann, *Public Opinion*, (1922; New Brunswick: Transaction, 1998), 92.
24 This view is advanced by Lena Johannesson in her study of the xylographic press picture (Johannesson, *Xylografi och pressbild* (Nordiska museets Handlingar, 97; Uppsala: Almquist & Wiksell, 1982, 298).
25 In Sweden, the telegraph station in Stockholm was described as 'a kind of telegraphic centre of Europe that came to function as a mediator of traffic between countries that no longer had any direct connections' (K.V. Tahvanainen, *Telegrafboken – Den elektriska telegrafen i Sverige 1853–1996* (Stockholm: Telemuseum, 1997). In Denmark, the telegraph station in Fredericia is now recognized to have been the communication hub:

'Fredericia developed into Denmark's most important telegraph station. It served both the Danish state lines and the foreign lines of Store Nordiske Telegraf Selskab. Here most of the internal telegrams and telegrams in transit through Denmark were dealt with. [...] Danish neutrality meant that the allies—France, Britain, Russia—could communicate via Fredericia without the Germany enemy being able to listen in as well.' (Post&Tele Museum, Copenhagen, <http://mini.ptt-museum.dk/150aar/popup.html>, accessed 24 September 2012). At the time, however, it was Copenhagen that was considered to be the hub of telegraphic communication: 'Copenhagen is fortunate enough to have connections with Berlin, Hamburg, Britain, Stockholm and Kristiania, and via Fredericia receives the British and Russian traffic' (*Hver 8. Dag*, 13 September 1914).

26 Poul Thestrup, *P&Ts historie 1850–1927*, iii: *Vogn og tog – prik og streg* (Copenhagen: Generaldirektoratet for Post- og Telegrafvæsenet, 1992), 339.

27 Torsten Gihl, 'Den svenska opinionen under världskriget. Aktivismen', in Nils Ahnlund et al. (eds.), *Den svenska utrikespolitikens historia*, iv (Stockholm: Norstedt, 1951), 93–119; Svenbjörn Kilander, *Censur och propaganda* (diss.; Uppsala: Uppsala universitet, 1981).

28 Frejlif Olsen (1868–1936), editor of *Ekstra Bladet*, stood out as early as August 1914 as a result of strongly critical articles about Germany and the Danish army. Although several MPs wished to have Olsen dismissed, no action was taken because of his close connections with powerful people in the Danish press and politics (see Gregers Dirckinck-Holmfeld, *Tør – hvor andre tier*, i (Copenhagen: Ekstra Bladets Forlag, 2003), 67–73).

29 Stig Hadenius, *Dagens Nyheters historia. Tidningen och makten 1864–2000* (Stockholm: Bokförlaget DN, 2002), 120, my translation.

30 Taylor 1991 (above, n. 5), 44.

31 Hadenius 2002, 125.

32 *Dagens Nyheter*, 9 August 1914, quoted in Hadenius 2002, 126.

33 This type of newspaper coverage was part of the special organization of the temporal and spatial relationships that, according to Anthony Giddens, characterizes modernity. Indeed, it is in connection with the emergence and use of the telegraph in journalism—in the form of news telegrams and up-to-date reports—that Giddens writes of the contraction of space because of 'the intrusion of distant events into everyday consciousness' (Giddens, *Modernity and Self-Identity* (Cambridge: Polity Press, 1991), 27), to which the newspapers' war coverage made a massive contribution.

34 Paul 2004 (above, n. 4), 117.

35 The absolute figures and percentages are listed in Tables 1.4–1.6. I do not give the percentage divisions, as the material, especially for the daily press in 1916, is extremely limited.

36 Gustafsson & Rydén 2001, 110.
37 See Paul 2004, 118–9; Lina Sturfelt, *Eldens återsken. Första världskriget i svensk föreställningsvärld* (Lund: Sekel, 2008).
38 Motif angle indicates the angle from which a given motif is viewed, and is thereby also an indicator of where the picture in question comes from. Since none of the media studied here indicated their picture sources systematically, this is the only method of getting an approximate value for the origin of the picture flow. Listed picture sources are (German) 'Frankl., Berlin', 'Berlin.Ill.G.', 'Ill. Zeitung' 'Boedeker, Berlin', 'Braemer, Berlin', and Leipz.P.B.'; (French) 'Branger, Paris', 'Meurisse, Paris', 'Chusseau Flaviens, Paris', 'Meurisse, Paris', and 'Trampus, Paris'; (British) 'Ill.Bur., London', 'Record Press, London', 'Alifieri, London', 'Off.Phot., London', and 'Ill. London News'; and (Dutch) 'Veren.Fotob., Amsterdam'. With regard to regulation of the flow of telegrams from the countries at war, Swedish studies show that the relationship between telegrams from the Entente Powers and the Central Powers was fairly balanced in the major morning papers, which meant that they lived up to the government's recommendation (Hadenius 2002, 126–7).
39 *Politiken*, 8 October 1914.
40 *Pressens Magasin*, 1916:1, 87.
41 See for example, *Illustreret Familie-Journal*, 10 (1916), 16; ibid. 31 (1916), 9; and ibid. 34 (1916), front page).
42 *Pressens Magasin* 1917, 21, 22.
43 *Illustreret Familie-Journal* 1914, 47 & 50; *Politiken*, 24 October 1914.
44 See Michael Billig, *Banal Nationalism* (London: SAGE; 1995; George L. Mosse, *Fallen Soldiers. Reshaping the Memory of the World Wars* (New York: Oxford University Press, 1991), 126–56.
45 *Kolding Avis*, 10 February 1905.
46 Biograf-Teatret, *Social-Demokraten*, 4 October 1914.
47 Very limited sections of this film material are available at <http://www.dfi.dk/faktaomfilm/nationalfilmografien/nffilm.aspx?id=36907>, s.v. 'War pictures', where it is also possible to watch a twenty-five minute film. Accessed 24 September 2012.
48 Vesterbros Teater, *Social-Demokraten*, 26 October 1914. An enthusiastic contemporary mention of the possibility of using these films to experience aspects of the war is to be found in Julius Magnussen's feature in *Politiken*, 1 October 1914, while Mosse 1991, 144–9 provides a description of various kinds of 'entertaining' presentations of the war in tableaux, theatre, and film.

CHAPTER 2

The secret battlefield

Intelligence and counter-intelligence in Scandinavia during the First World War

Nik. Brandal & Ola Teige

'War is not an intellectual activity,' writes the British military historian John Keegan. 'War is about doing, about the application of brute force.'[1] The First World War, however, was the first war where the systematic gathering of intelligence by professional agencies influenced military decisions. In fact the very concept of a 'spy' was not codified until the Brussels Declaration of 1874, and while the collective European intelligence agencies before 1914 employed but a handful of people, the number had grown to several thousand when the war ended.[2] This development reflected that a steep process of professionalization and the use of new technology such as wireless radio and the telegraph had given greater credence to information gathered through covert intelligence.[3] The outbreak of war on 28 July 1914 also led to a sharp increase in intelligence activities in the neutral countries of Sweden, Denmark, and Norway. Thus, while devoid of trenches, gas clouds, or pitched battles, even Scandinavia became a battlefield in the Great War.

Scandinavia's importance for the warring parties derived from its natural resources and its geographical position. Scandinavia produced goods that were valuable for the warring parties—fish, agricultural products, and minerals used in the manufacturing of ammunition—while in a Europe split in two there was but a limited number of routes available for the transportation of people, goods, and information. Scandinavia offered fast and open lines of communication between the warring parties as well as from the eastern to the western theatre of war. As the alternative routes ran either through the Iberian Peninsula, North America, or the Netherlands, Scandinavia rose in importance, and its ports became information and transportation hubs, providing conduits to enemy territory.

This chapter explores three main questions regarding intelligence activities in Scandinavia during the First World War, with special emphasis on Norway. Firstly, what were the aims of the various intelligence agencies and Norwegian counter-intelligence? Secondly, how did they organize and conduct their work? And thirdly, how successful were the various agencies in achieving their desired outcome?

German intelligence

German intelligence operations against enemy states and neutral countries were organized and run by two different organizations: the Nachrichten-Abteilung N of the Admiralty Staff and Abteilung IIIb of the General Staff. The senior agency was IIIb, established back in 1889 to collect non-battlefield information of strategic interest for the army, but until 1914 it was still rather small and staffed by gentleman amateurs rather than professional agents.[4] However, in the run-up to the war, and especially after the appointment of Major Walther Nicolai as head of IIIb in 1912, this was rapidly changing. The N-Abteilung, meanwhile, was modelled on IIIb, and had been set up as late as 1901 to gather information on the navies of foreign powers, chiefly the British Royal Navy. Accordingly, it was responsible for all espionage in Great Britain. Unlike IIIb, N-Abteilung was an integrated part of the German navy and all its staff members were naval officers. Its field agents, on the other hand, were a mix of reserve officers and foreigners. While there was some competition between the two agencies, a broad division of labour existed from early on. N-Abteilung also established close links with the German Foreign Office, with the latter practicing a 'don't ask, don't tell' policy of leaving it up to individual diplomats to decide their level of involvement in covert activities, although stressing the need for plausible deniability should such involvement be discovered.

Before 1914, German intelligence activities in Scandinavia had been few and far between, reflecting the region's status as peaceful and neutral, posing little threat to Germany. The only known operations were a limited number of mapping tours by German naval officers along the coastlines of Norway and Denmark, more or less in disguise. In addition, the German General Staff had contingency plans for an occupation of Denmark. These plans of course rested on specific information about that country, collected by various means.[5]

British intelligence

Compared to Germany, Great Britain was late in establishing a professional intelligence organization. In fact, the creation of the Secret Service Bureau (SSB) was prompted by the spy mania whipped up by the publication of several works of popular fiction depicting an aggressive Germany secretly plotting to attack Great Britain.[6] The agency was established in 1909 to gather intelligence on German activities. From the outset, its activities were divided between two separate divisions: MI5, responsible for domestic counter-intelligence, and MI6, in charge of espionage. Similar to the development within the German intelligence agencies, the outbreak of war vastly increased the pressure on MI6 to provide information on enemy activities. With the recruitment of agents in and around Germany, as well as collecting information on the German arms industry, fortifications, and military installations, MI6 was to create an early warning system for a future German attack.

The threat of imperial Germany also led to cooperation with Britain's old enemies, the French, who suggested that the British should 'use people from third countries—Norwegians, Swiss and so on'.[7] MI6's initial focus in Scandinavia was on naval intelligence. Pre-war efforts to follow German warship movements were renewed, and with the imposition of the wartime blockade on the enemy MI6 was also deployed to monitor this and help plug gaps which the Germans might exploit.[8]

Norwegian counter-intelligence

In the period immediately preceding the outbreak of war, for the first time since the country gained its independence in 1905, foreign espionage became a challenge for Norwegian authorities. A related problem was the large influx of foreigners to Norway, and especially its capital Kristiania, as the warring countries expelled thousand of aliens from their territories and thousands more chose to leave on their own account to seek refuge in neutral countries. By 1917 more than 25,000 aliens had settled in Norway, most of them in Kristiania. At the same time, Norway's ports were a transit area for everyone from deserters, wounded soldiers, and escaped prisoners of war to diplomats, journalists, and businessmen. Just the sheer number of immigrants and people in transit alone became a cause for unrest among the general public. In 1914 Norway was still a small and homogenous country on Europe's periphery, its experience of such large-scale immigration limited. Xenophobia was widespread, and in particular the perceived increase in the number of Jews and other migrants from Germany and Eastern Europe was given much attention.[9]

As a consequence, the Norwegian Storting in August 1914 passed the *Lov om forsvarshemmeligheter* (Act on Defence Secrets) or—as it was widely known—the 'Spy Act', which throughout the war provided the main authorization for the police in matters of espionage. For the first time, all espionage activity on behalf of a foreign power on Norwegian soil was criminalized, regardless of the origins of the perpetrator or whether the target was Norwegian interests or not. The act also made all military areas off limits, and forbade the drawing of sketches and maps as well as photographing in military areas. In many ways, this was an attempt to stop Norway from becoming a battlefield in the war, as the activities of spies from foreign powers were not merely a source of embarrassment for the Norwegian government—they could also lead to severe difficulties in relations with Germany and Great Britain, thus potentially endangering Norway's status as a neutral country.[10] In June 1915, the Storting passed amendments to the law on the control of aliens, which made it easier for the police to expel foreigners and to investigate their mail and telegram correspondence. Later followed regulations making it compulsory for all foreign citizens to register, authorizing the police to ban foreigners from residing in certain municipalities, and making passports mandatory.

Like their foreign counterparts, and perhaps even more so, the Norwegian agencies charged with carrying out these new policies were yet in their infancy. Information about perceived external and internal threats were collected by *Generalstabens etterettningskontor*, the General Staff's Intelligence Office, manned by only two officers. And while this office collected and analysed information received from the police or from open sources, it had no independent means with which to carry out investigations. Counterintelligence and surveillance were the responsibility of the police, but no centralized direction or coordination existed before the war. Responsibility for counteracting the activities of foreign intelligence agencies fell to *Opdagelsespolitiet*, the detective departments of the local police forces. By far the largest and most important was the department in Kristiania, headed by the energetic *Opdagelseschef* (Chief of Detectives) Joh. Søhr. His assistant in cases pertaining to espionage and aliens was the veteran Detective Inspector Redvald Larssen.[11]

The early years (1914–16)

After the outbreak of war, both N-Abteilung and IIIb set in motion pre-planned operations known as the *Kriegsnachrichtenwesen*. This entailed establishing a number of posts along the borders of the Reich, with those belonging to the army termed *Kriegsnachrichtenstellen* (war intelligence posts, or KNSt) and those operated by the navy termed *Zweigstellen der Admiralstab* (Admiralty auxiliary posts), charged with establishing spy networks in enemy states, as well as collecting information from open sources.[12] Army operations were directed against Russia, and Scandinavia played only a minor role for IIIb. Swedish and Norwegian territories were used mainly as bases for these operations, and all of Sweden and Norway were left to a single desk staffed by only two officers at the Berlin KNSt.[13]

However, one of the first German agents caught in Norway was Friederich W. Katsch from the Berlin KNSt in the spring of 1915. The former businessman had travelled extensively throughout Norway, recruiting locals as observers and setting up listening posts from the autumn of 1914 onwards. His mission was first and foremost to collect information about Norway, and only secondly to receive and transmit information sent from spies inside Great Britain. In so far as he was able to continue his work until his arrest and deportation in March 1915, the mission was a limited success.

Most of German intelligence activity in Scandinavia, however, was directed by N-Abteilung's Zweigstelle in Gothenburg, established in July 1915 with substations in Kristiania, Bergen, Copenhagen, Malmö, and Stockholm. The Zweigstelle operated under the guise of the firm Handelsaktiebolaget Emptio AB, and was under the command of Lieutenant Captain Edwin Nordmann. Before the war Nordmann had been in the merchant navy, as had several others on his staff. The steadily growing number of incoming intelligence reports—from 740 in 1915 to 1,410 in 1916, and 2,066 in 1917—is testament to a high level of activity.[14]

From these substations a large number of agents were sent into Great Britain over the next couple of years. But the poor quality of the intelligence they gathered as well as the high discovery rate soon led to a change in policy. In fact, open sources such as newspapers had yielded as much, if not more, valuable information, and as early as 1915 a decision was made to put less emphasis on the placing of agents inside Great Britain. Instead, resources were reallocated to the gathering of intelligence from open sources and establishing a greater presence in neutral countries, especially the Netherlands and Scandinavia.

A contributing factor was the submarine war launched in February 1915, defining the waters surrounding the British Isles as a war zone, rendering all ships found inside this zone, regardless of their flag and cargo, liable to be attacked by German U-boats. One of the main shipping lanes ran from western Norway across the North Sea to Great Britain, and during 1915 the N-Abteilung set up a ship-watching service (*Schiffbefragungsdienst*) in the harbour cities of the Netherlands, Norway, Sweden, and Denmark in order to collect such intelligence. The most important of these networks of agents and informants were found in Rotterdam, Esbjerg, and Bergen. Local agents, mostly disguised as businessmen or journalists, were charged with setting up a system of ship-watchers in harbour towns from Trelleborg to Narvik. While the agents running the substations were mostly German nationals, the ship-watchers were generally Norwegian and paid per report submitted. The substations in Copenhagen and Kristiania were also given additional tasks, the most important being the surveillance of British intelligence, checks on expatriate Germans, the collection of information about the national governments, investigations of companies trading with the enemy, and the recruitment of spies who could be sent over the North Sea.[15]

The German operatives were divided into three groups: 'Agenten'—German intelligence operatives and locally recruited spies who, undercover, collected information inside enemy territory; 'Ausfrager'—people who provided information and reports, but who did not work undercover and, for the most part, operated in neutral territory; and 'Helfer'—people who assisted N-Abteilung by providing cover addresses, safe houses, information, and equipment. While many of the Helfer and Ausfrager were Scandinavian citizens, German expatriates were also extensively recruited by appealing either to their patriotic duty or by offering them trade licenses, exemption from military service, or simply money.[16]

From January 1916 on, German intelligence began to provide individual operatives with a number identifying his or her status. Numbers 1–299 were given to Agenten, 300–599 to Ausfrager, and 600 upwards to Helfer. By 1918 the Zweigstelle in Gothenburg had given out 242 numbers to Agenten and Ausfrager and 341 Helfer numbers. However, not all of these operatives ever produced any reports as many, especially among the Danes, turned out to be swindlers, some had changed their minds after being recruited, while others were unable to obtain passports to enter Great Britain, or had been arrested or fallen sick. According to a report from February 1918 there were also more than 50 spies that N was unable to re-establish contact with.[17]

Shortly after Katsch's arrest in March 1915, the Norwegian

police also uncovered their first naval operative, a German language school principal in Bergen by the name of Heinz Clarenz Bauermeister. His main task was to pass messages between Great Britain and Berlin, and among the operatives he had received letters from was Carl Lody, who in November 1914 had been the first German spy to be executed in Great Britain. Bauermeister was put under surveillance by the Norwegian police after having received a suspiciously large number of letters, and they soon noticed that he often visited British ships in Bergen's harbour. However, because the case became public knowledge when a police request for his expulsion was rejected by the government, Bauermeister lost value as a spy and chose to leave Norway.[18]

After Zweigstelle Gothenburg became fully operational in the summer of 1915, the navy took over control of Scandinavian operations. At this point Abteilung-N's agents set up the ship-watching base 'Organisation Bergen', which monitored shipping and obtained information by engaging travellers in conversation. Its leaders were frequently changed so as not to expose them to Norwegian and British counter-intelligence, and a number of Norwegians and expatriate German were recruited to do the legwork.[19]

The second base, 'Organisation Kristiania', also functioned as a logistical support centre for German activity in Norway as a whole, collecting information on Norwegian politics and military affairs, companies trading with the British, Germans expatriates, and British agents, while also providing a base for recruiting and dispatching spies to Great Britain. This organization was broken up by the Norwegian police in 1916 and the German agents expelled from Norway. A new base was soon established, and only six months later the Norwegian police yet again had to arrest the leaders of the Kristiania organization, after noticing a newspaper advertisement seeking young men or seamen willing to travel to England. In police custody the highest-ranking officer confessed that his mission had been to obtain military and commercial information concerning Germany's enemies.[20] The operation had already succeeded in recruiting several destitute young sailors, who were supplied with money, a list of questions, secret ink hidden in handkerchiefs, and a cover address. At least nine Scandinavians were sent to Great Britain, two of them women. After confessing, all the Germans were allowed to leave Norway quietly.[21]

Given that N-Abteilung was able to establish several bases and networks on Norwegian territory, the German activities there can be counted moderately successful. Also, as long as the consequences of being discovered were relatively mild—expulsion for non-Norwegians and a warning for Norwegians—recruiting agents and establishing new bases was a relatively easy task. However, the information gathered was by and large of mediocre quality, mostly stemming from open sources and second-rate agents. Moreover, the deficiencies of German intelligence become even more obvious when compared to its opposite number.

MI6's operations in Scandinavia in the first couple of years of the war were led by Frank Stagg, a former Navy officer, and his assistant Richard Carlyle Holme, a British artillery captain who lived in Kristiania. From the very start MI6 had a double mission: monitor Norwegian trade in order to compose a 'black list' of Norwegian companies and businessmen trading with Germany, and run a ship-watching network monitoring German and neutral ships in Norwegian waters. Similar organizations also existed in Sweden (nine agents) and Denmark (twelve agents). Like their German counterparts, MI6 numbered its agents, giving each a national prefix—N, D, or S—followed by a number. Come the spring of 1915 as many as twenty Norwegians, spread along the coast, worked for Holme. By that time his activities had come to the attention of the Norwegian police, and he was subsequently arrested, whereupon he immediately confessed to being an agent and explained that his job was to monitor enemy activity in Norway. As in the German cases, it all ended with Holme and the other Britons being expelled and their Norwegian agents being given warnings.[22]

Holme was then relocated to Copenhagen, freeing up Stagg to travel more widely. However, late in 1915, after the Germans had registered serious complaints against him with the Danish government, Stagg was pulled out of Denmark altogether and brought back to London. Over the following years he spent more and more of his time in Norway, travelling on an American passport, and there he developed a productive liaison with the Norwegians, particularly the police and the navy. A major coup for MI6 came when Stagg travelled to northern Norway in the autumn of 1916 to survey and monitor the transport of goods from Finland and became acquainted with Redvald Larssen of the Kristiania police. According to Stagg, Larssen agreed that 'he would always help in any way he could without letting down his superiors if we passed word to him.'[23] Stagg and Larssen became close friends, and this was the starting point of a close collaboration between MI6 and the Norwegian police.[24] Stagg also gained access to reports from the Norwegian navy's own costal observation stations and radio listening posts. The British Admiralty went so far as to send technicians to a Norwegian naval base to improve its listening technology. The liaisons between British and Norwegian officials were unofficial and based on personal ties. It is not possible to determine from available sources whether they were sanctioned by the Norwegian government, though it is probable that an acceptance of sorts had been obtained.

MI6's success rate in monitoring and banning companies that traded with Germany seems to have been considerable, especially measured against the delicate balancing act of maintaining accord with governments in the neutral countries where these activities took place. Also, taking into account that MI6 had to start from scratch and immediately became locked in a turf war with other government agencies, its construction of an intelligence network in Scandinavia might more aptly be described as an outright success. That said, this was due in large measure to its more limited aims when compared to the Germans.[25]

The increasing number of spy cases uncovered in 1914 and 1915 led to demands for the centralization of Norwegian counter-intelligence, and in the summer of 1915 the Ministry of Justice decided that counter-intelligence efforts should be coordinated under the leadership of the Kristiania Detective Department. Joh. Søhr now became the head of Norwegian counter-intelligence in addition to his duties as Chief of Detectives in Kristiania, and the staff at the Kristiania immigration office was tripled from two to six officers. However, due to the lack of manpower and resources, most of the activity was still confined to the cities of Kristiania, Bergen, and

Trondheim. As head of the counter-intelligence, the conservative, anti-Semitic, and anglophile Søhr kept a high public profile, constantly calling for more resources and men, while complaining that the existing laws were too lax and failed to provide the police with the necessary tools.[26]

An investigation of the spy cases uncovered by Norwegian counter-intelligence in the first two years of the war leads to the following conclusions. Firstly, Norway, and indeed all the Scandinavian countries, were of limited importance to the warring states, as most of their activities were directed towards one another. They mostly used the Scandinavian countries as a launch pad for moving spies and information back and forth across the front lines, or using the coast and harbours to observe the movement of people, goods, and ships.

Secondly, the efforts of the German and British intelligence services in Norway were in retrospect rather amateurish. The informants and spies were recruited in a hurry, and were a mix of expatriates already living in Norway and former officers, mariners, and businessmen, none with any intelligence experience. This was especially evident in the way the agents tended to draw unwanted attention by receiving large amounts of mail or being overly inquisitive or lax in their security measures. But, having said that, both MI6 and N-Abteilung rapidly became more professional.

Thirdly and finally, there was the question of Norway's response to foreign intelligence activity on its soil. The Norwegian police's counter-intelligence grew in size, capability, and effectiveness in 1915 and 1916, as the implementation of the 1914 Spy Act provided them with the necessary tools to prosecute spies operating in Norway. To the frustration of the police, the prosecutors tended to release spies who were caught with nothing more than a slap on the wrist; foreigners were expelled and Norwegians let off with a warning. Furthermore, such cases were kept under wraps by the government, and did not as a rule become public knowledge.[27] As a result, MI6 and N-Abteilung could operate more or less unrestricted.

This, however, was beginning to change. The last German spy to merely be extradited was a Swedish citizen in German service, baron Otto von Rosen, who was arrested in northern Norway in

January 1917. The Norwegian police were acting on a tip received from MI6 that von Rosen and two assistants were travelling northbound in the direction of Russian-controlled Finland through the Swedish and Norwegian wilderness. In his possession the police found Norwegian, Finnish, and Russian currency, a box of sugar lumps, a pistol, a map of Northern Finland, explosives, fuses and percussion caps, and several bottles of the poison curare. As was customary, von Rosen was soon released and expelled, and it was only later that the police discovered that the sugar lumps contained anthrax germs.[28] These were most likely to be used to sabotage the transport of British weapons to the Russians in Finland. Unlike previous cases the discovery became public knowledge, and the police's decision to do no more than expel von Rosen came under heavy criticism.[29] Furthermore, it added to the building British pressure on Norwegian authorities to put an end to such activities on its soil.

Hollow neutrality (1917–18)

More than any other year of the First World War, 1917 was characterized by 'spy mania', when real and imagined plots of sabotage and espionage dominated the public discourse. There were three reasons for this. German submarine warfare provoked anti-German sentiment, as Norwegian ships were targets for the German navy. Similarly, the image of the German spy threat was enhanced by a number of high-profile public court cases against German agents and their Norwegian confederates. And third, but not least, the Russian Revolution in November caused a widespread fear that the Russian Bolsheviks would try to spread their revolution to the rest of the world.

The British, on the other hand, kept a low profile. In an MI6 report, only ten British agents were listed as active in Norway in 1917—rather on the low side compared to its German counterpart, and reflecting the different working environments of the two agencies. In fact, after the break-up of the Holmes spy ring in 1916, no British agent or Norwegian citizen in British service was ever prosecuted. In some cases British agents were asked to keep a lower profile, but the mutual cooperation and understanding that had developed between the Norwegian police and British intelligence, especially after Stagg and Larssen's meeting in late 1916, meant that the Norwegians mostly turned a blind eye.[30]

On 1 February 1917, just weeks after the expulsion of baron von Rosen, the Germans resumed and intensified the submarine warfare in the Atlantic Ocean and the North Sea that had been suspended since the autumn of 1915 so as to not provoke neutral countries, in particular the Americans. The change in strategy was a response to a stalemate in the trenches, where the German military campaign in France had once more been bogged down. The German navy's strategy was to sink merchant ships so that Great Britain would run out of food and be forced to sue for peace. Initially the campaign was a success, as Britain's food supplies shrank to only six weeks' worth in April 1917, but it also led to the US joining the Allies. And towards the end of 1917, the Entente Powers' losses were significantly reduced through the introduction of convoys and submarine hunting by British and American warships, causing Germany to lose more submarines than it could replace.[31]

Few nations felt the consequences of the submarine war as hard as Norway. Between July 1914 and February 1917 it had lost 336 ships, the majority sunk by German submarines, and nearly 400 sailors had lost their lives. Now the number grew at an alarming rate. In the first six months of 1917 alone the Germans sank 300 ships and killed close to 450 sailors. That was bad enough, but several ship captains reported that the Germans had been lying in wait and seemed to know their course. While the majority of the Norwegian public had been more or less supportive of the Entente throughout the war, public opinion now definitely turned against Germany. Local Germans were actively shunned and became objects of suspicion, as the anti-Semitic image of a German equals a Jew equals a spy was cultivated even in the mainstream press, in a number of high-profile cases of espionage. Several prominent Norwegians returned honours and medals previously bestowed upon them by Germany and openly condemned the Kaiser. Until this point, all foreign agents had been treated equally, regardless of their country of origin, but now German submarine warfare and its dire consequences for Norway paved the way for more severe punishment for German agents, as news of ship losses and deaths came on a daily basis. When the Norwegian police discovered a new spy ring in early 1917, it was no longer possible to keep such news under wraps.[32]

The spy ring in question was N-Abteilung's 'Organisation Bergen', and the case, soon dubbed the 'Major Bergen Spy Case' by the media, created a public outcry. The Norwegian Detective Department became aware of German activities in Bergen in late 1916, and in the spring of 1917 fourteen Norwegians were arrested. While the German instigators had managed to escape before the arrests took place, it only served to increase the disgust of the public that among the Norwegians there were several seamen. According to the local Bergen paper *Bergens Tidende*, 'there is hardly any difference between treason and commercial espionage leading to Norwegian ships being torpedoed'.[33] The conservative newspaper *Aftenposten* led the attack on the government and demanded action: 'We can see that spies have surrounded us on all sides and worked in our midst. ... A change to the system is necessary! Spies have been arrested, extensive spying affairs investigated. The public has been kept totally unaware, all doors closed in this respect too.'[34] The sentences were handed down in early June: ten of the accused were imprisoned for up to nine months, while four were acquitted.[35]

A year earlier, N-Abteilung had established a new department, NIV, to run sabotage operations against the Allies. A sub-office named 'Organisation S' (for sabotage) was set up in Stockholm and disguised as a medical supplies business, and seems to have been kept separate from the Zweigstelle in Gothenburg. The targets were ships carrying food to Britain and Russian industry in Finland, and most of the personnel were Finnish exiles. In 1917 Finnish agents controlled from Stockholm built up a large cache of explosives in Kristiania. As in the von Rosen case, it is not entirely clear what their actual purpose was; whether the explosives were intended for blowing up British and possibly Norwegian ships, or Finnish factories. That several bombs were disguised as lumps of coal may point to the former. NIV used a Finn, Walther von Gerich, to transport the explosives to Kristiania. He travelled as a diplomatic courier under a false identity as baron Walther von Rautenfels, and the explosives were transported in sealed diplomatic bags. The operation was discovered by MI6 in Stockholm, who in turn tipped off the Kristiania Detective Department. Soon after von Gerich arrived in Kristiania in June 1917, they apprehended him and his associates, and they also located a cache of nearly 1,000 kilos of explosives and fire bombs, or 'infernal machines' as the press soon labelled them. Because of von Gerich's diplomatic immunity the Norwegian government had to release him, albeit along with a sharply worded protest, but a number of his accomplices were tried in a large public trial later in 1917 and given severe sentences. This effectively shut down NIV in Norway, and there are no confirmed reports of sabotage against Norwegian ships after this date. The Rautenfels case also alerted Norwegian and Swedish police as well as the press to the Germans' operations in Stockholm, and the NIV office was soon forced to shut down as its staff had to return to Germany.[36]

N-Abteilung continued to run its ship-watcher network as before, and a new organization was soon set up in Kristiania under the leadership of Erich Lawendel. He was also supposed to reestablish the ship-watching organization in Bergen, and in the spring of 1917 he dispatched a butcher's apprentice, Karl Schwartz, to Bergen. Schwartz was rewarded with money and exemption from German military service. In April 1917, after he had boasted to other Germans about being a spy, the Bergen police duly arrested Schwarz. In custody, he soon confessed, and named not only Lawendel but also Alfred Hagn, a Norwegian painter recruited by Lawendel and sent to Great Britain disguised as a journalist. Søhr, or possibly Larssen with the implicit acceptance of his superior, then tipped of MI6 about the Norwegian agent currently working in London. For Søhr this was probably a *quid pro quo* for the information leading to the von Rosen and Rautenfels arrests, but he also expected the British to extradite Hagn back to Norway. This was a miscalculation, and after Hagn was arrested by British police on 24 May he was swiftly sentenced to death, only escaping execution after the intercession of Norwegian officials and because the British government wanted to appease Norway in matters of trade policy. Lawendel and Schwartz were tried in late 1917, in what was labelled the 'Minor Bergen Spy Case'. They were the first foreign citizens prosecuted for espionage in Norway, and were sentenced to five and four years in prison respectively after a trial that was widely reported in the press.[37]

Soon afterwards several more German agents were apprehended. Perhaps the most important was Hugo Gramatski, an engineer who had previously completed two missions to Great Britain, earning him an Iron Cross. Gramatski was working for a recent addition to the N-Abteilung stable: Department G. This had been set up in 1916 to conduct *Abwehrspionage* or *Gegenspionage*—counter-intelligence and surveillance of local Germans—and at the time of his arrest several *G-stellen* had been established across Europe, including Gothenburg and Malmö. Gramatski's mission was to set one up in Kristiania, and before coming to Norway he had carried out similar work in Denmark and Sweden. In November 1917 he was sentenced to eight months' imprisonment.[38]

Throughout the war, but increasingly towards the end of 1917 and onwards, the losses of German personnel in Norway were significant, although not totally crippling. In late 1917 agents 665 and 114 were reported as being active in Kristiania, the latter being the new spy leader there. He was never identified by the Norwegians, and sent valuable reports to Gothenburg throughout 1918. Operational changes took place in this cell too. The front company, Emptio AB, was struck from the register of companies in 1916, as the tax authorities were unable to determine its actual business. Nordmann was then given a new cover as the local vice-consul, while other agents posed as businessmen or clerks at the consulate. While the local police were well aware of what was going on, they turned a blind eye as long as it did not harm Swedish interests. This was an interesting parallel to MI6's activities in Norway. However, as the increasing number of disclosures in Norway became public knowledge, it eventually forced the hand of the Swedish police, especially as the connections to Sweden were evident, most noticeably in the Rautenfels case. As we have seen, the NIV office in Stockholm was forced to shut down, and in June 1917 the Gothenburg police arrested and expelled several other German agents.

Nordmann was still protected by his diplomatic immunity, and he now voiced his growing annoyance with the Norwegian policies to his superiors in Berlin. Not only were the sentences given to his agents overly harsh, especially in the case of Lawendel, they also bore witness to a great hatred of Germany. He pointed out that no British agent had ever been punished, even though several had been caught and many were still active. The Admiralty certainly agreed that the Norwegian police was working in the British interest in a brutal and ruthless manner, and to counter this, the G-stelle in Gothenburg started to collect evidence of British espionage in Norway in order to provoke the arrest of MI6 agents. The project failed, as no MI6 agents were arrested or even had their work impeded in any serious way. [39]

The Norwegian police continued to receive reports of imaginary spies from all corners of Norway, as everyone who looked even remotely German was treated with deep mistrust. German intelligence, however, for the time being preferred to keep a low profile, and large operations such as sabotage were avoided. Instead, they concentrated on running the more mundane, day-to-day espionage. The *Schiffbefragungsdienst* was still operative, with bases in Kristiania and Bergen, but the recruitment and dispatch of agents to Great Britain was mostly dropped. If one takes into account the lowered ambitions, these operations went quite well. Large amounts of information were sent back to Germany, although in the event there was little of any significant value.

Towards the end of the war the feverish work of *Opdagelspolitiet*, MI6, and Nachrichten-Abteilung in Norway, indeed across Scandinavia, waned. The Detective Department in Kristiania, which had grown so much in the war years, was dissolved, and its staff returned to their pre-war assignments. Many of them were put to work investigating the new danger of Communism.

This development was also reflected in the reorganization of other intelligence agencies. Nordmann eventually dismantled the Zweigstelle in Gothenburg and returned to Germany. And while the N-Abteilung continued to send in junior agents to Norway, and a number of them were caught and tried, the court cases no longer produced a media storm. Moreover, the main interest was no longer British activities, but rather the growing fear of a communist revolution spreading from Bolshevik Russia. One instance was the arrest of a Norwegian-Dutch businessman sent by Zweigstelle Gothenburg to Bergen in April 1918, equipped with a detailed questionnaire in order to chart communist activities.[40] MI6 also kept up a discreet presence in Scandinavia, and in 1918 agents with numbers as high as D.62, N.20, and S.76 were working in the field. And like its German counterpart, and in addition to its previous activities against imperial Germany, MI6 now increasingly sought information about the Bolsheviks, and Scandinavia was seen as a good base for working inside Russia.[41]

Thus, as German and British intelligence operations in Norway ceased, the triangle of the German–Jew–Spy was gradually erased and replaced, both in the minds of the public and the Norwegian police, with a new triangle of a Bolshevik equals a Jew equals a Spy, as the threat of communist Russia was to dominate intelligence activities in Norway and elsewhere in Western Europe for the next seven decades.[42]

A neutral ally?

From the earliest times, military leaders have sought information about the enemy—his strengths, his weaknesses, his intentions, and his dispositions. Unlike previous wars, the First World War was the first major conflict where the belligerents were able to transmit such information over vast distances in real time. However, the intelligence agencies' effectiveness in fulfilling their purpose, especially when measured against the resources poured into such agencies, has been questioned in recent years by historians.[43] Scandinavia in the First World War seems to be a case in point.

In hindsight, the intelligence war in Scandinavia as a whole, and certainly in Norway, had no real victors, as it never went beyond a war of attrition. Germany had few gains of any real value, the British merely succeeded in hindering the Germans, and the Norwegians were generally unsuccessful in preventing both sides from operating on its territory. In fact, as we have seen, the major triumphs of the Norwegian police—the von Rosen and Rautenfels cases—were results of information from MI6. If anything, the greatest success of Norwegian counter-intelligence was its close cooperation with MI6. For Norway, the increased attention paid to its territory by the warring powers meant it had to strike a delicate balance with its counter-measures. On the one hand, it was dependent upon exporting and importing goods to both the Entente and the Central Powers. On the other hand there was an inherent danger that a failure to heed to the demands of either side could threaten Norway's status as a neutral country. Cooperation with MI6 provided a back channel which was used to promote understanding for Norway's official foreign policy in British government circles. While the Norway of this dual approach has been described by the historian Olav Riste as 'the neutral ally', Riste was referring to the praxis of the state remaining neutral while the private sector functioned as an allied partner of the British.[44] Here, however, we have a case of a government agency undermining public policy and—as in the case of Hagn—actually endangering a Norwegian citizen.

When judging the success, or rather lack of success, of the various agencies, it must be measured against their aims. In this respect, Germany lost. Norway was supposed to be a bridgehead both towards Russia to the east and Great Britain to the west, and while several agents were sent into Great Britain from Norway, the available evidence does not indicate that information of any real value was gained. And even if the ship-watching operation had some successes, the British soon learned to take appropriate counter-measures. Similarly, German sabotage efforts came to nothing. On balance, German intelligence operations in Norway were rather counter-productive, especially as they worked to turn public opinion decisively against Germany.

While there was no clear victor in the intelligence war, if anything the win by default would go to the British. With its rather limited and mainly reactive war aims, MI6 was able to hinder the Germans from using Norwegian territory with any real effectiveness, all while keeping the Norwegians on the straight and narrow.

SCANDINAVIA IN THE FIRST WORLD WAR

Notes

1 John Keegan, *Intelligence in War. Knowledge of the Enemy from Napoleon to Al-Qaeda* (London: Pimlico 2003), 369.

2 Dietrich Schindler & Jiří Toman, *The Laws of Armed Conflicts: a collection of conventions, resolutions, and other documents* (Dordrecht: Martinus Nihjoff, 1988), 30; cf. Hugo Kerchnawe, 'Werdegang der Spionage', in Paul Lettow-Vorbeck et al. (eds.), *Die Weltkriegsspionage* (Munich: Justin Moser, 1931), 15.

3 Fritz Karl Roegels, 'Die Technick im Diensten des Agenten', in Lettow-Vorbeck et al. 1931, 125–39.

4 Rudolf von Borries, 'Spionage im Welten vor dem Kriege', in Lettow-Vorbeck et al. 1931, 77–84.

5 Thomas Boghardt, *Spies of the Kaiser. German Covert Operations in Great Britain during the First World War Era* (London: Palgrave Macmillan, 2004), 6–20 & 80–8; Tim Greve, *Spionjakt i Norge. Norsk overvåkningstjeneste i tiden før 1940* (Oslo: Aschehoug, 1982), 31–33 & 80–88; Jürgen W. Schmidt, *Gegen Russland und Frankreich. Der deutsche militärische Geheimdienst 1890–1914* (Ludwigsfelde bei Berlin: Ludwigsfelder Verlagshaus, 2006); Michael H. Clemmesen, *Den lange vej mod 9. april. Historien om de fyrre år før den tyske operation mod Norge og Danmark i 1940* (Odense: Syddansk Universitetsforlag, 2010), 8–59.

6 The best-known works of these anti-German invasion fantasies are William Le Queux's two novels *The Great War in England in 1897* (1894) and *The Invasion of 1910* (1906) as well as Robert Erskine Childers's *The Riddle of the Sands* (1903) and Saki's *When William Came: A Story of London Under the Hohenzollerns* (1913).

7 Michael Smith, *Six. A History of Britain's Secret Intelligence Service*, i: *1909–1939* (London: Dialogue, 2010), 20; Alan Judd, *The Quest for C. Mansfield Cumming and the founding of the Secret Service* (London: HarperCollins, 2000), 150, 229 & 255.

8 Judd 2000, 25–26, 70–72, 89–111, 150, 203, 229 & 255; Keith Jeffery, *MI6. The History of the Secret Intelligence Service 1909–1949* (London: Bloomsbury, 2010), 87; Smith 2010, 35–36.

9 Knut Kjeldstadli, Jan Eivind Myhre & Einar Niemi, *I nasjonalstatens tid 1814–1940* (vol. ii of Knut Kjeldstadli (ed.), *Norsk innvandringshistorie*) (Oslo: Pax 2003), 376–82; Hans Fredrik Dahl, 'Antisemittismen i norsk historie', in Bernt Hagtvet (ed.), *Folkemordenes svarte bok* (Oslo: Universitetsforlaget, 2008), 444 ff.

10 Roald Berg, *Norsk utenrikspolitisk historie*, ii: *Norge på egen hånd 1905–1920* (Oslo: Universitetsforlaget 1995), 182–215; Knut Einar Eriksen & Trond Bergh, *Den hemmelige krigen. Overvåking i Norge 1914–1997*, ii:

Overvåkingssystemet bygges opp, 1914–1955 (Oslo: Cappelen akademisk forlag, 1998).

11 Nik. Brandal, Eirik Brazier & Ola Teige, *Den mislykkede spionen. Fortellingen om kunstneren, journalisten og landssvikeren Alfred Hagn* (Oslo: Humanist forlag, 2010), 112–14.

12 August Urbanski von Ostrymiecz, 'Aufmarschpläne', in Lettow-Vorbeck et al. 1931, 85–8.

13 Markus Pöhlmann, 'German Intelligence at War 1914–1918', *Journal of Intelligence History*, 5/2 (2005), 35–37; Schmidt 2006; Boghardt 2004, 159.

14 Greve 1982, 34–35; Bundesarchiv Abteilung Militärarchiv (BAM), Freiburg, RM/5 3680.

15 Boghardt 2004, 12–20 & 80–94; Pöhlmann 2005, 23–38 & 47–54; Greve 1982, 31–49 & 69; Joh. Søhr, *Spioner og bomber. Fra opdagelsespolitiets arbeide under verdenskrigen* (Oslo: Tanum, 1938), 47–62, 99–107 & 126; BAM, RM 5/2700, 3650, 3680, 3708, 4663 & 4677; National Archives (TNA), London, KV 1/42, KV 1/43–44.

16 BAM, RM 5/2700, 3680 & 4677.

17 BAM, RM 5/2700, 3680; Riksarkivet (Norwegian National Achives – NRA), Oslo, Generalstaben, 1814–1940, IV avdeling, pk. 216 Yngve Nielsen; Statsarkivet i Bergen (Bergen Regional Archives), Bergen (SAB), Bergen politidistrikt, O.a Diverse, Henlagte spionsaker 1915–20, pk. 2 1916.

18 NRA, Generalstaben, 1814–1940, IV avdeling, pk. 65 register over mistenkelige personer 1914–1916 and pk. 193 Spionsaker 1915; SAB, Bergen politidistrikt, O.a Diverse, Henlagte spionsaker 1915–20, pk. 1 1914–15.

19 Greve 1982, 31–49; Søhr 1938, 47–62 & 99–126; NRA, Generalstaben, 1814–1940, IV avdeling, pk. 192 Spionsaker 1915, Rush and Emden, pk. 194 Spionsaker 1916, pk. 208–209 Tyske spioner 1917–18, pk. 211 Dokumenter om mistenkelige personer, pk. 214 Holzhüter and Borgen, and pk. 216 Yngve Nilsen; SAB, Bergen politidistrikt, O.a Diverse, Henlagte spionsaker 1915–20, pk. 1 1914–15 and pk. 2 1916; BAM, RM 5/3650 and 3680.

20 NRA, Generalstaben, 1814–1940, IV avdeling, Pk. 214 Holzhüter and Borgen.

21 Greve 1982, 31–49; Søhr 1938, 47–62 & 99–107; NRA, Generalstaben, 1814–1940, IV avdeling, pk. 191 Spionsaker 1915, pk. 193 Spionsaker 1915 and pk. 196 Spionsaker 1916; BAM, RM 5/3680, 4664 and 4673.

22 Smith 2010, 123; Jeffery 2010, 87–9; NRA, Generalstaben, 1814–1940, IV avdeling, pk. 212 Kaptein R. C. Holme 1914–15; SAB, Bergen politidistrikt, O.a Diverse, Henlagte spionsaker 1915–20, pk. 1 1914–15.

23 Quoted in Smith 2010, 129.

24 Judd 2000, 264, 282, 301, 318–22 & 350; Smith 2010, 129; Redvald Larssen, *Fra vekterstuen til Møllergaten 19* (Oslo: Aschehoug, 1946), 96–7.

25 Smith 2010, 35, 123–8; Jeffery 2010, 87–9 & 94–7; Judd 2000, 264, 282, 301, 318–22 & 350.

26 Brandal, Brazier & Teige 2010, 13, 96–105 & 136–137; Søhr 1938, 24–34, 115–16 & 148–151; Kjeldstadli et al. 2003, 376–382; Greve 1982, 27–31, 57–59 & 72–76.

27 NRA, Generalstaben, 1814–1940, IV avdeling, pk. 214 Holzhüter and Borgen; *Aftenposten*, 19–21 April 1917.

28 K.-G. Olin, *Tärningkast på liv och död* (Jakobstad: Olimex, 2009), 202–32.

29 Greve 1982, 35–46; Søhr 1938, 46.

30 Judd 2000, 264; NRA, Generalstaben 1814–1940, IV avdeling, pk. 198 Spionsaker 1917; TNA, FO 272/1289.

31 Paul G. Halpern, *A Naval History of World War I* (London: Routledge, 1995), 329–441.

32 Berg 1995, 182–215; Riste, Olav, *The neutral ally. Norway's relations with belligerent powers in the First World War* (Oslo: Universitetsforlaget, 1965), 126–191.

33 *Bergens Tidende*, 28 June 1917, 'Ti nogen væsensforskjel paa landsforræderi og handelsspionage med torpedering av norsk skib som følge kan der neppe siges at være.'

34 *Aftenposten*, 15 May 1917, 'Vi ser, at spioner har omgivet os paa alle kanter og drevet sit arbeide midt blant os. … I dette system maa der nu ske en forandring! Spioner har været arresteret, vidløftige spionaffærer behandlet. Almenheden har været sat heldt udenfor, alle døre lukket ogsaa der.'

35 Greve 1982, 44–57; Søhr 1938, 32–46, 66–71 & 108–142.

36 Boghardt 2004, 15–16, 120–140, 158 & 170; BAM, RM 5/2582, 3708–3709, 3650, 3680, 4663, 5024 & 5126; TNA KV 1/42; NRA, Riksadvokaten, Diverse saker, D saksarkiv 1886–1956, pk. 4 and 5 Bombesaken 1917.

37 Søhr 1938, 90 & 110–114; Greve 1982, 57; NRA, Riksadvokaten, Diverse saker, D saksarkiv 1886–1956,6 Straffesak mot Karl Schwartz m.fl. 1917–25; NRA, Utenriksdepartementet, eske 5819, P25–K 02/17 Alfred Hagn; NRA, Utenriksstasjonene, Legasjonen/Ambassaden i London, Rettssaker, A 1 Alfred Hagen (pk. 481).

38 Boghardt 2004, 153–155; Greve 42–43 & 74; Statsarkivet i Oslo (Oslo Regional Archives), Oslo, Oslo politikammer, Straffefullbyrdelse, pk. 940, sak.9/1918 and Domsjournaler, 26 1917–1918, 4.1 1918; NRA, Generalstaben, 1814–1940, IV avdeling, Pk. 194 Spionsaker 197; BAM, RM 5/3708–3709; RM 5/3650; RM 5/3680; RM 5/4663; TNA, NA KV 1/42.

39 Søhr 1938, 51; Greve 1982, 31–49 & 69; SAB, Bergen politidistrikt, O.a Diverse, Henlagte spionsaker 1915–20, pk. 2 1916; BAM, RM 5/3680, 3705, 4604, 4662–5 and 4677; Politisches archiv des Auswärtiges Amt, Berlin, R 8412 Spionageprozesse in Norwegen, bd. 2, L24576, L253931, L253933 and L253937–8.

40 Søhr 1938, 130–131; SAB, Bergen politidistrikt, O.a Diverse, Henlagte spionsaker 1915–20, pk. 5 1918; NRA, Generalstaben, 1814–1940, IV avdeling, pk 205, Spionsaker 1918.

41 Jeffery 2010, 87–109, 134–138, 172–178 & 193.

42 Per Ole Johansen, *Oss selv nærmest. Norge og jødene 1914–1943* (Oslo: Gyldendal, 1984), 9–26.

43 See Keegan 2003; and Ronen Bergman, *The Secret War with Iran. The 30-Year Clandestine Struggle against the World's Most Dangerous Terrorist Power* (New York: Free Press, 2008).

44 Riste 1965.

CHAPTER 3

Rats and anthills

The First World War
in the Scandinavian spy novel

Claes Ahlund

The spy novels that were published in Denmark, Norway, and Sweden during the First World War are of interest as a documentation of the war's mental impact on neutral Scandinavia. They should not only be considered a passive impression of the war, however, since they also actively contributed to the formation of public opinion. The prelude to the war and the German invasion of Belgium are recurring themes in the novels of the first year of the war, later to be followed by variations on the dominant theme of foreign intelligence activities in Scandinavia. The novels are largely adapted to the conventions of formula fiction. As a consequence, they have many common traits on the level of plot structure as well as on the thematic level. Nevertheless, they express contrary and competing interpretations of the political course of events. These interpretations can be compared to the political propaganda distributed in other media; to pro-German or anti-German sentiment; and to conservative, liberal, or socialist opinions. The object of this chapter is to relate the Scandinavian spy fiction of the war years to the discursive war that was fought in the neutral states as elsewhere, actively supported by the belligerent powers. Different ideological positions will be discussed, and different ways of conveying the political message will be examined. In popular literature, this message was sometimes stated explicitly, but it could also be implicitly indicated.

In Sweden, voices were heard calling for the country to enter the war, but, as in Denmark and Norway, such a scenario was feared by an overwhelming majority. Nevertheless the war split public opinion in two. In Sweden, sympathy for Germany were stronger than in Denmark and Norway, but even in these two countries there were advocates for a benevolent attitude towards the Central Powers.

The rapid expansion of intelligence activity in Europe in the years immediately preceding the war was closely connected to the dramatically increasing attention paid to spies in the press and in popular literature. During the war, more or less paranoid ideas prevailed among all the belligerents, claiming that military failures were the consequence of infiltration, espionage, and treason rather than inadequate preparation or miscalculation. There were common patterns of national chauvinism directed against the culture of the opponents or against individuals with an ethnic attachment to the enemy, but there were also local variations in the manifestation of spy mania.[1] In more than one case, notably in Great Britain, the establishment of a professional intelligence organization was realized only after the publication of a number of successful *literary* accounts of operations by foreign intelligence agencies—fiction once more demonstrating its persuasive capacity.[2]

This climate of suspicion and anxiety certainly influenced attitudes towards the stream of foreigners arriving in Copenhagen, Kristiania, and Stockholm. In Sweden, reports of supposed espionage by Russian travelling saw-doctors had appeared in the press since the turn of the century. A Swedish intelligence agency, Underrättelsebyrån (UB), had been established in 1905, and in the last years before the outbreak of war rumours of foreign secret agents working in Sweden had caused a marked increase in the activities of Swedish counter-intelligence.[3] In addition, new espionage legislation was passed in 1913. In August 1914, the Norwegian Storting passed the Act on Defence Secrets, commonly known as the 'Spy Act', authorizing the police to intervene against all espionage, regardless of the target of the activity.[4] Even in neutral Scandinavia there was in the summer of 1914 a sense of being involved in secret international machinations, unavoidably leading to war. This atmosphere is well expressed by the detective Asbjørn Krag in the novel *Tindebestigerklubben* (1915) by Stein Riverton (Sven Elvestad):

> Krag was standing in the open front door of the hotel … listening to the yells of the newspaper boys. Their cries hit him like rocks, and he suddenly experienced an unsettling and sickening feeling that the menacing stillness of Central Europe … was about to give way to a dreadful advance of great, fateful events.
>
> One of the newspaper boys called out as he walked past: 'Austria and Serbia! The latest telegrams!' Further down the street came the cry: 'Austria wants war! The World War is coming! The World War is coming!
>
> Krag closed the door. He was beginning to see clearly the undercurrent in world events that had brought all these mysterious and dangerous people to this neutral capital. Like rats sensing approaching catastrophe, they had fled the sinking ship. Peace was about to be broken out there in the big world.[5]

The individual perspective confronts that of international politics when Krag listens to the cries of the newspaper boy. This narrative device was not restricted to popular literature, as the well-known example of Sigfrid Siwertz's novel *Eldens återsken* (1916) shows. In *Tindebestigerklubben* the function is more specific. The war that is announced is not only waged on the Continent. The many spies at work demonstrate that Kristiania is also a battlefield, as are the other Scandinavian capitals. The foreigners, characterized as 'mysterious and dangerous people', are in the service of one of the great powers, competing for intelligence and trying to exert influence. Asbjørn Kragh is no ordinary Norwegian, but in this passage he nevertheless represents the anxiety of the general public. As a writer of fiction, Riverton/Elvestad is building up suspense, but at the same time he is planting suspicion. Who are these peculiar foreigners who can be seen everywhere in the city? What intrigues are they involved in? Is the country at risk?

The growing cosmopolitan element in neutral Scandinavia is depicted as even more sinister in the novel by Radscha (Iwan

Aminoff), *De ljusskygge. En spioneriroman från huvudstaden* (1917).
In the following passage, the Swedish capital is apostrophized in
order to be blamed for not having stood the moral test of the war:

> The Stockholmers have had to yield the way to the cosmopoli-
> tan element. Dozens of tongues are spoken on your streets, in
> your squares, in your hotels. His Highness Gold rules more or
> less openly. You sacrifice to the profiteers, to the golden calf. Your
> blood has become unhealthy, contaminated, and yet livelier than
> ever before.
>
> Stockholm has become an immense anthill with an addition
> of foreign intruders. You have sacrificed morals, codes of honour,
> and customs in exchange for the bountiful gifts of mammon. Yet
> inside the anthill schemes and stratagems are being plotted, often
> of the most complicated nature—an abundant field of study. The
> many-armed polyp of the World War has put out not one but
> several arms over the city, sucking greedily wherever it can.[6]

The international element is not only described as mysterious, but
as menacing. The foreign presence is not only politically dangerous;
the 'many-armed polyp' of war is also threatening the economy and,
not least, the morals of the country. Using an imagery of sickness
and disease, Radscha suggests that traditional Swedish morals are
disintegrating, suborned by filthy international lucre. Here, as in
Riverton/Elvestad's novel, foreign spy rings are described. The spy is
a threat to peace as well as to the economy and morals of the neutral
country, but at the same time he serves another purpose; he permits
the neutral but nevertheless curious Scandinavians to be a part of
the great course of events.

From invasion stories to spy fiction

At the turn of the century, increasing concern caused by international industrial competition and an escalating arms race had already created a market for historical novels illustrating the clash of
nations. At the same time, a new genre developed where thrilling
political plots were placed not in the past, but in the future. These

stories rapidly became extremely popular after the Franco-German War, starting with *The Battle of Dorking* (1871), where the Prussians, having defeated France, successfully invade England. During the following decades, a great number of short stories and novels of this type were published all over Europe, relating local, hair-raising details of invasion.[7] A parallel genre also developed; the spy story situated not in the past but in the present, often extending into the immediate future. The invasion story and the spy story are in fact inseparable. In the invasion novel, the enemy's attack is regularly preceded by espionage. In an atmosphere of mental militarization, the spy novel on the other hand very often describes clandestine activities that are preparing for a war that appears to be unavoidable. A French novel of 1905, *La future invasion prussienne et l'espionnage à la frontière*, led with both topics to be on the safe side.[8]

Both genres were continuously developed in close connection with international politics as well as with current mentalities. Franco Moretti has pointed out that the British invasion novels are located in the same south-eastern part of England that Sherlock Holmes prefers to visit when leaving London. Even more interesting, the murder cases are much more frequent here, among 'parks and country-houses and estates', than in the city, and so is the proportion of foreign perpetrators.[9] This pattern can be found all over Europe, the invasion novels being in many cases set in rural parts of the country, and particularly in places connected to national history and thus likely to appeal to patriotic sentiment. A typical Swedish example was *Hvarför vi förlorade slaget vid Upsala den 18 maj 1900* (1890).[10]

After the outbreak of war, the international and political polarization sharpened. The invasion novels of the pre-war period had in most countries portrayed several nations as potential invaders. These alternative scenarios were now replaced by a stable cast corresponding to the roles played in the real war. Naturally, Germany played the part of the villain in British and French spy novels published during the war.[11] In the neutral Scandinavian countries, the political situation was more complicated. Different national histories provided different points of departure. In the case of Denmark, the harrowing experience of the Second Schleswig War in 1864 provided an interpretative frame that resulted in wide-spread anti-militarist sentiment. The Swedish pre-war invasion novels invariably expressed a Russophobia deeply rooted in history.[12] The Russian threat was also depicted in Norwegian novels such as Vilhelm Nagel's *Et skjæbnesvangert dokument* (1905), or *Kaptein Skugge. Fantastisk forteljing um krigen millom Russland og Noreg i 1950* (1911), by Olav Gullvåg writing as Johan Visionary. Several Norwegian adventure novels featured espionage related to the dissolution in 1905 of the union between Sweden and Norway: Ludvig Larsen's *En spionhistorie fra 1905* (1909), Engebret Amundsen's *Spionen paa Fredriksten* (1910), and Olaf Wilhelm Erichsen's *Naar lænkene brytes* (1915).[13] The spy story was a flexible form that could easily be adapted to changing political circumstances. Amundsen had previously written a historical spy novel, *Bonaparte og den østerrigske spion* (1909). Erichsen, using the signature 'Kaptein Munk', moved on from the dissolution of the Union to the world war. In *Den hvite races selvmord* (1915), the course of events corresponds roughly with that of the ongoing war, with the exception that it is explained as a part of a Japanese scheme for dominion over the West.

Besides Russia and the Yellow Peril, Germany also appears in a threatening role in the Norwegian spy fiction of the war years, which can be seen in Finn Lie's *Naar krigsfaklen luer* (1915) and Aksel Akselsson's *Undervandsbaatens hemmelighet* (1918).[14] Denmark also had its share of invasion novels with Germany in the role of the invader. There are striking differences on more than one level between Karl Larsen's *Dommens dag* (1908) and Emil Bønnelycke's *Spartanerne* (1919), but in both novels Denmark is invaded by Germany.

In Sweden, the traditional fear of an imminent Russian invasion led to a series of misjudgements at the outbreak of war, in fiction as well as in politics. Axel Kerfve's novel *Allt för fosterlandet* (1914) was published in the first week of the war, launched with the hastily added subheading *Krigsutbrottets roman* ('A novel of the outbreak of war'). The plot, dealing with Russian espionage culminating in an invasion of Sweden, was soon overtaken by the course of events in Europe.[15] After this, the traditional Russian enemy lost much of its popularity, but no other nation took over the part of villain in the invasion stories published during the war. The danger of Sweden's close relations to militarist Germany was a recurrent theme in the liberal and socialist press, but this threat had no impact at all on popular literature. Even in socialist papers, it was rarely expressed in an invasion scenario, but rather as unease at the spread of militarism to Sweden or the potentially disastrous consequences if Sweden entered the war on Germany's side.[16]

In Sweden as well as in Norway and Denmark, political persuasions often corresponded with attitudes towards the belligerent powers. Socialists and liberals, inclined to sympathize with the Allies, judged the German invasion of neutral Belgium as a heinous crime and accused the German army of repeated acts of cruelty against Belgian civilians. In Britain, the same version of the story was often used to justify the decision to go to war, as in Asquith's graphic image: 'It is impossible for people of our blood and history to stand by ... while a big bully sets to work to thrash and trample to the ground a victim who has given him no provocation.'[17] In the opinion of writers and debaters such as Marika Stiernstedt and K. G. Ossiannilsson in Sweden, Johannes Jørgensen and Kr. Nyrop in Denmark, and Johan Bojer in Norway, the German invasion was regarded as an anti-democratic act and a violation of international law. The same interpretation was also expressed in fiction, as in Erich Erichsen's novel *Den tavse dansker* (1916), in which a soldier from Schleswig bears witness to his complicity in war atrocities committed against Belgian civilians.[18]

Meanwhile in the pro-German camp, often but not always corresponding to a conservative political standpoint, the German invasion was described as the unavoidable and legitimate prevention of a long-planned and impending attack on Germany by the united strength of Britain, France, and Belgium. A number of spokesmen for this theory, and thus for Germany, were to be found in Scandinavia: in Sweden, Per Hallström and Fredrik Böök; in Norway, Knut Hamsun; and in Denmark, Karl Larsen. In both camps, the rhetoric of ethos was much used, portraying the Belgians either in a favourable light or as sly criminals.[19] In her pamphlet *Från Berlin till Brüssel* (1916), Annie Åkerhielm idealizes the Germans and paints a very black picture of the Belgians, characterized as a 'bigoted, ignorant, and backward race'. The German occupation of Belgium is consistently described as 'an act of self-defence forced by bitter necessity'.[20] Marika Stiernstedt, in contrast, depicts German soldiers as bestial in *Den grymma läxan* (1915),[21] while exerting herself to make it possible for Swedish readers to identify with the Belgians. This she achieved by stressing that both countries were neutral and by discussing the emigrant Walloons, 'the ancestors of many of our most prominent Swedish families, and thus binding us with ties of blood to the valiant Belgian people'.[22]

Scandinavian spy novels

Kanonernes sjel (1915), written by the Norwegian writer of suspense fiction Øvre Richter Frich, is not a traditional spy novel, but it includes espionage and the first half of the plot takes place in Belgium. Frich criticizes parliamentarianism and socialism, and repeatedly describes war as a badly needed purge for modern civilization. Nevertheless, his analysis of the hidden motives for the war resembles that of the socialists, and he repudiates nationalist propaganda. Frich's ideal is in fact a radical, individualistic vitalism. Modern war is described as a threat to individuality because it turns men into soulless machines. Conversely, the fight between individual men is proclaimed as one of life's greatest virtues. One effect of Frich's individualism is that he does not side with any of the two competing representations of the Belgians.[23]

Willy Dahl has characterized the ideology of Frich's novels as fascist, pointing out that Norway in particular provided all the necessary prerequisites of the anti-capitalist variety of fascism.[24] *Kanonernes sjel* certainly contains passages that could be described as proto-fascist. An ideological position such as this often leads to a pro-German standpoint, but Frich differed from this pattern, keeping his distance to the controversial issue of Belgium.

A departure from the standard opinions on Belgium's fate can also be found in another Norwegian novel, *Den gule marquis. Ei soga fraa storkrigen 1915* (1915) by Kaare Gullveng (Olav Gullvåg).

This is definitely a pro-Belgian novel, but at the same time, a highly individualistic brand of opportunism is portrayed in a sympathetic light. Captain Falk of Svanhild carries on business with the British and the Germans alike, declaring that he keeps a neutral position. He is soon provided with a twofold reason for turning against the Germans: a growing liking for an eccentric, exiled Belgian million-aire who is waging a private war on the Germans, and his love for a Belgian woman. His increasing dislike of Germany has dramatic consequences when he decides to get himself and his ship out of a difficult situation by ramming a German submarine escort, caus-ing it to go down with all hands.

In Belgium, Falk joins the resistance led by the Belgian million-aire, the 'Yellow Marquis'. The anti-German position is now much more evident, with German lootings and rapes strengthening the motivation. The much-debated question of whether the behaviour of the Belgian *francs-tireurs* justified the German's harsh treatment of civilians is also settled, the Germans being described as suffering from hysterical paranoia and the Belgians as completely innocent victims. Nevertheless, the Yellow Marquis and his men are doing exactly what the Germans accused the Belgian *francs-tireurs* of: not only do they spy and carry out sabotage, sometimes disguised as Belgian farmers, sometimes as German soldiers,[25] they even carry out proper attacks on German troops. Gullvåg's novel is highly biased, but his message is undermined not only by the protagonist's profiting by the war, but also by the inconsistent portrayal of the relations between Germans and Belgian *francs-tireurs*.

Interesting points of comparison are offered by three spy nov-els, two Swedish and one Norwegian, that deal with the German invasion of Belgium: *Spionernas mästare* (1915) by Radscha (Iwan Aminoff); *Mannen från Liège* (1914) by Frank Heller (Gunnar Serner); and, already quoted, Riverton's *Tindebestigerklubben* (1915). In Heller's novel, we enter a world of secret German prepa-rations for the invasion, a plot reversed by Radscha, who writes of a Germany threatened by imminent attack. In Riverton's novel, the partiality is not as outspoken: hidden conspiracies certainly exist in *Tindebestigerklubben*, but it is only in the very last sentence that he finally comes down on one side. These particular novels illustrate the two main explanations of the outbreak of the war, thus entering the controversy about the responsibility for the war that was formulated in many different media. They also demonstrate that popular literature can shape public opinion in more than one way. It can be heavily biased, but it can also deliver its message in a more subtle way. Read in isolation, Riverton's novel does not provide us with an explanation to the mystical agreement deciphered by the detective Asbjørn Krag. The pattern only appears if we use the German propaganda as cipher key. In the pro-German press, there was much speculation about a secret plan for an attack on Germany signed by Britain, France, Belgium, and, sometimes, Russia. In an effort to make this theory more credible there were often references made to 'well-informed sources', claiming to have first-hand knowledge of the document.

The role of the villain may be played by different nations, but there are nevertheless many similarities between the plot structures of the three novels. In *Spionernas mästare*, secret plans for an invasion of Germany are exposed; in *Mannen från Liège*, a secret plan for a German invasion of Belgium. Radscha makes use of several techniques to make the pro-German story credible.[26] One of these is to avoid using a German protagonist. Instead, the action is carried forward by the French spy Croz, who is loyal to his country, but nevertheless has access to secret information making it possible for him to see through the Allied propaganda. In 1916, Germany was to have been the victim of a secret and long-planned invasion; the German invasion of Belgium in 1914 was therefore a legitimate and necessary attempt to forestall the Allies before they were fully armed.

An altogether different scenario is used in the anti-German fiction. Sir Arthur Conan Doyle's short story, 'His last bow' (1917), in which Sherlock Holmes outwits a German spy, is a typical example. The combination used to open the lock of the German's safe is 'August 1914', and we are told that this combination was chosen in 1901! The plot of *Mannen från Liège* is similar, featuring a young Swede who is drawn into a life-and-death struggle between the Belgian intelligence service and a band of German spies. The clues consist of a mysterious figure drawn on matchbox and a coded message in a stolen letter. The letter concerns classified information about Belgian fortifications and is in the process of being smuggled over the border into Germany.[27] The mysterious drawing finally proves to be a map of the fortifications protecting Liège—the target of an attack planned by a treacherous industrialist.

Both Heller's and Radscha's novels were published after the German invasion of Belgium and the subsequent international outcry, making Heller's version of events the more marketable one. In time, Radscha's urgent efforts to convince his readers of Germany's innocence became increasingly unfeasible. Yet for all that, political developments were not the only reason behind the Swedish publisher's decision in the autumn of 1915 finally to stop the series. More important was a general and growing war-weariness, making war novels more difficult to sell, irrespective of their political message.[28]

A political subtext is also often much in evidence in novels published after the dramatic first year of the war. Witness three Danish novels: Jørgen Bast's *Spioner* (1916, published under the pseudonym Willy Stone) and *Det elskelige København* (1917), and Erik Hansen's *Det nevtrale hjerte* (1918). In *Spioner*, Copenhagen is depicted as one of the neutral capitals where a merciless struggle for intelligence is fought under the unconcerned surface. The German spy Moses Auerstein and his accomplices confront a Russian organization using the Danish capital as a centre for the collection of information. The Russians are confident that they will soon be able to put an end to Germany's economic influence in Russia.[29] To achieve this, they bring pressure to bear on a French businessman as well as on a Danish officer. In this secret struggle between Russia and Germany, Denmark is far from neutral. To start with, the Russians are aided as a matter of course by a captain Hage of the Danish secret service. Another mysterious helper acting behind the scenes is eventually recognized as 'the head of secret intelligence in a country whose credentials we respect'.[30] The German spy ring is defeated and forced to leave Denmark. The friendship between Denmark and Russia is then symbolically confirmed by the love between Prince Ivan Trubetskoj and Else Marker, a young Danish woman initially duped into running the Germans' errands.

In *Spioner*, the anti-German position stems not from any sympathies with Britain or France, but with Russia; a very unusual position in Scandinavia during the First World War. Bast's next novel, *Det elskelige København* (1917), has no Russian connection, but the political undertone is the same as in *Spioner*. The role of the villain is once more taken by a German Spy called Moses, and once more the novel ends when this sly creature is defeated and forced to flee—this time not to Germany but to Malmö. The objective this time is different too: the smuggling of bombs ('*helvetesmaskiner*', or infernal machines) to Norway to blast Norwegian ships, an extension to a blockade of Denmark trying to stop all exports to Britain. Russia is once more threatened, when the Germans smuggle anthrax to Finland via Norway. These spectacular episodes can be seen as typical of the creative sensationalism of popular literature, but they are based on reality. There are close points of similarity between them and two episodes much discussed in the press in 1917 and discussed by Nik. Brandal and Ola Teige in their contribution to the present volume. The first case was an attempt to smuggle anthrax from Germany to Finland via Norway by a Swedish citizen acting as a German spy; the second that of another German spy, this time a Finnish citizen, caught in the act of smuggling explosives, described in the press with the very word '*helvetesmaskiner*', to a hiding-place in Kristiania discovered by the Norwegian police. The possible reason may indeed have been to smuggle them to the Finnish resistance.[31]

In both novels, *Spioner* as well as *Det elskelige København*, the connection between espionage and the economy is underlined. Profiteers who made a killing selling tinned food ('*gulaschbaroner*') are often satirically portrayed in comical popular fiction during the war. Bjarne S. Bendtsen has pointed out that they nevertheless represented far smaller returns than those made by speculating on the stock market, where shipping companies were particularly lucrative.[32] In this respect, the spy novels display a better sense of economic essentials. *Det elskelige København* uses two parallel plots, the one concerning the smuggling of explosives and anthrax by the German spies, the other dealing with speculation on the stock exchange, the two plots eventually merging when the sabotage of the Norwegian merchant vessels causes a dramatic fall in shipping shares. In the novel the Danish police are described as incompetent; the Norwegian police force, on the other hand, stands out as energetic and efficient. The censure of the Danish police is related to criticism of the Danish preference for 'Neutrality at any price', a position maintained even after the German blockade: 'Any nation not opposing this unparalleled injustice would simply be doomed.'[33]

Erik Hansen's *Det nevtrale hjerte* brings ingredients from the traditional adventure novel and early science fiction to the spy novel. The adventure is based on spectacular elements: a hidden German submarine equipped with an epoch-making radioactive accumulator, a giant German ocean liner bound for home after the outbreak of war, long marches across the Greenland icecap, and a Japanese spy disguised as a woman. The novel's sympathies lie plainly with France, the anti-German sentiment being as evident as in Jørgen Bast's novels. One example of this is the heavily biased and evidently authorized summary of the course of the war provided by one of the Danish protagonists.[34] An important role is given to a secret document providing 'a complete plan for Germany's secret intelligence activities in Japan, France, England, and the Baltic provinces of Russia'.[35]

Germany is cast as the arch-enemy, but there are other threats against Denmark. Just as 'Kaptein Munck' in *Den hvite races selvmord*, Erik Hansen warns against 'the Yellow Peril'. The Japanese spy accordingly delivers a hateful monologue in which he expresses his joy at the European powers' mutual destruction, making Japanese dominion so much easier to accomplish.[36] In the last part of the novel a young Dane goes to France in order to join the resistance against the Germans, a device for linking a neutral country to the shooting war that was also used by Olav Gullvåg in *Den gule marquis*. In Jørgen Bast's analysis, despicable Danish neutrality resulted from naïvety and a widespread fear of repeating the catastrophic mistakes of 1864. Erik Hansen adds an anti-democratic flavour by stressing 'the parliamentary gelatine' that results not only in neutrality, but in irresponsibility and amateurism as well.[37]

The uses of popular literature

The spy novels under consideration here build on a dualistic conception of the world. They are adventure stories that align themselves with either pro-German or anti-German ideology, the latter being the dominant pattern in neutral Scandinavia. Reader identification with the protagonists was facilitated by the novelists' black-and-white political map—a map used by Kaare Gullveng in *Den gule marquis* as well as in Frank Heller's *Mannen från Liège*, where several factors guide the reader into sympathizing with Belgium and repudiating Germany: the insistence on the deceitful attack on a small neutral country, the physical and moral repulsiveness of a Belgian traitor of German descent, the protagonist's falling in love with a young Belgian woman. The political message may be spelled out in Gullveng's and Heller's novels, but next to Aminoff's pro-German *Spionernas mästare* they could be described as positively restrained. Stein Riverton's *Tindebestigerklubben*, on the other hand, appears to be completely neutral; that is, until the very last sentence of the novel, when the sudden appearance of the secret German invasion plan makes it an irrefutable fact. In this novel at least, Riverton's conception of the world appears to be pro-German. Nevertheless, *Tindebestigerklubben* is not a book with a purpose; many readers were not sufficiently well informed to decipher the hidden pattern, and were thus likely to miss the point altogether.

The communication of unity and a sense of belonging is a fundamental function of popular culture, particularly important in a time of crisis. Kim Salomon has characterized the Swedish magazines as 'an arena where cultural community is created and maintained', and Lina Sturfelt adopts a similar perspective in her thesis on the coverage of the First World War in Swedish magazines.[38] Nevertheless, there was no dominant ideological position in the Swedish media during the war. The situation could rather be described as a discursive struggle in a transitional period. Radscha's novels propagate conservative and pro-German beliefs deeply rooted in civil service departments as well as in the officer corps. The novels of Frank Heller represent the rival, liberal, anti-German ideology, growing stronger with every passing year. Neither in Denmark nor in Norway was there a political polarization as sharp as that in Sweden. The Danish and Norwegian spy novels discussed in this chapter demonstrate a certain political variation, from the liberal position adopted by Kaare Gullveng to the anti-parliamentary message of Erik Hansen. Despite these differences, they all have the same pronounced anti-German tendency, the one exception being Stein Riverton's sophisticated staging of the secret invasion plan used in German propaganda.

The spy novel was used by all combatants in the discursive war fought in the neutral nations to convey liberal opinions as well as conservative and anti-parliamentary messages. In *Spionernas mästare*, Radscha invites his readers to join a much more exclusive cultural fellowship than that proposed by liberal writers such as Frank Heller and Kaare Gullveng. The ideological appeal of the spy novels was an integral part of a discursive war, but the conditions varied according to media and genre. In contrast to the guarded-ness of most magazines, the spy novels in many cases explicitly took sides. This does not agree with Sofi Qvarnström's conclusion that the anti-war literary fiction of the First World War problema-tized the war to a greater extent, whereas non-fictional anti-war writing was in many cases programmatically biased.[39] Unlike the novels discussed by Qvarnström, the spy novels fall into the category of popular literature, which means that they reflect a set of much more stable genre conventions, favouring an unequivocal political message. Nevertheless, popular literature does not differ from 'serious literature' in its capacity for public debate as well as for escapism.[40] The proportions may vary, but both tendencies can certainly be found in all of the spy novels discussed in this chapter. Yet behind the apparent similarities at the level of the plot struc-ture, there is great variation in the political message.

Notes

1 See Thomas Boghardt, *Spies of the Kaiser: German Covert Operations in Great Britain during the First World War Era* (Houndmills: Palgrave Macmillan, 2005); William C. Fuller, *The Foe Within. Fantasies of Treason and the End of Imperial Russia* (Ithaca: Cornell University Press, 2006); Matthew Stibbe, *German Anglophobia and the Great War, 1914–1918* (Cambridge: CUP, 2001).

2 See David Trotter, 'The Politics of Adventure in the Early British Spy Novel', in Wesley K. Wark (ed.), *Spy Fiction, Spy Films and Real Intellligence* (London: Frank Cass, 1991), 31; Boghardt 2005; Philip Knightley, *The Second Oldest Profession: Spies and Spying in the Twentieth Century* (London: Pimlico, 2003), 17; Michael Smith, *Six. A History of Britain's Secret Intelligence Service*, i: *1909–1939* (London: Dialogue, 2010), 20.

3 Gunnar Åselius, 'Militärattachéerna i S:t Petersburg. En undersökning av det svenska underrättelseväsendets professionalisering 1885–1917', *Militärhistorisk Tidskrift* (1990), 7–44; cf. Jan Ottoson & Lars Magnusson, *Hemliga makter. Svensk hemlig militär underrättelsetjänst från unionstiden till det kalla kriget* (Stockholm: Tidens Förlag, 1991), 42 ff.

4 See Nik. Brandal & Ola Teige in this volume.

5 The novel by Stein Riverton (Sven Elvestad), *Tindebestigerklubben*, was serialized in a Norwegian paper in 1915 and was not published as a novel in Norway until 1940, under the title *De excentriske herrers klubb*. A Swedish translation of the novel published in 1915 has been used here: 'Krag stod i den öppna hotellporten … och lyssnade till tidningspojkarnas skrän. Dessa rop träffade honom liksom stenar och han erfor plötsligt en oroande och beklämmande känsla av att den hotande stillheten i Mellaneuropa … var nära att brytas och ge plats för en ohygglig frammarsch av stora ödesdigra händelser. En av tidningspojkarna ropade när han gick förbi: "Österrike och Serbien! Sista telegrammen!" Längre bort på gatan hördes skriken: "Österrike vill ha krig! Världskriget kommer! Världskriget kommer!" Krag stängde porten. Nu började han klart förstå, den underström i världshändelserna som hade fört alla dessa mystiska och farliga människor hit till denna neutrala huvudstad. Liksom råttor, vilka ana katastrofens närhet, hade de flytt från det sjunkande skeppet. Freden var nära att brytas därute i den stora världen.' (*De excentriska herrarnas klubb* (Stockholm: Dahlberg, 1915), 248)

6 Radscha (Iwan Aminoff), *De ljusskygge. En spioneriroman från huvudstaden* (Karlskrona: K. L. Svenssons, 1917), 7, 'Stockholmarna ha fått vika tillbaka för det kosmopolitiska element[et]. Dussintals tungor talas på dina gator, dina torg, dina hotell. Hans höghet guldet reg[er]ar mer eller mindre öppet. Du offrar åt gulaschen, åt den gyllene kalven.'

Ditt blod har blivit osunt, nedsmittat och dock livligare än någonsin tillförene. Stockholm har blivit en oerhörd myrstack med ett tillskott av utländska inkräktare. Moral, hedersbegrepp, plägseder har du offrat i utbyte mot mammons rika gåvor. Men inom myrstacken utspinnas ränkor och intriger, ofta av den mest komplicerade beskaffenhet, ett rikt fält för studier. Världskrigets mångarmade polyp har sträckt ej blott en utan flera armar över staden och suger girigt, där sugas kan.'

7 See I. F. Clarke, *Voices Prophesying War 1763–1984* (London: OUP, 1966); Cecil Degrotte Eby, *The Road to Armageddon: The Martial Spirit in English Popular Literature, 1870–1914* (Durham, NC: Duke University Press, 1987); Johan A. Höglund, *Mobilising the Novel. The Literature of Imperialism and the First World War* (diss.; Studia Anglistica Upsaliensia, 99; Uppsala: Uppsala universitet, 1997), 94 ff. Swedish invasion novels are discussed by Claes Ahlund, 'Den svenska invasionsberättelsen – en bortglömd litteratur', *Tidskrift för litteraturvetenskap*, 32/3 (2003), 82–103.

8 Edouard Rousseaux, *La future invasion prussienne et l'espionnage à la frontier* (Mayenne: C. Collin, 1905); see Margaret H. Darrow, *French Women and the First World War: War Stories of the Home Front* (Oxford: Berg, 2000), 304.

9 Franco Moretti, *Atlas of the European Novel 1800–1900* (London: Verso, 1998), 137 ff.

10 [Christian Gernandt], *Hvarför vi förlorade slaget vid Upsala den 18 maj 1900* (Stockholm: Henrik Sandberg, 1890).

11 See John Buchan, *The Thirty-Nine Steps* (1915) and *Greenmantle* (1916); Gaston Leroux, *Rouletabille chez Krupp* (1917); and Léon Daudet, *La Vermine du Monde. Roman de l'Espionage Allemand* (1916).

12 Ahlund 2003.

13 Bjørn Carling, *Norsk kriminallitteratur gjennom 150 år* (Oslo: Gyldendal Norsk Forlag, 1976), 79.

14 Ibid. 81.

15 Ahlund 2003, 95–6.

16 This can be seen in an invasion story published in *Brand* in 1916, describing Sweden's gruesome fate having entered the war on Germany's side and consequently being invaded ('Sverige i kriget', *Brand*, 2 September 1916).

17 Quoted in Niall Ferguson, 'The Kaiser's European Union. What if Britain had "stood aside" in August 1914', id. (ed.), *Virtual history: Alternatives and Counterfactuals* (London: Picador, 1997), 231.

18 Erichsen's novel is discussed by Bjarne Søndergaard Bendtsen, 'Mellem fronterne. Studier i Første Verdenskrigs virkning på og udtryk i dansk kultur med særligt fokus på litterære skildringer 1914–1939', Ph.D. diss. (Syddansk Universitet, 2011).

19 See Sofi Qvarnström, *Motståndets berättelser. Elin Wägner, Anna Lenah Elgström, Marika Stiernstedt och första världskriget* (diss.; Skrifter utgivna av Avdelningen för litteratursociologi vid Litteraturvetenskapliga institutionen i Uppsala, 58; Hedemora: Gidlunds förlag, 2009), 309.

20 Annie Åkerhielm, *Från Berlin till Brüssel* (Stockholm: Hugo Gebers förlag, 1916), 107, 85. See Claes Ahlund, 'Krig och kultur i konservativ och radikal belysning. Annie Åkerhielm och Frida Stéenhoff från sekelskiftet till första världskriget', *Samlaren*, 126 (2005), 97–150 at 132, 'en bigott, okunnig och efterbliven ras', and 'en af den bittraste nödvändighet framtvingad akt af självförsvar'.

21 Qvarnström 2009, 327.

22 Marika Stiernstedt, *Den grymma läxan* (1915), quoted in Qvarnström 2009, 324, 'från vilka många av våra duktigaste nu svenska släkter härstamma, och som sålunda också med blodsband knyta oss till det tappra belgiska folket'.

23 Øvre Richter Frich, *Kanonernes sjel* (Kristiania, 1915), 92, 149–50, 89, 33, 289, 63.

24 Willy Dahl, *Blå briller og løsskjægg i Kristiania* (Oslo: Gyldendal Norsk Forlag, 1975), 70.

25 Kaare Gullveng (Olav Gullvåg), *Den gule marquis. Ei soga fraa storkrigen 1915* (1915), 139.

26 *Spionernas mästare* is discussed by Claes Ahlund, *Underhållning och propaganda. Radschas (Iwan Aminoffs) romaner om första världskriget 1914–1915* (Skrifter utgivna av Avdelningen för litteratursociologi vid Litteraturvetenskapliga institutionen i Uppsala, 61; Uppsala: Uppsala universitet, 2010).

27 *Mannen från Liège* was serialized in 1914 and published as a novel in 1915, then with the title *Monsieur Jean-Louis Kessels papper*.

28 Ahlund 2010, 167 ff.

29 Willy Stone (Jørgen Bast), *Spioner. Billeder fra de sidste dages København* (Copenhagen: Steen Hasselbalchs forlag, 1916), 24.

30 Stone 1916, 137, 'Chefen for det hemmelige Efterretningsvæsen i et Land, hvis Legitimation vi respekterer her.'

31 Brandal & Teige in this volume.

32 Bendtsen 2011, 126 ff.

33 Jørgen Bast, *Det elskelige København. En roman fra dette aar* (Copenhagen: Nyt Nordisk Forlag, 1917), 158, 'Neutraliteten for enhver Pris'; 'Den Nation, der ikke rejste sig som een Mand mod dette uhørte Overgreb, vilde simpelthen være dødsdømt.'

34 Erik Hansen, *Det nevtrale hjerte. Roman* (Vamdrup: O. Sparre Ulrichs Forlag, 1918), 93–4.

35 Ibid. 101, 'en fuldstændig Plan for Tysklands hemmelige Efterretningsvæsen i Japan, Frankrig og England og de russiske Østersøprovinser.'

36 Ibid. 123–4.
37 Ibid. 188, 'denne parlamentariske Gelatine.'
38 Kim Salomon, *En femtiotalsberättelse. Populärkulturens kalla krig i folkhemssverige* (Stockholm: Atlantis, 2007), 36, 'en arena för skapande och upprätthållande av kulturella gemenskaper'; Lina Sturfelt, *Eldens återsken. Första världskriget i svensk föreställningsvärld* (diss.; Lund: Sekel Bokförlag, 2008), 217.
39 Qvarnström 2009, 347 ff.
40 Dag Hedman, 'Samhällsdebatterande förryttare eller eskapistiska eftersläntrare? Populärlitteraturens status exemplifierad med sekelskiftets brittiska invasions- agent- och spionfiktion, främst av William Le Queux', *Tidskrift för Litteraturvetenskap*, 30/1 (2001), 95, 108.

CHAPTER 4

Scandinavian collaboration for peace during the First World War

Per Jostein Ringsby

The outbreak of war in 1914 was a massive setback for the members of the international peace organizations. But while most of Europe was at war, the three Scandinavian countries remained neutral throughout. As a result, the Scandinavian peoples were brought closer together through joint declarations of neutrality and the first meeting of the Scandinavian kings since the peaceful dissolution of the union between Norway and Sweden in 1905. In this chapter I will focus on Scandinavian collaboration for peace through the activities of three peace organizations, and delve into two definite outcomes of their group efforts: the erection of a monument to peace and the foundation of the Nordic Peace Association. Both came to fruition during the war, both are examples of close Scandinavian collaboration, and as such are important milestones in Scandinavian peace history.[1]

A fortnight after the outbreak of war, a crowd of 12,000 gathered on the border between Norway and Sweden for the unveiling of a peace monument in commemoration of a century of peaceful Scandinavian coexistence. Two weeks before the war ended, the Nordic Peace Association was constituted at a meeting in Copenhagen. These two clear markers of the Scandinavian peace movement's work are a gateway to a closer study of how the war affected the peace cause and Scandinavian collaboration in particular.

What brought about the collaboration? Did it arise due to or despite of the war? How does this development align with developments in society at large? Are there other instances of similar contemporary monuments being erected and how common was close, formal collaboration between Scandinavian associations in this period?

International background

Toward the end of the nineteenth century, the liberal idea that international conflicts could be solved peacefully rather than by using military force gained ground very rapidly. A number of liberal peace societies were formed, and international collaboration between peace societies, MPs, and even at governmental levels, was expanded and institutionalized in the years running up to 1914.

In 1880 a peace society, the International Arbitration and Peace Association, was formed in Great Britain. Scandinavia's three peace societies were inspired, and indeed prompted, by Hodgson Pratt, the founding member of the British society: *Dansk fredsforening* (the Danish Peace Society) in 1882,[2] *Svenska freds- och skiljedomsföreningen* (the Swedish Peace and Arbitration Society) in 1883,[3] and *Norges fredsforening* (Norwegian Peace Society) in 1895.[4]

In 1889 the Inter-Parliamentary Union, the first permanent forum for multilateral negotiations, was founded, and in the same year, for the first time since 1853, a peace conference was held; meanwhile, in 1891 the International Peace Bureau, the first international peace federation, was established in Berne. Two other international peace conferences, not arranged by the International Peace Bureau, should also be mentioned: the first two Hague conferences in 1899 and 1907. With these two conferences the peace effort was taken to a higher political level, while perhaps their most significant outcome was the foundation of the Permanent Court of Arbitration in The Hague in 1899. There were plans for a third Hague conference in 1915, but it was cancelled because of the outbreak of the First World War.[5]

The three Scandinavian peace societies supported the international efforts and joined the International Peace Bureau in Berne. True, only a small number of the Scandinavian peace activists participated regularly at the international peace congresses, but the politically active members of the societies were also active at the inter-parliamentarian level. The early 1890s saw the foundation of inter-parliamentarian groups in the three Scandinavian national assemblies, and in 1907 the Nordic Inter-Parliamentarian Association was constituted. From 1910 this association held annual meetings, including throughout the war, and for this reason became an important arena for peace politics. The Scandinavian peace activists further supported the initiatives of the two Hague conferences in 1899 and 1907.[6]

Scandinavian collaborations before the war

The Scandinavian peace activists were looking for collaboration from the very outset. In 1885 the First Nordic Peace Congress was arranged, and by 1918 a total of nine Nordic peace congresses had been held. Prior to 1910 the average interval between meetings was five years, but after this the meetings were held every two to three years.[7] Furthermore, the three Scandinavian peace societies shared an interest in a few central issues, the most important of which were questions of neutrality, arbitration, a new international legal system organized through a league of nations, disarmament, and the organization of the armed forces. For the peace societies these issues were of vital importance, be it at the national, Scandinavian, or international level.

The pacifists' ultimate goal was a world without war. In order to attain this, they believed the creation of a new international system based on law instead of force was a fundamental prerequisite. This could come about in a number of ways, but principally they envisaged the establishment of an international court of arbitration and a league of nations, accompanied by general disarmament. There were disagreements within the peace societies, however, about the best means to reach the ultimate goal of world peace. One bone of contention was whether all military forces would have to cease to exist before a new international system based on a court of law was achievable, or if the reverse might be possible. This led to a series of internal power struggles in the three Scandinavian peace societies as elsewhere. Put simply, one group, the relative pacifists, were opposed to closing down the military, or possibly supported doing so gradually after the introduction of new international legal systems, while the other group, the absolute pacifists, wanted to root out militarism at any cost.[8]

Even if their ultimate goal was world peace, the three Scandinavian peace societies were also concerned with protecting national interests. The three societies considered their respective countries to be minor players in the international power struggle, and it was important for them to avoid being drawn into international conflicts. Preserving national sovereignty was vital; peacetime non-alignment and wartime neutrality were their watchwords. At the same time, the position of the small Scandinavian countries was seen as an advantage in terms of peace politics. The main reason for this was the fact that the countries refrained from engaging in international power struggles and from pursuing their interests aggressively.

The three Scandinavian peace societies developed in the same direction organizationally—an elected leadership, paying members, annual meetings, and membership publications—and all proceeded according to specific statutes and policy programmes. All three societies chose a more radical path after the turn of the century, and their respective statutes gradually came to resemble one another.[9] Again, all three had a relatively stable, if small, circle of committed peace activists, who constituted the societies' leadership. We may easily identify certain common characteristics among the key players in the societies: they were generally highly educated males (the societies encouraged female participation, but they only joined in small numbers); many of them were deeply religious, although more so in Norway and Sweden than in Denmark; a great many were also teetotallers; and, finally, a number of them were also politically active. They were primarily affiliated with liberal and radical parties, but after 1905 many of the old guard switched allegiance to the social democratic parties. They were not exclusively concerned with issues of peace, but also other contemporary liberal concerns such as women's and workers' rights.[10]

Preliminaries for a peace monument
and the Nordic Peace Association

At the Sixth Nordic Peace Congress in 1910 two matters were addressed which would strengthen the bonds between the Scandinavian peace activists, and both of which would come to fruition
during the First World War. Already at the commencement of the
congress those present stressed the importance of a close collaboration between the Scandinavian peace societies. The chairman of the
Danish Peace Society, Niels Petersen, asserted that the Scandinavian
countries were particularly suited to take on the role as pioneers
within the peace movement.[11]

On the last day of the congress, the Swedish peace activist Arvid
Grundel tabled two propositions to be discussed at future Nordic
peace meetings.[12] The first called for a collection for a peace fund
to be used to mark a century of Nordic peace in 1914, as well as
to promote the cause of peace in general. Grundel argued that this
extended period of peace—fifty years in the case of Denmark and
a hundred years in the case of Sweden and Norway—was historically unprecedented, and that a commemorative fund of this kind
would secure the three Scandinavian countries a place among the
champions of peace.

Grundel's other suggestion was to establish a permanent, pan-
Nordic organization for the grassroots peace movement. This
was not a new suggestion. As early as the First Nordic Peace
Congress in 1885 there were loud calls for a joint organization
for the Scandinavian peace activists.[13] In 1896 the following was
incorporated into the policy programme of the Norwegian Peace
Society: 'Together with the Swedish and Danish peace societies the
Norwegian Peace Society constitutes a Nordic Peace Association,
which seeks to arrange ordinary joint meetings every three years,
alternating between the three countries.'[14] The question of organizing this was brought up for discussion at four subsequent Nordic
peace congresses, but without any concrete results.[15]

Grundel was inspired by the fact that the Nordic inter-parliamentarian peace effort had become better organized back in 1907.
He considered it a great advantage to be able to promote and discuss

the pacifists' future tasks jointly instead of separately. Furthermore, he was of the opinion that Nordic meetings should be arranged at regular intervals, and that each peace society should be given an equal number of elected delegates with decision-making authority. A commission would prepare the meetings and continue work on approved issues between each meeting. These thoughts show a clear resemblance to the statutes of the Nordic Inter-Parliamentary Association of 1907.[16]

The congress in 1910 expressed sympathy with both of Grundel's proposals, but not much happened until the summer of 1912, at the Seventh Nordic Peace Congress in Kristiania.[17] At this meeting, a unanimous assembly agreed that a century of peace between Norway and Sweden was a cause for celebration, and that it should be commemorated with the construction of a peace monument on the border between the two countries, erected jointly by the three peace societies.[18] The autumn of 1912 therefore saw work on the peace monument begin to make headway. However, work on the foundation of a Nordic peace association lay more or less dormant until 1917.[19] One of the reasons Grundel's suggestion to organize was not followed up may have been the fact that the pacifists were focused on getting the monument erected on the border in August 1914. Moreover, the outbreak of war brought other matters than the organization of Nordic collaboration to the fore for a time.[20]

In the winter of 1912–13, two proclamations were published. Norwegians and Swedes were called upon to participate in a nationwide rally to collect money for the erection of a peace monument in 1914.[21] By this time it had already been decided that it would be located on the border crossing between Magnor and Charlottenberg, where it would be clearly visible from the main road and the railway alike. Since the intention was to make the site a venue for Swedish–Norwegian peace, temperance, and youth arrangements, the peace societies in both countries applied for permission to buy a sufficiently large area surrounding the peace monument from the two owners, Eda glassworks and the landowner Hans Raastad. Both parties were willing to sell, and thus the two peace societies became the owners of a plot of almost five acres. The next obstacle required the help of the two countries' politicians. After the dissolution of the union between Norway and Sweden in 1905, a neutral zone between the two countries had been created where all construction required the authorization of the government. This was forthcoming without any problems worth mentioning, however.[22]

The inscriptions intended for the monument were made public in December 1912: 'Henceforth war between Scandinavian brothers is inconceivable' and 'The people of Scandinavia erected this stone in 1914 in commemoration of 100 years of peace.'[23] The first quote was taken from the Swedish–Norwegian King Oscar I's speech during a student meeting in Uppsala in 1856.[24] The peace activists hoped that the inscriptions would have a mobilizing effect on the Scandinavian population as a whole. The monument would also show the world that the Nordic people were an exceptionally peaceful people, united in the struggle for a better and more peaceful world.[25]

What was the Danish attitude to all this? The Danish Peace Society had at an early stage given their endorsement to the idea of a peace monument, yet when the plans became more concrete towards the end of 1912, the leadership of the Danish society nevertheless rejected the invitation to participate further. Even if there had been a century of peace between the three Scandinavian countries, Denmark had participated in two wars which still lingered in Danish memory. 'The painful loss, which the last war has caused Denmark, does not diminish the joy of the 100 year peace. Nevertheless, it renders a collection of monetary funds in this country to a monument celebrating a 100 year period of peace impossible.'[26] In particular, Denmark's defeat in the war with Prussia and Austria in 1864 was still fresh in their minds. In 1914, fifty years after the defeat, a great deal of the Danish Peace Society's work consisted of preventing the memory of this war from being exploited by militaristic agitators.[27] But even if the Danish pacifists refrained from active participation in raising funds or erecting the peace monument, they still supported the effort. In *Fredsbladet* they expressed their 'vibrant satisfaction and joy that our Norwegian and Swedish brothers have been able to realise the beautiful plan of building a peace monument at the

Swedish–Norwegian border.'[28] As a result of the Danish withdrawal, the inscription on the monument was changed to the following: 'Norwegian and Swedish peace activists erected this monument in the year 1914 in gratitude for 100 years of peace.'[29]

What would this monument look like? Early in the process the discussion turned on whether the peace monument should be given the shape of Christ. The Scandinavian peace activists had taken the idea of a Christ monument from South America: in 1904 a statue of Christ, known as Christ the Redeemer of the Andes, was erected on the border between Chile and Argentina as a reminder of the peaceful outcome of the border dispute between the two countries.[30] In 1912 the thought of a monument depicting Christ was rejected, and instead one without religious connotations was chosen.[31]

Norwegian and Swedish artists and architects were invited to submit proposals for the monument's design.[32] Twenty-four proposals were submitted, but none of them satisfied the monument committees in the two countries.[33] The problem was solved when a unanimous monument committee decided on a proposal, submitted after the deadline, by the architect Lars Johan Lehming. A sketch of the peace monument was displayed publicly for the first time in September 1913.[34] The work of the erecting the monument encountered no further obstacles, and the monument committee was exceedingly pleased with the final result, both in terms of design and cost.[35]

The peace societies would not have been able to carry out this project but for the assistance they received from their governments and the population at large. In Norway it was straightforward business for the peace society to gather support from the country's politicians: they were enthusiastic from the beginning, and both the permit to build the monument and funding to the tune of 2,000 *kroner* were passed without debate in the Storting. The Swedish peace activists had to walk a more difficult path. They also received a building permit and a donation of 2,000 *kronor*, but none of it came easily. In addition, the Swedish peace activists were actively opposed by the conservative, right-wing press. The national differences were also reflected in the fashion in which the funds were acquired. In Norway the amount was collected with relative ease because of the generosity of a few individuals. In Sweden, however, the peace societies were forced to spend a great deal of time and resources in order to collect the full amount. Fortunately, the results were reassuring: 20,000 Swedes donated money.[36]

A few people may be singled out as the driving force in this process. In Norway, the chairman of the peace society, Bernhard Hanssen, was undoubtedly the mastermind behind the project.[37] In Sweden, it may have been Arvid Grundel who hit upon the idea of commemorating the hundred years' peace, but there were two other Swedes, Knut Sandstedt and Carl Sundblad, who distinguished themselves in the work on the peace monument.[38]

A unique peace monument
at the outbreak of the world war

On Sunday 16 August 1914 some 12,000 people were gathered at the border between Magnor in Norway and Charlottenberg in Sweden to attend the dedication of the peace monument. A century had gone by since the signing of the Convention of Moss, and since that time the two countries had been at peace.[39] At the outbreak of the First World War several people raised the question of whether the dedication ceremony should be delayed until a more appropriate time. However, in *Fredsfanans ekstranummer*, which was published shortly after the outbreak of war, all peace activists were encouraged to appear on the Norwegian–Swedish border on 16 August. The gathering would now not only mark a century of Nordic peace, but also the Scandinavian pacifists' protest against the war, the publication proclaimed.[40] Enclosed with the printed programme handed out at the dedication was a postcard depicting the peace monument.

The artist, one J. Swedin, was inspired both by symbols from antiquity as well as more recent peace symbols. Palm leaves encircle the entire picture, and form a victory wreath where a young, athletic man rests a broken sword on his knee. The peace monument is pride of place in the middle of the picture. In the background, the sunrise is flanked by the Peace Palace in The Hague. The Norwegian and Swedish flags are placed in the two top corners.[41]

Souvenir de l'inauguration du monument de la paix sur la frontière entre la Suède et la Norvège le 16 août 1914.

FIGURE 1: A postcard by J. Swedin. This was handed out at the dedication of the peace monument, 16 August 1914.

The monument itself consisted of a solid plinth with two columns culminating in two figures, and is 17 meters high in its entirety. The plinth, which is shaped to function as a pulpit, symbolizes the two countries' mutual origins, both culturally and historically. Two columns reach up from the plinth to symbolize the peoples of the two independent nations. At the top of the monument are two male figures—Norway and Sweden—holding hands. Several fasces are also carved around the two figures. The whole monument thus symbolizes peace and good neighbourliness between two independent nations with common cultural and historical origins.[42]

The Norwegian Peace Society and the Swedish Peace and Arbitration Society, which were responsible for arrangements, had expected a turnout of 3,000, but the number proved to be much larger, around 12,000. This was a significant number compared to other large, popular gatherings both before and after at peace society arrangements and elsewhere—clear evidence that the pacifists had succeeded in mobilizing the people. The visitors made their way either independently from nearby areas or by train from Kristiania and Stockholm. Among those present were as many as seventy Norwegian and ten Swedish MPs. On the other hand, neither country's prime minister nor representatives of the royal families were present.[43]

The programme was long and varied. National anthems were sung, and a festival cantata was performed in honour of the occasion. In addition to the musical interludes, a series of telegrams were read out and speeches were given, by the Norwegian MP Jørgen Løvland among others.[44] He called attention to the fact that the Scandinavian position of neutrality was the reason that everyone was willing to go through with the dedication as planned, despite the outbreak of war. His speech was marked by optimism: 'This is one of the greatest solemn occasions any of us present have ever experienced! Norwegian and Swedish men and women have come together in their thousands to greet one another beneath this sign of peace. A beautiful dream has come true.'[45]

Denmark was also included as part of a joint Scandinavian peace effort by Løvland and other speakers at the dedication. 'Denmark belongs in this commemoration. The country has seen its share of affliction, but the three Nordic countries have long been at peace with one another, and we hope and wish it will always remain so,' Løvland declared.[46] The Swedish MP A. Åkerman asked that they spare a thought for Denmark, since the country was closer to the fighting in Europe than were Norway and Sweden. He concluded his speech with 'a cheer for Nordic agreement and a happy future for the Nordic people.'[47] Even if the Danish Peace Society had declined to participate actively in the process leading up to the dedication, the Danes were also represented among the speakers: 'Denmark has experienced a great deal of affliction, but we joyfully welcome the *free* friendship and brotherhood between Sweden and Norway—which have been displayed so beautifully in these difficult times beneath the gathering storm,' the Danish MP Andr. Th. Grønborg proclaimed.[48]

Unlike the Swedish Peace and Arbitration Society, the Norwegian Peace Society had faced neither challenge nor criticism from the conservative right. A telegram was sent to dedication from both the Norwegian royal family and the government, while neither the Swedish royal family nor the Swedish government sent one. The large turnout of Norwegian MPs, as well as the Norwegian Storting's unconditional support prior to the dedication, shows that there was greater and broader political support for the peace monument in Norway than in Sweden. Militarism was much stronger in Sweden, where the national peace association met with active resistance from the conservative Right, both in the press and the Riksdag.[49] However, the upper crust of Swedish politicians was not entirely absent. A telegram arrived from former Prime Minister Karl Staaff, who had resigned on 17 February 1914.[50]

The circumstances of the dedication lent a solemn air to proceedings. The dedication of the peace monument did not go unnoticed in the Scandinavian press. Most of the leading newspapers and many of the local ones filed reports on the occasion. A point repeatedly made was the contrast between the unveiling of a peace monument while at same time European soldiers met in battle on the Continent.[51]

A drawing that illustrates this well appeared in the Norwegian satirical publication *Tyrihans* after the dedication. Entitled 'In war and peace! 1814–1914', with the subtitle, 'They knew what they did, these people of Moss. Hereafter impossible for the brothers to fight! Motto: Yes, we love Thou old and free!', it refers to the Convention of Moss of 1814 and blends together the two countries' national anthems. The drawing shows a model of the peace monument being threatened by dark clouds while warplanes drop bombs. A Norwegian farmer in tattered national dress and somewhat better turned-out Swede, both drunk, symbolize Norway and Sweden. Between them we see a smiling and unsuspecting sheep with closed eyes, and the symbolism is clear. The pacifists are being referred to as 'peace sheep', unable to face reality (see Figure 2 next page).[52]

Of course, the building of monuments was not a phenomenon limited to the beginning of the twentieth century, and their purpose has also remained much the same down the ages: to serve as a reminder of important people, ideas, and events for their own and future generations. However, monuments were most often erected to celebrate victory in war or to remember the fallen. This was especially evident after the First World War. Peace monuments pure and simple, however, were far less common.[53] Only the aforementioned example from South America can be considered a similar effort. Thus the Scandinavian peace monument was quite unique in a European context in the period around the First World War.

The Scandinavian activists wanted to introduce a tradition of annual peace rallies on the border. This was to prove difficult, but several major peace gatherings were arranged after 1914.[54] In September 1915, 5,000 people attended the first large gathering after the dedication. The following year a new peace rally was held that numbered almost 10,000. In 1917 and 1918 no rallies were held, largely due to the course of the war. In the summer of 1919 again 4,000 people met at the border, where they also could celebrate that the war was finally over.[55]

After 1919 it seems there was a steep decline in the popularity of the peace rallies, with a few exceptions. In 1934, the peace publications could inform their readers that approximately 1,000 people had shown up at the border to commemorate the twentieth anniversary of the monument's unveiling, and in 1939 6,000 people were gathered to mark its twenty-fifth anniversary. The chairman of

FIGURE 2: A satirical drawing of the peace monument in *Tyrihans* 34/1914.

the Norwegian Peace Society, the headmaster Ole Fredrik Olden, emphasized in his 1934 speech that there were an abundance of war monuments in the world, while only two peace monuments existed: one on the border between Sweden and Norway and the other on the border between Argentina and Chile. The same point was made by the Norwegian foreign minister, Halvdan Koht, in his speech five years later.[56] After the gathering in 1939, the Norwegian peace publication *Verden Venter* announced that when Germany had declared war on Poland it was a repetition of events in 1914, with the only difference that now war had broke out a fortnight after the meeting, instead of a fortnight prior, as had been the case in 1914.[57] In 1945, at the end of the Second World War, again approximately 13,000 people gathered to attend a large peace rally at the border.[58]

The peace monument and surrounding area have gradually declined in use by the Scandinavian peace societies, and in 2005 the land they had purchased in 1914 was sold to the counties of Eda and Eidskog.[59] The jubilee in 2014 could be an opportunity for a new historic border meeting. Would it be possible to gather well over 10,000 people here once again, just as in 1914 and 1945?

Peace societies—membership and peace gatherings

How large was the membership of the three societies during the First World War? When it comes to the International Peace Association's growth in membership, Nigel Young has drawn attention to the fact that they experienced an increase until 1914, and then declined during the war.[60] Is this pattern mirrored by the three Scandinavian peace societies in this period?

The Danish Peace Society had a relatively stable membership of approximately 3,500 during the war. In contrast to the Danish society, the Norwegian Peace Society and the Swedish Peace and Arbitration Society saw an increase in membership after 1905, which reached a peak towards the end of the First World War. There was, however, a significant difference between the two, in that the Norwegian Peace Society probably never reached more than 800 active members in this period, while the Swedish Peace and Arbitration Society could proudly point to a membership of more than 20,000 in 1917, of whom approximately half were direct members. Both the Swedish and the Norwegian societies quickly lost ground after the war, ending up with 4,000 members in the case of the Swedish Peace and Arbitration Society, and fewer than 200 in the case of the Norwegian Peace Society. The Danish Peace Society only experienced a marginal increase in membership during the war, having actually reached its peak as early as 1899 with an estimated 9,000 members. However, the Danish society did not experience any dramatic decrease after the war.

Nigel Young's conclusions about developments in membership of the European peace associations are therefore not borne out by the Scandinavian peace societies. All three societies, and in particular the Norwegian and Swedish, went through a period of decline around the turn of the century, at a time when the peace movement in Europe was otherwise growing rapidly. In addition, the Scandinavian societies saw their membership increase throughout the First World War, in particular the Swedish society, while the international peace movement in general declined sharply from 1914 onwards. The Scandinavian peace societies only faced dwindling numbers after the war, at a time when the tide was turning in the rest of Europe.[61]

Peace was discussed thoroughly at Nordic peace congresses and by the peace societies during the First World War. Before the outbreak of war the Danish peace activists were the leading lights of the Scandinavian peace discourse. This changed during the war. The Danes grew more sceptical and passive, while the peace effort was further developed and supported to a larger extent by the Norwegian Peace Society and the Swedish Peace and Arbitration Society. It was vital for Danes after 1914 to avoid provoking Germany, since they had an unresolved border dispute with their considerably larger neighbour on their hands.

The Eighth Nordic Peace Congress in Copenhagen in 1915 was the first such to be held after the war began, a fact that dominated proceedings. The Danish chairman emphasized that the peace activists should take care not to lose courage due to the war, referring specifically to the neutrality policy of the three countries: 'The war has created a common bond between the Nordic people like never before. The *absolute* neutrality policy that all three countries subscribe to has contributed to this to a large extent.'[62]

Two years later the Ninth Nordic Peace Congress took place in Kristiania. During his opening speech the Norwegian chairman, Bernhard Hanssen, pointed out that the main goals of this congress were organizational. First, they were to discuss, and hopefully adopt, his proposals for Nordic Peace Association statutes, as a more tightly constructed organization would tie the three peace societies closer together. The second organizational matter had a larger objective related to foreign policy, namely the establishment of a league of nations.[63] During the war, thoughts of a future peace confederation were put in more concrete terms, and the peace activists realized that it might be up to the great powers to take the first step.[64]

The establishment of the Nordic Peace Association in 1918

The Nordic Peace Association was founded at a meeting in Copenhagen in 1918. From the outset the association comprised the Norwegian Peace Society, the Danish Peace Society, and the Swedish Peace and Arbitration Society—it had been a long process for the three peace societies to reach this point. In 1917 Bernhard Hanssen had presented a proposed set of statutes for a future alliance between the peace societies. Hanssen largely continued Grundel's line from 1910, both having been inspired by the foundation of the Nordic Inter-Parliamentarian Association in 1907. Indeed, Hanssen used the statutes of this association as a model when drawing up his proposal, which was adopted more or less unaltered.

The purpose of establishing the Nordic Peace Association was mainly to provide the Scandinavian collaboration with a tighter organization, forge closer bonds between the three peace societies, make more effective use of the meetings' time, and instil greater continuity into their peace work. This would give the three societies a stronger position through joint statements to national governments, as well as with international peace congresses and the International Peace Bureau in Berne.

The main difference now was the adoption of statutes that would ensure the agendas for Nordic meetings were properly prepared, while an elected board of nine would see to it that the decisions taken at Nordic meetings were edited and followed up afterwards. The meetings were to be held every three years, and the societies would be represented by an equal number of appointed delegates. Despite pressure from the Swedish society, which was far larger than the other two at that point, the Danes and Norwegians insisted on equality between the three societies—it would contribute to giving the decisions of the Nordic meetings greater impact. The similarities between the statutes of the Nordic Peace Association and the Nordic Inter-Parliamentary Association led to some disagreement between the three peace societies. Both the Norwegians and the Danes supported Hanssen's proposed statutes; the Swedes were rather more sceptical, however. They felt that having an elected board with an equal number of delegates would put power in the hands of a small number of people and make the association undemocratic, and they thus made several—unsuccessful—attempts to have the statutes changed before eventually acceding to the wishes of the two other societies. This capitulation may seem surprising, considering the fact that Sweden's was decidedly the largest society. In this context, however, their strength in numbers may in many ways have constituted a weakness in the negotiations: they already collaborated well with other societies in Sweden, and were therefore less dependent on a Nordic association to increase their influence. This, instead, was far more important for the smaller societies in Denmark and, in particular, Norway. The difference in relative strength, and what the various societies could hope to gain from the formation of a Nordic association, may have given the Norwegian and Danish societies an incentive to take quicker action and be more interested in driving the process forward. The Swedish society thus found itself in a situation where it was forced to accept or reject a proposal from the other parties, and as it was equally interested in forming a Nordic alliance, it therefore chose to accept the proposal despite the differences of opinion regarding the organizational model.[65]

How unique was the founding of the Nordic Peace Association? The Scandinavian activists were certainly inspired by the foundation of the Nordic Inter-Parliamentary Association in 1907. However, few other Nordic alliances were formed in the period immediately after 1905: the decade prior to 1905 having been something of an Indian summer for pan-Scandinavian collaboration, the dissolution of the union between Norway and Sweden put a decisive stop to this collaboration, and the period after 1905 has therefore been described as a Nordic winter. The reluctance over Scandinavian collaboration was particularly pronounced in

Sweden, which experienced a wave of anti-Scandinavianism after the dissolution of the Union that was to last until after the outbreak of the First World War.[66] The generally poor climate for Scandinavian collaboration between 1905 and 1914 did not apply to the peace societies, however: their collaboration for peace did not stagnate; it only increased in intensity and vigour after 1905. After the peaceful dissolution of the Union, the Norwegians could put aside the fight for national independence and focus on the peace effort. The dissolution of the Union also provided the Swedish peace activists with a practical goal. Besides, they were presumably the least disappointed Swedish group when it came to the disruption of the union and its peaceful end. Therefore the break did not create lasting enmity between the three peace societies—rather the opposite.

The experience of the First World War brought the three countries closer together again, in this and in other respects. As early as 8 August 1914 the three countries signed an agreement jointly expressing their desire to stay out of the conflict by maintaining their neutrality. During the war, the countries' ministries of foreign affairs collaborated closely, and the first meeting of the Scandinavian kings since 1905 was held in December 1914; in 1917 another such meeting was arranged; and there was frequent contact between the three countries' inter-parliamentary groups throughout the war.[67]

Due to this closer alliance, several new Nordic associations had been formed by war's end: 1916, for example, saw the foundation of the Nordic Women's Suffragette Coordinating body; 1918 the foundation of Nordic Administrative Society, the Nordic Cooperative Society, and the Nordic Music Union; while the following year saw least eight more associations come into existence, among them the Nordic Writer's Council, the Nordic Tuberculosis Society, and the Nordic Prohibition Committee. In addition, the first three Nordic societies were formed in Denmark, Sweden and Norway this year.[68] Thus the founding of the Nordic Peace Association cannot be said to be a unique in its day, but rather part of a general trend towards a closer and more formalized collaboration between the three Scandinavian countries on a wide range of issues during the First World War.

Developments after 1918

The peace activists had gradually adjusted to the international situation during the course of the war. This is most evident in connection with the subsequent foundation of the League of Nations. After the US joined the war on the side of the Entente Powers and all signs pointed to German defeat, the Danes, for example, changed strategy on a future peaceful alliance between states, shifting from a passive to an active attitude in the matter. After the Tenth Nordic Peace Congress in 1919 the activists therefore urged their respective governments to join the League of Nations, thus departing from the principle of absolute neutrality, given the fact that the League Covenant required member states to support a policy of collective security. The idea that it was necessary to participate in order to steer the League of Nations in a more pacifist direction carried the most weight.[69]

In March 1920 the Danish Rigsdag voted unanimously to join the League of Nations. The neighbouring countries displayed no such agreement. In Norway, 100 MPs voted for and 20 against joining, while in Sweden 238 MPs voted for and 114 against.[70] As seen, the Scandinavian peace activists supported the decision to join even if they differed on several counts as to how the world should be organized in order to achieve a lasting peace. However, the foundation of the League of Nations after the war changed the role of the peace societies, as issues related to making peace policy were moved to a higher and more formalized political level. However, the three peace societies still continued arranging Nordic peace congresses at regular intervals during the interwar years.[71]

Increased Scandinavian collaboration for peace during the First World War

The First World War was a time when the three Scandinavian peace societies flourished, and with them their collaborative efforts. Since the three countries managed to remain neutral and therefore stayed out of the actual fighting, the peace effort found excellent conditions for growth and was politically important to many Scandinavians during this period. The First World War therefore brought the pacifists closer together. Further, the outbreak of war led to closer collaboration between the three Scandinavian countries on the inter-parliamentarian and government levels, and between the three royal houses. These developments were supported by the Scandinavian peace activists.

16 August 1914 was the date for the dedication of the peace monument. The outbreak of the First World War put a damper on the occasion and could have caused a delay; that this did not happen was largely due to the advanced stage reached in the planning. It was considered important that the monument be unveiled a hundred years almost to the day after the signing of Convention of Moss. In addition, the Scandinavian countries' declarations of neutrality played a part. Ultimately the dedication turned out to be both a celebration of a century of Scandinavian peace and an occasion for anti-war protest. The peace activists wanted to unite the Scandinavian people through the peace monument, and remind them to stand together as a people of peace. The monument was the fruit of thorough preparations and remains one of the most prominent examples of the close collaboration between the Scandinavian peace societies—it may have been the Norwegians' and the Swedes' show, but they were assisted by the Danes. Thus the peace monument on the border between Norway and Sweden is unique in the sense that it is the result of collaboration between peace activists that transcended borders, commemorating an extended period of piece. As such it is unrivalled in Europe in the period between 1900 and 1920. The other monuments of the day were largely war memorials.

The foundation of the Nordic Peace Association in 1918 represents, aside from the construction of the peace monument, the most obvious example that the Scandinavian peace activists developed even closer and more formalized collaboration during the world war. With the foundation of the Nordic Peace Association the three peace societies secured a more cohesive organization, and the goal for the future was for the groups to stand more united in their efforts after the end of the war. However, the process leading up to the foundation of the Nordic Peace Association was both long and arduous. An important initiative was taken in 1910, but until 1914 the peace activists focused on the peace monument.

What concerned the societies after the outbreak of war was in particular the question of a future league of nations. Thus organizational matters remained in the background for a time. If it had not been for the outbreak of war in 1914, the Nordic Peace Association would most probably have been created much earlier. It was quite common to form various Scandinavian associations in the time around 1918, and in this respect the formation of the peace activists' alliance is only one of many in this period.

The Scandinavian countries' entry into the League of Nations guaranteed that the peace effort moved up to a higher political level, and the three peace societies ended up with less influence after the war. Thus it could be useful to consider the period from 1914 to 1918 as the heyday of the peace activists in Scandinavian peace history. In the peace monument they had a tangible symbol of their struggle for peace; their total membership reached its peak; and they were certain of a more formalized collaboration thanks to the foundation of the Nordic Peace Association. After the First World War, membership dwindled and the delegates to the League of Nations took up many of the societies' core concerns. Nevertheless, the peace monument still exists, and 2014 may be an appropriate moment to acknowledge the peace activists' legacy.

Notes

1 This article is based on my Ph.D. dissertation, *40 års kamp for fred. Tre fredsforeninger i Skandinavia 1882–1922* (diss.; Oslo: Universitetet i Oslo, 2011).

2 *Freden*, Tillæg A/1883; Fredrik Bajer, *Dansk fredsforenings historie* (Copenhagen: Gjellerup, 1894), 5–7; Kurt Risskov Sørensen, *Fredssagen i Danmark 1882–1914* (Odense: Odense universitetsforlag, 1981), 18–20; Arne Hytter Nørregaard, *Fredsbevægelsen i Danmark 1864–1914* (MA diss.; Copenhagen: Københavns Universitet, 2008), 24; Niels Petersen & Ingvard Nielsen, *Halvtreds aars fredsarbejde* (Copenhagen: Levin & Munksgaard, 1932), 11–14.

3 Per Anders Fogelström, *Kampen för fred. Berättelsen om en okänd folkrörelse* (Stockholm: Bonnier, 1971), 34–40; Svenska Freds- och Skiljedomsföreningen, *Jubileumsskrift 1883–1933* (Falun: Svenska freds- och skiljedomsföreningen, 1933), 13.

4 Mats Rønning, *Fredsfaar i gjentatt strid – historien om den folkelige freds-*

bevegelsen i Norge før 1914 (MA diss.; Oslo: Universitetet i Oslo, 2005), 28–30; Jens Evang, *Norges fredsforening 1894–1937* (MA diss.; Oslo: Universitetet i Oslo, 1938), 19–28; Halvdan Koht, *Freds-tanken i Noregs-sogo – Noreg i den samfolkelege rettsvoksteren* (Oslo: Samlaget, 1906), 111–114; Oscar J. Falnes, *Norway and the Nobel peace prize* (New York: Columbia University Press, 1938), 50–54.

5 Christian Lous Lange, *Det interparlamentariske forbund. Tyve aars historie* (Kristiania: Det norske Stortings Nobelkomité, 1909), 9–10; Rainer Santi, *100 years of peace making* (Geneva: International Peace Bureau, 1991); *Danske Voldgiftskonventioner* (Copenhagen: Udenrigsministeriet, 1912), 5–6; Anna Nilsson, *Fredsrörelsens ABC: data och fakta* (Stockholm: Informationsbyrån Mellanfolkligt samarbete för fred, 1934), 61. Between 1889 and 1914 the Interparliamentary Union arranged 18 congresses, as opposed to 20 international peace congresses during the same period.

6 Santi 1991, 13–15; Nilsson 1934, 20–21; *Årsbok för de Nordiska interparlamentariska grupperna, andra årgången 1919* (Stockholm, 1920), 35; *Aarbog for de Nordiske interparlamentariske grupper, fjerde aargang 1921* (Copenhagen, 1922), 5; Edvard Wavrinsky, *Några personligen minnen från det interparlamentariska arbetets första tid* (Stockholm, 1920); Fredrik Bajer, *Det nordiske interparlamentariske delegeretmødes forhistorie* (Copenhagen: Schultz, 1908); Ruth Hemstad, *Fra Indian Summer til nordisk vinter, Skandinavisme, skandinavisk samarbeid and unionsoppløsningen* (diss.; Oslo: Universitetet i Oslo, 2008), 473–5, 541, & 548; Ringsby 2011, 116, 208–210, & 382–383.

7 The Nordic peace meetings are discussed at length in Ringsby 2011, 119–174. The nine Nordic peace meetings until 1918 were as follows: Gothenburg (1885), Copenhagen (1890), Stockholm (1895), Skien (1901), Copenhagen (1904), Stockholm (1910), Kristiania (1912), Copenhagen (1915), and Kristiania (1917).

8 Historical research has utilized several terms in explaining the difference between the two movements. In Scandinavian peace research, a line has been drawn between realists and idealists, or between those who advocated defence and those who advocated peace. Those wedded to peace have also been considered utopists, radicals, and pacifists. See Nils Ivar Agøy, 'The Norwegian Peace Movement and the Question of Conscientious to Military Service 1885–1922', in Katsuya Kodama & Unto Vesa (eds.), *Towards a Comparative Analysis of Peace Movements* (Aldershot: Dartmouth, 1990), 89–104; Martin Ceadel, *Thinking about Peace and War* (Oxford: Oxford University Press, 1987), 4–5 & 101–165; Martin Ceadel, *Semi-Detached Idealists—The British Peace Movement and International Relations 1854–1945* (Oxford: Oxford University Press, 2000), 7; Ringsby 2011, 2–3.

9 Ringsby 2011, 40–49.

10 Ibid. 115–116 & 382–383.

11 *Fredsbladet,* 7/1910. Niels Petersen (1858–1933) was chairman of the Danish Peace Society between 1910 and 1928, and a Danish MP between 1913 and 1929 for the Danish Social Liberal Party (Det Radikale Venstre).

12 Arvid Grundel (1877–1959) was active in the Swedish Peace and Arbitration Society until 1911, when he became one of the founders of the new Swedish Peace Society.

13 *Freden,* 32/1885; *Beretning om det* første nordiske *fredsmøde, holdt i Gøteborg den 17.–19. August 1885* (Ringsted, 1885), 19–20.

14 *Det Norske Fredsblad* 15/1896.

15 Ringsby 2011, 123–35.

16 *Fredsbanneret,* 6/1911; Ringsby 2011, 208–210.

17 *Freden* 8/1910; *Fredsfanan,* 9–10/1910; *Fredsbanneret,* 8/1910; Carl Sundblad, *Svenska fredsrörelsens historia: åren 1904–1919,* iii (Stockholm: Svenska freds- och skiljedomsföreningen, 1919), 139.

18 *Fredsbanneret,* 7–8/1912; *Fredsfanan,* 7–8/1912; *Fredsbladet,* 8/1912.

19 *Sundblad* 1919, 138–139; *Fredsbladet,* 8/1910; *Fredsbanneret,* 6/1911 & 9/1911.

20 Ringsby 2011, 214–215.

21 *Fredsbanneret,* 12/1912; *Fredsfanan,* 2/1913; Sundblad 1919, 236–240. In Sweden, fifty-four people had signed the petition, while the Norwegian petition was signed only by the chairman of the Norwegian Peace Society, Bernhard Hanssen.

22 *Fredsfanan,* 2/1913; Carl Sundblad, *Fredsmonumentet på norsk-svenska gränsen* (Stockholm: Wilhelmsson, 1916), 4; Sundblad 1919, 243.

23 *Fredsfanan,* 12/1912; see also *Invigningen av fredsmonumentet å svensknorska gränsen den 16 august 1914* (Stockholm: Wilhelmssons, 1914), 3.

24 Bo Stråth, *Union og demokrati: dei sameinte rika Noreg–Sverige 1814–1905* (Oslo: Pax, 2005), 209.

25 *Fredsfanan,* 12/1912.

26 *Fredsbladet,* 1/1914.

27 *Fredsbladet,* 8/1914; Claus Bjørn & Carsten Due-Nielsen, 'Fra helstat til nationalstat: 1814–1914', *Dansk udenrigspolitisk historie,* iii (Copenhagen: Danmarks Nationalleksikon, 2003), 236–263.

28 *Fredsbladet,* 1/1914.

29 *Invigningen av fredsmonumentet* 1914, 3.

30 *Nya Vägar* 1/1922; *Fredsfanan,* 3/1913; Nilsson 1934, 57–8.

31 *Fredsfanan,* 3–4/1911, 5/1911 & 7–8/1911; *Fredsbanneret,* 7–8/1912 & 12/1912; *Invigningen av fredsmonumentet* 1914, 10–11;Ringsby 2011, 176–80.

32 *Fredsfanan,* 12/1912; *Invigningen av fredsmonumentet* 1914, 12.

33 Sundblad 1919, 246.

34 *Fredsfanan*, 9/1913 & 10/1913; *Fredsbanneret*, 10/1913; *Fredsbladet*, 1/1914; Johan Lindström Saxon, *En tidningsmans minnen* (Stockholm: Nutiden, 1918), 265. Lars Johan Lehming (1871–1940) worked as an architect in Stockholm, and was committed to the peace cause—he did not charge anything for his work designing the peace monument.

35 Carl Sundblad, *Minnesskrift med anledning av 110-årig fred i Norden samt fredsmonumentets tioårsjubileum* (Stockholm: Wilhelmsson, 1924), 22; Carl Sundblad, *Fredsmonumentets Historia* (Stockholm: Wilhelmsson, 1929), 23–4; *Fredsfanan*, 10/1914; *Fredsbanneret*, 8/1914. The cost of the peace monument came to less than 27,000 *kroner*, including the purchase of the site.

36 Magnus Rodell, 'Monumentet på gränsen', *Scandia*, 74/2 (Lund, 2008), 37–8; Ringsby 2011, 180–7; Sundblad 1919, 277; *Freden*, 13/1964.

37 Bernhard Hanssen (1864–1939) founded the Norwegian Peace Society in 1895. From the outset he served both as the society's chairman (for fourteen of its first twenty-seven years) and as editor of *Det Norske Fredsblad*. Hanssen also served several terms as an MP between 1900 and 1921, initially for Venstre, and later for Frisinnede Venstre

38 Carl Sundblad (1849–1933) worked as a teacher all his life. He served more or less continuously in the leadership of the Swedish Peace and Arbitration Society until 1925. Knut Sandstedt (1858–1944) served continuously in the leadership of the Swedish Peace and Arbitration Society from 1897 to 1930, primarily as the society's secretary and treasurer. Both men were deeply religious, but not politically active.

39 Stråth 2005, 91–95.

40 *Fredsfanans ekstranummer* 8½/1914; Sundblad 1919, 258–9.

41 The French caption reads 'In memory of the dedication of the peace monument on the border between Norway and Sweden, 16 August 1914'. See *Invigningen av fredsmonumentet* 1914; Nilsson 1934, 62; and Irene Andersson, 'Att gestalta fred. Fredsrepresentationer mellan 1885 och 1945 i ett genusperspektiv', in Lars M Andersson, Lars Berggren & Ulf Zander (eds.), *Mer än tusen ord. Bilden och de historiska vetenskaperna* (Lund: Nordic Academic Press, 2001), 163–4.

42 *Fredsfanan*, 10/1913; *Fredsbladet*, 1/1914; *Fredsbanneret*, 10/1913 & 8/1914; *Freden*, 13/1964; Saxon 1918, 265; Sundblad 1924, 27–30. *Fasces*, the Latin for bundle or stack (*sädeskärven* in Swedish), were a mark of power in ancient Rome. Fasces were originally a bundle of beech or elm sticks, tied together with a red band, with an axe bound in among the sticks. An axe was not used in the case of the peace monument.

43 *Fredsfanan*, 9/1914; *Fredsbladet*, 9/1914; *Fredsbanneret*, 8/1914.

44 *Invigningen av fredsmonumentet* 1914.

45 *Fredsbanneret*, 8/1914.

46 *Fredsfanan*, 10/1914.

47 *Fredsbanneret*, 8/1914.

48 *Fredsbladet*, 10/1914.

49 Rodell 2008, 37–8; Ringsby 2011, 184–7.

50 *Fredsfanan*, 9/1914; see also *Fredsbladet*, 9/1914; *Fredsbanneret*, 8/1914; Sundblad 1924, 17; Sundblad 1929, 19.

51 Rodell 2008, 39–40.

52 *Tyrihans* 34/1914. 'Ja, vi elsker dette landet' ['Yes, we love this country'] is the Norwegian national anthem, with words by Bjørnstjerne Bjørnson (1832–1910) and music by Rikard Nordraak (1842–1866). 'Du gamla, du fria' ['Thou ancient, Thou free'] is the Swedish national anthem, with words by Richard Dybeck (1811–1877) to a traditional melody.

53 See Tønnes Bekker-Nielsen, 'Mellem antidyrkelse og nationalromantik', *Den jyske Historiker*, 29–30 (Aarhus, 1984), 13–32; Mari Seilskjær, 'Identitet og erindringspolitikk – en analyse av Fridtjof den frøkne som historisk monument', *Fortid*, 3 (Oslo, 2006), 63–8; Ulf Zander, 'Läroböcker i sten', in Klas-Göran Karlsson & Ulf Zander (eds.), *Historien är nu. En introduktion till historiedidaktiken* (Lund: Studentlitteratur, 2004), 103–123 for a general introduction to the use of monuments as historical sources.

54 *Fredsfanan*, 2/1913; *Fredsbanneret*, 9/1915. There are no indications that the temperance movement, the youth movement, or other societies started using this location regularly.

55 *Fredsfanan*, 9/1915, 9/1916 & 9/1919; *Fredsbanneret*, 8/1916; *Folkefred*, 9/1919.

56 *Freden*, 14/1933, 15/1933, 8/1939, 11–12/1939, 15–16/1939 & 15–16/1940; *Verden Venter*, 7/1934, 4/1939, 6/1939 & 7/1939, *Arbeiderbladet*, 14 August 1939.

57 *Verden Venter*, 7/1939.

58 *Verden Venter*, 1–2/1945; *Freden*, 17–18/1940, 8/1944, 5/1945, 7/1945 & 8/1945.

59 *Freden*, 13/1964; *Över alla gränser. Fredsmonumentet i radioriket Morokulien vid svensk-norska gränsen, Eda–Magnor* (Stockholm: Svenska freds- och skiljedomsföreningen, [n.d.]); *Fredsmonumentet. En milstolpe i historien* (Stochholm: Svenska freds- och skiljedomsföreningen, [n.d.]); <http://www.fredsmonumentet.com/>, accessed 24 September 2012.

60 Nigel Young, 'Why do Peace Movements Fail? An Historical and Sociological Overview', *PRIO Working Paper*, 10 (Oslo, 1983), 10.

61 Ringsby 2011, 76–106.

62 *Fredsbladet*, 9/1915.

63 *Folkefred*, January 1918. See also *Folkefred*, August & November 1917; *Fredsbladet*, 9/1917; *Fredsfanan*, 46/1917.

64 Karen Gram-Skjoldager, *Fred og folkeret. Internationalismens status og rolle i dansk udenrikspolitik 1899–1939* (diss.; Aarhus: Aarhus Universitet, 2008), 119–148; Ringsby 2011, 273–97 & 313–15.

65 *Folkefred*, 12/1917 & 11/1918; Knut Sandstedt, *Nordisk fredskalender 1919–1920* (Stockholm: Svenska freds- och skiljedomsföreningen, 1920), 87–90; Ringsby 2011, 208–210 & 233–6.

66 Hemstad 2008, 264–75 & 502–503.

67 Svein Olav Hansen, 'Foreningene Norden 1919–94 – ambisjoner og virkelighet', *Den jyske Historiker*, 69–70 (Aarhus, 1994), 114–15; Roald Berg, 'Nordisk samarbeid 1914–1918', *IFS Info*, 4 (Oslo: Institutt for forsvarsstudier, 1997), 8; Karen Gram-Skjoldager & Øyvind Tønnesson, 'Unity and Divergence: Scandinavian Internationalism 1914–1921', *Contemporary European History*, 17/3 (Cambridge: Cambridge University Press, 2008), 307–310.

68 Hemstad 2008, 536–56; Hansen 1994.

69 Ringsby 2011, 165–7 & 298–304.

70 Gram-Skjoldager 2008, 156–70; Gram-Skjoldager & Tønnesson 2008, 319–20; Fogelström, 1971, 169; Odd-Bjørn Fure, 'Mellomkrigstid 1920–1940', *Norsk utenrikspolitikks historie* (Oslo: Universitetsforlaget, 1996), iii. 183–184; Nils Yngvar Bøe Lindgren, *Norge og opprettelsen av Folkeforbundet* (MA diss.; Oslo: Universitetet i Oslo, 1993), 175–98; Erik Lönnroth, *Den svenska utrikespolitikens historia 1919–1939* (Stockholm: Nordstedt, 1959), v. 30–54. Sixteen of the Norwegians who voted against belonged to Arbeiderpartiet, while the opponents in Sweden belonged to the far Right and the far Left alike.

71 Eight Nordic peace meetings were held in the interwar years: Stockholm (1919), Copenhagen (1922), Oslo (1925), Stockholm (1928), Copenhagen (1931), Oslo (1934), Helsingfors (1937), and Arvika (1939). This arrangement was more or less discontinued after the Second World War.

CHAPTER 5

Restoring the strident female voice

Selma Lagerlöf and the women's anti-war movement

Anna Nordlund

The Nobel Laureate Selma Lagerlöf (1858–1940) stands out in public as peaceable, never hysterical. She protected her reputation as an author, and played the role of the balanced and worthy queen of Swedish literature very well, starting with her 1891 début *Gösta Berlings saga.*[1] When Lagerlöf, as the first woman and the first Swede, received the Nobel Prize in Literature in 1909, her role as 'Sweden's noble daughter' was reaffirmed, and she was seen as the international intermediary of the new Swedish identity, based on the long period of peace in Sweden and the soundness and morality of the Swedish people, which this enduring peace was thought to stand for.[2]

With such international successes as *Jerusalem* (1901–1902) and *Nils Holgerssons underbara resa genom Sverige* (*The Wonderful Adventures of Nils*) (1906–1907), Lagerlöf was welcome to represent these new, chauvinistic ideas about a peaceful and progressive Swedish people, ideas that were in political agreement with the peaceful dissolution of the Union in 1905.[3] Swedish self-esteem was rebuilt on a new story of an honourable country, where the people had turned their backs on the barbarities of war, and now looked ahead to Scandinavian reconciliation across the social divide and the establishment of good cross-border relations.[4] In this story, Liberals and Social Democrats were united in the struggle for universal suffrage, introduced for men and men only in Sweden

1909, which merely increased Selma Lagerlöf's commitment to the women's liberation movement. Similarly, inimical to Sweden's new self-esteem as a peaceful and neutral state, the 1906 Liberal government had legislated against anti-militarism, and Conservative politicians along with King Gustav V and his German wife Queen Victoria made no secret of their support for Germany, at the time closely linked to Sweden historically as well as economically and culturally.

At the outbreak of war in August 1914, the German invasion of Belgium had the full support of the majority of the Swedish upper classes. Swedish opinion was divided into the conservatives' pro-German claims for 'active neutrality' (that is, 'neutrality' that held Germany to be the more innocent party in the war) and more liberal and labour-oriented, Entente-friendly claims for 'real neutrality' (that is, 'neutrality' that regarded Germany as the aggressor).[5] The chauvinistic Swedish peace identity that had slowly formed during the nineteenth century was thus put to the test by the politics of neutrality. At the same time, Selma Lagerlöf's role as an author was sorely tried, and during the first years of war she frantically searched for a new voice that would challenge chauvinistic ideals and recognize international pacifism and democratic ideals, associated with the worldwide women's suffrage movement, which now also took the shape of a strong political opinion in favour of peace.

In this chapter I use Selma Lagerlöf's authorship during the war years to illuminate the connection between women's liberation and the peace movement. In particular, I consider the anti-war novel *Bannlyst* (*The Outcast*) from 1918 and Lagerlöf's construction of an ignored and silenced female voice, which urgently speaks against all war. Just like the suffragettes, Lagerlöf argued through her authorship that the repressed female voice could offer a new and humane order of society, if only it was given credence. The repressed female voice in *Bannlyst* is juxtaposed here with Fredrika Bremer's famous emancipation novel *Hertha*, published in 1856 and written during the Crimean War. Bremer (1801–1865) was the leading Swedish novelist at the time, recognized internationally as one of the greatest pioneers of women's liberation. Her novel *Hertha* is a *Bildungsroman* in which the growth and maturity of society is ineluctably connected to the growth and maturity of women. Young Hertha has a theological mission: she wants to change the world, revive Christianity's true commandments on the sanctity of human life, and give women the same rights as men. Hertha speaks from the position of the nineteenth-century bourgeois woman. The novel had also prompted a series of reforms that gave bourgeois women, including Lagerlöf herself, increased freedom, much like the daughters who are apostrophized by the dying Hertha in her orations at the end of the novel. In Lagerlöf's novel, meanwhile, the female voice is projected through Lotta Hedman, a lonely working-class woman from the far north, at a time when working-class literature was just beginning to emerge in Sweden. Thus the female voice in *Bannlyst* speaks from a searching new position, far removed from the bourgeois women's sphere in earlier feminist literature that had been so despised by Strindberg and others.

Lagerlöf's creative crisis during the war was clearly connected to a politicization of authorship in the 1910s due to massive class conflict throughout Europe,[6] compounded by a general doubt about the place of serious, non-realistic fiction as a vehicle of debate and opinion, prompted not least by the fact that war, in the rapidly changing media scene, for the great majority was now increasingly mediated as experienced reality—experienced through pictures and news reports in the press, and romanticized war stories in popular novels and short stories.[7] The disastrous war thus had a paralysing effect on Lagerlöf, like other authors of the time.[8] But more specifically, Lagerlöf's creative crisis can also be connected to her ideological roots in the liberal women's movements dating back to the nineteenth century and Fredrika Bremer, and the demands that leading figures placed on Lagerlöf to be part of the international women's movements' campaign for peace.

A 'peace sheep'?

Not speaking out against the war meant letting emotions die and inspiration dissipate: this was the lament in several of Lagerlöf's unpublished drafts and published sketches during the war.[9] So, why let herself be called a 'peace sheep'?[10] At the beginning of her career,

159

Lagerlöf had received a great deal of support from both the Swedish and the Danish women's liberation movements, and she had contacts with leading representatives of the women's movements.[11] But not until she stood up for women's right to vote did Lagerlöf speak publicly in favour of women's liberation. She became a member of the suffrage committee in her hometown of Falun 1905, and wrote the committee's petition for universal suffrage to the Riksdag, in which she referred to the national appeal for women's suffrage, at the beginning of 1906.[12] In 1911 she held her speech 'Hem och stat' ('Home and State') in Stockholm at the International Congress for Women's Suffrage.[13] It was quite an unassuming speech, with ideas that heralded those espoused by the Social Democrats—that the state would build a safe welfare state, in Lagerlöf's vision by dint of woman's hard-won experience and devotion to creating a safe and happy home. Because of her presence, the congress was treated more exhaustively and respectfully by the press than it probably would have otherwise.[14]

When the war broke out in 1914, women had the right to vote in Finland (since 1906)—the first country in Europe where women were enfranchised at the same time as universal male suffrage was introduced—and in Norway (since 1913). The women's suffrage movement in Europe and Sweden had been well organized since the beginning of the 1900s, as a result of the fact that general suffrage organizations did not pursue the issue of women's right to vote persistently enough. When the war started, the women's suffrage movements swiftly mobilized into strong organizations for peace, and it was important to get the world-famous and widely respected Selma Lagerlöf to join these movements.[15] She was under a lot of pressure.

Speak up against the war

Letters came by the sackful to her home in Falun and her childhood home, Mårbacka. Selma Lagerlöf was the country's darling; yes, even the world's. The letters were mainly from Swedes in need, asking for money. But could Dr Lagerlöf perhaps also make the war come to an end?[16] Hers is a constant search for a narrative voice that could speak out against the war. In her 1916 short story 'Dimman' ('The Fog'), Lagerlöf condemns the main character, 'den fridsamme' ('the peaceable'), who, ironically echoing neutral Sweden, expresses a desire to continue his life unaffected by the Great War then raging:

> Let me work in the way that is my own, do things that I can take care of! Let me be excused from running around the country as if deranged, trying to put things right that I am not man to master![17]

But the price is high for such wilful self-isolation and self-deceit. Later in the same story, the character describes himself as being surrounded by 'cold and darkness and silence and petrification and a haze which makes one apathetic'.[18] It is not this creature, longing for a peaceful existence, who finds favour in the eyes of the Lord, but a mad woman constantly reminding him and others about the atrocities of the war. This short story has a very critical attitude towards neutral Sweden's passivity. It was written in time for Christmas 1915 for the Neutral Conference for Continuous Mediation that was to be held in Stockholm in February 1916 on the initiative of the mayor of Stockholm, Social Democratic MP Carl Lindhagen and his sister Anna Lindhagen, one of the leading Swedish suffragists.

In the sketch 'Ödekyrkan' ('The Church Ruin') written the same year for the International Committee of Women for Permanent Peace, a ruined church becomes the symbol for Lagerlöf's creative paralysis. The narrator, in misery over her lost creative powers, compares herself to the ruin: 'I have been a minstrel and a jester, but out of my soul no more jesting or playing will emerge. My soul has become like you, mute, without bells, without song.'[19]

Throughout the war years, Lagerlöf was constantly aware that some voices of protest, particularly from the women's suffrage and anti-war movements—scorned as peace sheep—were stifled or censured, while simultaneously regarded as often naïve and inconsequential. In the peace movement's protests, she saw women taking politicized responsibility for human life, but personally she declined to actively take part in any other way than writing stories. To the great disappointment of many intellectuals—such as Ellen Key and Elin Wägner—Lagerlöf thus refused to get more personally involved in the Neutral Conference for Continuous Mediation in Stockholm and the international pacifist Henry Ford Peace Expedition, organized by famous London-based Hungarian suffragist and pacifist Rosika Schwimmer and named for its financial supporter, the American industrialist Henry Ford. Repeated calls from members of the expedition did not convince her to participate, and only succeeded in irritating her intensely. Selma Lagerlöf saw the expedition as vanity.[20] Also, the participating women from neutral nations all over the world ended up splitting into antagonistic national factions, and the expedition was judged a failure.

Unlike her colleagues Key and Wägner, as well as the preceding generation of female authors, Lagerlöf kept her distance from official political rhetoric. As the war raged on, however, Lagerlöf began to doubt the effectiveness of her authorial image, although she still remained reluctant to embrace a more conventionally political discourse. In a poem that probably dates to February 1918, when she had started work on her anti-war novel *Bannlyst*, she laments the separation of body and soul during the years of war, and the loss of inspiration. The poem describes how soul and body fuse together again when the author to whom they belong has come to terms with her approach to the atrocities of war.[21]

A disturbing work

Over the course of a few months in the spring of 1918, Selma Lagerlöf completed the writing of her new novel. *Bannlyst* is arguably Lagerlöf's most disturbing work. Emotional excess is laid out side by side with realistic, goal-oriented narrative to function as a manifesto of ideas against the war. The thought behind *Bannlyst* was to create a new taboo. If people could be made to feel the same feelings of disgust toward the killing of people in war as toward the eating of dead human flesh, then all wars might be avoided.[22]

The complex narrative chiefly spans the years 1909 to 1916 and is largely set in a rural fishing community on the rocky shores of the Swedish west coast, as well as rural parts inland. The hero of the novel, Sven Elversson, an English gentleman in his late twenties, has returned to his native Sweden after a British polar expedition.

His English parents adopted him when he was nine years old. They have now rejected him, after rumours spread that Sven and his crewmates, shipwrecked and starving in the Arctic, ate the flesh of a dead comrade. Wishing to hide from the world, Sven returns to his biological parents, Joel and Thala, farmers on the island of Grimön on the west coast.

Sven, the Swedish-born outsider who has been a member of an English expedition, brings some kind of horrible contagion back with him to the country of his birth. The local minister, Rhånge, accepts Sven's existence in the county, living with his parents on a remote island. But he would never accept Sven as an active parishioner in the church where he holds sway. Rhånge's condemnation of Sven in church sparks off the inhabitants' mistreatment of Sven in the name of disgust. But Sven proves to be more gracious and righteous in his ways than any of the churchgoers. Rhånge's spiritual charisma gradually leaves him after he condemns Sven. Lotta Hedman, a simple servant girl, who has the powerful gift of second sight, reveals the minister as a fake and shallow man. Rhånge falls deeper into rage and depression, before he realizes that he has to renegotiate his beliefs in spiritual powers and taboos. Two competing discourses of narrative consciousness thus clash within the novel: rationalist realism represented by the authoritarian Lutheran minister Rhånge, and untrammelled supernaturalism represented by a poor and simple woman born and raised in peripheral Lapland.

Bannlyst raises questions about the nature of reality and its apparent failure to represent the corporeal perceptions of war, and mirrors Lagerlöf's own struggle to balance her wish to live in ignorance of the atrocities of the war with her urge to use her artistry to fight them and ultimately to break out of the box of genteel, National Romantic writing in which she had been long confined. When waves of swollen corpses of young men float ashore after the Battle of Jutland, people begin to re-evaluate Sven's crime. His brother Joel, a seaman who has encountered thousands of corpses floating out at sea, now sick with despair asks Sven for forgiveness. Sven reminds him of the time Joel and his friends forced him to eat a snake. With eye-witness accuracy, Lagerlöf goes on to describe the sights Joel has seen:

They did not lie flat on the water, but were held upright by their lifebelts, with heads above water, so their features could be seen. And Ung-Joel told how the vessel had sailed for hours among the dead–thousands and thousands of dead. The sea was covered with them.

He described many terrible sights he had seen, but what seemed most terrible of all to him was that all those dead men had their eyes torn out by innumerable seagulls that hovered about their heads.[23]

Lagerlöf was on holiday in Strömstad on the west coast in June 1916 when corpses from the battle floated close to the shore. She then immediately started to work with the idea of connecting the disgust at dead human flesh with a taboo against war.[24] The community's disgust with Sven is redirected towards the corpses from the slaughter of battle. *Bannlyst* thus offers a new, more adequate perception of the ultimate repulsiveness of war than the conventional descriptions of the battles as a contest mainly between Germans and British offered in newspaper reports. The two major national newspapers in Sweden at the time, the liberal *Dagens Nyheter* and the conservative *Svenska Dagbladet*, routinely reported on the war by way of the propaganda headquarters in Berlin, London, Paris, and Amsterdam; the conservatives with a huge emphasis on Berlin and great sympathy for the Germans.[25] The newspaper reports recast hand-to-hand slaughter, shooting, shelling, or bombing as the protection or defence of comrades, and always in national—never individual—terms.

Lotta Hedman's supernatural sight appears as a cultural corrective. A prophetess from the rural north of Sweden, Lotta's haunted visions, irrational compulsions, and dramatic public outbursts construct her as a kind of madwoman–outsider capable of seeing beyond dominating discourses. Her initial appearance on a train a third of the way through the novel signals a disorientingly abrupt change in the text's tone and direction. Dressed in black, shy and inhibited, she nonetheless directs at her fellow passenger Sven a rapid-fire, half-mad, half-rhapsodic monologue that slowly attracts the other passengers as well. Finally, as she has finished her proclamations of the world coming to an end after the Great War, she starts talking about her love for her childhood friend and the minister's wife Sigrun, and her notion, confirmed in a series of visions, that the minister Rhånge is a man capable of killing Sigrun's soul.

Lotta's presence, voice, and vision constantly threaten the novel's realist conventions and narrative stability. She is the consistently uncontainable and destabilizing element in this fictional universe, one whose excessive inner visions and prophetic powers keep exploding outwards and keep creating unexpected dislocations at the levels of plot and formal coherence.

Fredrika Bremer and the women's international peace movement

The repulsive yet captivating Lotta Hedman appears in the novel as a personification both of a rejected position in society and a female literary tradition from which the Establishment had dissociated itself—especially at the time of Lagerlöf's literary début in 1891— and which Lagerlöf herself considered harmful to be too strongly associated with: a tradition of politically radical, sentimental novels with reformist ambitions, where their message could be dismissed as sentimental and banal.[26] All through the war, Lagerlöf's drafts and short stories contained the insight that some voices were not to be heard, and if they were heard they were dismissed by the authorities of the world as silly and naïve. She lamented her fear that her great reputation as a humane and honourable author would collapse if she did not deliver an outburst against the war, while also fearing such an outburst would be associated with femininity and silliness. In the peace movements she saw women who took a certain responsibility for life, but she never took part in the worldwide manifestations arranged by women's international peace movements. Lagerlöf protected her reputation as an author and her fear of public debate is well known.[27] But at the same time she felt compelled throughout the war to reflect over the significance of her authorship in sketches and drafts, written at the request of various peace movements. She searched for a completely new format to be able to mediate a message of peace that would make an impact and all the while might restore the once-repressed female voice to literature and society. 'Once, I sacrificed my good name as an author for them. I am happy that I knew what I sacrificed, and still did it.' This is what Swedish author Fredrika Bremer says in a sketch by Lagerlöf from 1891. It is Christmas morning and she is in church, surrounded by the spirits of ageing spinsters. Lagerlöf's short story 'Mamsell Fredrika' ('Miss Fredrika') was published in the women's liberation periodical *Dagny*, and paid tribute to Bremer and her feminist novel *Hertha*.[28] Thus, very much in line to her own début, Lagerlöf shows consciousness of a female author's vulnerability in public, as well as an awareness of the political reforms in women's right to self-determination and education that made her own career possible. Undoubtedly, Lagerlöf also knew that Bremer, after the Crimean War battle on the Åland Islands in the summer of 1854, had published an appeal in *The Times* on 28 August 1854, calling for the women of the world to unite in an alliance for peace: 'May the earth thus become encircled by a chain of healing, loving energies, which neither ocean nor event, neither discord nor time, can interrupt.'[29] The women's organization's main purpose would be to educate women to be responsible and competent citizens. Education would be a part of the emancipation of women from spiritual and physical oppression, and would change the world. Bremer's conviction was that if women participated in public life it could fundamentally change world politics.

Lagerlöf was clearly formed in the spirit of Fredrika Bremer. Like many women in the Swedish suffrage movement and peace movement, she had a degree from the prestigious Kungliga Högre lärarinneseminariet (College for Women Teachers) in Stockholm, which was established by some far-seeing educationalists in 1859, after women's lack of education opportunities had been debated in *Hertha* and by other intellectuals in Fredrika Bremer's circle.[30] The college had been run by the state under royal patronage since 1861 and was a unique, public higher educational institution for women in a country where women were not admitted to public grammar schools until 1927. That women's limited opportunities for education and self-support troubled Lagerlöf in her youth is evident from her writings.[31] Furthermore, it was older women in direct contact with Fredrika Bremer who had encouraged Lagerlöf to make use of her talent by going out into the world and getting an education.[32] During the years Lagerlöf attended the college (1882–5) the peace issue was much discussed by the liberal women's movement, which had connections to the college. Internationally as well, women's commitment to peace and peace education was widely discussed. An international conference for peace had been held in 1878, where women were urged to engage in peace work. In a number of countries this led to women's peace organizations being formed, with education and fosterage to peace on the programme, which also characterized the education on offer at the College for Women Teachers from the start.

When the war started in August 1914, suffragists all over Europe quickly organized peace rallies. The International Women's Suffrage Alliance sent protests against the war to various countries' legations in London, and in New York thousands of women dressed in black demonstrated in a silent procession to the sound of muffled drums.[33] In Sweden, women of various political affiliations gathered in a help committee, and in the autumn of 1914, some of the Swedish suffragists secretly began to prepare an action they called Women's Peace Sunday, planned for February 1915. The idea was that women in the neutral Scandinavian countries would gather in as many places as possible, pass a joint resolution against the war, and recommend neutral intervention between the belligerent states. When fully organized, the whole action suddenly had to be cancelled, as news of it reached the Swedish royal family and Queen Victoria considered it improper.[34]

However, plans for a pan-Scandinavian women's manifestation for peace resurfaced after a legation of sixteen Swedish women participated in the International Women's Congress for Peace and Freedom in The Hague in April 1915. In The Hague, the International Committee of Women for Permanent Peace was founded, with the influential American suffragist Jane Addams elected chairwoman (Addams, a forerunner in modern social politics, had useful contacts with President Wilson). The conference resulted in a resolution to send women's delegations to governments involved in the war and thus work for a dialogue between the belligerent states. With the resolution, they also aspired to show that women were taking active responsibility for the development of society; that they could contribute to a better world, and thus should be enfranchised. The manifestation failed. But towards the end of June 1915, Women's Peace Sunday gathered over 88,000 women in 343 different places in Sweden.[35]

Preparing for this Sunday, 27 June 1915, Selma Lagerlöf tried to write a speech for peace. A halting draft has been saved in her collection at the National Library in Stockholm: she wonders why the peace movement does not have more supporters, cannot sort it out, and suddenly her pencil starts writing a prayer of utter despair: 'Jesus Christ, come and help me! Say what I should write. I am sitting here, listening for God's voice.' And she continues:

> I have been wondering for quite some time whether the peace movement ought to change its name.
>
> It is the word. Peace movement sounds as if we were seeking something unreasonable, something that will never come about, something so unthinkable as peace on earth being possible. ... Why lay yourself open to being called a peace sheep.[36]

There was an anonymous speech given on Women's Peace Sunday, published and delivered to the rallies all over the country. Present in person in Strömstad, Lagerlöf read the speech and it is possible that it was she who had written it.[37]

Hertha and *The Outcast* as novels of ideas

The voice of Lotta Hedman in *Bannlyst* restores the female voice and the female literary tradition of the sentimental novel, for decades silenced as naïve and sentimental in political debates and intellectual discussions.[38] Through the character of Lotta Hedman, Bremer's fundamental message in *Hertha* is stressed: women have the same right as men to preach the word of God, and are perhaps even closer to God's plan for mankind. As the novel unfolds, Lotta finally preaches outside the church, and the crowd turns its attention to her. It is stressed that Lotta has been called in her own right, and that she did not come to the church with Rhånge. The portrayal of Lotta throughout the novel alludes to Fredrika Bremer's criticism of the strict Swedish Lutheran church, far from Bremer's radical Christianity and the visions in *Hertha* of women possessed of divine wisdom that is renounced by men. Lotta's concluding sermon is a clear parallel to the depiction of Hertha as a saviour and Hertha's closing speech in Bremer's novel. Here Bremer's much-mocked, radical suggestion of a peaceful alliance between the peoples of the world, initiated by Christian women in a network of philanthropic women's organizations, is also redressed. The fact that Bremer, by appealing for peace, had made a fool of herself was something the Swedish newspapers had diligently reported.[39]

With the characters' reaction to the raft of corpses at sea and the novel's two concluding sermons, where Rhånge's and Lotta's visions are joined, *Bannlyst* emphasizes the limitations of realism and documentary as a depiction of reality. In that sense, Lagerlöf also puts her authorship to the test, questioning its distance to a conventional realism and approaching Bremer's ability to write a feminist novel of ideas with a pacifist message. In *Hertha*, her most radical work, Bremer depicts her feminist ideas, closely related to her radical, Christian view of society, through dreamlike apparitions and visions, cutting through the realistic accounts in the novel and pleading for women's rights to an education and society's need for female preaching. Hertha stands out as God's human daughter called to turn fettered women into disciples. In a famous passage, Hertha has a challenging radical and satirical dream with mythical dimensions. In the dream she travels all over the world to seek help to solve the curse that lies upon women who have no rights. But among men of learning, all she meets is a lack of interest in her cause. They dispose of all their time and strength in the invention of bombs and disputes on theological and scientific trivialities; all while the world is on fire in the burning Crimean War, in Sweden's immediate vicinity. In Hertha's dream the men's excitement prefigures the First World War propaganda:

we are now so occupied with the oriental war in the East, and are at this very moment doing our best to perfect a huge projectile, a gigantic projectile, which, when it explodes, will poison a whole city with its stench. It is a great matter, a very great matter. This is, my good girl, a great time for humanity, and if you and your sisters will come hither and help to cast bullets or to give lessons in the French language, then...[40]

Just like Hertha, Lotta has an inner calling, but external constraints obstruct her. She is still unlearned and is locked out from the ministry, but because of this, 'My head's not heavy with knowledge. Not all confused with doctrines of error. I am as an unwritten page; as the white scroll on which God Himself writes His own thoughts.'[41]

Like Hertha, Lotta delivers a sermon at the end of the novel, in which earthy schooling is severely criticized for its apparent failure to give mankind the proper means to listen to their inner voices and fulfil their true vocations. Her sermon concentrates on the essential elements of religion: the commandments concerning people's inviolable worth and social rules. The sermon she delivers is a vision in which she sees how the bodies found in the ocean meet God in the hereafter, and God asks: '"Ye souls that have passed through the school of earth," says the man to them, "can you say my Ten Commandments as they are said on earth to-day."'[42] The men haltingly rattle off the four commandments that speak to the formal side of the Church, but all the commandments concerning ethical rules for life are distorted in their mouths into warlike summons.

Bannlyst re-established Lagerlöf in the twofold female literary tradition that was founded on Bremer's ideas of emancipation: realist allusions to substantial changes and political debate and visionary, mythical allusions to spiritual liberation and theological debate. In *Bannlyst*, Lagerlöf's solution in the face of the realist tradition, which at the time of her début had never been greater nor more influential, and because of this began to be despised as simple, everyday realism—tendentious, inartistic—is to bring it almost to the level of expressionistic realism in its accounts of the community's abhorrence at Sven's cannibalistic crime; Lotta Hedman's appearance on the train; Sigrun's escape from her raging husband; rafts of swollen corpses drifting on the North Sea. Moreover, in *Bannlyst* Lagerlöf renews Bremer's provocative, visionary, mythical allusions and her liberation theology. In both novels, the oppressed female voice has a messianic edge to it, and the message is worded with the hope that the world will change for the better when all people are given the freedom to determine their own circumstances, and can no longer be tamed and forced into submission by the formal regulations of power. Bremer and Lagerlöf show how, as long as women are excluded from formal power structures, the formal dictates of power result in a direct contradiction of the Christian tenet of the sanctity of human life.

However, the intention behind *Bannlyst*, that of creating a new taboo, admittedly ended up being modified and de-fanged in the final version. Lagerlöf's influential friends Valborg Olander and Sophie Elkan were so upset by the shunned hero Sven Elversson's cannibalistic crime that Lagerlöf finally surrendered to their advice. At the last moment she modified the idea of the novel by deleting the word äckel (disgust) where she could, and by adding to the plot a letter in which a dead comrade of Sven's confirms that Sven was innocent of the cannibalism committed by the others on the polar expedition.[43] The author desperately wanted to get the book published. *Bannlyst* finally reached Swedish bookshops in the middle of December in 1918, only a little more than a month after the armistice was signed on 11 November. The reception disappointed her. Not one critic drew a parallel with the women's peace and suffrage movements.[44]

In the aftermath

Europe changed after the armistice and with time the women in Germany, Great Britain, the US, and Sweden received the vote. The League of Nations was founded in 1919 on President Wilson's initiative, with the Women's International League for Peace and Freedom (WILPF) as an example and in consultation with Jane Addams.

For many women, however, the franchise was a disappointment. It did not change society to the extent the suffragists had argued it would. Already in 1919, Selma Lagerlöf spelled out the risks for decreased political commitment, in her speech on a suffrage festive just a couple of days after the full introduction of general suffrage in Sweden on 24 May, last of all the Scandinavian countries.[45] She also foresaw the severity of the Entente Powers' peace terms, and immediately after the armistice she appealed to the women of the Entente Powers to work for reconciliation. The article 'Till mödrarna i ententeländerna' ('To the mothers of the Entente Countries') was published in a number of major Swedish newspapers on 29 November 1918 and had an impact on the WILPF. Although the women's peace movement had no effect on the peace negotiations, the WILPF is still active and has consultative status with a number of UN organs. Three of its members have received the Nobel Peace Prize: its first chairwoman, Jane Addams, in 1941; its first secretary-general, Emily Greene Balch, in 1946; and the Swedish politician Alva Myrdal in 1982.

Notes

1 For more on Lagerlöf's reputation in Swedish literary criticism and history, see Anna Nordlund, *Selma Lagerlöfs underbara resa genom den svenska litteraturhistorien 1891–1996* (diss.; Stockholm/Stehag: Brutus Östlings Bokförlag Symposion, 2005).

2 '*Sveriges ädla dotter*' is an epithet in the Nobel prize speech given in honour of Lagerlöf, which drew a clear connection between Sweden's role as peacekeeper and Swedish literature in general, and with Lagerlöf in particular. The speech was published in *Les Prix Nobel en 1909* (Stockholm: Norstedts, 1910), 31–33.

3 For the cultural development of a new nationalism around 1905, see Rikard Bengtsson, *Trust, Threat, and Stable Peace. Swedish Great Power Perceptions 1905–1939* (diss.; Lund Political Studies, 114; Lund: Statsvetenskapliga institutionen, Lunds universitet, 2000); Magnus Ericson, *A Realist Stable Peace. Power, Threat and the Development of a Shared Norwegian–Swedish Democratic Security Identity 1905–1940* (diss.; Lund Political Science, 113; Lund: Statsvetenskapliga institutionen, Lunds universitet, 2000); Inger Hammar, *För Freden och rösträtten. Kvinnorna och den svensk-norska unionens sista dagar* (Lund: Nordic Academic Press, 2004), 145–78.

4 Much has lately been written on Sweden's peaceful self-image slowly formed during the 1800s. See Mats Hellstenius, *Krigen som inte blev av. Sveriges fredliga officerskår vid 1800–talets mitt* (diss.; Lund: Lunds universitet, 2000); Lars I. Andersson, *Fred i vår tid. Sverige, krigen och*

Freden, 1870–1945 (diss.; Lund: Sisyfos, 2003); Magnus Jerneck, 'Modernitet och småstadsidentitet – mönsterlandet Sverige som fredlighetens land', in id. (ed.), *Fred i realpolitikens skugga,* (Lund: Studentlitteratur, 2009), 77–93; Kim Salomon, 'Synen på krig och fred. En greppshistoria', in Jerneck 2009, 66–76.

5   Nils-Olof Franzén, *Undan stormen. Sverige under första världskriget* (Stockholm: Albert Bonniers förlag, 1986); see also Lina Sturfelt, *Eldens återsken. Första världskriget i svensk föreställningsvärld* (diss.; Lund: Sekel, 2008), 185–218.

6   For more on Lagerlöf's creative crisis in the 1910s, see Ulla-Britta Lagerroth, *Körkarlen och Bannlyst. Motiv- och idéstudier i Selma Lagerlöfs 10-talsdiktning* (diss.; Stockholm: Albert Bonniers förlag, 1963), 3–35.

7   For more on narratives and images of the war in the Swedish popular press, see Sturfelt 2008.

8   However, recent research has shown how in particular explicitly politically active authors in Sweden responded to the war in prose and poetry in various ways. See Claes Ahlund, *Diktare i krig. K. G. Ossiannilsson, Bertil Malmberg och Ture Nerman från debuten till 1920* (Hedemora: Gidlunds förlag, 2007); Sofi Qvarnström, *Motståndets berättelser. Elin Wägner, Anna Lenah Elgström, Marika Stiernstedt och första världskriget* (diss.; Hedemora: Gidlunds förlag, 2009); and Qvarnström in this volume.

9   The drafts are in the Mårbacka Foundation's collection of manuscripts, held at Kungliga biblioteket, Stockholm, under the heading 'Stämningar från krigsåren' ('Moods of the War Years').

10   Peace was commonly associated with sheep, and '*Fredsfår*' (lit. peace sheep) was used across Scandinavia to disparage peace activists. It is also found in Lagerlöf's lamentations over her reluctance to support the peace movement, discussed below.

11   See, for example, her correspondence with her Danish translators Elisabeth Grundtvig and Ida Falbe-Hansen, and with the Norwegian dentist and pacifist Kaja Hansen, in Selma Lagerlöf, *Brev 2. Utgivna av Selma Lagerlöf-sällskapet,* ed. Ying Toijer-Nilsson (Lund 1969).

12   For Lagerlöf's commitment to the suffrage movement, see Bertil Björkenlid, *Kvinnokrav i manssamhälle. Rösträttskvinnorna och deras metoder som opinionsbildare och påtryckargrupp i Sverige* 1902–1921 (diss.; Skrifter utgivna vid avdelningen för litteratursociologi vid Litteraturvetenskapliga institutionen i Uppsala, 29; Uppsala, 1982), 197–2004. For the dissolution of the union and its influence on the Swedish suffrage movement and Lagerlöf in particular, see Hammar 2004, 188. From Lagerlöf's correspondence with her close friend Sophie Elkan it is evident that the dissolution of the union was a political reawakening for Lagerlöf, which resulted in her commitment to women's right to vote, hoping that women

would be able to contribute to a fresh start for Sweden (see Selma Lagerlöf, *Du lär mig att bli fri. Selma Lagerlöf skriver till Sophie Elkan*, ed.
Ying Toijer-Nilsson (Stockholm: Albert Bonniers förlag, 1992), 262, 266–7.

13 Published in Selma Lagerlöf, *Troll och människor 1* (Stockholm: Albert
Bonniers förlag, 1915).

14 Elin Wägner, *Selma Lagerlöf*, ii: *Från Jerusalem till Mårbacka* (Stockholm:
Albert Bonniers förlag, 1943), 86.

15 See further Sif Bokholm, *I otakt med tiden, om rösträttsmotstånd, antipacifism och nazism bland svenska kvinnor* (Stockholm: Atlantis, 2008), who
also shows the strong political engagement among women against the
right to vote and, during the First World War, the suffrage movement's
division into a militarist grouping with less interest in the right to vote
and a dominant pacifist grouping for whom the commitment to the franchise remained or increased during the war: See also Irene Andersson,
Kvinnor mot krig. Aktioner och nätverk för fred 1914–1940 (diss.; Studia
Historica Lundensia; Lund, 2001), 73–84.

16 The more than 40,000 letters Lagerlöf received from the general public
are held at Kungliga biblioteket, Stockholm, in the Mårbacka Foundation collection. Jenny Bergenmar and Maria Karlsson are currently studying the letters for the research project 'Reading Lagerlöf. Letters from
the public to Selma Lagerlöf '.

17 All translations are mine unless otherwise indicated. Lagerlöf, *Troll och
människor 2* (Stockholm: Albert Bonniers förlag, 1921), 180, 'Låt mig
verka på det sätt, som är mitt eget, syssla med ting, som jag kan sköta! Låt
mig slippa att som en sinnesrubbad löpa kring landet för att söka ställa
till rätta det, som jag inte är man till att behärska!'

18 Ibid., 'köld och mörker och tystnad och förstening och förslöande töcken'.

19 Lagerlöf 1921, 169, 'Jag har varit en lekare och en gycklare, men ur min
själ framgår inte mer varken gyckel eller lek. Min själ har blivit som du,
stum, utan klockor, utan sång.'

20 Lagerlöf 1992, 438–9; for further evidence in her unpublished letters
to Elkan and her companion Valborg Olander from December 1915
until August 1916, see Kungliga Biblioteket, Stockholm (hereafter
KB), Ep L 45.

21 The poem was published after Lagerlöf's death in Selma Lagerlöf, *Från
skilda tider 2*, ed. Nils Afzelius (Stockholm: Albert Bonniers förlag,
1946), 17–20.

22 KB, Ep L 45, Lagerlöf to Olander, 14 & 19 October 1918; Lagerlöf
1992, 474, Lagerlöf to Elkan.

23 *The Outcast*, trans. W. Worster (London: Gyldendahl, 1920, 257); Selma
Lagerlöf, *Bannlyst* (Stockholm: Albert Bonniers förlag, 1918), 315, 'De
hade inte legat utsträckta i vattnet, utan de hade hållits i upprätt ställ-

ning av sina korkvästar. Deras huvuden hade varit upplyfta ovan vattnet, så att man hade kunnat urskilja anletsdrag och uttryck. Och ung-Joel berättade, att ångaren hade gått fram i timtal genom tusenden och åter tusenden av döda. Hela havet hade varit betäckt av dem. Han skildrade för brodern många fasans syner, som han hade sett, men det, som tycktes värst ha gripit honom, var, att alla de döda hade fått sina ögon uthackade av de otaliga skaror av måsar, som kretsade över dem.'

24 Lagerroth 1963, 375.

25 I have looked through *Dagens Nyheter* and *Svenska Dagbladet* with an eye to the battlefields of Champagne, Neuve-Chapelle, and Ypres in February and March 1915, the sinking of *Lusitania* on 7 May 1915, the Battle of Jutland on 31 May and 1 June 1916, and the battlefields of Cambrai–St Quentin and Amiens for 21 March and April 1918.

26 For more on the sentimental novel in connection with Lagerlöf's debut, see Lisbeth Stenberg, *En genialisk lek. Kritik och överskridande i Selma Lagerlöfs tidiga författarskap* (diss.; Skrifter utgivna av Litteraturvetenskapliga institutionen vid Göteborgs universitet, 40; Gothenburg, 2001), 169–82; Nordlund 2005, 33–8, 48.

27 Wägner 1943, 395.

28 Also published in Selma Lagerlöf, *Osynliga länkar* (Stockholm: Albert Bonniers förlag, 1894), 156–68, 'Jag offrade en gång mitt författaranseende för dem. Jag är glad, att jag visste vad jag offrade och ändå gjorde det.' This taken almost word for word from a letter Bremer wrote a fortnight before her death. See further Carina Burman, *Bremer. En biografi* (Stockholm: Albert Bonniers förlag, 2001), 393.

29 Quoted in Burman, 362.

30 Nothing has yet been written on the College for Women Teachers as a hotbed of intellectual women.

31 See, for example, *Ett barns memoarer* (Stockholm: Albert Bonniers förlag, 1930); *Dagbok för Selma Ottilia Lovisa Lagerlöf* (Stockholm: Albert Bonniers förlag, 1932).

32 Namely Eva Fryxell and Sophie Adlersparre.

33 Andersson 2001, 67–8.

34 Ibid. 84–90.

35 Ibid. 90–101.

36 KB, Mårbacka Foundation collection of manuscripts, 'Stämningar från krigsåren': 'Kristus Jesus kom och hjälp mig! Säg vad jag ska skriva. Jag sitter och lyssnar efter Guds röst.' 'Jag har gått och undrat sedan någon tid om inte fredsrörelsen borde byta om namn. Det är ordet. Fredsrörelsen låter ju som om vi eftersträvade något orimligt något som aldrig ska komma, något så otänkbart, som att det skulle kunna skapas fred på jorden. … Varför utsätta sig för att bli kallade fredsfår.'

37 A letter to Valborg Olander indicated she did (KB, Ep L 45, 30 June 1915); see also Lagerroth 1963, 427–8.

38 Through Julia Kristeva's psychoanalytical theory of abjection Birgitta Holm suggests that Lagerlöf's aesthetics in *Bannlyst* represent discoveries of cultural powers surrounding 'the female' as a collective unconscious. See Birgitta Holm, *Selma Lagerlöf och ursprungets roman* (Stockholm: Norstedts, 1984), 248–73. For the female literary tradition and the sentimental novel in Sweden between 1830 and 1880, see Elisabeth Mansén, *Konsten att förgylla vardagen. Thekla Knös och romantikens Uppsala* (diss.; Lund: Nya Doxa, 1993); in connection with Lagerlöf, see Stenberg 2001, 169–215, 264–5; and for Lagerlöf and the melodramatic imagination, see Maria Karlsson, *Känslans röst. Det melodramatiska i Selma Lagerlöfs romankonst* (diss.; Stockholm/Stehag: Brutus Östlings bokförlag Symposion, 2002).

39 Inger Ekbom, *Den kvinnliga fredstanken. Fredrika Bremer och andra i kamp för fred* (Stockholm: Carlssons, 1991), 21.

40 *Hertha*, trans. Mary Howitt (London: Arthur Hall, Virtue & Co., 1856); Fredrika Bremer, *Hertha eller En själs historia. Teckning ur det verkliga livet*, ed. Victor Svanberg (Aktuella klassiker; Stockholm: Askild & Kärnekull, 1974), 113, 'Vi ha så mycket att göra med orientaliska kriget; vi hålla som bäst på att tillverka en stor bomb, en jättebomb, miss, som, när den exploderar, skall kunna förgifta en hel stad genom sin stank. Det blir en stor sak, en mycket stor sak! Detta är en stor tid, miss, för mänskligheten, och om ni och era systrar vilja komma hit och stöpa kulor eller ge lektioner i franska språket, så …'

41 *The Outcast* 1920 (above, n. 23), 111; Lagerlöf 1918, 133–4, 'Mitt huvud är inte tungt av vetande. Det är inte förvirrat av irrläror. Jag är som det oskrivna papperet. Jag är som det vita bladet, där Gud själv skriver ner sina tankar.'

42 *The Outcast* 1920, 292; Lagerlöf 1918, 347, 'I själar, som haver genomgått livets skola, kunnen i läsa upp för mig mina tio bud, sådana som de i dessa dagar lyda på jorden?'

43 KB, Ep L 45, letters to Valborg Olander, 14, 24 & 28 October 1918; Lagerlöf 1992, 476, letter to Sophie Elkan, 28 October 1918; Lagerlöf 1969, 343, 391–395, letters to Kaja Hansen, 5 April 1919.

44 Nordlund 2005, 158–63.

45 Published in *Från skilda tider 1*, ed. Nils Afzelius (Stockholm: Albert Bonniers förlag, 1945), 156–9.

CHAPTER 6

Recognizing the Other
The Armenian Genocide
in Scandinavian literature

Sofi Qvarnström

Soon the world was a gaping wound,
The two became thousands. Day became year.

But you never forget them—the first two,
who were borne ashore at Galata Bridge.[1]

What does it take to recognize another life? Under what circumstances
is it possible to recognize it as valuable, important, and grievable? Is
it only when we are able to apprehend a life that it matters to us if
it is lost; is it only then that we can act to save or protect it?

Judith Butler argues in her book *Frames of war. When is life grievable?* (2009) that we need to recognize life as precarious, conditional, and that this requires support in social relations and institutions.[2] But we must also try to see what determines and defines
what kind of life is recognized, because this recognition is not
equally distributed. Butler discusses the example of the photographs of the torture carried out in the Abu Ghraib prison, and
she asks why war tends to make some lives grievable and others
ungrievable. She focuses especially on the media framing: how the
photos are shown, how they are named and described, when they
are shown. These framings all 'work together to produce an interpretative matrix for what is seen.'[3] In other words, Butler wants to
discuss the ways in which suffering is presented to us, and how this

177

presentation affects our responsiveness. In particular, she wants to understand 'how the *frames* that allocate the recognizability of certain figures of the human are themselves linked with broader *norms* that determine what will and will not be a grievable life'.[4]

In this chapter, I take the perspectives presented by Butler on the grievability of images and texts, and pose the question of what function the act of criticizing war has. Can the criticism be an attempt to recognize all lives as grievable, or to recognize the lives that hitherto have been denied? As Butler writes, 'What would it take not only to apprehend the precarious character of lives lost in war, but to have that apprehension coincide with an ethical and political opposition to the losses war entails? … How is affect produced by this structure of the frame?'[5] How do we avoid human catastrophes becoming abstractions for us? And how do we avoid the paralysing effect of habit when the world is 'a gaping wound', 'two became thousands', and in suffering 'day became year'?

These questions are examined here in relation to the Scandinavian commitment for the Armenian people during the mass exterminations by the Turkish army in the 1910s. The Armenian Genocide took place during the First World War, and the simultaneity of the two events poses an interesting problem for the question of Swedish engagement and the possibility of communicating grievable life in the shocking torrent of death and suffering. From a European perspective, the outskirts of Europe were hit by another tragedy, which was partly over-shadowed by an already shattered everyday life. However, it is not the public engagement as such that will be explored, but rather a specific medium, namely fiction.

The aim of this chapter is to explore how the Danish teacher and writer Inga Nalbandiàn tried to get the Scandinavians to commit to the Armenian cause. Through a reading of her three novels published as *Den store Jammer* ('The Great Lamentation') (1917–18), I will show how fiction can create *or* fail to create compassion for unknown lives, and thus, in Butler's words, to make those lives grievable. To do so, a close text analysis is combined with an examination of the publishing context and the reception of the books—ultimately the question touches on the significance of literature in the making of public opinion.

The Armenian Genocide
and the Scandinavian public opinion

Armenia has a long history of conflicts and has repeatedly been subjected to the great powers' attempts to wrest control and influence.[6] In the beginning of the nineteenth century, most of the country belonged to the Ottoman Empire, but the eastern part was under Persian influence. Soon another great power, Russia, became interested in Caucasus for political and economic reasons. At the end of the nineteenth century, under the influence of European ideas and goods, tensions increased between the Muslim ruling class and an Armenian middle class with considerable influence on commerce and banking. Armenians and other Christian minorities had strong positions in urban areas, and they demanded the same civil rights as Muslims had. As in Europe, national movements fighting for independence were growing stronger. The Turkish–Russian War of 1877–8 brought an intensification of their demands, but the war only led to Russia's increased influence over the country's northern regions. In the 1880s, new revolutionary political parties were formed, clashes took place, and eventually the authorities' response was direct attacks and massacres of Armenian villages. About 300,000 Armenians were killed in 1895–6. After several relatively quiet years, the turbulence increased around 1910. The Sultan was removed in a bloodless *coup d'état* and a group of reform-oriented and well-educated officers, the so-called Young Turks, took over. Their goal was to create a modern nation founded on an ethnic and authoritarian nationalism. But Russia stood in the way of their dream of Pan-Turkism, and Armenia constituted a real threat as the region bordering on Russia. Ottoman society became militarized, and opposition was met with violence and terror.

In early November 1914, Turkey joined Germany in the First World War. At the same time, what later came to be known as the Great Genocide began—an attempt at the systematic extermination of an entire people.[7] Government employees were fired, Armenian soldiers in the Turkish army were disarmed and sent to labour battalions, and officers were imprisoned. At the end of March 1915, deportations began, first of men, then of women and children. Many were sent southwards, toward the Syrian Desert, and most of them died on the way or were killed upon arrival. Nearly half of the Armenian population in the Ottoman Empire was killed, with estimates ranging from at least 800,000 up to 1 million people.[8] Some managed to escape to Russia, others were forced to convert to Islam, and a few survivors were found in the Syrian Desert after the war.[9]

Both European and American media reported on the genocide. Strong condemnations were directed against the Turks; already in May 1915 the Entente Powers threatened the Ottoman government that it would be held personally accountable if the crimes against humanity continued. However, in the subsequent peace negotiations in 1920, no UN member state wished to accept the role as mandate power over Armenia.[10]

The Scandinavian countries were not unaware of what was happening. Already in the 1880s, Swedish, Danish, and Norwegian missionaries stationed in Armenia had reported on the killings, and when the great deportations began, several missionaries and aid workers still remained in the country. Many of them testified to the most brutal acts of violence against the Armenian people.[11] The Scandinavian foreign ministries received reports from diplomats, and the Danish envoy Carl Ellis Wandel in particular seems to have understood with perfect clarity what was going on. Wandel interpreted the deportations as an openly cruel, opportunistic, political and economic project, fuelled by a nationalist ideology.[12] The Swedish ambassador in Constantinople, P. G. A. C. Anckarsvärd, also reported in detail on Turkey's increasingly violent actions and described it as 'the Extermination of the Armenian nation'.[13]

The Swedish policy on Armenia and the commitment to the Armenian cause have been characterized as strongly linked to the peace movement against the First World War, which of course was redoubled during the war years and then weakened at the end of the war.[14] In Stockholm, a protest meeting in support of the Armenians was held in the autumn of 1917, with the author Marika Stiernstedt and the Social Democratic leader Hjalmar Branting as speakers. Stiernstedt's speech was published afterwards, and she went on a lecture tour in the provinces.[15] The Swedish press reported on the events in Armenia, but the reports were, not surprisingly, over-shadowed by the news from the World War.[16] Information and knowledge about the situation in Armenia thus existed in Scandinavia, as did some commitment and aid work. However, it did not lead to much concrete action.

To apprehend the lives of others

Inga Nalbandiàn (née Collin, 1879–1929) was a teacher, journalist, and writer, married to the Armenian Paul Mardiros Nalbandiàn. They met in Switzerland and in 1909 they settled in Constantinople when Mardiros Nalbandiàn received an appointment as lecturer at the Armenian National High School. The situation became more and more precarious as the deportations intensified, and in the summer of 1916 they sent their two children back to Denmark. Paul Mardiros Nalbandiàn died shortly afterwards, and Inga Nalbandiàn returned to Denmark that same autumn. Once in Denmark, she started writing her books about Armenia: *Den Store Jammer, De Hjemsøgte* and *Den Hvide Mark* ('The Great Lamentation', 'The Haunted', and 'The White Field') (1917–18). The books comprise seemingly independent stories linked by their setting, as they take place at the same hospital, in the same village, or the same city. Eventually, however, the reader discovers that the stories relate to one another, characters return, kinship is revealed, and destinies are intertwined. The composition alternates between narration, dialogue, diary notes, and letters.

Some themes in the novels recur. The first touches upon the atrocities committed by the Turks, and the innocent victims' suffering. A second theme depicts the national character of the Armenians and the Armenian nation, and a third history and politics. All these discourses are linked to the epideictic rhetorical genre, as they reinforce certain values and norms and thus indirectly renounce others.[17] A fourth theme belongs to the judicial genre since it sharply criticizes Turkey's (and Europe's) actions. In addition to these themes, others emerge when the novels are considered as a whole. Among other things, women's vulnerability appears to be an important theme, as it turns out that all the main female characters die. The small group of Armenians who in the very last chapter are headed for what at least looks like freedom consist of men and boys only.

The variation in narrative perspective is a key factor when discussing literature as addressed to an implied reader. But a text's ability to induce action in others depends on the reader as much as on the text itself. A text can only provide the prerequisites for action; for that action to become reality, it takes a meeting with a reader who is willing to listen, reconsider, and act upon it.[18] A text calls upon its readers in different ways, but of course it is not only text-internal factors that matter, but also material contexts. Butler discusses related issues as she emphasizes how frames 'seek to contain, convey, and determine what is seen'.[19] Norms and frames restrict the visions and attention of the one reading, and leave the reader to a greater or lesser extent ethically responsive in apprehending life as precarious and grievable.[20]

What are the frames that capture Nalbandiàn's novels? Do they facilitate or prevent the recognition of Armenian life and suffering? The author's good intentions do not necessarily mean that the frames have the desired effect. Butler emphasizes that such frames are politically saturated operations of power.[21] In the present context, the frames include the literary composition itself, the author's status, and the whole media context—its publication, translation, and reception.

Perspectives on a boy

The choice of narrative perspective is a crucial frame when it comes to the reader's perception of events and characters. Nalbandiàn alternates between first and third person narrative and between points of view in the different stories. While the many diary entries and letters give the reader the possibility to empathize and identify with the characters, this is counteracted by the novella structure, the reverse chronology, and the many disparate human destinies. For a Scandinavian reader, such a trivial thing as the many Armenian names can obstruct and create distance (and sometimes, to make it even more complicated, when a name reappears, it belongs to a different person than the first time). The ambivalent function of shifting perspectives is clearly seen in the story about the boy Karnig. He is one of the main characters in the work, since he returns in all three parts. He may not be one of the characters who take up the most space, but he happens to be related to several other characters, and therefore comes to be something of a focal point in the narrative web. Karnig is a young man who is midway between childhood and adulthood. The reader meets him for the first time in the Armenian hospital where he works. Then he is deported, but the reader remains unaware of what happens to him. Much later, we are told that he managed to escape death by hiding in a cave with some other refugees. At the end of the third book, he is saved from starvation and joins some other boys on their escape over the Russian border.

In the very short story 'Revenge', Karnig is talking to the younger boy Humajàk, telling him about the Armenian volunteers who fight in the Russian Eastern Army against the Turks. He is described entirely from the younger boy's hero-worshipping perspective. We get glimpses of his previous life, but the focus is on his 'proud and silent despair' at being confined to the hospital as a nurse, and on his longing for the 'brothers at the Russian Front'.[22]

Next time, Karnig is also depicted from an external perspective, this time through the gaze of the chief of the hospital, Garekin Effendi. Night has fallen, and Karnig stares at the sky where bombers are circling. The dialogue between them reveals that Karnig fought in the First Balkan War, on the Turkish side, and that he is guilt-ridden over the unspeakable actions there. Karnig appears as a frightened animal, uncertain, anxious, and wild-eyed.

After the deportation of the children from the hospital, the reader does not meet Karnig again until the very last story in the second book ('The Dripstone Cave'). This is a story about a group of starving and dying people who have sought shelter from their pursuers in a cave. Karnig feels responsible for the others, but the hunger and exhaustion are overwhelming: 'The fatigue makes him see flashing lights. The bayonet wound in his shoulder hurts. Sleep—Sleep!'[23] Here, for the first time, the narrative is told from Karnig's point of view, and the reader gets to meet his inner struggle. Equally important for the reader's view of Karnig is his encounter with the starving woman who finds her way to the cave with a child. She gets a few grains to chew on, and she tells him her story while Karnig holds the child in his arms. The roles become reversed here and Karnig is the adult, and the woman is a child. The next morning, both the woman and her son are dead, and the story ends with Karnig's words: 'Stepan ... Come and help me carry them out.'[24] These lines are a distillation of what war forces people to endure. The scene brings the reader closer to Karnig as everything is seen from Karnig's point of view. The fact that not everything has to be said to be understood strengthens the sense of presence. His sorrow becomes the sorrow of the reader.

In one of the last stories in the third book ('When Karnig came'), Karnig is found lying on a river beach by another boy. The boy takes him to a hut where he and some others are planning an escape. The dialogue between the two dominates the narrative, but the main intrigue is really something else. When the boy goes to fetch bread, he sees, 'as usual', corpses floating down the river.[25] But this time he recognizes one of them. It is Araksi, a girl who lived with her grandmother in the village. The reader has met her in several of the previous stories. She was an orphan, but had a brother who left home several years ago, and she still hoped to see him again. His name is Karnig. In this way, the story depicts a meeting that never happens, a meeting that comes too late, and creates an imagined gap in the narrative, emblematic of the kind of postponed reunions and lack of reunions that war causes.

How, then, does this frame, consisting of shifts and changes in narration and points of view, affect the reader's responsiveness? The different and sometimes contradictory images of the young man emphasize human's complex nature. He is the young, brave hero fighting for his country; he is the abused child forced to grow up all too fast; he is the chosen one; he is the silent soldier with dark secrets. The distant relationship between the reader and Karnig, which slowly develops into something else, mirrors the relation-ship between Scandinavian readers and the Armenians. It was not until 1917 that Scandinavian popular support for Armenia made heard of itself, through books, pamphlets, and manifestations— the protest meeting in Stockholm mentioned earlier was held that autumn. The composition and overall structure of Nalbandiàn's books—the many different destinies that the reader encounters and quickly leaves behind for yet more others—thus reflect the difficulty in apprehending the suffering of lives in another part of the world, and to see them as subjects, as individuals. In the beginning, Karnig is just one of many to be pitied, much like the characters that quickly pass by in a newspaper article. It is only as the reader continues reading that relationships appear and characters transform from abstractions into real human fates. The geographical and cultural distance from Armenian suffering can thus in time be overcome by a committed reading of the novels. The rapid and fluid narrative that creates distance is renegotiated over time, and suddenly the narrative becomes more consistent and familiar. Perhaps this is how literature, in Butler's words, can make us recognize the divergent lives of others as precarious and grievable. What is familiar is also grievable. In other words, the reading of Nalbandiàn's novels requires a perseverance much like that required for political commitment. In that way, the frame of narrative perspective can both approach and distance the Scandinavian reader in relation to Armenian lives.

To tell the truth – witness literature and fiction

There are several stories in the books that function the same way as Karnig's, but sometimes with a reversed chronology. This is seen, for example, when Dr Delacombe tells Garekin Effendi what happened when the young, promising doctor Haïk Hovsephian was abducted, put in prison, and eventually shot. The prelude to the abduction is related in the second book, which takes place in spring 1915. Most of the stories in this book are set in the city of Pera and the characters are urban and middle class. The abduction has already been described by Dr Delacombe in a letter in the first book: 'they are all gone, friends and colleagues, politicians, members of the National Assembly, editors, professors, all the "intellectuals": practically all have been deported or hanged or at best been shot in the dark deserts of Asia Minor; the patriarchate is closed, the newspapers withdrawn—'[26]

The instructive tone of this and similar passages must be attributed to the genre as such. This literature has a message; it is literature with a political purpose. In such genres, the imminent risk is that the political dimension overshadows the aesthetic, or, if you will, telling dominates over showing.[27] This way of writing can also be linked to the text's claims to truth, or at least to authenticity. The parallel to witness literature is illustrative. The historian Peter Englund has written about the difficulties of this genre; about the conflict between the literary and the testimony, between form and function. He calls witness literature a 'mongrel form of literature', for

> in spite of appearances, the genre is a difficult one, both in form and function. There are more failures than triumphs. The problem is that instead of a union of the best of two distinct literary worlds, we often get a union of the worst. The outcome functions neither as a source nor as literature. The requirements of veracity distort the literary form, while the literary form distorts the testimony. Auden wrote that every attempt to create something that could be at once beautiful and functional was doomed to fail, and this may even apply to witness literature.[28]

At the same time, the fragmented and disorganized is an effective counterweight to the tendentious and one-sided. Englund comments on the deformation that inevitably occurs when we make a narrative of the past: 'We gain, of course, coherence, totality, and flow but at the risk of forcing narrative and teleological unity on to something that in reality is diverse, confused, and contradictory. The very form of narrative tempts us to tidy things up.'[29] In his discussion of three testimonies from the First World War he points to the lack of concision and composition—it is not a linear story—as an indirect, 'truer' form. The same could be said of Nalbandiàn's work. Thus, fragmented and disordered, the aesthetic in itself might be a way of approaching the Armenian experience. It is a frame that, perhaps paradoxically, does not try to define or delimit, but rather to unclose; that makes double and partially incompatible demands on the reader, for it is for the reader to arrange and organize events and human fates, or to accept chaos and incoherence.

There are great similarities between the testimonies of Nalbandiàn's fictional characters and the testimonies of violence, abuse, and persecution in actual Scandinavian reports. The Swedish author Marika Stiernstedt quoted directly from the Bryce Report, which comprised of hundreds of documents on the deportations and described executions, rape, and drowning. The descriptions are often straightforward and brutal. Sexualized violence against women is mentioned, explicitly but briefly: 'The girls were almost without exception violated by the soldiers or their henchmen'; a woman has 'been left in the hands of ten officers, to their delight—"to be their sport"'.[30]

In comparison, the young boy Humajàk's account of the deportation of his family is given the same outer frame by Nalbandiàn, but the perspective is a child's and the descriptions more indirect:

> And so all the women were gathered in ox-wagons and taken to boats, which lay down by the river. And they screamed and wept. But the young and those who the Turks liked were put aside. And they were sold, all of them, and many of the children too. And the children, who had their mother sold to others, they were running around crying—[31]

It is as if the boy, with his personal involvement in the event, is unable to describe his family in an all too brutal or frank language. It is often said that direct and crude language arouses repugnance and disgust, but what if it is the other way around? Perhaps such language coarsens in a way that makes it harder to apprehend the victims as human beings? Are they deprived of their humanity and dignity in this way? Butler discusses the pornographic gaze fixed on pictures of torture and scenes of violence—an objectifying and dehumanizing gaze, which, in Butler's words, prevents us from becoming ethically responsive and instead makes the lives depicted inhumane and ultimately ungrievable.[32] Why should not verbal language function in a similar way? It is a parallel sign system, symbolic instead of iconic. If so, then Nalbandiàn's narrative style can be said to be an attempt to move away from the pornographic style of direct, crude, and matter-of-fact language use to one of greater tenderness and fluidity.

Furthermore, the power of the fictive testimony lies in its coherence—that the reader gets a brief but seemingly whole story, instead of disjointed fragments. Humajàk's story does not end when he is separated from his mother, but continues there and then, and again later as a story within the larger narrative. This extension in time allows the reader to establish a relationship with him, and he thereby becomes someone the reader in one way or another has to relate to.

Contexts – the writer's ethos, publication, and reception

Butler emphasizes that responsiveness is not 'a merely subjective state, but a way of responding to what is before us with the resources that are available to us.'[33] Following this argument, it is not surprising that the Scandinavian commitment to the Armenian cause was not that strong, as events in Turkey had to compete with the media reports on the First World War. Nalbandiàn's project can be seen as an attempt to break with certain frames. Or to use Butler's words, 'it is only by challenging the dominant media that certain kinds of lives may become visible or knowable in their precariousness.'[34] But to succeed, Nalbandiàn had to reach out to a broad audience, which is not the easiest task for a relatively anonymous author. Her personal connection to the subject will certainly have helped. Regarded as fictive testimony, the deliberative appeal is also strengthened by her personal involvement. She herself commented on the relation between fact and fiction in the preface to her first book: 'I must see with the eyes of others and feel with the hearts of others in order to depict the events, which are the most dreadful and unbelievable of all the irrevocable horrors caused by the world war. The events that have set the indelible mark of death on my own and my young children's lives.'[35]

In a later text she confirmed that several of her characters were based on real-life people, and on her husband's nieces and nephews who disappeared during the deportations. One of them was called Humajàk: 'And if it is our own little Humajàk—him or one of the many wandering, homeless, half-naked children who in the tracks of the deportations' train of death are picked up by merciful travellers now and then, searching for barleycorn in the dung of horses and mules…—that I do not know, and it does not matter.'[36] The quotation is from an open letter addressed to the women of Scandinavia, published in the Danish newspaper *Berlingske Tidende* in 1919. The exhortation is explicit: read my books as a testimony of what actually happened, read, react, and respond: 'And now in the eleventh hour, let the Scandinavian Women's Association help one another so that the light can again be lit deep in the dark eyes of the children'.[37] In other words, the fictive contract between reader and novel does not entirely apply. It can be seen as an attempt to challenge the medium and break the traditional frame of literary narrative. As will be discussed further on, the books' reception shows that they were, in fact, read and judged by somewhat different criteria than usual.

One frame that delimits and weakens the deliberative appeal is Nalbandiàn's relatively weak ethos and status as a writer. She could not take publication for granted. Judging from the fragmentary correspondence preserved, she hoped to get her manuscript published by Gyldendal, one of Denmark's largest and oldest publishing houses, with a good reputation. That is where she had made her début as a writer in 1905, with a collection of poems, *Bølgesang. Digte om Drøm och Liv* ('Billow Song. Poems on Dream and Life'). Her next book, *Børn* ('Children', 1913) was a kind of handbook for mothers in essay form, or 'studies in practical pedagogy' as one of the reviewers put it. Moreover, she had, from her home in Constantinople, reported on the political and cultural situation in Turkey for the Danish newspaper *Dagbladet*. In the autumn of 1914, she tried to convince the author and editor Peter Nansen to accept two manuscripts: a book she called 'Balkan—or short stories of war', and another book about children. She did not get the answer she wished for and wrote disappointedly that Nansen had now beheaded her twice in the most amiable way.[38] She tried again to invoke the letter of recommendation by the author and literary critic Wilhelm Østergaard, in which he emphasized the artistic qualities of her short stories.[39] Østergaard worked at Gyldendal and edited, among other things, the Gyldendal Library series (1899–1916). In February 1915, having revised the short stories, she made a new attempt to attract Nansen's interest, but without success. The short stories were not picked up by a publisher until 1918.[40] However, her other manuscript was finally accepted in 1915, with the title *Barndom. En Bog om Børn* ('Childhood. A book about children').

Without further research it will be difficult to determine why Gyldendal did not publish her three Armenian books. Instead, they were published by the relatively newly established Aschehoug Dansk Forlag A/S, a branch of the Norwegian H. Aschehoug & Co. The Norwegian publisher had been running a general bookshop and a publishing house since 1872, and had been in Denmark since 1908. The publishing house grew rapidly during the first decades of the twentieth century.[41] Nalbandiàn wrote in a late letter to Nansen that she did not even send her manuscript to Gyldendal at the time because Nansen was abroad. But considering the limited interest Nansen showed in her manuscript, other factors were probably involved. Nevertheless, Nansen's opinions and judgement continued to matter to Nalbandiàn. Two weeks before the publication of *Den Store Jammer*, she wrote to Nansen to ask him if he would reread her preface to the book: 'Is the language good? What is there to correct when it comes to language and content? Is something unclear? Something too political or too personal? Is there too little or is there too much?'[42] Her letters to Nansen reveal that she was struggling with her identity as a writer, but also that she had literary and political ambitions. She wanted to be recognized as an artist, but just as important, she wanted her writings to reach a wide audience and spur them to action.

There is an interesting tension between her difficulties in getting her books published and the books' subsequent reception and circulation. None other than Georg Brandes, Denmark's leading literary critic, remarked on the first book in an article in *Politiken*.[43] Now, Brandes was already involved in the Armenian question and was one of the founders of the aid organization Danske Armeniervenner (Danish Armenian Friends), and as early as 1900 he had written a long article on the atrocities Armenians had suffered in the 1890s. Brandes's article in *Politiken* is no regular review of Nalbandiàn's book, but rather an article that, prompted by the release of her book, seizes the opportunity to direct attention to the Armenian situation. But regardless, to be acknowledged by such an influential critic had significance. Brandes also wrote a foreword to one of the later editions, in which he praised the combination of artistry and politics: 'It looks reality in the eye, depicts the events as they were and are, without parading feeling or indignation.'[44] It is also worth noticing that by May, when Brandes's article was printed, the book had already run to five editions, which gives an indication of the demand. Several translations were already underway, and the book was soon published in Swedish, French, and Dutch. *Berlingske Tidende*, one of Denmark's largest newspapers, did a feature story on Nalbandiàn, remarking that the many editions were a sign of the public's interest in the cause 'and that it is treated in a way that makes it appeal'.[45]

Finally, to broaden the perspective, I will look at the Scandinavian reception of the books by examining some of the literary reviews in Swedish newspapers. Nalbandiàn's first book was reviewed in several of the major Swedish newspapers. On Christmas Eve 1917, the Social Democrat Anna Lindhagen—also committed to the Armenian question—wrote a detailed review of the first two books in the conservative *Svenska Dagbladet*.[46] The review is rather conventional. It largely consists of a plot summary, and the judgement is altogether positive. Lindhagen adopts what might be called a functionalist perspective on literature, and suggests that anyone who considers it a duty to find out what is happening in Armenia should read these books. But she also emphasizes what is characteristic about literature: it can teach us in a much more efficient way than the reports available, since it can give us insight into the hearts of the Armenian martyrs. The review's aesthetic arguments are sketchy, but she praises the lack of sensation, and highlights the mildness of the stories.

Reading between the lines in Lindhagen's review, we see a hope that readers' compassion will be transformed into political action. The same idea is found in her review in the social-democratic women's magazine *Morgonbris*, but there she focuses on actual events and on the importance of the outside world finding out what was going on.[47] Something similar is seen in the unsigned review in the liberal *Dagens Nyheter*, albeit from a different perspective. While Lindhagen argues that the death toll is even greater than what is being said, this critic objects: 'it may be doubted that the extermination of the Armenian race is so complete as Inga Nalbandiàn fears and thinks. But undoubtedly, this people's history of suffering during the First World War marks one of its most horrible chapters. Unspeakable atrocities, a whole singular culture devastated; that is the content of this book written in tears.'[48] Also in the long, largely positive review in the conservative *Stockholms Dagblad*, a large section is devoted partly to the background and reasons for the conflict, partly to political debate. Turkey's attacks are not excused; however, the reviewer objects to Nalbandiàn's way of portraying Germany's role in the conflict. And as for the book's intention, as understood by the reviewer, 'to arouse the readers pity and interest for the unfortunate Armenian people … the author has succeeded admirably.'[49] The most detailed literary judgement is found in the conservative *Lunds Dagblad*. Like the other critics, Vilhelm Buhre discusses the political situation and Nalbandiàn's personal ties with Armenia, but he also emphasizes that this is a book of 'high poetic value': it is well composed, has a graceful style, and is narrated vividly but without excess.[50]

It becomes clear, having examined the reception of the books, that the critics' judgements were based on somewhat different criteria than were usually applied to fiction. At times, critics confused literary or aesthetic value with subject matter. Elsewhere, aesthetics were suppressed, or a book was said to be worth reading despite its compositional shortcomings because of its important topic. The latter is evident in several of the critics' detailed accounts of Armenian history and their discussion of the current political situation. The addressivity is all about enlightenment and compassion. Although the critics' judgement is a frame that partly reduces a text's aesthetics, it is not just a restricting frame, because at the same time they place the book in a wider context with political implications. The critics emphasize literature as part of a larger media system, attempting to influence and change the society it is a part of. The judgements on a book clearly point to the complicated relationship between aesthetics and politics, and the fact that the myth of the non-political or purely aesthetic text is definitely not valorized here. Instead, the reviewers' various responses show that the frame of politics and the frame of aesthetics are inseparable and contingent. In this case, it is as if the political anticipates the aesthetic and influences its expression.

Conclusion

In this chapter I have discussed how literature, together with the frames that determine its interpretation and circulation, can create ethical and political opposition to the losses of war. The challenge, according to Butler, is to make the lives of others human and grievable. But there are also frames that inhibit and delimit. The first frame discussed here is an enabling frame and has to do with narrative perspective. The reader's possible identification with the Armenians is strengthened when characters are described from a first-person perspective. It is as if the reader, by adopting the same point of view, almost becomes one with the character in question. The second frame has to do with the composition and overall structure of the three books. On the one hand, the fragmentary structure forces the reader to a greater degree of co-creation; yet on the other, the reader risks losing interest if there are too many sketchy characters and disparate plots, especially since the text is not aesthetically very interesting. The third enabling frame is connected to genre, to the texts' closeness to witness literature, and the claim to authenticity. Nalbandiàn's texts are given a special charge by the fact that they were written by someone who 'had been there'. This is evident in several reviews, where the books are characterized as a moving testimony. The fourth frame both opens and forecloses, and is also related to genre, particularly the texts' informative and instructive features. It reveals a will on the author's part to teach the ignorant Scandinavians. This frame alienates the text from the literary genre and brings it closer to the many pamphlets and reports on Armenia written at the time. The determination to provide knowledge creates credibility, but weakens the literary form. At the same time, knowledge of what is happening is the first step towards action.

Concerning the fifth and final frame, the publishing context, there are several different factors that work in both directions. The fact that Nalbandiàn was not an established author is a disadvantage, as is the fact that a small, relatively unknown publishing house published the first two Swedish translations. Neither did the Swedish newspapers' most important critics review her work. The enabling frames are the many editions and translations, and Georg Brandes's positive judgement of her work.

The textual analysis reveals the author's address to a relatively ignorant Scandinavian audience that through reading will be brought to knowledge, compassion, and commitment. However, the somewhat challenging composition requires a persevering reader. This fact, combined with the analysis of publishing context and reception, suggests that the books reached out on a relatively broad spectrum, but that they probably mainly attracted the attention of people already committed to the peace movement and human rights issues. Nalbandiàn's books on Armenia were above all noticed by a Scandinavian movement that brought together war critics and pacifists—the likes of Georg Brandes, Anna Lindhagen, and Marika Stiernstedt.

Finally, Nalbandiàn's books on Armenia can also have forward-looking function. At the end of the review in *Morgonbris*, Anna Lindhagen downplays her belief in what this type of literature is capable of. Instead, she suggests that this literature is written as much for future generations as for contemporaries:

> It is expensive to buy books. However, let us agree to buy this book together, for perhaps, by bravely keeping in our hearts the consciousness of the terrible things that have happened, then we can in some small degree hope to alleviate the pain of grief. Maybe thoughts perhaps might reach their mark. And if they cannot, still one day it will be good for the survivors to know that the world that could not help nevertheless suffered with them.[51]

Thus, literature can act as a kind of memory, as a way to preventing all the lives lost from drowning in the sea of oblivion. And if the books cannot be proven to have made life grievable, to have reduced the distance between people, it can at least be shown, be it here in this chapter or in the enduring testimonies, that they can serve to reduce the gap in time between what was then and what is now.

Notes

1 Translations are mine if not otherwise indicated. 'Snart var Verden eet gabende Saar, | De To blev Tusinder. Dag blev Aar. | Men du glemmer dem aldrig – de *første* To, | som bares i Land ved Galata Bro.' From the poem 'The First Wounded', Inga Nalbandiàn, *Dønninger* (Copenhagen: Aschehoug & Co., 1919), 23.

2 Judith Butler, *Frames of War. When is Life Grievable?* (2009; London: Verso, 2010), 21.

3 Butler 2010, 79.

4 Ibid. 63–4.

5 Ibid. 13.

6 The following is largely based on Kristian Gerner & Klas-Göran Karlsson, *Folkmordens historia. Perspektiv på det moderna samhällets skuggsida* (Stockholm: Atlantis, 2005).

7 The international research on the Armenian Genocide is extensive. A selection: Vahakn Dadrian, *The History of the Armenian Genocide. Ethnic Conflict from the Balkans to Anatolia to the Caucasus* (Providence, RI: Berghahn Books, 1995); Tancer Akcam, *A Shameful Act. The Armenian Genocide and the Question of Turkish Responsibility* (New York: Metropolitan Books, 2006); Richard Hovannisian (ed.), *The Armenian Genocide in Perspective*, (New Brunswick, NJ: Transaction Books, 1986); Richard Hovannisian (ed.), *The Armenian Genocide. History, Politics, Ethics* (Houndmills: Palgrave, 1992).

8 Gerner & Karlsson 2005, 128.

9 For a discussion of the Armenian Genocide as the archetypal genocide, see Gerner & Karlsson 2005, 134–5.

10 Gerner & Karlsson 2005, 137; Erik Lindberg, 'Svensk armenienpolitik', in Göran Gunner & Erik Lindberg (eds.), *Längtan till Ararat. En bok om armenisk identitet* (Religionshistoriska studier, 1; Gothenburg: Gothia, 1985), 273.

11 Alma Johansson, *Ett folk i landsflykt. Ett år ur armeniernas historia* (Kvinnliga missionsarbetare, 1; Stockholm, 1930); *Armeniskt flyktingliv* (Kvinnliga missionsarbetare, 2; Stockholm, 1931); Maria Jacobsen, *Diaries of a Danish Missionary. Harpoot 1907–1919* (London: Gomidas Institute, 2001); Amalia Lange, *Ett blad ur Armeniens historia. Danska K.M.A. 1910–1920* (Stockholm: Kvinnliga missions arbetare, 1920); see also Maria Småberg,

'Witnessing the Unbearable. Alma Johansson and the Massacres of the Armenians 1915', in Karin Aggestam & Annika Björkdahl (eds.), *War and Peace in Transition. Changing Roles of External Actors* (Lund: Nordic Academic Press, 2009).

12 Matthias Bjørnlund, 'When the Cannons Talk, the Diplomats Must be Silent. A Danish Diplomat during the Armenian Genocide', *Genocide Studies and Prevention*, 1/2 (2006), 197–224; see also Bjørnlund, '"Et folk myrdes". Det Armenske folkemord i Danske kilder', MA diss. (Copenhagen University, 2005).

13 Vahagn Avedian, 'The Armenian Genocide 1915. From a Neutral Small State's Perspective: Sweden, MA thesis, Department of History, Uppsala University, 2008, 39, available at <http://www.armenica.org/material/master_thesis_vahagn_avedian.pdf>.

14 Lindberg 1985, 268. For Scandinavian commitment in Armenia, see also Helle Schøler Kjær, *1915: Danske vidner til Det Armenske Folkemord. Maria Jacobsen, Karen Jeppe, Carl Ellis Wandel* (Copenhagen: Vandkusten, 2010); Göran Gunner, *Folkmordet på armenier – sett med svenska ögon* (Skellefteå: Artos, 2012); Svante Lundgren, *I svärdets tid. Det osmanska folkmordet på kristna minoriteter* (Otalampi: Sahlgren), 2010.

15 Marika Stiernstedt, *Armeniernas fruktansvärda läge* (Stockholm: Svenska Andelsförlaget, 1917); see also Sofi Qvarnström, *Motståndets berättelser. Elin Wägner, Anna Lenah Elgström, Marika Stiernstedt och första världskriget* (Skrifter utgivna av Avdelningen för litteratursociologi vid Uppsala universitet, 58; Hedemora/Möklinta: Gidlund, 2009), 267–8, 324–5.

16 Britt Sturve, Reidar Sunnerstam & Ebon Sönnergren, 'Armenienfrågan i svensk press under första världskriget', in Gunner & Lindberg 1985.

17 Chaïm Perelman & Lucie Olbrechts-Tyteca, *La nouvelle rhétorique. Traité de l'argumentation* (Paris: PUF, 1958).

18 Qvarnström 2009, 353.

19 Butler 2010, 10.

20 Ibid. 12.

21 Ibid. 1.

22 Inga Nalbandiàn, *In i natten. Bilder från Armeniens undergång* (Stockholm: Hjalmar Lundberg & Gösta Olzon, 1917), 71 & 73. All quotations are my translations from the Swedish translations.

23 Inga Nalbandiàn, *Bakom förlåten* (Stockholm: Svenska förlaget, 1918), 153, 'Det gnistrar för ögonen på honom av matthet. Det gör ont i bajonettsåret i skuldran. Sova – sova!'

24 Nalbandiàn 1918, 160, 'Stepan … Kom och hjälp mig att bära ut dem.'

25 Inga Nalbandiàn, *Det vita fältet* (Lund: Gleerups, 1919).

26 Nalbandiàn 1917, 77, 'de äro borta allesammans, vännerna och arbetskamraterna, politikerna, medlemmarne af nationalförsamlingen, redaktörerna,

professorerna, alla 'de intellektuella': så godt som alla ha deporterats eller hängts eller i bästa fall skjutits inne i Mindre Asiens mörka ödemarker; patriarkatet är stängdt, tidningarna indragna –'.

27 Wayne C. Booth, *The Rhetoric of Fiction* (1961; 2nd edn., Harmondsworth: Penguin, 1983).

28 Peter Englund, 'The Bedazzled Gaze: On Perspective and Paradoxes in Witness Literature', in Horace Engdahl (ed.), *Witness Literature: Proceedings of the Nobel Centennial Symposium* (River Edge, NJ: World Scientific, 2002), 52.

29 Ibid. 51.

30 Stiernstedt 1917, 36 & 35, 'Flickorna blevo (på vägen) så gott som utan undantag våldförda av soldaterna eller deras hantlangare'; 'lämnats i händerna på tio officerare, till deras förnöjelse – "to be their sport"'.

31 Nalbandiàn 1917, 50, 'Och så blefvo alla kvinnorna samlade i oxvagnar och körda till båtar, som lågo nere på floden. Och de skreko och gräto. Men de unga och de, som turkarne tyckte om, de fördes för sig själfva. Och de såldes allesammans och många af barnen såldes också. Och de barn, som fått sin mor såld till andra, de sprungo omkring och gräto –'

32 See Butler 2010, ch. 2, 'Torture and the Ethics of Photography: Thinking with Sontag'.

33 Ibid. 50.

34 Ibid. 51.

35 Nalbandiàn 1917, foreword, 'Jag måste se med andras ögon och känna med andras hjärtan för att kunna skildra de tilldragelser, som äro det förskräckligaste och det otroligaste af allt obotligt, som världskriget vållat. De tilldragelser, som satt dödens outplånliga spår i mitt eget och mina små barns lif.'

36 Inga Nalbandiàn, 'Aabent Brev til Skandinaviens Kvinder!', reprinted in *Berlingske Tidende*, 1 February 1919, 'Og om det er vor egen, lille Humajàk – den eller den af de vildfarne, hjemløse, halvnøgne Børn, der i Sporene af Deportationernes Dødstog nu og da opsamles af barmhjertige Rejsende, søgende efter Bygkorn i Hestenes og Muldyrenes Ekskrementer ... – jag véd det ikke, og det spiller ingen Rolle.'

37 Nalbandiàn, 'Aabent Brev', 1919, 'Og lad nu i den 11t Time skandinaviske Kvindeforeninger hjælpe hinanden til, at Lyset igen kan tændes dybt inde i de mørke Barneøjne'.

38 Det Kongelige Bibliotek, Copenhagen (DKB), Gyldendal B4a, letter from Inga Nalbandiàn to Peter Nansen, 22 September 1914.

39 DKB, Gyldendal B4a, Vilhelm Østergaard to Inga Nalbandiàn, 15 September 1914, a letter held in Peter Nansen's collection of letters.

40 Inga Nalbandiàn, *Balkan-noveller. Tyrkiske typer* (Copenhagen: Aschehoug & Co., 1918).

41 *H. Aschehoug & Co.s Forlag 1872–1922. Jubilæumskatalog*, (Kristiania: Aschehoug & Co., 1922). The focus of their publication was scientific literature, particularly language and cultural history, and fiction, both Danish and translations.

42 DKB, NKS 4043, 4, Inga Nalbandiàn to Peter Nansen, 24 February 1917.

43 Georg Brandes, 'Armenierne. Kronik', *Politiken*, 15 May 1917.

44 Quotation from the back of Nalbandiàn's second book in the series, *De Hjemsøgte* 1917, 'Den ser Virkeligheden under Øjne, skildrer gribende, uden at lægge hverken Følsomhed eller Indignation for Dagen, Forholdene som de var og er.'

45 'Et Dameportræt hver Uge', *Berlingske Tidende*, 22 April 1917.

46 Anna Lindhagen, 'Armeniernas undergång. En dansk-armeniskas berättelser', *Svenska Dagbladet*, 24 December 1917. Lindhagen was a leading member of the Swedish section of the Women's International League for Peace and Freedom (WILPF), which published a call to aid the Armenian people in the Christian newspaper *Svenska Morgonbladet* in February 1919. Lindhagen was also in contact with the Turkish diplomat in Stockholm, Galib Kemali Bey, concerning a planned protest meeting organized by the Norwegian and Swedish Women's Association; however, the protest seems not to have taken place (Stockholm City Archive, Anna Lindhagens arkiv, Anna Lindhagen to Galib Kemali Bey (n.d.) and Galib Kemali Bey to Anna Lindhagen, 22 May 1922.

47 Anna Lindhagen, 'Litteratur', *Morgonbris*, 1917, 11.

48 'In i natten', *Dagens Nyheter*, 10 December 1917.

49 Lt–s, 'In i natten. Ett nödrop från Armenien', *Stockholms Dagblad*, 21 October 1917.

50 Vilhelm Buhre, 'Litteratur', *Lunds Dagblad*, 26 October 1917.

51 Lindhagen 1917, 11, 'Det är dyrt att köpa böcker. Men kom dock överens att köpa denna bok tillsammans, ty kanske ändå genom att modigt hålla medvetandet av det förfärliga som skett vaket i våra hjärtan, så kunna vi hoppas att i någon liten mån mildra sorgens sveda. Måhända kunna kanske tankar gå fram. Och om ej de kunna det, skall det dock för de överlevande en gång bliva gott att veta att den värld, som icke kunde hjälpa, dock led med dem.'

CHAPTER 7

The call of the blood

Scandinavia and the First World War
as a clash of races

Lina Sturfelt

Is it not of real importance that the 11 million Scandinavian
Teutons have found one another and decided to stand together
as one in the great global struggle between Slavs, Romans, Anglo-
Saxon Teutons, and Germanic Teutons?[1]

In scholarly and popular historiography the First World War is
often pictured as a clash of nations. Nationalism, ideas of national
sovereignty, and the right to self-determination are seen as the ra-
tionale of the conflict in terms of both origins and outcome. Conversely, Stephan Audoin-Rouzeau and Annette Becker argue that
to better understand the meaning of the war to its contemporaries,
we should see it as a perceived war of civilization(s), an absolute,
binary 'crusade' of eschatological dimensions.[2] Daniel Pick likewise
claims that it is hard to underestimate the notion of 'civilization'
as a cultural key to the war.[3] To him, 'The First World War was
justified and rationalized as a fundamental conflict, a historically
and anthropologically inevitable struggle between two inalienably
different forces'.[4] Aggression on the part of the enemy was seen as
innate and due to racial instincts. On a deep level, the defensive
war of civilization was thus imagined as a clash of races: of Teuton
and Slav, of Teuton and Latin/Celtic, of European (white) and non-
European (yellow/black), and finally of the European elite and the
racially inferior lower classes. These seemingly different conceptions

of race intersected in a complicated web of meaning. According to Frank Füredi, the First World War was represented as both an internal and an external racial battle. To contemporaries, the racial factor was also to count for the war's extreme and unexpected brutality. In the general understanding of history as a racial struggle, conflict was pictured as a zero-sum game, and success for one race must thus mean the total subjection or even annihilation of the other.[5]

For a century prior to the outbreak of war in 1914, race had been a central social motif for the Western world. The Europeans expressed their world in the language of race. The domination of the world by the West was seen as a proof of white racial superiority. Race was a significant element in the composition of Western identity, and shaped the definition of Western culture. At the turn of the twentieth century, race was believed to explain the character of individuals, the structure of social communities, and the fate of human societies. The sense of race was central to the prevailing Social Darwinist outlook and biological explanations of social phenomena. Typologies of race, class, and gender were virtually interchangeable in the discussion of social inferiority, often linked to ideas of a special national destiny. In racial thinking, the revulsion at the 'inferior' European classes and at non-European races could not be told apart.[6] In a similar way, the category of race was virtually inseparable from and intimately interrelated to images and ideas of gender. For example, 'inferior' races and classes were feminized and equated to Western women.[7]

Scandinavia was no exception, as witnessed by the quotation above about a special Nordic or Scandinavian racial solidarity, taken from the Swedish weekly magazine *Hvar 8 dag* in 1915. Culturally speaking, Sweden, Norway, and Denmark belonged to the Western hemisphere, to a common European community where ideas of a civilizing mission, white racial superiority, and colonial domination were taken for granted. Even if Sweden and Norway did not have much of an imperialist record, colonial and racist discourses were prevalent in all three countries. Within the European community, Sweden and Denmark both had a history of a strong cultural affinity with Germany, even if the Danish defeat and territorial losses of 1864 had made Danish–German relations more strained. Norway, on the other hand, was generally more oriented towards Great Britain.

These different affinities were both emphasized and challenged by the First World War. At the outbreak of war in August 1914, the three Scandinavian countries issued similar declarations of neutrality and they all managed to stay out of the conflict. But the emotional and discursive battles were nevertheless intense and often infused with ideas of race. For example, Sweden's so-called *aktivister* (activists), who pressed for Sweden to enter the war to help its Germanic counterpart fight the Russians, saw the conflict as a racial contest, a struggle for the survival of Western civilization against the threatening, barbaric Asiatic East.[8] It would be a mistake, however, to consign ideas of a racial war to the militarist, conservative, and pro-German wing alone. Rather, a racialized interpretation of all things national was part of a much wider Scandinavian discourse—after all, eugenic and racist ideas and practices had struck a popular chord in all Scandinavian countries by the time of war. The existence of a racial hierarchy topped by a biological and culturally defined Nordic (or Germanic) 'master race' with its contemporary core in Scandinavia was widely taken for granted.[9] Racial thinking bridged the Left–Right divide as well as the pacifist–militarist divide in both Sweden and Norway, and was commonplace in the pro-Entente and pro-German camps alike.[10]

The aim of this chapter is thus twofold. The first part is an attempt to examine and locate the meaning of race and racial war within the historical context of the First World War by discussing the international historiography of the war as a race war. The second part is a case study in which I analyse the themes of the war as a clash of races and 'the sense of race' from a Scandinavian—and primarily Swedish—perspective by surveying the Swedish popular press of 1914 to 1919.

The meaning of race

Today—in sharp contrast to the period considered here—biological explanations of race are no longer valid, and the common scholarly position is to view race as a social construct. Seen as a social category, race is a complex and amorphous concept that has been repeatedly recast and reformulated in different contexts over a long period of time. As Kenan Malik points out, race cannot be reduced to a single property or relationship, but is better understood as a 'medium' through which the changing relationship between humanity, society, and Nature has been socially and historically constructed.[11] To analyse the Scandinavian meanings of race in the historical context of the First World War, it is necessary to broaden the understanding beyond both the narrow Nazi ambit and its contemporaneous association with colour. It is essential to acknowledge that the modern discourse of race also partly developed through the racialization of social differences *within* Europe. Racial theories accounted for these social inequalities by attributing them to nature. According to Malik, the construction of non-Europeans as inferior races was but an extension of already existing views on the lower classes at home. In this he diverges from the post-colonial and Orientalist tradition associated with Edward W. Said, where the origins of race and racism are intimately connected to imperialism, European conquest, and the construction of the colonial Other.[12] Perhaps more accurately, Pick speaks of a dialectical, interconnected process where the European elites proclaimed their racial superiority to non-European peoples and simultaneously revealed the inferiority of the masses within their own nations: 'The 'other' was outside and inside.'[13] At the turn of the century, race gradually became more associated with colour, and at same time racial thinking became part of popular culture, as evident from the burgeoning mass press and entertainment industry.[14]

Thus on the eve of the First World War the concept of race could and did refer to many different social categories. Distinctions between perceived social, biological, and cultural entities were constantly blurred. Differences between individuals and groups were naturalized and racially encoded. Not only were the colonial peoples categorized and differentiated according to racial hierarchies and evolutionary standards, so were the Europeans. This did of course become more evident during the Second World War, when the Nazis—to whom Europe was a racial rather than a geographical entity—tried to recast the entire Continent as a new racial order, with terrible results.[15] But the same kinds of ideas—that some European nationalities, ethnicities, or races were superior and civilized and others inferior and barbaric—also permeated the conflict of 1914–18 and its aftermath.[16] In conflict, racial awareness was heightened, as was the focus on physical and cultural borders, defining the 'insider' and the 'outsider'. For example, Vejas Gabriel Liulevicius has convincingly shown how German images and conceptions of the East and its peoples were increasingly radicalized and racialized under the impact of the war experience: the occupied lands and peoples of the East were mentally transformed into alien races and strange spaces, which the Germans had to colonize and civilize.[17]

The First World War as a race war

The war generally reinforced pre-existing racial sentiment. Pick shows how race formed a language of war with which the atrocities and violence could be negotiated and explained. Audoin-Rouzeau and Becker talk of a 'war culture' in which the general desire to exterminate the enemy and his culture stemmed from the overwhelming conviction of belonging to a superior civilization. Social Darwinism and racism underpinned popular representations of the conflict. It also permeated wartime propaganda and rhetoric on both sides. The Allies frequently paralleled German atrocities in Belgium and northern France to the Armenian Genocide of 1915, referring to 'Muslim methods', and thus implicitly likening the Germans to barbarians and non-Christians. In French propaganda, ideas of special racial traits such as particular bodily odours or hairiness dehumanized the enemy and shaped the image of the war as a crusade against barbarous or even animalistic Germans.[18]

Differences between the French and the Germans were drawn from a biological standpoint, as race was identified with nation. In France, German culture was said to be at the same level as half-savage tribes in Congo. The German race was degenerate to begin with, and during the war it had regressed to the level of 'inferior people'. French writers and scholars deemed the German civilizing process to be superficial. The war had revealed the ancestral barbarism in the German race and unleashed its racial hatred. Atrocities were interpreted as signs of barbarity and the instincts

of race. Underneath their veneer of civilization and modernization, the Germans had remained biologically different—an inferior race. The enemy was thus hereditary and permanent; he could
not change or amend, but must be punished and kept in place
forever.[19]

British propaganda also stressed the degeneration and deterioration of the Germans, but more frequently blamed the Prussian
influence. The Prussians were deemed the betrayers of the 'real'
Germany, an alien race of Slavic origin within the German nation.
The brutality and ruthlessness of the Germans were down to their
Slavic blood, to an Eastern, even Asiatic, atavism and barbarity,
best captured in the common concept of 'the Hun'.[20]

The German propaganda, on the other hand, frequently accused Great Britain of treacherous miscegenation by forging alliances with the black and yellow races, polluting the purity of the
Continent, and blurring the lines of division between European
and non-European. The Germans protested about prisoners being
held in French colonies in Africa, arguing that it was inhuman and
degrading to be guarded by 'negroes' and fanatic Arabs debasing
Christians. But above all, the Germans focused on the deployment
of colonial troops on European battlefields. The African and Asian
soldiers were a recurring focal point in wartime German polemics on barbarism, civilization, culture, and race. In October 1914,
German scholars addressed an 'Aufruf an die Kulturwelt' ('Appeal
to the civilized world')—with the neutral parties especially in
mind—where they turned the accusations of barbarism against the
Allies. Using racial arguments they pictured the conflict as a fratricidal war, a European civil war. The troops of colour were seen as a
cause of depravity in war, and they were accused of especially cruel
and barbarous warfare, even cannibalism.[21]

A related German argument was to accuse the British of blurring
the line between superior and inferior Europe by their unholy alliance with barbarous Russia, instead of forming a true Anglo-Saxon
union. The Anglo-Russian alliance was especially demeaning to the
Germans, since in the German imagination the war was primarily
seen as a defensive struggle against the East, a great racial conflict between Teutonic and Slavic. The racial argument—especially

ideas of a superior Nordic 'master race' and white supremacy—was central in the German propaganda that attacked the neutrals, particularly the US. As Pick notices, the perception of the inferiority and separateness of the Slavs was shared by the British, Americans, and Germans alike.[22] In imagination at least, they were all fighting on the Eastern Front, trying to define the outer borders of Europe and Western civilization and debasing the enemy to non-Europeans.

Pick, Audoin-Rouzeau and Becker, and others demonstrate how widespread and common racial arguments were in all the main Western belligerent countries during the war—by no means was 'race' a marginal or exclusively German concept—and illustrate how notions of race and civilization were applied to both Europe and its colonies, and were discursively woven together in the construction of the self and the Other. Since all underline the importance of wartime violence and propaganda for spurring on this racist, binary thinking, the question is how their findings correspond to the Scandinavian context of neutrality and non-participation.

In wartime, the cultural meanings and implications of neutrality and its relation to national and racial identities became vital.[23] In the Social Darwinist thinking of the day, war was the antidote to decadence, unfitness, and degeneracy; a cure for both national and individual lethargy and degeneration. It was to alter the physical and moral emasculation produced by modernization and 'over-civilization'. War was a test of racial virility and 'the right to live'. It was an illustration of the natural selection of 'the survival of the fittest'. Peace and neutrality were subsequently associated with cultural castration, national sterility, and feminine passivity. But under the impact of the mass slaughter of the First World War, it became more common to speak of the relation between war and racial fitness and survival in negative terms. There was a racial dimension to the famous trope of the 'Lost Generation'. In interwar racial thinking, war was increasingly seen as a racial catastrophe, killing off the nation's noblest, manliest specimens, while the racially unfit and degenerate—the chronically ill, handicapped, criminals, neurasthenics, deserters, and the like—survived and were left to breed uncontrollably.[24]

Race, war, and neutrality
– the Swedish popular press 1914–19

Most international literature on race and the First World War focuses on either the intellectual and academic discourse or on state-sanctioned propaganda. When it comes to the Swedish historiography of race there is still a lack of research on popular racial discourses.[25] Regarding Sweden's First World War experience, Claes Ahlund has examined popular conceptions of different ethnicities and nationalities in the war novels by Radscha (Iwan Aminoff), a prolific Swedish writer of popular literature. Evidently, ethnicity was an important element in portraying the different parties. The colonial soldiers in particular were repeatedly pictured according to very crude racist stereotypes.[26] According to Sofi Qvarnström, racist images and ideas were also prevalent in the Swedish anti-war literature and press.[27]

To discuss some illustrative examples of how race was articulated and imagined in relation to the war in the case of neutral Sweden, I will turn to another popular context: the contemporary popular press, notably the weekly magazines *Allers Familj-Journal* (*Allers*), *Hvar 8 dag* (*H8D*), *Idun*, and *Vecko-Journalen* (*VJ*) for the years 1914–19.[28] The mass-circulation popular press's extensive war coverage offers a window on how race and racial war were imagined and represented on a more everyday basis in wartime Sweden.[29] Unfortunately, I have not had the opportunity to examine similar weekly magazines in Denmark and Norway, but when possible I will compare my findings from the Swedish sources with literature on the other Scandinavian countries. My intention here is to tentatively point to some trends that might stimulate further discussions and research on the subject. I will analyse the problematic of race from different angles, further testifying to the ambivalence and ambiguity of the concept in this period.

Troops of colour and the yellow peril

In the popular press, the existence of distinct human races and racial differences was taken for granted. So was the idea of a racial hierarchy between European and non-European on the one hand, and between North European (Nordic) and East/South European on the other, based on notions of evolutionary progress and standards of civilization. Notable, though, is the fact that 'the Jew' did not figure prominently in the racial imagination of the Swedish popular press considered here.[30]

As noted earlier, the Allies' deployment of troops of colour on European soil heightened racial awareness and fears in the belligerent countries. In the Swedish popular press, meanwhile, the colonial troops were considered more a curiosity or an amusement than a racial threat. Several picture reports of these 'picturesque troops' were published, usually focusing on their exotic uniforms or weapons. The descriptions stick to well-established racist and colonial stereotypes. Indigenous Canadian soldiers are thus presented as 'a couple of redskins' with feathers in their hair, and Indian soldiers were captured riding camels.[31] A half-naked, African soldier is labelled a 'man-eater' and a 'nigger' in a short notice about German accusations of him belonging to a cannibal tribe.[32] Even if the magazine dismissed the cannibal story as propagandistic and possibly fake, at the same time it still fed on and entrenched widespread popular atrocity stories about the inhuman battlefield behaviour of colonial soldiers.[33]

The colonial soldiers were commonly referred to as 'barbaric ', 'primitive', 'savage' and 'wild'. The Indians are cruel and display a special 'Asian savagery', to quote *Allers* in 1915.[34] They were also infantilized, as the magazines stated they do not really understand what they are fighting for. But in contrast to the Africans, the 'higher-standing' Indians were at the same time considered beautiful, brave, and excellent soldiers.[35] Time and again, big losses on the colonial front were said to be expendable, since there was enough 'human material' in Africa and Asia anyway.[36] This might be seen as a reflection of the common idea of the higher fertility of the coloured races and the subsequently declining white race. It also implies that colonial lives counted for less than European ones.

At other times, the trope of the noble savage is used, as in a review in *Idun* where the death of an African soldier serves to highlight the breakdown of the European order: 'Of the sketches from the prisoner-of-war camp, easily the best is the dying Negro, whose helpless alienation and silent heroism the author captures in a couple of pages … You do not forget this sharp but completely unbiased picture of the supposed barbarian, with all his true inner culture, against the backdrop of the barbaric civilization of the rich, the bankruptcy of European humanity.'[37] This perceived breakdown of Western civilization and the war's blurring of lines between civilized and barbarian, European and non-European, was a general theme frequently elaborated on in the popular press.[38] Fears of racial decline and a changing global balance in favour of the (Far) East were also found in the contemporary Swedish war discourse, as the rising power of Japan and 'the new yellow peril' gained attention.[39] In 1918, *Vecko-Journalen* warned that the war had exposed the weakness of the West and enabled other races to 'cut their teeth'.[40] While the white man was about to exterminate himself, the yellow man lurked in the shadows, supplying him with weapons for his own extinction, *Allers* cautioned in 1916: 'How the Jap must feel his heart swell with pride and secret joy as he watches his born rival play into his hands'.[41] Once Europe was totally devastated by the war, the peoples of East Asia would take over their leading role.[42] Like Füredi, I would say the war shattered European racial confidence and heightened the sense of a threat from without. In contrast to the Swedish press reports from the Russo-Japanese war of 1905, there were no positive images of the Japanese expansion to be found in the First World War material.[43] The fear of an expanding Japan and the threat of the advancing 'yellow race' were also frequent themes in Danish war literature.[44]

The Teutons struggle for existence

Like the belligerent countries, the Swedish press represented the conflict as a clash of races and civilizations, a Social Darwinist struggle for existence of gigantic and sometimes apocalyptic magnitude. As *Vecko-Journalen* solemnly stated at the outbreak of war: 'The first of August was to be the doomsday of Europe when … the Teutons' struggle for existence began.'[45] Another example, cited at the very beginning of this chapter, was when *Hvar 8 dag* discussed the mutual

Scandinavian interest of neutrality in terms of a 'Nordic' racial community in 'the great global struggle'.[46] In an additional war column, the same magazine called the war a 'release of tensions of historical dimensions' between two incompatible opponents and hereditarily predestined adversaries, Russia and Germany.[47]

When constructing a Swedish identity in racial terms, the Swedes were firmly placed in the Germanic 'family'. Metaphors of kin were frequent: the Germans were 'our admirable kinsmen', 'noble kinsfolk', or 'this host of a million heroes … that … dams up the flood of real barbarians, who are eager to launch themselves on Europe and its culture … and thus secure for all us Teutons space to live in according to our innermost nature and essence'.[48] In a short story entitled 'A dream about the war', Sweden (or rather, the gendered national symbol of Mother Svea) is figured as the pet of the Germanic family, the favourite daughter of the ancestress Germania 'since she is the most fair-haired of them all'.[49]

This Germanic sense of race was elaborated upon in an essay by Carl Larsson i By, dated August 1914. The writer vividly describes his own experiences of 'the call of the blood' as an irrational passion, a commanding instinct that makes man forget his morale, his will and his independence:

> I saw an endless row of fiery hosts pass by like dark shadows on a lemon-yellow sky. … And I was no longer myself; I was barely Swedish; I was a Teuton. It was the Teutons marching to the border. It was the blue-eyed, unconquerable Teutons I saw before me. Did they march to their last battle? … the war! I could feel my hands clenching and unclenching as if they were hungering for a weapon. The Teutons marching to war.'[50]

Deep down in his heart Larsson i By is bound by blood to the greater Germanic community and cause. This is his primordial identity, stronger and more genuine than the articulated, civilized Swedish one. And even if Larsson i By condemns both his own instinctive reactions and the war itself, the imagined connection between the ancient Teutons and contemporary Germany is made explicit. The same goes for the age-old bond between the Swedes and the

German(ic)s, further stressed by the writer's thoughts on his German friend in battle and his final benison on the two nations. Other contemporary articles underline in the same way that the Swedes and the Germans are united by race, by a common history, and, last but not least, by an ancient struggle for civilization and *Kultur*.[51]

In sum, Germany and the Germans are represented in terms of family and kin, as blood relations. In the construction of Swedish identity, they are the positive counterparts, the manly ideal. The Swedes and the Germans—'us Teutons'—are bound by blood and destiny to a common cause. On the opposite, negative side of this identity construction we find the inherent Other: the Russians. The Russians are generally represented as different and inferior in relation to the Swedes and Germans, often in a racialized, evolutionary vocabulary. The Russian enemy embodies the barbaric, un-civilized, dirty and backward East.[52]

The call of the blood

As we have seen, racial and national belonging was associated with blood, genealogy, and biology, and imagined as natural and predetermined. In this section, I will further expand on this topic by discussing constructions of race in three short stories that were published in the magazine *Hvar 8 dag* in 1915. They all confirm yet somehow complicate the emphasis on blood as the basis for identity and sympathy. In 'The heart and the blood' the protagonist is a German soldier, Rogen. In the first scene he is left injured on the battlefield together with a young Frenchman. At first, they try to kill each other, since 'even unto death national hatred is stronger than the pain'. But then Rogen is filled with a sudden compassion for his enemy, who soon dies in his arms. Just before dying with the name of his beloved Marianne on his lips, he gives Rogen a photograph and asks him to tell his fiancée. When later recovered, Rogen goes to the occupied French town where Marianne serves in a pub. To his surprise, he finds her laughing and flirting with the German soldiers. Once told of her fiancé's fate, she just jeers and stamps on the photograph. When the agitated Rogen asks why, she says the answer lies 'in the blood'. Marianne was born German, and the war has made her despise her former lover and everything French: 'the blood—the blood is stronger than anything else. ... the blood made me hate him.' The moral of the story is that blood—race—is thicker than the water of romantic love. Marianne is thus described as a woman 'who became unfaithful to her heart, but stayed true to her blood and put Germany above all'. In the final scene, Marianne stands proudly crying in the middle of the German crowd, singing *Deutschland, Deutschland über alles*. Her eyes are described as glowing with a fire that comes from the blood, not from the heart. Overwhelmed by Marianne's deceit, the treachery of women in general, and the insignificance of romantic love compared to patriotism 'now, at the time of the great reckoning', Rogen faints. 'No one paid heed to him, for the national anthem grew and grew—the blood sang and the heart remained silent'. In sum, the story holds racial belonging to be the strongest of all bonds, an ineluctable community of blood and birth. The passion for the nation runs much deeper than individual, romantic love. But race is also figured as something deeply irrational and perhaps even dangerous, on the verge of a mass hysteria, and consequently positioned as primarily belonging to the home front and the female sphere. For the fighting men, having shared a baptism of fire in battle, the racial differences are obviously not as crucial.[53]

The second case is 'The Orchestra', a short story about a family orchestra touring Europe in the summer of 1914. Here national belonging and identity are also racialized and described in biological terms. Race is imagined as something inescapable, irrational, passionate, and uncontrollable. The main character is a German woman. Interestingly, her name and appearance do not fit the Germanic stereotype: Juanita, star of the orchestra, is a black-haired girl with heavy eyelids. Yet to her and her wandering, dark-complexioned family, Germany is everything: 'Oh, home, home? Yes, she longs for her own race, her own people, her own language.' The news of the outbreak of war is described—'Germany was at war. Have you ever received a telegram saying your father or mother was dying? Then you know how they felt.'—and the nation likened to a parent, a living organism. 'The Orchestra' also ends with the band playing a patriotic hymn (*Die Wacht am Rhein*), 'the song from their own *Volksgeist*', with Juanita weeping for her beloved nation. The sense of race is represented as something immortal yet primeval, a sort of 'terrible and eternal power' that reason and rationality cannot count for; an emotional chain that links the musicians to earlier generations of Germans in a community of kin outside time but firmly wedded to one territory.[54]

The final example, 'Beyond good and evil', is the story of a Swedish doctor volunteering in a German war hospital in occupied Belgium, who is caught in a moral dilemma when asked to report a suspected spy. The doctor cannot fully convince himself that the suspect should be considered a traitor and not a patriot. He is subsequently dismissed and sent home. Recalling a conversation with his superior at the hospital, a German professor, his moral doubts are considered neither ethical nor political, but due to a lack of racial instincts. The Swedish doctor is simply not German enough, despite a German mother and wife, many years spent in Germany, and his choice to volunteer and fight for Germany. In the words of the professor: 'Yes, you see, there is a difference between us. I am certain you love Germany. … But the war takes us far, far beyond good and evil. And it is then the goats will be separated from the sheep, the friends of the nation from the children of the nation.'[55] In wartime, *pro patria* is all that counts. To be a friend is not enough; you have to be 'a child of the nation', bound by blood. The half-blood doctor stands out as a particularly treacherous and dangerous figure, whose true loyalties are always disputable and divided. In a racist discourse, where national identity is absolute and exclusive, he is an anomaly. This is racial thinking in its most essentialist form.

Scandinavian supremacy – the purest race of all?

For numerous writers in the contemporaneous popular press, neutrality was a complicated issue, especially in relation to ideas of national virility and racial fitness. To many, the permanent peace after 1814 and Sweden's decision to stay neutral in the First World War were signs of national degeneration and decay. In the contemporary European discourse, the Germanic race was represented as a warrior race, a particularly manly nation of conquerors. Here, the discursive intersection of race and gender became painfully clear. Fears were raised of Swedish emasculation on both the national and the individual level due to the lack of war experience.[56] In Denmark, the loud and firm neutral stand of the internationally renowned writer Georg Brandes was feminized and ridiculed in cartoons picturing him as a terrified woman.[57]

But in other cases, the racial argument was used as a reason to stay out of war. As Helge Pedersen has shown in his study of the Norwegian anthropologist Jon Alfred Mjøen, the total war of 1914–18 confirmed his pre-war theories on the anti-selective and racially damaging nature of modern, industrialized war.[58] In a Swedish context, the shared experience of wartime neutrality also meant a reorientation towards things Scandinavian and a Scandinavian (racial) identity. In the popular press, 'Swedish', 'Scandinavian', and 'Nordic' were often used interchangeably. To the Swedish author K. G. Ossiannilsson writing in *Vecko-Journalen*, the Swedes were bound by blood to both belligerent parties, although the German blood was definitely the thicker; yet the racially mixed German nation, with its influx of Slavic and Jewish blood, was no longer as pure as it once was: 'we Scandinavians' now represented the purest, most 'unpolluted' and 'untainted' Teutons, and therefore had the highest standing of all Germanic races. This was also a reason why Sweden should remain neutral and totally independent to best protect its unique racial purity and pursue its own 'national destiny'.[59] To avoid becoming but a province of 'Greater Germania', the Scandinavian nations should 'secure ourselves with both military and cultural ramparts against any aggressor'.[60] The same argument was put in one of *Hvar 8 dag*'s weekly war columns, denying that any bloodlines between the Swedes and the Russian emperors remain, but acknowledging that it was very hard to tell whether the Anglo-Saxon Germanic or the Teuton Germanic race was closest to the Scandinavian heart. While accusing the prime defenders of Western civilization, France and Great Britain, for their seemingly 'unnatural' alliance with 'Eastern despotism', the article is also critical of 'the politics of iron and blood on the Spree' that actually places Germany east of Europe, on the other side of the border, in 'half-Asia'. Hence, 'we Scandinavians' did not wish to take sides in 'the giant struggle', but defended their independence and absolute right 'to be true to us', *Hvar 8 dag* goes on. Instead of the greater Germanic community, the smaller Scandinavian family with its unique 'distinctive character' is invoked, the kinship of the neutral 'sibling kingdoms' and 'people of the cross-banners', who as never before feel that they ultimately belong only to one another, and even 'stand and fall' together and are 'doomed to live and die together'.[61]

As the war dragged on, the racial benefits of peace became even more prominent. In a series of articles in *Vecko-Journalen* of 1916, the war was said to have given the neutrals 'a big step ahead' in the global struggle for the survival of the fittest, and the already noble Swedish race could—in contrast to the belligerents—look forward to a prosperous future. That there was no race like the Swedish race was even considered 'statistically verified'. To protect the future virility and purity of Swedish stock, the nation should stand firm in its splendid isolation.[62] Such racial images of 'the Nordic lead' fitted into a broader contemporary media narrative of war and neutrality, in which Sweden, and to some extent Scandinavia, was constructed as a moral great power. Within this discourse the Scandinavians were figured as a chosen (spared) people with a common destiny; as superior, civilized, peaceful, and forward-looking, in stark contrast to the barbaric belligerents.[63] Similar images and ideas of the culturally superior, progressive, and more 'clear-sighted' neutrals were also prevalent in wartime Denmark and Norway.[64]

At the twilight of the white race

The image of war as an evolutionary breakdown of biblical dimensions took on a new aspect at the end of the war. Neutral Scandinavia might have survived, but what about European civilization as a whole? In the face of total war and revolution, metaphors of 'European suicide' and 'civil war' became more widely used in Scandinavia to convey the war's meaning.[65] Danish intellectuals turned to these terms to bewail the fact that their 'natural racial allies' were meaninglessly fighting one another instead of the 'racially alien' and expansive Japan.[66] And in Sweden at the beginning of 1919, the fervently pro-German Annie Åkerhielm expressed a deep sense of pessimism and disillusion regarding the survival of Western civilization. In *Idun*, under the headline 'At dusk', she paralleled the ruin of contemporary Europe to the fall of the Roman Empire. The situation was actually worse, she claimed, since there was no source of renewal, 'no race, young and unspoilt as once the Germanic race' to take the lead and build up a new civilization. This time, Europe, and with it civilized Man, was inevitably doomed. To Åkerhielm, the main threat came from barbaric, racially inferior Russia, with bolshevism as its latest incarnation: 'We do not any longer … have to ask ourselves from whence the new barbarians will come. We see them take form right in front of us, the fusion of darkest Asia and darkest Europe, as real and evident as the Huns in their day, but advancing in far greater numbers.'[67] Here, the external and internal racial threat merge into the Bolshevik—the modern Hun—an amalgamation of the worst of Asia and Europe.

In a response, the Finland-Swedish author and literary historian Henrik Hildén tried to prove Åkerhielm wrong. To him, the world war was not the end of Western civilization, but only the righteous fall of the Industrial Age and its inherent horrors. The revolting working classes were in fact only destroying themselves and their way of life. Once this inferior race was erased from history, the true heir to the ancient Germanic conquerors, the Farmer, would step forward. The Farmer had survived the war, and he would outlive the Bolshevist mob. Under his rule, Europe will be rebuilt and renewed as an agricultural, aristocratic civilization.[68] The debate is a Swedish example of how the lower classes were seen through the prism of race, as argued by Malik and Pick. The use of colonial tropes such as an internal European (or Swedish) *mission civilisatrice* also testifies to the adaptable and inter-discursive application of the race concept. For Åkerhielm and Hildén, the barbarian hordes of Asia were inevitably connected to hoi polloi of the European homeland. This symbolic connection was also indicated in articles dealing with the Red violence of the Finnish Civil War of 1918 and the perceived Swedish civilizing mission in Finland.[69]

This sense of the decline of the white race was part of a more general post-war crisis of confidence about the future of the Western civilization, articulated in works such as Oswald Spengler's *Decline of the West*. According to Füredi, the experience of the First World War resulted in a radical change in the dynamic between Western identity and racial thinking, from racial confidence to racial fear. The conflict was seen as a sign of Western weakness, white feebleness, and the demise of racial solidarity. It seriously undermined the presumed moral superiority and authority of the West. By now, the war was also frequently represented as a 'civil war' between white nations—a fratricidal war at the heart of European civilization.[70]

In the long run, the war was also a serious blow to the eugenics movement, and not least to the cherished idea of the Nordic 'master race'.[71] At the same time, it was not until after the war that these racial ideas were institutionalized and put into practice in Scandinavia. Sweden was a pioneer with the establishment of the world's very first eugenic institute in 1922 and extensive sterilization laws and policies from the early 1930s onwards. Denmark and Norway followed suit. In the interwar years, huge anthropological censuses were undertaken of the Swedish and Norwegian populations as a whole, as well as particular groups such as conscripts and the indigenous Sámi minority. The results were published internationally, for example in *The Racial Character of the Swedish people* in 1927, and also spread and popularized nationwide through schools and a stream of educational lectures, pamphlets, films, and books.[72] As Tommy Gustafsson has shown, state-sanctioned racism was mirrored in Swedish popular films of the 1920s, where constructions of white supremacy, black subordination, and the superior manly Germanic/Nordic race versus the infantile, feminine, Eastern/Southern species prevailed.[73] In the 1930s, the concept of race became increasingly politicized with the spread of Nazi ideology.[74]

Blood and belonging in wartime

Notions of race were thus widespread in the war narratives of the Swedish popular press during the First World War. It was commonplace in neutral Sweden to imagine the war as a great war for civilization, fought between opposing races struggling for survival and supremacy. Concepts of blood, race, people, nation, civilization, evolution, and barbarity permeated the language of war in the intense 'discursive battle' that took place in non-belligerent Scandinavia as elsewhere. Race was considered a biological fact, and national belonging was comprehended in terms of blood and breeding, not of will or consent. But there was also a certain ambiguity about the concept: it was considered irrational and primordial, a potentially destructive passion. It was also evident how notions of the inferior, colonial, and 'coloured' Other were interwoven, interrelated to, perhaps inseparable from, ideas about a racial threat from within and below, and both undermining European civilization. The imagined racial borders of the mental map of Europe did not necessarily correspond to the geographical or political ones. Here Swedish war narratives were very much part of a wider, Western, colonial and racist discourse on civilization. Within the overarching European community, the Scandinavians were considered to belong to the German(ic) camp, as opposed to the Eastern Russians, who were constructed as racially different and distant. Although the self-positioning as 'Germania's favourite daughter' or allusions to 'we Teutons' did not always reflect bellicosity—since ideas of racial superiority could also serve as a foundation for Scandinavian solidarity and isolationism—this 'racial affinity' should nevertheless be regarded an important strand in the cognitive web that made neutral Sweden 'a cultural ally' of Germany in the First World War.

It is not within the scope of this chapter to make a more systematic comparison between the Scandinavian countries. In the belligerents' eyes they were often considered a single unit—as small neutral states on the European periphery with a long, common history and a large number of cultural and societal similarities. My findings show that at least from a Swedish point of view, Scandinavia was also considered a racial entity, a biological and cultural family of 11 million Nordic Teutons. Suffice to say, ideas of 'white supremacy' and a 'Nordic master race' went more or less unquestioned in Scandinavia. But given the countries' different political positions during the First World War—for example, Norway's alignment as 'a neutral ally' of Great Britain, or Denmark's fears of being engulfed by the 'German(ic) big brother'—it would also be interesting to trace if racial images, identities, and arguments *differed* from one Scandinavian nation to another, and how the pre-existing concepts of blood and belonging were complicated and reformulated under the impact of this devastating war.

Notes

1 'Ledarne af Nordens utrikespolitik', *Hvar 8 dag* (*H8D*), 1915/14, 'Hvad betyder dock icke detta, att de 11 millionerna nordgermaner funnit hvarandra och beslutit bilda en grupp för sig i den stora världskampen mellan slaver, romaner, anglosaxgermaner och tyskgermaner?' All translations from the Swedish are mine.

2 Stéphane Audoin-Rouzeau & Annette Becker, *14–18. Understanding the Great War* (New York: Hill & Wang, 2003), 9, 92–171, 228, 236–7; see Daniel Pick, *War Machine. The Rationalisation of Slaughter in the Modern Age* (New Haven: Yale University Press, 1993), 140–1, 148–51; Svante Nordin, *Filosofernas krig. Den europeiska filosofin under första världskriget* (Nora: Nya Doxa, 1998), 214–17, 227–40.

3 Pick 1993, 153.

4 Ibid. 141.

5 Frank Füredi, *The Silent War. Imperialism and the Changing Perception of Race* (New Brunswick, NJ: Rutgers University Press, 1998), 60–2. See also Pick 1993, 153; Audoin-Rouzeau & Becker 2003,154; Ian Ousby, *The Road to Verdun. France, Nationalism and the First World War* (London: Jonathan Cape, 2002), 22–5; Jon Røyne Kyllingstad, *Kortskaller og langskaller. Fysisk antropologi i Norge og striden om det nordiske herremensket* (Oslo: Scandinavian Academic Press/Spartacus Forlag, 2004), 25–6, 92–111.

6 Füredi 1998, 1, 64–6; Ousby 2002, 142–50; Kenan Malik, *The Meaning of Race. Race, History and Culture in Western Society* (New York: NYUP, 1996), 1–2, 39; Barbara Caine & Glenda Sluga, *Gendering European History 1780–1920* (London: Leicester University Press, 2000), 87–142.

7 See Caine & Sluga 2000; Anne McClintock, *Imperial Leather. Race, Gender, and Sexuality in the Colonial Contest* (London: Routledge, 1995).

8 Nils-Olof Franzén, *Undan stormen. I Sverige under första världskriget* (Stockholm: Bonniers, 1986), 119–59; Ulf Zander, *Fornstora dagar, moderna tider. Bruk av och debatter om svensk historia från sekelskifte till sekelskifte* (diss.; Lund: Nordic Academic Press, 2001), 137–44; Claes Ahlund, *Underhållning och propaganda. Radschas (Iwan Aminoffs) romaner om första världskriget 1914–1915* (Skrifter utgivna av Avdelningen för litteratursociologi

vid Litteraturvetenskapliga institutionen i Uppsala, 61; Uppsala: Uppsala
University, 2010), 44–53, 62, 81, 157–64.

9 Kyllingstad 2004, 10–11, 90–1; Helge Pedersen, *'Gud har skapat svarta och
vita mäniskor, djävulen derimot halfnegeren'. En komparativ analyse av Jon
Alfred Mjöen og Herman Lundborgs rasehygieniske ideer i Norge og Sverige
ca 1900–1935* (diss., Oslo University, 2003), 2, 41–2, 69–75 (available
at <http://www3.hf.uio.no/1905/publikasjon18.php>, accessed 28 May
2012); Håkan Blomqvist, *Nation, ras och civilisation i svensk arbetarrörelse
före nazismen* (diss.; Stockholm: Carlssons förlag, 2006), 326–7; Gunnar
Broberg & Nils Roll-Hansen (eds.), *Eugenics and the Welfare State. Sterilization Policy in Denmark, Norway, Sweden and Finland* (East Lansing, Mich.:
Michigan University Press, 1996); Lene Koch, *Racehygiejne i Danmark
1920–56* (Copenhagen: Informations Forlag, 2010); Maja Hagerman, *Det
rena landet. Om konsten att uppfinna sina förfäder* (Stockholm: Norstedts,
2011).

10 Blomqvist 2006; Patrik Hall, *Den svenskaste historien. Nationalism i Sverige
under sex sekler* (Stockholm: Carlssons förlag, 2000); Sofi Qvarnström, *Motståndets berättelser. Elin Wägner, Anna Lenah Elgström, Marika Stiernstedt
och första världskriget* (diss.; Hedemora: Gidlunds förlag, 2009), 313–5,
327–30; Kyllingstad 2004, 11; Pedersen 2003, 2.

11 Malik 1996, 39, 71, 265; see Mark Mazower, *Dark Continent. Europe's
Twentieth Century* (London: Penguin Books, 1998), 102.

12 See Edward W. Said, *Orientalism* (London: Penguin, 2003); Edward W.
Said, *Culture and Imperialism* (London: Vintage Books, 1994).

13 Daniel Pick, *Faces of Degeneration. A European Disorder, c.1848–c.1918* (Cam-
bridge: CUP, 1989), 39. See Malik 1996, 8, 70, 81, 91, 99, 115–19, 225;
Pick 1989, 20–1, 37–42; Ousby 2002, 136–93; Mazower 1998, 77–105;
George M. Fredrickson, *Racism. A Short History* (Princeton: PUP, 2002);
Ivan Hannaford, *Race. The History of an Idea in the West* (Washington,
DC: Woodrow Wilson Center Press, 1996); Imanuel Geiss, *Geschichte des
Rassismus* (Frankfurt am Main: Suhrkamp, 1988).

14 Malik 1996, 91, 115–19.

15 Mazower 1998, 161–84.

16 Fredrickson 2002, 105–106, 114–20, 158–65; Ousby 2002, 136–93.

17 Vejas Gabriel Liulevicius, *War land on the Eastern Front. Culture, National
Identity and the German Occupation in World War I* (Cambridge: CUP,
2000); Vejas Gabriel Liulevicius, *The German Myth of the East. 1800 to the
Present* (Oxford: OUP, 2009), 130–70.

18 Audoin-Rouzeau & Becker 2003, 48–49, 68, 103–104, 154; see also Paul
Fussell, *The Great War and Modern Memory* (New York: OUP, 1975), 77–8.

19 Audoin-Rouzeau & Becker 2003, 108, 154–5.

20 Pick 1993,146–8, 153–7. See Ousby 2002, 156–9, 181–2.

21 Audoin-Rouzeau & Becker 2003, 88–9, 148–58, 131; Christian Koller, 'Feindbilder, Rassen- und Geschlechterstereotype in der Kolonialtruppendiskussion Deutschlands und Frankreich, 1914–1923', in Karin Hagemann & Stefanie Schüler-Springorum (eds.), *Heimat–Front. Militär und Geschlechterverhältnisse im Zeitalder der Weltkriege* (Frankfurt am Main: Campus, 2002); see Ahlund 2010, 57, 72, 180–1.

22 Pick 1993, 152, 157; Audoin-Rouzeau & Becker 2003, 258; Kyllingstad 2004; Bjarne S. Bendtsen, 'Colour-blind or Clear-Sighted Neutrality? Georg Brandes and the First World War', in Johan den Hertog & Samuël Kruizinga (eds.), *Caught in the Middle. Neutrals, Neutrality and the First World War* (Amsterdam: Aksant/AUP, 2011), 26.

23 See Lina Sturfelt, 'From Parasite to Angel. Narratives of Neutrality in the Swedish Popular Press during the First World War', in den Hertog & Kruizinga 2011, 105–20.

24 Pick 1993, 2–3, 30, 203–204; Mazower 1998, 92–3; Sturfelt 2011; Bendtsen 2011, 130; Ainur Elmgren, *Den allrakäraste fienden. Svenska stereotyper i finländsk press 1918–1939* (diss.; Lund: Sekel bokförlag, 2008), 201–216.

25 See Björn Furuhagen, *Den svenska rasbiologins idéhistoriska rötter, en inventering av forskningen* (Forum för Levande Historia, 2007), 40–1, available at <http://www.levandehistoria.se/files/rasbiologi_inventering.pdf>, accessed 22 December 2011; regarding Swedish popular anti-Semitism during this period, see Lars M Andersson, *En jude är en jude är en jude… Representationer av 'juden' i svensk skämtpress omkring 1900–1930* (diss.; Lund: Nordic Academic Press, 2000).

26 Ahlund 2010, 68–95, 156–7, 161–2, 164, 180–1.

27 Qvarnström 2009, 313–15, 327–30.

28 I have examined the general war narratives of these magazines more thoroughly in Lina Sturfelt, *Eldens återsken. Första världskriget i svensk föreställningsvärld* (diss.; Lund: Sekel, 2008).

29 As already seen, racial solidarity was used as a propaganda tool. It is worth noting that the German influence on the Swedish press was quite extensive, especially in the early war years (see Ahlund 2010, 44–53).

30 The term 'Aryan' is also largely absent, in contrast to 'Germanic', 'Teuton' and 'Nordic' (see Andersson 2000).

31 'Frankrikes svarta armé', *H8D* 1914/48; 'Englands måleriska trupper', *H8D* 1914/8, 'ett antal rödskinn'; 'måleriska trupper'; 'Fred, hurra!', *Vecko-Journalen* (*VJ*), 1918/48.

32 'En människoätare på "ärans fält"', *VJ* 1915/7, 'människoätare', 'nigger'.

33 Variations on such stories figured in Swedish popular literature; see Ahlund 2010, 57, 72, 180–1.

34 'Asiens folk på Europas slagfält', *Allers Familj-Journal* (*Allers*), 1915/40, 'barbarisk', 'primitiv', 'vilda', 'asiatisk vildhet'; see 'Frankrikes svarta armé', *H8D* 1914/48; see Ahlund 2010, 52, 57, 180–1.

35 'Himalajas folk på Europas slagfält', *Allers* 1914/44; 'Asiens folk på Europas slagfält', *Allers* 1915/40.

36 'Asiens folk på Europas slagfält', *Allers* 1915/40, 'människomaterial'; 'De svarta soldaternas fana', *Allers* 1919/28.

37 E. Norling, 'En läsvärd krigsbok', *Idun*, 1918/29, 'Bland skisserna från fånglägren tas utan tvifvel priset af den döende negern, hvars hjälplösa främlingskap och stumma heroism författaren fått fram på ett par tre sidor … Man glömmer icke denna skarpa men alldeles tendenslöst hållna bild af den förmente barbaren med all sin äkta inre kultur mot bakgrunden af de rikas barbariska civilisation, den europeiska humanitetens bankrutt.' See 'Den sårade negern', *VJ* 1915/7; see Qvarnström 2009, 75.

38 Sturfelt 2008, 176–7.

39 See Torsten Burgman, *Svensk opinion och diplomati under rysk-japanska kriget 1904–1905* (diss.; Stockholm: Norstedts, 1965), 43–54; Malik 1996, 118–19, 123.

40 'Vad väntar ni av 1918?', *VJ praktupplagan* 1918/2, 'blodad tand'.

41 'Då mikadon blef krönt', *Allers* 1916/5, 'Hvad japanen måtte känna sitt hjärta svälla af stolthet och hemlig glädje öfver att se sina födda motståndare arbeta honom i händerna'.

42 'Den nya gula faran', *Allers* 1916/1.

43 See Burgman 1965. Even if this difference might partly be explained by the fact that Japan in 1905 defeated the Swedish 'arch-enemy', the change is still notable.

44 Bendtsen 2011, 130, 133.

45 'Lördagen den 1 augusti blev Europas ödesdag', *VJ* 1914/32, 'Lördagen den 1 augusti blev Europas ödesdag då … germanernas livskamp började.'

46 'Ledarne af Nordens utrikespolitik', *H8D* 1915/14, 'den stora världskampen'; see Mathilde Serao, 'Civiliserade och barbarer', *Idun*, 1919/18.

47 'Världskriget', *H8D* 1914/45, 'en utlösning af spänningar mellan världs-historiska tendenser'.

48 Annie Åkerhielm, 'Krigssommar', *Idun* 1915/23, 'beundransvärda stam-fränder'; E. Norling, 'Svensk lifsglädje', *Idun*, 1915/14, 'det ädla frändefolket'; Annie Åkerhielm, 'Soldater bakom fronten', *Idun*, 1916/38, 'hela denna här af miljoner hjältar … som … dämma tillbaka den flodvåg af verkliga barbarer, som vill störta sig in öfver Europa och dess kultur … de skaffa oss alla germaner rum att lefva i världen efter vårt innersta väsen och egenart.'

49 Hilding Barkman, 'En dröm om kriget', *Idun* 1914/34, 'ty hon är ju den mest ljuslockiga'.

50 Carl Larsson i By, 'Ut i kriget', *Idun* 1914/34, 'Jag såg en ändlös rad af
lågande härar draga förbi som svarta skuggor mot en citrongul himmel.
... Och jag var inte längre mig själf, jag var knappt längre svensk, jag var
german. Det var germanerna, som tågade mot gränsen. Det var de blåögda,
okufliga germanerna, som jag såg i synen. Tågade de mot sin sista strid?
... kriget! Jag kände mina händer öppnas och knytas som om de hungrat
efter ett vapen. Germanerna tåga till strid.' See K. G. Ossiannilsson, 'Mitt
läger i kostallet och en sömnlös natts fantasier', *VJ* 1914/39, where the
author feels his 'Germanic blood speak' ('Å andra sidan talar det germanska
blodet').

51 'På Gustaf Adolfs-dagen 1914', *Idun*, 1914/45. See Sebart, 'Hjälteminnets
makt', *Idun*, 1914/45; 'Lützen den 6 november', *Idun*, 1914/48; 'Lützen
den 6 november', *H8D* 1914/8; cf. Zander 2001, 142.

52 Sturfelt 2008, 55–156, 209–18. See Ahlund 2010, 81–6; Blomqvist 2006,
308–30; Liulevicius 2009, 137.

53 John Hellman, 'Hjärtat och blodet', *H8D* 1915/25, 'in i döden kände
nationalhatet starkare än smärtan', 'blodet – blodet är starkare än allt an-
nat ... Då gjorde blodet att jag hatade honom', 'som blef otrogen mot
sitt hjärta, men förblef trogen mot sitt blod och satte Tyskland öfver allt-
ing', 'nu i den stora uppgörelsens tid', 'Ingen brydde sig om honom, ty
nationalhymnen växte och växte – blodet sjöng och hjärtat teg.' Another
example with a similar metaphor and message is Ulla Linder, 'Monsieur
Pellegrins mörkrum', *H8D* 1916/14.

54 Signe Lagerlöw, 'Musikkapellet', *H8D* 1915/49, 'O hemlandet, hemlandet? Ja, dit längtar hon, till sin egen ras, sitt eget folk, sitt eget språk',
'Tyskland stod i krig. Har du fått ett telegram någon gång, hvari stått att
far eller mor varit döende? Då förstår du hvad de kände', 'sången ur deras
egen folksjäl', 'det aldrig utreddas fruktansvärda och evinnerliga makt'.

55 Hjalmar Bergman, 'Bortom godt och ondt', *H8D* 1915/13, 'Ja, ser du,
det finns en skillnad oss emellan. Jag är säker om, att du älskar Tyskland
... Men kriget för oss långt, betydligt långt bortom godt och ondt. Och
det är där getterna skola skiljas från fåren, landets vänner från landets egna
barn.'

56 Sturfelt 2011; Sturfelt 2008, 185–248; Caine & Sluga 2000, 121–2,
143–59; Pick 1993, 204; Audoin-Rouzeau & Becker 2003, 120–1, 139;
Ousby 2002, 67, 189–93; Louis Clerc, 'The Hottest Places in Hell? Finnish and Nordic Neutrality from the Perspective of French Foreign Policy,
1900–1940', in den Hertog & Kruizinga 2011, 139–153 (above, n. 22).

57 Bendsten 2011, 130.

58 Pedersen 2003, 44–5.

59 K. G. Ossiannilsson, 'Söner av ett folk som blött...', *VJ* 1914/40, 'vi

THE CALL OF THE BLOOD

skandinaver'; for Ossiannilsson and the war, see Claes Ahlund, *Diktare i krig*. K. G. Ossiannilsson, *Bertil Malmberg och Ture Nerman från debuten till 1920* (Hedemora: Gidlunds förlag, 2007).

60 K. G. Ossiannilsson, 'Mitt läger i kostallet och en sömnlös natts fantasier', *VJ* 1914/39, 'befästa oss med både militära och kulturella vallar mot varje angripare'.

61 'Världskriget', *H8D* 1914/45, 'onaturligt', 'österländsk despotism', 'järn- och blodspolitiken vid Spree', 'half-Asien', 'jättarnes kamp', 'vi skandinaver', 'att få vara och förblifva oss själfva i vår svenska, danska och norska egenart', 'syskonrikena', 'korsfanornas folk', 'står och faller', 'dömda att lefva och dö med hvarandra'. See K. G. Ossiannilsson, 'Klockorna kalla', *VJ* 1914/35; see Sturfelt 2008, 203–205.

62 Gunnar Frostell, 'Svenska folkstammens kraft', *VJ praktupplagan* 1916/45, 'ett verkligt försteg'; Gunnar Frostell, 'Svensken söker sin like' *VJ praktupplagan* 1916/47, 'statistiskt säkerställt'.

63 Sturfelt 2011.

64 Monika Janfelt, *Stormakter i människokärlek. Svensk och dansk krigsbarnshjälp 1917–1924* (Åbo: Åbo Akademis Förlag, 1998); Monika Janfelt, *Att leva i den bästa av världar. Föreningarna Nordens syn på Norden 1919–1933* (Stockholm: Carlssons, 2003); Bendtsen 2011; Clerc 2011, 139–53.

65 Jane Gernandt-Claine, 'Amerikanska Röda Korset', *Idun* 1918/52, 'europeiskt själfmord', 'inbördeskrig'; see Ahlund 2010, 57, 72; Bendtsen 2011, 126,130, 133.

66 Bendtsen 2011, 130, 133.

67 Annie Åkerhielm, 'Det skymmer', *Idun*, 1919/4, 'inte någon ras som, ung och ofördärvad som den germanska rasen då', 'Vi behöva icke längre … fråga oss varifrån de nya barbarerna skola komma. Vi se dem livslevande inför oss, sammansmältningen av det mörkaste Asien och det mörkaste Europa, reella och påtagliga som hunnerna på sin tid, stadda i ett anryckande som hotar att bli vida mer omfattande än dessas.' For Åkerhielm and the war, see Sif Bokholm, *I otakt med tiden. Om rösträttsmotstånd, antipacifism och nazism bland svenska kvinnor* (Stockholm: Atlantis, 2008); Claes Ahlund, 'Krig och kultur i konservativ belysning. Annie Åkerhielm och Frida Stéenhoff från sekelskiftet till första världskriget', *Samlaren* (2005), 97–150.

68 Henrik Hildén, 'Det skymmer—skymmer det?', *Idun*, 1919/11.

69 'Nyaste bilder från Finland', *VJ* 1918/9; Ruth Hellström, 'Var det människor?', *Idun*, 1919/2; John Landqvist, 'Det fria Finland', *Idun*, 1918/3; 'Fänrik Ståls land', *Allers* 1918/12. See Elmgren 2008, 209–210.

70 Füredi 1998, 2, 17, 31–55. See Pick 1989, 230–4; Pick 1993, 155–6; Malik 1996, 123, 147; Mazower 1998, 77–105.

223

71 Kyllingstad 2004, 150–3, 178–85; Pedersen 2003, 83–5.

72 Gunnar Broberg, *Statlig rasforskning. En historik över rasbiologiska institutet* (Lund: Avdelningen för idé- och lärdomshistoria, Lunds universitet, 1995); Broberg & Roll-Hansen 1996; Kyllingstad 2004, 108–110, 130–58; Koch 2010.

73 Tommy Gustafsson, *En fiende till civilisationen. Manlighet, genusrelationer, sexualitet och rasstereotyper i svensk filmkultur under 1920-talet* (diss.; Lund: Sekel bokförlag, 2007), 210, 273, 293–6.

74 Kyllingstad 2004; Broberg 1995; Fredrickson 2002; Malik 1996.

CHAPTER 8

Money talks

Failed cooperation over the gold problem of the Scandinavian Monetary Union during the First World War

Gjermund F. Rongved

The Scandinavian Monetary Union (SMU) initiated in 1873 constituted one of history's very best examples of Scandinavian cooperation. The initial agreement regarding common coins was gradually extended to include increasingly new means of payment and settlements, in the hope of establishing a basis for increased trade and integration. The cooperation of the union's three central banks—Riksbanken in Sweden, Nationalbanken in Denmark, and Norges Bank in Norway—was exposed to a number of setbacks over the ensuing forty years. However, the SMU was by and large a well-functioning institution of cooperation by the outbreak of the First World War; it was as wartime experience uncovered important economic differences between the three countries that the union gradually dissolved.

In 1917 the leading contemporary Danish economist and central bank critic, Axel Nielsen, ended his book on the Scandinavian Monetary Union thus: 'What is left of it, however, is difficult to see. Apparently all the economic cooperation that was built up in the nineteenth century through more than 30 years' tireless work has been laid waste in the course of only two years, and this at a time when a new movement for a more intimate economic cooperation is growing.'[1] In the midst of an incomplete development imposed by the war, Nielsen obviously was neither able to see the full picture nor know the details of what had been going on in the past couple of years; however, his defeatism was certainly pertinent.

The reasonably smooth operation of the SMU had run into a stonewall, and despite apparent efforts to maintain cooperation, each of the three central banks was basically working for their own financial or national considerations. The 'new movement' Nielsen was referring to was most likely the Scandinavian emergency measures of 1917, which saw trade representatives of the three countries set out to help one another out by exchanging commodities. Yet this was at a time when Scandinavian monetary cooperation was approaching its nadir. During the war, cooperation within the union continued successfully only as long as it was to all the partners' advantage—on matters that were costly and really mattered it was virtually absent. Thus it was wartime experience that dealt the union its death blow, despite the futile attempts to restore the union that were initiated alongside the broader, international moves towards economic cooperation in the 1920s. Officially, however, the SMU existed until its termination in 1973.

This chapter will provide a short introduction to the main features and historical development of the SMU's heyday prior to the First World War, which earned the union its reputation as 'the most successful of all European currency unions'.[2] The main focus, however, is the union's 'gold problem' after gold convertibility was suspended in August 1914. Despite the fact that the value of the three currencies started to deviate on the world markets, Scandinavian gold coins still had to be bought by the central banks at the old, fixed price; gold was still legal tender at full value—par value—within the union. This implied that someone—for example, individuals, central banks, or governments—could take advantage of the situation and profit by differences between the market and the legal values. This moreover happened at a time when commodities were scarce and the role of gold as *the* measure of value was under attack. The point of departure in this chapter is the attempt to maintain central bank cooperation on gold policy within the SMU, with chief focus on a number of meetings—'money talks'—between the three countries' central banks.

The gold standard, central banks, and the SMU

During the second half of the nineteenth century, the national banks were in the midst of becoming 'central banks', a process which we will be returning to below. At this time the most important task of these banks was to uphold the value of money. A common way of achieving this was to fix the national currency to a precious metal such as silver or gold—or both. Coins thus had a specified metal content, and paper money was made legal tender, which meant that the central banks were obliged to sell or buy their notes for metal at a fixed price. From the 1860s gold gradually replaced both silver and bimetallism, and when the first talks about a Scandinavian union were held, there was hardly question of anything but the gold standard. Even though the Norwegian Storting rejected the 1873 convention for the Scandinavian Monetary Union, it eventually joined Sweden and Denmark in 1875.[3] From its very start the SMU involved common coins containing gold at a quantity that made it easy to convert from the previous three different silver standards. The new currency and legal tender in all three countries was the Scandinavian gold *krone/krona* containing 0.44803 grams of gold, and the three central banks were obliged to buy and sell gold at a fixed price: 2480 *kroner/kronor* per kilo, against a 0.25 per cent fee covering expenses. This price was the same in 1873 as it was in 1914, and by keeping this fixed gold price the SMU was simultaneously part of the international gold standard framework of fixed interchangeable currencies.

Another task of these 'central banks' was to facilitate trade. This could be done either by selling or buying bills of exchange from individuals and companies, and thus acting like a normal bank, or by rediscounting bills of exchange or drafts from the expanding field of commercial banking. A bill of exchange was the most common means of payment in business transactions of the nineteenth century, a financial document by which the issuer bound himself to pay the holder an amount of money on a given date—both specified in the document—while a draft was a bill where the issuer ordered a third party to pay the holder. In international trade these bills and drafts to a large extent made the physical payment of gold or silver superfluous, and a single bill could be used in numerous business transactions and could even cross borders.[4]

In 1885, the SMU expanded its scope considerably when it was decided that all three central banks could sell drafts upon one another and transfer them at par value without paying a fee. This meant that, for example, Nationalbanken thus could 'draw' on Riksbanken by issuing a draft to a Danish importer that Riksbanken ultimately would have to pay to the Swedish exporter, which simultaneously increased Nationalbanken's debt to Riksbanken. The decision was intended to facilitate larger settlements between the countries. In 1894, business and trade benefited further when Riksbanken and Norges Bank agreed to accept each other's notes at par value. Nationalbanken, however, was reluctant, and did not join this part of the union until 1901, at which time the SMU was at its height. This heyday only lasted a few years, as Riksbanken in 1905 terminated the 1885 agreement. The decision was undoubtedly encouraged by the political tensions of the year, as Norway broke out of the personal union with Sweden. However, considering the development of imbalances in drawing between the banks, Riksbanken probably had good financial arguments. The 1885 agreement had made it illegal to charge a fee on drafts, although a fee might have helped to relieve Riksbanken of the demand and ultimately the need to ship gold to cover its debt. Thus bilateral replacement agreements were concluded in 1905, introducing limits for the normal interest-free debts the central banks could have on their books. Where the debt was not paid by shipping gold, it was left to the banks to decide if a fee was to be introduced for any debts exceeding these limits.

So what can be said of the status of the SMU at the outbreak of the First World War? There obviously had been setbacks, something the 1905 turmoil bears witness to: for shorter periods, fees on drafts had been introduced, although admittedly not until 1910; there is evidence that the SMU did not facilitate trade integration, as inter-Scandinavian trade actually declined; and it is difficult to distinguish between the effects of the monetary union and adherence to the gold standard. Yet all this notwithstanding, the SMU in 1914 is probably correctly described as well-functioning. When it was 'at its best' between 1901 and 1905 it has been labelled a 'complete system' of payment.[5] Until this point, monetary cooperation had strengthened on an almost year-by-year basis, and the reversals of 1905 and 1910 do not alter the fact that coins and notes were still traded at par. The fees charged on drafts were temporary arrangements, and despite a fall in central bank drawing after 1905, the use and circulation of the different Scandinavian banknotes consequently expanded considerably. In addition, central bank cooperation was facilitated by, for example, the sharing of information on changes in discount rates. Recent work has also pointed to the fact that even though the SMU did not facilitate trade, it did have an important function in fostering financial integration through short-term financing.[6] Finally, the SMU's very existence and continued survival was important politically, being a major accomplishment of Scandinavianism.

By the outbreak of war, Riksbanken, Nationalbanken, and Norges Bank had all become true central banks. This first of all meant that the banks had gained a monopoly on issuing notes, something that was not that common during the nineteenth century. In fact it was not until 1897 that Riksbanken was given a note-issuing monopoly.[7] Moreover, the banks had mostly withdrawn from competing with—or covering for the lack of—private commercial banks, which thus resulted in a growth in the private banking sectors of the three countries, albeit with somewhat differing outcomes. For instance, where Sweden's financial sector saw a move towards fewer, yet bigger banks, Norway had an increasing number of small private banks. Furthermore, the three were central banks by dint of their role as lender of last resort; during times of crisis, they would come to the assistance of the financial sector—and thus the state.

This notwithstanding, there were differences in the banks' relationships with their respective states. Where Riksbanken was state-owned, Nationalbanken and Norges Bank were privately owned, although a substantial part of their shares were held by the state and central bank legislation guided their actions. The Swedish Riksdag's control of Riksbanken gave the governor Victor Moll (1912–29) a rather weak start. Moll, having worked his way up in private banking, was the Liberal's chosen candidate. In the

Riksdag, Moll and the Conservative's candidate received the same number of votes, and Moll was thus elected governor by the solid foundation of drawing lots. Even though he was a Liberal MP, Moll's counterpart at Norges Bank, the entrepreneur Karl Gether Bomhoff, was in many respects a contrast. Bomhoff had been on the Board of Directors since 1885, and in 1893 he became the first permanent, government-appointed governor of Norges Bank. It was under Bomhoff that Norges Bank had stepped in as lender of last resort in 1899 following the burst of Kristiania property bubble that year. At Nationalbanken, meanwhile, Marcus Rubin had scarcely taken the governor's seat before war broke out, having been appointed by the government, thanks to his connections with the Liberal Party, as recently as 1913. Rubin had extensive management experience, having served as head of both the statistical bureau and the tax authorities, and his background seemed promising—he was both a statistician and an historian, and he had published several works on economic history—and although lacking formal banking experience, he seemed well equipped for the task. However, neither experience nor background could prepare the three men for what was to come in 1914.

Diverging exchange rates and the gold problem

The outbreak of the First World War had a massive impact on international business and trade. Production in the belligerent countries—the large economies of Europe—was directed towards materiel, while transportation by land and sea was made difficult by the endless trenches scarring European soil and the lurking dangers of submarine warfare. Commodities were scarce and insufficient to meet demand in the belligerent and neutral countries alike. The scarcity naturally added to the hardships of the populations of the main belligerent countries. Despite intermittently severe problems in obtaining the necessary imports, the Scandinavian countries overall experienced a favourable trade cycle up until 1917. The export sectors fared well, trading with the belligerents. During the course of the war, however, the hardships were felt increasingly strongly in neutral countries as well. Many governments ultimately found it necessary to expand the once small-scale and passive modus of the liberal, nineteenth-century state into new areas of economic affairs. Thus neutral countries, like the belligerent countries, introduced rationing in order to be able meet the demands of their beleaguered populations. And the difficulty of obtaining a vast range of commodities had an important financial knock-on effect: it laid a solid foundation for massive inflation after the suspension of the gold standard.

The war brought with it the collapse of international finance, and there was an abrupt halt to the world's stable monetary system when most of the gold standard countries suspended gold convertibility to protect their gold reserves from a run. The Scandinavian countries were no exception. On 2 August 1914, Riksbanken and Nationalbanken were relieved of the obligation to redeem their banknotes with gold, while Norges Bank followed suit three days later. It should be noted, however, that the obligation to *buy* gold was still in effect; what is more, this obligation was regulated by the convention of the SMU. During the autumn of 1914 all three countries went on to ban gold exports.[8] The Scandinavian countries thus followed the pattern seen across the world, where the international exchange rate stability of the gold standard soon vanished and a period of violently fluctuating exchange rates followed; the value of each country's currency was no longer determined by the fixed price of gold but by supply and demand on the world markets.

What were the effects on the intra-Scandinavian exchange rates? Compared to the Swedish *krona*, the Norwegian and Danish *krone* soon started to lose value on the markets. The Scandinavian currencies were still traded at par well into 1915, albeit with a small, yet increasing, exchange fee charged by the banks for buying Norwegian and Danish *kroner* as of 1914.[9] With the exception of a short period in the spring of 1916, the Swedish *krona* was stronger than its Norwegian and Danish equivalents for the remainder of the war— frequently far, far stronger—as can be seen clearly in Figure 1. The other two currencies had a much more uniform development.[10]

What were the reasons for the diverging Scandinavian exchange rates? This issue has been the subject of some debate.[11] The most likely explanation is the fortuitous trade cycle, which helped the Swedish export sector and thus increased the demand for Swedish

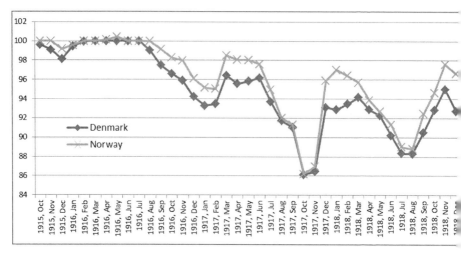

FIGURE 1: Riksbanken's avista DKK and NOK exchange rates October 1915–December 1918, monthly averages. Source, Riksbanken's yearbook 1918.

kronor compared to the other two currencies.[12] Norwegian and Danish exports, mainly generated by the two countries' primary sectors, did experience price increases; however, compared with important Swedish exports such as lumber, pulp, iron, steel, and iron ore—many of which were crucial to the belligerents' production of war materiel—the demand for Norwegian and Danish products was simply not as great.[13] Hence, greater demand for Swedish products in turn pushed up demand for the Swedish *krona* compared with the other Scandinavian currencies, thus resulting in a higher market price.

Riksbanken watched these developments with increasing concern. In 1915 Riksbanken's holdings of Scandinavian notes increased substantially, and the surplus of notes returned came to more than 72 million *kroner*. The main worry was the Danish notes; whilst the quantity of notes sent back to Norway actually dipped slightly between 1914 and 1915, the quantity of Danish notes increased massively.[14] As we have seen, the central banks had started charging a fee on one another's notes that reflected their market value, so why did these developments pose a problem for the Swedish monetary authorities? Was not the normal clearing mechanism for these central bank debts—payment in gold—a satisfactory solution for Riksbanken? The problem was that the increase was not confined to Riksbanken's holdings of Norwegian and Danish paper money. The massive inflow of gold during the last weeks of 1915 and the first weeks of 1916 was a new concern for the bank.[15]

Riksbanken's problem was the combined effect of the obligation to buy gold at the full legal value set by the SMU convention *and* the banks' right to settle their debts with one another using Scandinavian gold coins. This was firstly a financial matter, for when the Swedish *krona* rose above its gold value on the currency markets, Riksbanken's obligation to buy gold at the convention's fixed price thus led to a loss compared to buying gold at market value: the 2,480 *kronor* the bank was obliged to pay for a kilo of gold could buy substantially more gold on the market. Additionally, the Norwegian and Danish *kroner* had lost value against the Swedish *krona*, and Riksbanken's board of directors noticed that the rate loss of private business as well as the two other central banks could be transferred to Riksbanken with the help of the convention.[16]

The Scandinavian obligation to buy gold at par value meant there was risk of accelerated inflation. If the market value of one of these currencies, say Swedish *kronor*, increased to a certain level, it would be cheaper to send gold for example from Britain or Germany than to buy this currency on the market. As the seller of gold had a right to be paid in notes, such a gold inflow could increase the money supply, and thus in turn threatened to create higher prices.[17] Moreover, belligerents could use the SMU's convention and have gold minted in Norway or Denmark, or sell gold to one of those central banks, and so obtain Danish or Norwegian banknotes, which were still legal tender in Sweden.[18] The gold problem was not solely a Swedish matter—all of the Scandinavian currencies were prone to this danger. However, because of the Swedish currency's increased value compared to the other Scandinavian currencies and the massive gold inflows, Riksbanken was rightly the most concerned of the three central banks. What is more, prominent Swedish economists had begun to criticize Riksbanken's gold policy in addition to questioning whether gold should be *the* standard of value. Their criticism was strengthened as long as Sweden's gold reserves kept piling up while commodities were scarce and prices rose.[19]

To sum up, the gold problem stemmed from having a monetary policy with one foot in the new world and the other left in the old. Firstly, the value of each country's money was suddenly decided by the market, since the obligation on the central banks to *sell* gold for banknotes at a fixed price had been suspended. Secondly, the central banks still had to *buy* gold for notes at the old, fixed price. As the value of gold started to fall and the price of paper money conversely started to increase, whilst commodities were scarce due to the war, the world's hitherto immobile gold reserves began moving. Gold was apt to go where it would be valued the most, and the Scandinavian countries—with interesting export products and an obligation to buy gold at a fixed price still in effect—were a natural haven. Of these three, Sweden stood out as the best option because of its products' indispensability to the belligerents' war industry. The inflow of gold risked causing massive inflation while at the same time commodities and necessities flooded out, to the extent that in Sweden there was a fear that the country would share the fate of King Midas. Hence, for the Swedes it was necessary to end the gold inflows, and if trade was to be maintained, goods thus had to be paid for with goods, not metal. To solve the gold problem it was necessary to change the legislation regulating Riksbanken, but even though Sweden could prevent the inflow of gold directly from other countries, the SMU was still in effect. This meant that without the help of its union partners, Sweden could block neither Scandinavian gold directly nor other countries from sending gold indirectly via Denmark or Norway. By the end of 1915 the SMU was obviously becoming a straitjacket for Riksbanken. But by then wheels were already in motion.

The first step – the Swedish gold blockade

In the first days of 1916 Riksbanken resumed gold convertibility and again sold gold for notes at the old, fixed price. The fear that had set off the emergency measures of August 1914 was long gone: the

Swedish notes were quoted higher than their par value and a gold run was hardly a likely outcome. Faced with the option of either holding a kilo gold or 2,480 Swedish *kronor*, almost anyone would have preferred the latter as the market price made it more valuable. Even though the market value of the Norwegian *krone* in December also was higher than its gold value, Norges Bank did not think the time right to follow the Swedish initiative; on the contrary, it sought a return to more normal conditions.[20] However, the Swedish response was hardly encouraging; on 8 February 1916 the Riksdag relieved Riksbanken of its obligation to buy gold at par value in an attempt to 'prevent an uncontrolled increase of the gold reserves', putting the so-called 'gold blockade' into effect.[21] As Norway and Denmark had not been subjected to comparable gold inflows, Sweden's change of policy was not followed by her two neighbours—gold was still bought at the convention's fixed price. [22]

To make the Swedish gold blockade effective the convention had to be altered. The Swedish authorities thus had to make sure that Denmark and Norway would follow their lead, and Riksbanken took steps to secure their cooperation. Riksbanken sent a professor of economics, David Davidson, to Copenhagen in an attempt to convince Nationalbanken to fall into line.[23] Perhaps this was also a pre-negotiation attempt to obtain the cooperation of Nationalbanken prior to tackling Norges Bank on a two-against-one basis, in the hope of undermining the hard stance against altering the conditions for gold shipments that had been signalled by Norges Bank.[24] A meeting between representatives of the three central banks was eventually held in Stockholm in February 1916. The outcome of these proceedings was that the right to mint gold was temporarily suspended, Norges Bank and Nationalbanken agreed to recommend to their respective governments that the obligation to buy gold at the fixed price should be suspended,[25] and gold was only to be exported after 'consulting' the receiving central bank. Although Riksbanken thus to some extent got its way in implementing Sweden's gold policy without terminating the convention of the SMU, the two other banks had not agreed to anything awkward.[26] The manner in which Norway and Denmark implemented the 'gold blockade' was reluctant, and ultimately prompted by financial considerations rather than by an urge to uphold the partnership. Hence, it was not until the Norwegian gold reserves had risen to unprecedented levels a month later that Norges Bank wanted to remove the requirement to buy gold at the fixed price.[27] Riksbanken had not either been able to make the gold blockade effective; as neither Nationalbanken nor Norges Bank was interested in removing the possibility of settling their debts in gold, the door was still wide open.

Second-class cooperation

The unsuccessful Swedish efforts to implement an adequate gold blockade policy would have been striking for anyone with access to Riksbanken's vaults in the autumn of 1916; having lain more or less stable since the turn of the year, from September the gold reserve had begun to increase yet again. The loose ends of the gold problem and the working of the SMU led Riksbanken to initiate a new meeting in October 1916, this time in Gothenburg. Riksbanken's agenda included a Danish suggestion from May—a common gold policy. Other topics included limitations on the redemption of banknotes and the question of imposing interest rates on the formerly interest-free central banks accounts. Although the exchange rates seemed to have stabilized at close to par during the spring months, developments since the summer had again contributed to divergent rates—most noticeably the value of the Swedish *krona* rose massively compared to the other two (see Figure 8.1). Thus, exchange rates became an important topic at this meeting, but not surprisingly it was made known to the press that one of the solutions proposed by the Norwegian and Danish representatives—settlement in gold—was not considered helpful by Riksbanken.[28]

Did Riksbanken come any closer to solving its problem? The three central banks were actually able to reach an agreement on some points, including that a fee could be charged when drawing on the other central banks. If the central banks were in future to buy gold on the international markets, they agreed to inform one another of price, amount, and where it was bought; similarly, information was to be shared if any were to mint gold. Nationalbanken was in addition asked to help arrange quotations of the Swedish *krona* on Copenhagen stock exchange, while Norges Bank was asked if interest of 3 per cent could be paid on amounts exceeding 3 million *kroner/kronor* when clearing the two central banks' mutual line of credit.[29] Although the Norwegians rejected this last request—which actually implied an increase in the normal interest-free debt from the 1905 agreement with Riksbanken—the other points were agreeable to both Norges Bank and Nationalbanken, and it seemed as if a common gold policy was largely established.

However, even though agreeing to share information about gold purchases and minting may seem like the intensification of Scandinavian gold policy cooperation, it might as well be seen as the opposite. The fact that the three central banks were to inform one another whenever buying or minting gold can be regarded as a rather suspect method of creating a barrier to the other countries (for which read Denmark and Norway) from speculating in gold shipments instead of paying the (Swedish) currency's full market value. Moreover, when Norges Bank refused to countenance paying interest rates on mutual credits, it simply argued that a debt amounting to more than 3 million *kroner* was unlikely to be long-lived, as long as the 'clearing could be done by gold or other means'.[30] At this point the mutual lines of credit had not yet become a problem. However, under pertaining conditions there were two solutions available if further imbalances should ever develop: increase the debt, or settle it in gold. The Norwegian and Swedish central banks were on a collision course over this issue, and by its answer the Norges Bank seems simply to have ignored Riksbanken's gold fears. Thus Riksbanken's more acute problem had not been solved by this meeting either: Scandinavian central bank debts could still be settled by means of gold shipments.

Third time's the harm

The effects of the unsuccessful Swedish efforts to ward off gold inflows were evident almost immediately after the October meeting, as both Norges Bank and Nationalbanken sent Riksbanken 5 million *kroner* in Scandinavian gold.[31] Even though there were some improvements in Riksbanken's accounts at the end of the year, including the halving of 1915's exceptionally large number of returned Danish notes, these were paltry sums compared to the gold accounts. Scandinavian gold coin had increased by nearly 18 million *kroner* and foreign gold by more than 40 million *kronor* during 1916. Although most of the increase predated February's gold blockade, the increase in the aftermath of the blockade was nonetheless 23 million. Thus Riksbanken explicitly stated that the gold received after 8 February was mostly Scandinavian gold coin 'to which the provisions of the law […] are not applicable'.[32]

To the uninformed contemporary observer, Nationalbanken was to blame for the massive inflow of unwanted Scandinavian gold into Riksbanken's vaults. The reason was that most of the inflow was as Danish gold coin, and in contrast to Norges Bank the Danish central bank had not stopped minting gold. This was the main reason why Swedish monetary authorities deemed it crucial to limit or cease minting when trying to solve its gold problem. Nationalbanken was exposed to harsh criticism when it was discovered that Swedish measures in effect came down to an attempt to stop Danish gold coin. The criticism was first made by Swedish economist Gustav Cassel in 1917; however, it was echoed by Cassel's partisan in Denmark, the economist Axel Nielsen.[33] In fact the outcry was so massive that Nationalbanken felt the need to defend itself publicly. However, it seems that it was not until Marcus Rubin's second in command, Carl Th. Ussing, published his book about Nationalbanken in 1926 that the beans were spilled; the real offender had been Norges Bank.[34] According to Ussing, the Norwegians wanted Nationalbanken's debt to Norges Bank to be settled by sending Danish gold to Riksbanken in order to cover Norges Bank's debt there. To Nationalbanken this was nothing more than a matter between Norges Bank and Riksbanken, and the Danish bank could obviously not refuse to settle its debts in the way its Norwegian creditor wanted—in legal tender.

Although Victor Moll in his New Year's greeting to Karl Gether Bomhoff hoped to come to a 'better understanding between the three central banks' and with 'good will' overcome the differences in their cooperation, any good will the Scandinavian central bank cooperation enjoyed was running out by 1917.[35] In the middle of January 1917, financial considerations once again showed its prominence over nice phrases when Norges Bank found it necessary to pay its debt to Riksbanken by sending 3-4 million *kroner* of gold. Riksbanken replied by admitting that it was not in a position to refuse the gold, but it appealed to Norges Bank's sense of decency, and asked not to be forced to buy expensive gold considering the market price.[36] However, as Norway did not have any commodities to spare it was necessary to cover the imbalance with gold—in Bomhoff's words, the present situation had become 'unbearable'.[37] A few days later he forced through the gold shipment.[38]

The situation clearly had become unbearable to Moll as well; the need to protect Sweden from expensive gold and inflation made him recommend governmental negotiations to limit each country's right to mint gold under the convention.[39] Thus, in contrast to the two meetings of 1916, the meeting of April 1917 became an official meeting with delegates representing the three countries' governments, with the obvious objective of altering the forty-year-old convention. Before negotiations commenced Riksbanken leaned heavily upon Professor Davidson, but as neither Nationalbanken nor Norges Bank was interested in terminating or suspending any of the convention's paragraphs as suggested by Davidson, negotiations came to revolve around a proposal from the Norwegian delegates.[40] Norway was willing to stop gold shipments on the condition that the three central banks would put credit on reasonable terms at one another's disposal, and this standpoint was supported by the Danish delegates. As sketched out, the export ban was to be strictly maintained, although gold could be sent on agreement; if one of the bank's debts exceeded 1 million *kroner* the creditor had the right to be sent gold; and a small interest rate would be charged if the deficit exceeded 3 million *kroner*, but if this rate were to exceed a certain level the debtor had the right to send gold. An agreement was reached only after omitting the paragraph defining interest rates—to be decided by mutual agreement between the various banks. Moreover, Moll had to urge Davidson to agree to the proposal and allowed him to state for the minutes that he did not find the agreement sufficient to achieve the aims of Sweden's gold policy.

Just a few days before leaving Copenhagen, Marcus Rubin had written that he was heading for Stockholm, where '"Scandinavianism" is to be submitted to a small practical test—which I doubt it will past'.[41] Did Scandinavianism pass the test, considering that an agreement actually was concluded? In the very short run one can probably regard the incident as Swedish gold policy being sacrificed on the altar of Scandinavianism. Although the preferred policy of the Swedish monetary authorities was to alter or suspend parts of the convention, the proposed changes were unacceptable to the SMU partners. To carry out its gold policy, Sweden thus would have to abandon the SMU, and the political costs of doing that were simply too high. However, Rubin was in many respects correct: 'Scandinavianism' barely passed the test, despite the agreement. The solution was far from sufficient as the basic problem had not changed—gold could ultimately still be sent to cover central bank debts. The only difference was that the agreement paved the way to make greater use of lines of credit. However, to the Swedish monetary authorities this was not satisfactory either; in fact, curbing international credit was precisely one of the matters that were at the centre of Swedish economic policy. Thus the economic and financial costs of upholding the SMU were almost as high as the political costs of abandoning it, and there were few indications of Scandinavian brotherhood in the interaction between the three banks. The final months of 1917, *annus horribilis* of Scandinavian monetary cooperation, was to bear witness to this.

1917—*annus horribilis*

The hardship inflicted by the war worsened in 1917, as a number of circumstances dramatically altered the economic conditions of the northern neutrals. Probably the most important was Germany's decision to unleash unrestricted submarine warfare from 1. February, which made transportation, and thus obtaining necessities, extremely difficult. All the Scandinavian countries duly imposed rationing on foodstuffs; the extremity of the situation even led trade representatives from the three countries to meet and agree to help one another by exchanging commodities.[42] To top it all, the gold problem was aggravated, as Sweden more than ever needed *commodities* in return for its commodities, while Norway had no commodities to spare—only gold.

The April 1917 agreement is usually seen as ending the turmoil and differences between the three central banks while solving Sweden's gold problem.[43] Nothing could be further from the truth. Although the three central banks had managed to come to terms bilaterally on the interest rates on debts, the quarrelling between Norges Bank and Riksbanken peaked this year.[44] The problem was that Norges Bank's debt to Riksbanken increased massively once they had agreed on the mutual lines of credit—and this to a degree that obviously was not expected by Riksbanken when concluding the April agreement. A central element in the bickering was the inability of Norges Bank and Riksbanken to reach a decision on which agreement should be adhered to. For the rest of the year Norges Bank solely referred to the agreement of April 1917 and the line of credit so obtained; Riksbanken felt this was unreasonable, and that the old agreement of 1905 with fees on drafts was more appropriate—particularly as Norges Bank's debt was constantly increasing. Norges Bank's debt to Riksbanken soon surpassed 3 million *kroner*—a sum that had been considered virtually impossible in October 1916—and by the end of June it had reached 7.6 million, a fact which made Moll write of his concerns to Bomhoff as this had 'attracted some attention'.[45]

During the summer months the situation became most uncomfortable, as the temperature in the correspondence between the two banks increased; the banks simply could not work out their differences. 'Our "Nordic cooperation"', Bomhoff complained to the deputy governor Haakon Monsen, 'does not always seem to be particularly effective!'[46] Thus by the end of July, Norges Bank's debt had increased to 8.2 million *kroner*, and by the end of August more than 10 million *kroner*. As Riksbanken believed the debt would only increase further, it abandoned its attempts to resist gold shipments from Norway and asked to be sent 5 million *kroner* in Scandinavian gold in September 1917.[47] This brought no relief, however; things in fact worsened. In the numerous letters between Moll and Bomhoff, the two conflicting understandings of the situation were repeated over and over again; the same arguments were made, whilst the tone deteriorated. Both banks stuck to their guns, while the Norwegian debt piled up. In the middle of October, Riksbanken yielded once more and agreed to accept another 10 million *kroner* in gold.[48] After this the letters became increasingly poisonous, and by the end of October Moll and Bomhoff no longer sent each other personal letters with polite greetings.[49] The banks could not find any common ground and Norges Bank's debt remained large; however, Riksbanken relented yet again, and accepted another 5 million *kroner* in Scandinavian gold in November.[50] At this point Riksbanken's repeated concessions made Norges Bank ask if it was to be assumed that Riksbanken in the future would accept Scandinavian gold when being drawn on, in which case 'the difficulties in essence would be at least temporarily removed'.[51] The reply was short but positive; Riksbanken gave in by accepting gold beyond the last 5 million *kroner* as well.[52]

At the end of 1917 Riksbanken thus chucked its cards in and Norges Bank won the zero-sum game. The abrupt halt in gold shipments the following year did not mean that Norges Bank and Riksbanken finally had come to terms; rather, it most likely reflected the smaller fluctuations in the two currencies in relationship to changes in the world's currency conditions and in the Scandinavian trade balance.[53] Over the course of 1917—a disastrous year for Scandinavian monetary cooperation—some 34 million *kroner* in Scandinavian gold coin was sent to Riksbanken from Norges Bank.[54] It seems likely that all of this gold was received in the teeth of Riksbanken's wishes, and during the year the Swedish central bank's gold reserve increased by more than 60 million *kroner* despite the attempts to solve the gold problem by implementing a policy that could shelter the country from gold inflows.[55]

Concluding remarks

The First World War effectively ended the SMU. It is often described as having been doomed from the moment gold convertibility was suspended in August 1914; however, the manner in which the union disintegrated reveals some interesting issues to do with international cooperation at times of stress. There were few obstacles to founding the union and making it work during the heyday of the international gold standard. Even the political turmoil of 1905 was overcome. However, upholding the SMU when its foundations were severely damaged—by the disbanding of the three currencies exchange rates and their relationship with gold—was a completely different matter. Thus the pursuit of national self-interest, be it financial or economic, became paramount for all three central banks when the world changed so fundamentally in 1914. The SMU was a relic of a different epoch, belonging as it did to the pre-1914, liberal era, but to the contemporaries this was not evident. The doomed efforts to maintain the partnership reflected the belief that as soon as international hostilities ended things would go back to normal.

Sweden's wishes to change the SMU's rules could be accommodated as long as the changes were to the satisfaction of all three parties. When desperate Swedish needs collided with desperate Norwegian needs the result was a stalemate, overcome only a slow return to 'business as usual'. The need to do something more drastic by altering the fundamentals of the SMU seems to have been postponed by the urge to maintain the union as a beacon of Scandinavianism. This is probably the reason why the SMU survived far beyond the 1920s—when efforts were made to develop international economic cooperation beyond the narrow scope of Scandinavianism—and existed as an anachronistic survivor of the old world, until it was finally terminated in 1973. However, the lesson of discussions about collaborating to solve the Scandinavian Monetary Union's gold problem during the First World War is painfully clear: money talks.

Notes

1 Axel Nielsen, *Den skandinaviske møntunion. Et historisk rids* (Copenhagen: Børsens forlag, 1917), 74, 'Hvad der er tilbage af den, er imidlertid vanskeligt at faa Øje paa. Tilsyneladende er alt det der i det 19de Aarhundrede gennem mer end 30 Aars utrættelig Virken byggedes op af økonomisk Samarbejde, nu lagt øde i Løbet af blot to Aar, og det paa et Tidspunkt, hvor e n n y B e v æ g e l s e for en mere intim økonomisk Samvirken er i Vækst.'

2 Marcello de Cecco, 'European monetary and financial cooperation before the First World War', *Rivista di storia economica*, 9 (1992), 67.

3 The following section is based on Robert J. Bartel, 'International Monetary Unions: the XIXth Century Experience', *Journal of European Economic History*, 3 (1974), 689-704; Eli Hecskcher, 'Sweden in the World War', in Heckscher et. al. (eds.), *Sweden, Norway, Denmark and Iceland in the World War* (Carnegie Endowment for International Peace; New Haven: Yale University Press, 1930); Ingrid Henriksen & Niels Kærgård, 'The Scandinavian Currency Union 1875–1914', in Jaime Reis (ed.), *International Monetary Systems in Historical Perspective* (London: Macmillan, 1995); Nielsen, 1917; Nicolai Rygg, *Norges Banks historie II* (Oslo, 1954); Krim Talia, *The Scandinavian Currency Union, 1873–1924* (diss.; Stockholm: Stockholm School of Economics, 2004); Lars Fredrik Øksendal, 'The impact of the Scandinavian Monetary Union on financial market integration', *Financial History Review*, 14 (2007a), 125-148; L. F. Øksendal, *Essays in Norwegian Monetary History, 1869–1914* (diss.; Bergen: Norwegian School of Economics and Business Administration, 2007b).

4 See, for example, Hans Chr. Johansen, 'Om at skrive bankhistorie', *Historisk Tidsskrift* [Denmark], 90 (1990), 383-404. I am grateful to Martin Austnes for making me aware of this article.

5 Which thus for all practical purposes can be extended to 1910 (Henriksen & Kærgård 1995, 109).

6 Øksendal 2007a.

7 Gunnar Wetterberg, *Pengarna & Makten* (Stockholm: Sveriges Riksbank/ Atlantis, 2009), 233–4.

8 Rygg 1954, 470.

9 Ibid. 471.

10 Jan Tore Klovland, 'Historical exchange rate data 1819–2003', in Øivind Eitrheim, J. T. Klovland & Jan Fredrik Qvigstad (eds.), *Historical Monetary Statistics for Norway 1819–2003* (Oslo: Norges Bank, 2004), Table A2.

11 Until recently, economic historians have mainly focused on the money expansion, arguing that as Norway and Denmark issued more paper money than Sweden, the value of the Swedish *krona* was higher simply because it was more rare. There is, however, reason to believe that this explanation is incorrect, especially in view of the years up to 1917. I am elaborating these debates in more detail in my forthcoming Ph.D. thesis.

12 See Talia 2004, 179–80.

13 Heckscher 1930, 173.

14 Riksbanken, Årsbok (Stockholm: Sveriges Riksbank, 1915).

15 After an increase between December 1914 and the last weekly report in February 1915, Riksbanken's reserve hardly moved until mid-December 1915 (see the Riksbanken's weekly reports 1914–1916 in *Ekonomisk Tidskrift*).

16 Talia 2004, 174

17 For the Norwegian experience, see Monica Værholm and L. F. Øksendal, 'Leaving the Anchor: Monetary Policy in neutral Norway during the First World War', *International History Review*, 32/4 (2010), 661-686.

18 Erling Olsen & Erik Hoffmeyer, *Dansk Pengehistorie 1914–1960* (Odense/ Copenhagen: Danmarks Nationalbank, 1968), 49; Carl Th. Ussing, *Nationalbanken 1914–1924* (Copenhagen: Gads Forlag, 1926), 88.

19 The severest critic was undoubtedly Gustav Cassel, for example, in his 1917 book *Dyrtid och sedelöverflöd*; however, the most influential of all contemporary critics was the economics professor David Davidson.

20 National Archives, Oslo (NA), Norges Bank's archives (NB), Archive of Board of Directors I (DI), Bomhoff's book of copies 1900–1918 (Bb0001), letter from Bomhoff to Moll, 4 January 1916.

21 NA, NB, Archive of Board of Directors II (DII), D0641, letter from Ministry of Finance to Norges Bank's Board of Directors, 14 February 1916, 'avværge en ukontrollert ökning av guldforraadet'; Talia 2004, 174.

22 Denmark's gold reserve had only shown a minor increase in 1915, and even though the Norwegian reserve had increased substantially this was mostly due to events up until August. Statistics from *Ekonomisk Tidskrift*.

23 Ussing 1926, 88; Olsen & Hoffmeyer 1968, 49.

24 NA, NB, DI, Bb0001, Bomhoff to Moll, 16 February 1916.

25 Ussing 1926, 88–9.

26 Ibid.

27 NA, NB, DI, E0017, Norges Bank to Ministry of Finance, 30 March 1916 (draft).

28 Rygg 1954, 477.

29 Riksbanken to Nationalbanken and Norges Bank, 11 October 1916 (in Ussing, 1926, 92–3 & Rygg 1954, 477–8, respectively).

30 Rygg 1954, 478, 'oppgjør kan skje ved gull eller på annen måte'.

31 NA, NB, DI, E0017, 'Valutaresume pr. 30/11-16', Norges Bank to Riksbanken, 26 October 1916, and from Norges Bank to Nationalbanken, 30 October & 10 November 1916.

32 Riksbanken, Årsbok (Stockholm: Sveriges Riksbank, 1916), 'på vilket bestämmelserna i lagen […] icke hade någon tillämpning.'

33 Ussing 1926, 101 ff; Olsen & Hoffmeyer 1968, 52 ff.

34 Ussing 1926, 94–5.

35 NA, NB, DII, D0642, Moll to Bomhoff, 31 December 1916, 'ökadt samförstånd de tre centralbankerna emellan', 'god vilja'.

36 Letter from Moll to Bomhoff, 19 January 1917, D0642-DII-NB-NA.

37 NA, NB, DII, D0642, Bomhoff to Moll, 20 January 1917, 'Den nuværende tilstand blir snart utaalelig'.

38 NA, NB, DII, D0642, Bomhoff to Moll, 30 January 1917.

39 NA, NB, DII, D0642, Moll to Bomhoff, 22 & 30 January 1917.

40 The following is based on NA, NB, DII, D0641, the official minutes of the Stockholm meeting, 17–19 April 1917, and the undated summary by Bomhoff and Rygg of the Scandinavian conference on those dates regarding the currency convention; NA, NB, DII, D0642, David Davidson, 'P.M. rörande den skandinaviska myntkonventionen', enclosed with Moll to Bomhoff, 13 February 1917; Ussing 1926, 99.

41 *Marcus Rubins Brevveksling*, ed. Lorenz Rerup (Copenhagen: Rosenkilde og Bagger, 1962), iii. 300, Rubin to Kr. Erslev, 19 April 1917, '"Skandinavismen" skal underkastes en lille praktisk Prøve—som jeg tvivler om, den bestaar'.

42 Einar Cohn, 'Denmark in the Great War', in E. Hecscher (ed.), *Sweden, Norway, Denmark and Iceland in the World War* (Carnegie Endowment for International Peace; New Haven, Yale University Press, 1930), 470–1.

43 See, for example, Bartel 1974, 702; Michael Bergman, Stefan Gerlach & Lars Jonung, 'The rise and fall of the Scandinavian Currency Union 1873–1920', *European Economic Review*, 37 (1993), 515.

44 See NA, Archives of the Ministry of Finance (FIN), Finance Office (FOc), Dca0099, Riksbanken and Nationalbanken to Norges Bank, 21 & 24 April 1917 respectively, and replies from Norges Bank to Riksbanken and Nationalbanken, 24 & 26 April 1917 respectively.

45 NA, NB, DII, D0642, Moll to Bomhoff, 2 July 1917, 'väckt en viss uppmärksamhet'; Rygg 1954, 486; the statistics here and in the following section are from *Ekonomisk Tidskrift* 1917.

46 NA, NB, DII, D0642, Bomhoff to Monsen, 21 July 1917, 'Vort "samarbeide i Norden" synes ikke altid at ville bli synderlig virkningsfuldt!'

47 NA, NB, DII, D0642, Moll to Bomhoff, 11 September 1917.

48 NA, NB, DII, D0642, Moll to Bomhoff, 17 October 1917.

49 See NA, NB, DII, D0642, Norges Bank and Riksbanken correspondence from 20 October 1917.

50 NA, NB, DII, D0642, Riksbanken to Norges Bank, 12 November 1917.

51 NA, NB, DII, D0642, Norges Bank to Riksbanken, 16 November 1917, 'vanskeligheterne, i det væsentlige, iethvertfald foreløpig være ryddet tilside'.

52 NA, NB, DII, D0642, Riksbanken to Norges Bank, 19 November 1917.

53 Rygg 1954, 489; the value of Norwegian imports from Sweden increased by 36 per cent from 1917 to 1918, while exports increased by 73 per cent (see *Norges Offisielle Statistikk XII 245*, (Historisk Statistikk 1968; Statistisk Sentralbyrå, 1969), Table 165).

54 Rygg 1954, 488.

55 *Ekonomisk Tidskrift*, 1917–1918.

CHAPTER 9

Military history in an age of military change

Carl Bennedich, the Swedish General Staff, and the First World War

Gunnar Åselius

This chapter discusses how the experience of the First World War helped introduce a broader and more modern, scholarly approach to the writing of official military history under the aegis of the Swedish General Staff. A central figure in bringing about this change was Carl Bennedich (1880–1939), at the time a lieutenant at the General Staff's Military History Section. There is an interesting contrast between Bennedich's personal, arch-conservative, and fiercely nationalistic ideological position and the progressive instincts he demonstrated as a military historian. As has been pointed out by Swedish author Jan Olof Olsson, the radical-nationalist, politicizing type of officer that Bennedich represented was untypical for Sweden in the early twentieth century but quite common in Germany. One can easily imagine Bennedich as a subaltern in the Imperial Army, as one of the dangerous officers who conspired to overthrow the Weimar Republic, but also as a member of the opposition against Hitler in July 1944.[1] Bennedich's unexpected role as a 'modernizer' of Swedish military history raises the question of how a romantic dreamer with seemingly little understanding for the century in which he lived could be among the first to realize the impact of total war in the twentieth century. As I will demonstrate here, this had to do with Bennedich's deep involvement in the ideological struggle over democracy and parliamentary rule in Swedish society at the time, as well as with his discontent with Sweden's position as neutral between the belligerent great powers.

Sweden did not differ from other European countries in that military history had played a significant role in the education of officers before 1914. The Swedish Army War College had been reorganized in 1878 by Colonel Hugo Raab, using as a model the Prussian *Kriegsakademie* in Berlin, where Raab had studied in the 1850s. During the two-year-long course at the college, military history—together with tactics—was the largest subject, with some 200 hours' teaching (15 per cent of the total teaching time). A thorough knowledge of warfare in the past, Raab argued, could supply the students with the war experience that they could not gain through personal service, improve their general *Bildung*, and compensate for the fact that officers—unlike other Swedish government officials—had no university education. The military study of history was not undertaken only to teach students some supposedly 'eternal principles of warfare'; it also aimed at exploring the Swedish experience of war from a more historicist perspective as an object lesson for future conflicts against the nation's 'hereditary enemies' and to help build a professional identity.[2]

At the same time, the decades before the First World War saw rapid technological change. By the early 1900s, it was generally agreed that the industrialization of warfare had made cavalry charges and massed infantry attacks more or less suicidal enterprises. This, in turn, cast doubt on the role of history in military education. However, the prevailingly Social Darwinist ideology among European officers also created a readiness to accept high losses. Any nation claiming influence in the twentieth century, it was argued, must be prepared to prove its moral strength through bloody sacrifice. The lessons of the Russo-Japanese War in 1904–05, for instance—a conflict which saw the extensive use of indirect artillery fire, trenches, barbed wire, and machine guns—may seem obvious in retrospect, but were not so to contemporaries. The massive display of modern firepower during the siege of Port Arthur made less impression than the fact that the Japanese ultimately defeated the Russians because they were prepared to suffer tens of thousands of casualties. More than anything else, Japan's victory seemed to confirm the popular belief that war was a contest of will in which the toughest would prevail.[3]

Although European military professionals before 1914 certainly studied the technical aspects of contemporary conflicts such as the Boer War or the Russo-Japanese War, they also spent considerable time analysing pre-industrial wars, as these seemed equally rich with regard to moral examples. The American Civil War, then the only war of attrition waged by an industrialized society in history, evoked little interest outside the US, and although the military history sections of the French and German General Staffs published monumental histories on the Franco-Prussian War of 1870, the campaigns of national heroes such as Napoleon or Frederick the Great interested them much more. Together with other great commanders in the past like Alexander the Great, Hannibal, Julius Caesar, or Sweden's Gustavus Adolphus, Napoleon and *Der Alte Fritz* played the leading roles in the story of the progression of (Western) warfare, a story that was told in more or less the same way at most European military colleges. Apart from demonstrating that the central principles of war had remained unaltered since antiquity, the aim of this grand narrative was to validate the importance of moral factors on the battlefield, emphasizing to the young officer that one day his personal contribution could make a difference.[4]

When war finally came in 1914, disappointment and frustration awaited the European military. It was not until March 1918, after an almost four-year-long period of deadlock on the Western Front, that the German Spring Offensive demonstrated that mobile warfare was still possible in the age of machines. However, the new German infiltration tactics differed substantially from traditional tactics. The dense, regular formations that had characterized European battle since antiquity had now vanished. The delimited battlefield had dissolved into a wasteland; a combat zone without clear perimeters, dominated by artillery fire, poison gas, tanks, and aircraft, where small, autonomous groups of soldiers wandered about in isolation, struggling to survive in a ravaged landscape. It has been suggested that if an officer familiar with combat on the Western Front in 1914 had been able to time-travel four years into the future to witness combat on the same front in 1918, he would have been unable to grasp what was going on. On the other hand, had an officer with experience from the Western Front in 1918 been able to travel further into the future, he could probably have made perfect sense of the battlefields of 1940, and possibly even those in Iraq in 2003. The main elements of modern three-dimensional warfare appeared during the final months of World War I and not—as is so often claimed—in France in 1940 or in the Persian Gulf much later.[5]

Needless to say, the experience of war in 1914–18 affected the use of history in military education. If young officers were to continue studying classical manoeuvres and learning about the great commanders, if General Staff history departments were to continue producing multi-volume works on the great captains and their triumphs in the seventeenth, eighteenth and nineteenth centuries, these activities could no longer be motivated by positivist arguments. It was not self-evident that the same principles of war that had governed the Battle of Marathon were still at work during the Meuse-Argonne Offensive in 1918, or that studies of past wars would disclose any relevant truths about the wars of tomorrow. This precipitated a major cultural crisis for the military educational system as developed in the post-Napoleonic era—a crisis that would cast its shadow over the military profession during the entire interwar period.

Now, when numerous new aspects of warfare (gas war, air war, mechanized war, propaganda war, economic blockade, industrial mobilization) had to be integrated into the teaching, the dominant position that military history had held in war college curricula since the nineteenth century could no longer be maintained. In 1926, time for military history was reduced substantially at the Swedish Army War College, and in the years after 1934 additional reductions followed. A group of younger General Staff officers around Major Helge Jung—who would be appointed Supreme Commander of the Swedish armed forces in 1944—were instrumental in effecting these changes. Privately, Jung shared the nationalist-conservative ideology of the officer-corps in general.

Moreover, he had a serious interest in history. He had studied the subject as a young man at the University of Lund in 1905 and later served as head of the General Staff's Military History Section. He realized, however, that the traditional identity of the Swedish officer as answerable only to King and Nation had no place in the twentieth century. Officers must accept democratization and learn how to communicate with elected politicians, in the same way as other officials in modern society, otherwise their professional influence over defence policy would be reduced to insignificance. The role of compensating for the lack of university education among officers, which had previously been played by military history, was in the 1930s taken over by a new subject at the Army War College called 'Sweden's strategic situation'. This subject focused on current affairs, and included diplomatic relations, military geography, and the armed forces of the countries in the Baltic Sea region. These studies would better prepare the officer-corps to communicate with the future-oriented and utilitarian decision-makers of the modern age than would studying Sweden's wars against Russia and Denmark centuries ago.[6]

It is quite certain that Carl Bennedich disapproved of these changes. Nor does he seem to have been particularly interested in the changes in military technology demonstrated by the First World War. Nonetheless, it was his activities at the General Staff Military History Section that had helped pave the way for this new order.

Bennedich, whose father owned a construction company in the city of Falkenberg in south-west Sweden, had received his commission in 1901 and been assigned to the Northern Skåne Infantry at the garrison of Kristianstad. He had been passionately interested in Swedish history since his youth, as was evident when he applied to the Army War College in Stockholm in 1908. Among the many hundreds of applicants to the college in its thirty-six year existence before World War I, he was the only one ever to receive a '10' for his entrance essay (the given subject that year was 'What were the main drawbacks of the great-power position maintained by Sweden in the seventeenth century?').[7] At the Army War College, Bennedich distinguished himself by his fervent admiration for

Sweden's eighteenth-century soldier king, Charles XII. One of his fellow students later claimed that Bennedich frequently made comparisons

> between Sweden's situation in the early eighteenth and early twentieth centuries. How much more fortunate the latter would have been if only HE [Charles XII] had been alive.[8]

After graduation in 1910, Bennedich was admitted to the General Staff officer-corps and assigned to the Military History Section in 1914. From 1916 to 1920, he served as a senior lecturer in military history at the Army War College. During this period, he also co-ordinated the work on the General Staff's four-volume history of the campaigns of Charles XII, *Karl XII på slagfältet* ('Charles XII on the battlefield'), personally writing a substantial portion of the text. Between 1922 and 1929, he served as commanding officer of the Military History Section. In 1932 he was promoted to colonel and died seven years later, when serving as commanding officer of the Life Grenadier Regiment in Linköping.[9]

One of the men who worked under Bennedich during the 1920s was the director of the Military Archives, Birger Steckzén. Steckzén, who was a self-conscious man and soon came into conflict with Bennedich, gives a highly unsympathetic portrait of him in his memoirs, which were written in the 1950s. According to Steckzén, Bennedich regarded the military profession as superior to all others and believed that an officer—especially a member of the General Staff—was competent to solve most of the mysteries in life. Steckzén even compared Bennedich to Adolf Hitler:

> Outsiders often found him a fascinating person because of his dynamic nature and his flight of ideas. For those who had to deal with him on a daily basis he was a trying and tiresome man. He could sit and talk late into the night—that is, he talked the whole time.

Still, even such a hostile witness as Steckzén could write of Bennedich that 'by virtue of his mind he was very talented', admitting that some of his ideas were simply 'sparkling'.[10]

Bennedich had been active in founding Karolinska förbundet (the Caroline Society) in 1910—dedicated to studying Swedish history in 1654–1718, when Charles XII, his father, and grandfather had ruled Sweden—and he was in constant correspondence with some of the leading Swedish historians of his time, including professors Harald Hjärne in Uppsala and Arthur Stille in Lund. In 1911, together with a colleague, he surveyed the battlefield of Poltava in the Ukraine (where his hero Charles XII had suffered his decisive defeat against Tsar Peter of Russia in 1709) on behalf of the General Staff. In his inspection report from the battlefield terrain, Bennedich, who was inspired by a recent, apologetic study of Charles XII's campaign in Russia by his friend Arthur Stille, largely exonerated the king of any blame for Sweden's defeat. Instead, Bennedich identified the commander of the infantry, General Lewenhaupt, as the main culprit.[11]

This reinterpretation of the battle was presented in print in Karolinska förbundet's yearbook in 1913, and would later reappear in Bennedich's article on the Battle of Poltava in the popular home encyclopaedia *Nordisk familjebok*. Through the encyclopaedia and Bennedich's later work on the General Staff official histories of the campaigns of Charles XII—which the author Frans G. Bengtsson would use for his account of the battle in a famous biography of the king in the 1930s—Bennedich's explanation of the defeat would find its way into hundreds of thousands of Swedish homes. It remained largely unchallenged until the late 1950s.[12]

Bennedich's greatest claim to fame, however, came not from his work as an historian but from his role during the 'Courtyard Crisis' in February 1914, when he and the Swedish explorer Sven Hedin secretly drafted the constitutionally controversial speech which King Gustav V gave to 30,000 farmers, who had gathered to protest against the defence policy of Karl Staaff's Liberal government. The explicit support for the protesters that the King expressed in his speech forced Staaff's government to resign a few days later.[13]

In November that year, Bennedich began his tour of service at the General Staff Military History Section in Stockholm. Since 1890, the section had been spending most of its resources on producing a history of Sweden's wars against Russia and Denmark in

1808–09. This conflict was a traumatic memory, for it had ended in catastrophic defeat, the cession of Sweden's Finnish provinces, and the termination of six centuries of common Swedish–Finnish statehood. As this was the latest war Sweden had fought against its 'hereditary enemy' Russia, it was also expected to contain useful military lessons for the future. After twenty-four years, the sixth volume—which treated operations on the Norwegian border until July 1808—was still under preparation, and work on the seventh—which dealt with operations against Norway and Denmark until March 1809—had proceeded quite far (although it would not appear in print until 1919). At least two more volumes were planned before the project would be completed.[14]

The reception of this official history had been generally benign in academic circles, although not entirely uncritical. In his review of the fourth volume in *Historisk tidskrift* in 1905, Professor Ludvig Stavenow expressed his great appreciation of its thorough research, the high quality of maps, and the profuse and interesting data presented in the appendices, while at the same time pointing out that the lack of scholarly training among the authors had resulted in a rather fragmented main text, overloaded with detail at the expense of context and inner structure.[15] From the viewpoint of a professional historian, there is little to add to this appraisal even a century later.

The lack of inner cohesion in the General Staff work was not surprising. The Military History Section had set out in the 1880s by collecting enormous quantities of documents—or copies of documents—from archives in Sweden and abroad. When the project was finally concluded in the early 1920s, there were more than 130 shelf metres of excerpts and working material. However, there had been little notion of previous research or particular research problems, and in reality each volume became a compilation of disparate studies undertaken by several authors over the course of many years. Clearly, there was no general idea behind the work, nor any ambition to emphasize certain aspects of the past before others.[16] To some extent, this intellectual void may not only reflect the peculiar conditions under which the work came into being, but also the growing uncertainty among military professionals in the years before World War I as to what lessons from history would be relevant in the modern age.

As preparations for the eighth volume began, the Chief of the General Staff General Knut Bildt ordered a special study, in view of the possibility of Sweden being dragged into the ongoing war. In contrast to the earlier volumes in the series, this volume was to deal with the defensive measures that had been put in place in the territory of present Sweden in 1808–09, and thus risked revealing information that might still be sensitive. What precautions should be taken with such a text that would eventually be published?

It so happened that the task of answering this question at the Military History Section was entrusted to the newly assigned Lieutenant Carl Bennedich. From Bennedich's perspective, the war of 1808–09 was a tragedy not only because it had ended in humiliation and the loss of Finland. The defeat had also led to the only successful military coup in Swedish history—the mutiny of the army on the Norwegian border in March 1809—the end of royal absolutism, and the adoption of a new constitution (which would remain in operation until 1974). While Swedish Liberals in the early twentieth century regarded this bloodless revolution of 1809 as the founding moment of modern Swedish society, to Bennedich it was a disgraceful moment when self-serving, un-patriotic bureaucrats had initiated the erosion of royal power and national greatness. To him, it was therefore self-evident that an official history of Sweden's catastrophic defeat in 1808–09 should leap at the opportunity to draw conclusions that could also be use-ful in the contemporary political debate on parliamentary rule and democracy, a struggle in which Bennedich himself had made his most important contribution as anonymous co-author of King Gustav V's Courtyard address some months before.

When Bennedich presented his report in March 1915, he began by listing the literature he had consulted on the period. Among the historians he had read was the Liberal history professor Nils Edén, an expert on the 1809 Constitution, who a few years later would lead the government of Liberals and Social Democrats that would introduce universal suffrage in Sweden. As Bennedich acid-ly remarked in his memorandum, however, he had only studied

Edén's work in order 'to become acquainted with the desires and needs of modern Swedish party politics when it comes to tainting the truth about the events of 1809'.[17] In spite of this openly expressed ideological bias, Bennedich's memorandum nonetheless contained a highly critical appreciation of those volumes on the wars of 1808–09 that had already appeared. Bennedich's criticism was in fact quite similar to that which had been expressed by professional historians since the 1890s.[18]

Although Bennedich was a great admirer of the German military, he also shared the German historian Hans Delbrück's critique of the history-writing of the Prussian General Staff. The writing of history, Delbrück emphasized, must always be founded in a critical analysis of the available sources. Bennedich even asserted that the Army War College, like any other academic institution, should 'teach its students to form their own opinion on the basis of their own researches into various fields of the art of war'. When it came to source criticism, this would mean nothing less than giving future staff officers the same kind of training that civilian undergraduates received at history seminars, according to Bennedich. Although one could argue that the Swedish General Staff should not aspire to produce histories of the same quality as those of great powers such as Germany and Austria with their superior resources, he said, scholarly quality was not necessarily a function of size. The Danish General Staff, Bennedich noticed, had in recent years published no fewer than four volumes of a high scholarly standard on the Great Northern War, with no more than three officers involved in the project, none of them full-time.[19]

To Bennedich, it was also clear that military history could not be written out of context. He therefore demanded that the proposed structure of the last two volumes should be revised. According to the existing plan, Volume 8 should deal with the remaining operations on land and Volume 9 with the remaining operations at sea. It would be better, Bennedich said, to have both volumes describe land and naval operations, and draw a chronological line between them in March 1809. On the domestic scene at this point, the overthrow of King Gustav IV Adolf and the return to constitutional monarchy introduced a system of government related to that of modern Sweden. From March 1809, the strategic situation was also that of modern Sweden, the Russians having conquered the Åland Islands and advancing across the northern border of Sweden proper.[20]

In addition, Bennedich pointed out the need for a thorough geographical description of the theatre of operations, something that had been missing from the earlier volumes. Such a description should contain data on economy and agriculture, population density, the availability of horses and wagons, the quality of roads and communications, shipping, and ice conditions in the Baltic Sea region. The war must be analysed in its full geographic, economic, and social context, Bennedich believed, expressing views that would only become fashionable among academics much later, inspired by the famous French school of *Annales* historians in the interwar period. In a sense, he also precipitated the change in the Army War College's curriculum in the 1930s, when the teaching of 'Sweden's strategic conditions'—consisting of current geographic and statistical data— replaced military history as a core subject in officer training.

Bennedich hoped that if this material was collected it could also be of use later when the Military History Section's attention shifted to Charles XII, who had fought most of his wars in the same North European setting as the wars of 1808–09. Although publicizing such information could prove harmful to Sweden's present defence, he wrote, a thorough geographic survey of the Baltic Sea region would still be necessary for a correct analysis of events. Even if only a few pages of such a survey proved fit to print in the end, it would still have served its purpose.[21] Further, the influence of winter conditions on operations merited further research, he thought, as did the role of the archipelago fleet. Bennedich also pointed out that the Russian army had in fact defeated the superior Swedish army in wintertime, although Russian equipment had been just as bad and Russian logistical support even weaker than that of the Swedes: 'If we are better than in 1808, the Russians are probably better too, and at least to the same degree.'[22]

Moreover, Bennedich called for a thorough investigation of Sweden's diplomatic relations with her ally in 1808–09, Great Britain. He claimed that the British had dealt with the Russians behind Sweden's back throughout the conflict, as they knew that Russia was the only power on the Continent worth mobilizing in the struggle against Napoleon. Sweden's will to resist the Russian invasion in 1808 had also been weakened by domestic financial interests that wanted to continue to trade with Russia, and therefore were prepared to sacrifice the eastern part of the realm for a quick peace. It would therefore be valuable, Bennedich argued, if the General Staff history could explain the true nature of British policy in 1808–09, as 'in the present situation there are certain delusions even at very high levels regarding the interests of foreign powers in Scandinavia'. According to Bennedich, 'Already in those days the ghost of 'neutrality' hung over us'.[23]

Bennedich's remarks were a direct comment on Sweden's foreign political situation in the winter of 1915. The country was neutral in the ongoing world war, in which Britain and Russia openly aligned against Germany. Influential groups with whom Bennedich sympathized wanted Sweden to abandon its bystander role and enter the war on Germany's side. The principal guardian of neutrality in the Swedish government was Foreign Minister Knut A. Wallenberg, who was also the head of Sweden's leading financial family. Many of the pro-German activists regarded Wallenberg's concern for neutrality merely as a way to protect his private financial interests. Bennedich belonged to those who saw the Wallenberg family as a modern successor to the forces that had brought down the fatherland during the Napoleonic Wars. Apart from a survey of the military geography of the Baltic Sea region, he therefore urged that an examination of Sweden's domestic conditions in 1808–09 should be included in Volume 8. Bennedich realized that it might seem inappropriate for the General Staff to publish a study on domestic politics, but if the work on the wars of 1808–09 was to be concluded in a satisfactory way, all factors that had undermined Sweden's national defences must be taken into consideration. As in the case with the geographic survey, full publication would not be necessary. The published account could well terminate in early 1809, 'when the shadow of revolution approaches'.[24]

In earlier histories, the king who had been overthrown by the revolution in March 1809, Gustav IV Adolf, had been given most of the blame for Sweden's defeat. According to Bennedich, the King's only real fault was his reluctance to take strong measures against his subordinates and to enforce the necessary obedience among them. He was not responsible for the breakdown of army logistics and the mass deaths suffered by Swedish militia conscripts during the war, Bennedich claimed—they had been caused by bureaucratic inertia and passive local officials.[25] These and other important truths about 1808–09 must be brought to light, Bennedich concluded. He therefore urged the General Staff historians to abandon their nineteenth-century ambitions of academic impartiality and instead write an account of the 'dangers and consequences of the self-delusions of a people, its bureaucracy, and its party bosses, and their negligence towards their real, most elementary duty.' He hoped that such an emphasis would also make the revered 1809-Constitution appear in a different light. The true lesson of 1809 was that the ideals of the French Revolution had eroded national consciousness and officialdom's sense of duty, which in turn had led to chaos in the governmental apparatus. Expressing the dominant conservative stereotypes of the belligerents in 1914–18, Bennedich described Sweden in 1809 as a country where 'The Gallic phrase had confused stern Germanic reason'.[26]

There is no doubt that Bennedich's views found fertile ground among the Swedish General Staff at the time. When Volume 8 finally appeared in 1921, most of his recommendations had been duly implemented. This volume covered operations on both land and sea until March 1809, and contained a short survey of military geography as well as some thirty pages of domestic politics (albeit somewhat more moderate in tone than Bennedich would have preferred).[27] Volume 9, which covered operations in Åland and Västerbotten and the end of hostilities in September, appeared the year after, and had been produced at record speed by a single author.[28]

For the rest of the First World War, Bennedich served as the senior lecturer in military history at the Army War College. He was also busy writing and editing most of the General Staff's next monumental official history, the four-volume series on Charles XII. Bennedich wished to portray his hero as one of the greatest generals of all time and to 'sell in' the notion of a special Swedish tactical tradition, dating from Sten Sture the Elder at the Battle of Brunkeberg in 1471 by way of Gustavus Adolphus to Charles XII and his field marshal, Rehnskiöld. This alleged 'Swedish school' of army tactics was focused on decisive action and victories of encirclement and annihilation, and of course was much ahead of its time.[29] Since the 1950s, military historians have convincingly dismissed Bennedich's interpretation.[30] But although the Charles XII volumes are highly biased and in some respects even unreliable with regard to historical facts, they must still be regarded as far superior to most of the General Staff's volumes on the wars of 1808–09. Not only does Bennedich's work contain detailed references to sources, it is written with considerable dramatic talent in clear and elegant prose, and approaches its subject from a consciously theoretical perspective.

In his capacity as senior lecturer in military history at the Army War College, Bennedich in May 1918 firmly opposed a proposal by the college commandant Lieutenant-Colonel Oscar Nygren to temporarily exclude the war against Russia in 1808–09 from the syllabus so that time could be made for a general overview of the Napoleonic Wars. Bennedich argued that the 1808–09 conflict was valuable to study in view of the many 'negative lessons' it contained. He was supported by his colleague, the senior lecturer in military geography, who expected that the teaching of Finland's geography would become an important part of his duties in future (an independent Finnish state had appeared on Sweden's eastern border a mere six months before). Students would come better prepared to geography classes if they had studied the campaign in Finland in 1808 beforehand.[31]

The college commandant accepted these objections, but ten years later the wars of 1808–09 still disappeared from the syllabus for good. Swedish officers in the late 1920s spent considerable time studying Finland's geography, but they did so without consulting the General Staff's histories of 1808–09.[32] Although the short survey of the Baltic Sea region's military geography had been included in Volume 8 on Bennedich's recommendations, it proved to be of little use for strategic planning in the 1920s as it did not contain any information about railways, airports, munitions industries, hydroelectric power stations, or other modern infrastructure. The officer who in 1929 succeeded Bennedich as head of the General Staff's Military History Section, Helge Jung, initiated the reorientation of the Swedish officer-corps and the teaching at the Army War College towards a more contemporary focus.

The outcome of the First World War, when Imperial Germany suffered defeat and parliamentary democracy triumphed in Sweden, constituted a serious blow to Bennedich and made him lose interest in current affairs. During his time as head of the General Staff Military History Section (1922–9) he would also play a surprisingly marginal role when it came to research, not least because he had a formidable rival in the civilian director of the Military Archives, Birger Steckzén (who was formally Bennedich's subordinate). In the last of the three great Swedish General Staff histories, dedicated to the wars of Gustavus Adolphus in 1611–32, Bennedich was initially involved in some of the research, but the project was dominated by Steckzén, who had written a doctoral dissertation on Sweden's military participation in the Thirty Years War and had a much better grasp of the relevant sources—in Swedish as well as in foreign archives. The volumes of the Gustavus Adolphus work, which began to appear in print only in 1936 when Bennedich had long since left the General Staff Military History Section and was serving as regimental commander in Linköping, were also more in tune with contemporary academic history than had been the earlier General Staff works. Although the idea that Gustavus Adolphus represented a unique 'Swedish school' of warfare is still discernable, this thought tends to drown in a mass of details. No doubt, the lack of surviving documents from Charles XII's campaign in Russia had facilitated Bennedich's one-sided argument in his work on *Karl XII på slagfältet*. It is perhaps revealing that Steckzén criticized Bennedich for being an historian who started with 'a predetermined thesis and then adapted his sources accordingly'.[33] To this day, this has remained a common accusation against theory-oriented historians from their more cautious colleagues.

As would later be the case with many historians from the 1968 generation, it was Carl Bennedich's ideological awareness which gave urgency to his pen and led him to look for the overriding structures in history at the expense of detail and nuances. In Bennedich's view, the cataclysm of 1808–09, which had led to Sweden's final fall from great-power status and the reduction of the monarchy to a predominantly symbolic institution in society, could not be satisfactorily analysed in a purely military context. Consequently, the battlefield narrative of traditional General Staff history had to be expanded into a larger 'history of war and society'. Paradoxically, this position made him more 'modern' in scholarly terms than most other military historians of his time (and even some military historians of *our* time).

It is also clear that Bennedich's position was formed by the Great War. As this conflict had developed into an unpredictable war of attrition, it seemed obvious that any serious military analysis should include a knowledge of communications and infrastructure, as well as of demographic, economic, social, and ideological factors in the belligerent countries. Recent experience from the conflict in which Sweden—to Bennedich's regret—refrained from actively participating had also highlighted the role of trade interests in foreign policy and the dangers for a small-power neutral of the undermining of its governmental authority. Consequently, all those aspects of 'total war' should be a part of the official history of Sweden's struggle in 1808–09, if the General Staff's efforts were to be of any relevance to future generations of Swedish officers.

Although the First World War revolutionized warfare and seemingly diminished the immediate value of centuries-old experience to Swedish officers in the interwar period, Bennedich's view that total war made the writing of 'total military history' necessary remains highly relevant even today.

Notes

1 Jan Olof Olsson, *1914* (Stockholm: Bonniers, 1964), 36.
2 Gunnar Åselius, 'Hugo Raab och den moderna högskoleidén', in Gunnar Artéus (ed.), *Hugo Raab. Förkämpe för ett modernt försvar* (Stockholm: Försvarshögskolan, 2003).
3 Michael Howard, 'Men against Fire', in Peter Paret (ed.), *Makers of Modern Strategy: from Machiavelli to the Modern Age* (Princeton, NJ: Princeton University Press, 1986).
4 Gunnar Åselius, 'Historien som vägvisare till framtida segrar. Om krigshistoriens roll i svensk officersutbildning', in *Inte bara krig. Nio föreläsningar i Krigsarkivet. Meddelanden från Krigsarkivet XXVII* (Stockholm: Krigsarkivet, 2006); Martin Raschke, *Der politisierender Generalstab. Die Friedrizianischen Kriege in der amtlichen deutschen Militärgeschichtsschreibung 1890–1914*, (Freiburg: Rombach, 1993); Jay Luvaas, *The Military Legacy of the Civil War* (Chicago: Chicago University Press, 1959); Carol Reardon, *Soldiers and Scholars: the US Army and the Uses of Military History 1865–1920* (Lawrence, Kan: University Press of Kansas., 1990); Azar Gat, *A History of Military Thought: from the Enlightenment to the Cold War* (Oxford: Oxford University Press, 2001), 393–9.
5 Cf. Jonathan B. A. Bailey, 'The First World War and the birth of modern warfare', in MacGregor Knox & Williamson Murray (eds.), *The Dynamics of Military Revolution, 1300–2050* (Cambridge: Cambridge University Press, 2001); on the Swedish reception of the new way of waging war, see Lars Ericson Wolke, *Krigets idéer. Svenska tankar om krigföring* (Stockholm: Medström, 2007), 321–49.
6 Gunnar Åselius, 'Krigshistoria i kris: historia, strategi och kampen om undervisningstimmar på Krigshögskolan under mellankrigstiden', in Gunnar Artéus, Karl Molin & Magnus Petersson (eds.), *Säkerhet och försvar. En vänbok till Kent Zetterberg* (Karlskrona: Abrahamsson, 2006).
7 Military Archives, Stockholm, KHS arkiv, Inträdesprov, serie F I, 1908, 'Vilka voro de främsta nackdelarna med den stormaktsställning Sverige upprätthöll i det sjuttonde århundradet?'
8 Torsten Söderquist, 'Kursen 1908–1910', *Kungl. Krigshögskolan 1878–1928. En minnesskrift* (Stockholm: Haeggström, 1928), 99, 'mellan Sveriges läge i början av 18. och 20. århundradet. Huru mycket gynnsammare skulle icke det senare ha varit om HAN levat'.
9 Biographic data from Frank Martin, 'Carl Bennedich', *Svenska män och kvinnor. Biografisk uppslagsbok* (Stockholm: Bonnier, 1942).
10 Birger Steckzén, *Personliga minnen från det svenska arkivväsendet* (Meddelanden från Krigsarkivet, 26; Stockholm: Krigsarkivet, 2005), 29, 'För utomstående var han med sin dynamiska natur och sin tankeflykt en

fascinerande person, för den som hade att dagligen göra med honom var han en prövande och tröttande man. Långt in på nätterna kunde han sitta och prata dvs han pratade hela tiden själv'; ibid. 28, 'å huvudets vägnar var han mycket begåvad och hade uppslag och idéer som ibland voro blixtrande'.

11 Gunnar Åselius, '"Poltava verkar inte förstämmande på en frisk människa". Med Carl Bennedich på slagfältet', in Lena Jonson & Tamara Torstendahl Salytjeva (eds.), *Poltava: krigsfångar och kulturutbyte* (Stockholm: Atlantis, 2009).

12 Bennedich's studies of Poltava were published as 'Om den svenska planläggningen av slaget vid Poltava och stridsledningen', *Karolinska förbundets årsbok* (Stockholm: Karolinska förbundet 1913); Carl Bennedich, 'Poltava', *Nordisk familjebok. Konversationslexikon och realencyklopedi* (Stockholm: Nordisk familjeboks förlag, 1915); Generalstaben, *Karl XII på slagfältet. Karolinsk slagordning sedd mot bakgrund av slagtaktikens utveckling från alla äldsta tider* III (Stockholm, 1918); Frans G. Bengtsson's account of Poltava can be found in *Karl XII:s levnad. Från Altranstädt till Fredrikshall* (1935; Stockholm: Norstedts, 1980), 146–185 (this work was also translated into English: *The Sword does not jest: the Heroic Life of King Charles XII of Sweden*, New York: S:t Martin's Press, 1960; on Bengtsson's dependence on the General Staff official histories, see Bengt Liljegren, 'Om Frans G Bengtssons Karl XII', in Lars M Andersson, Fabian Persson, Peter Ullgren & Ulf Zander (eds.), *På historiens slagfält. En festskrift tillägnad Sverker Oredsson* (Uppsala: Sisyfos förlag, 2002), 62, 66; the first major reinterpretation of the battle came only with Gustaf Petri's article 'Slaget vid Poltava', *Karolinska förbundets årsbok* (Stockholm: Karolinska förbundet 1958).

13 Bennedich's activities in Karolinska förbundet and in connection with the Courtyard Crisis (when the king intervened directly in parliamentary politics) are described by Jarl Torbacke, *'Försvaret främst'. Tre studier till borggårdskrisens problematik* (Stockholm: Almquist & Wiksell International, 1983), 43–113.

14 Bertil Broomé, 'Krigshistoriska avdelningens förhistoria och verksamhet t o m 1917', *Aktuellt & Historiskt* (1973), 180–205.

15 L. S. [Ludvig Stavenow], 'Sveriges krig åren 1808–1809', *Historisk tidskrift* 25/1 (1905), 57–58.

16 Broomé 1973, 188–192; Krigsarkivet, *Beståndsöversikt* (Meddelanden från Krigsarkivet 11/2; Stockholm: Krigsarkivet, 1987), ii. 557.

17 Military Archives, Stockholm, Sveriges krig 1808–1809, vol. 398, 'Vilka särskilda synpunkter böra göra sig gällande vid utarbetandet av Del VIII av "Sveriges krig åren 1808–1809", dels på grund av att denna del, i motsats till övriga delar av ifrågavarande arbete, behandlar försvarsåtgärder inom eget land, dels med hänsyn till verkets avslutning inom rimlig tid?', Carl

Bennedich, 5 March 1915, preface, 'endast för att lära känna modern svensk partipolitiks önskningar och behov ifråga om färgläggning av sanningen om 1809 års händelser'.

18 Ibid. 21–24, 27.

19 Ibid. 20–21, 26, 'lära sina elever att på grundvalen av egna forskningar inom olika grenar av krigskonsten bilda ett eget omdöme'.

20 Ibid. 9–11.

21 Ibid. 32–9.

22 Ibid. 57; ibid. 67, 69, 'Äro vi bättre än 1808, torde ryssarna även vara det, och åtminstone i lika proportion'.

23 Ibid. 42, 'Redan då stod 'neutraliteten' som ett hotande spöke över oss'; ibid. 62, 'särskilt med tanke på vissa under nuvarande läge ännu även på mycket ledande håll rådande fullständiga vanföreställningar om utländska makters intressen i den skandinaviska norden'; ibid. 63–4.

24 Ibid. 6–7, 39, 40, 'då revolutionens skugga möter'.

25 Ibid. 41–7.

26 Ibid. 72, 'vådorna i och följderna av ett folks, dess byråkratis och dess partihövdingars självbedrägeri och åsidosättande av sin verkliga, mest elementära plikt'; ibid. 73, 'Den galliska frasen omtöcknade det sträva germanska förnuftet.'

27 Generalstaben, krigshistoriska avdelningen, *Sveriges krig åren 1808 och 1809*, viii (Stockholm: Norstedts, 1921), 44–47, 220–254.

28 Generalstaben, krigshistoriska avdelningen *Sveriges krig åren 1808 och 1809*, ix (Stockholm: Norstedts 1922); Willy Kleen, *Ur skuggan av min dal* (Stockholm: Bonnier, 1954).

29 Generalstaben, krigshistoriska avdelningen, *Karl XII på slagfältet. Karolinsk slagordning sedd mot bakgrund av slagtaktikens utveckling från alla äldsta tider I–IV* (Stockholm: Norstedts, 1918–1919).

30 Folke Wernstedt, 'Lineartaktik och karolinsk taktik. Några reflektioner med anledning av framställningen i "Karl XII på slagfältet"', *Karolinska förbundets årsbok* (Stockholm: Karolinska förbundet, 1957); Gunnar Artéus, *Krigsteori och historisk förklaring*, ii: *Svensk och europeisk stridstaktik 1700–1712* (Gothenburg: Historiska institutionen i Göteborg, 1972).

31 Krigsarkivet (KrA) [Military Archives of Sweden], Stockholm, KHS arkiv, serie A II, vol. 2, avd I, Exp. lärarkollegiets protokoll [faculty meeting minutes], 21 May 1918.

32 *Reglemente och övriga bestämmelser för Kungl. Krigshögskolan, 1926 års upplaga* [War College Regulations, 1926 edition] (Stockholm, 1926), §§ 2, 3 & 10; Militärläroverksinspektionens arkiv, Krigsundervisningskommissionen [Board of Military Education] serie A, vol. 5; KrA, Äldre lärokursen 1928–1929, C. A. Ehrensvärd 31 August 1928, 'Förslag till undervisningsprogram i läroämnet Sveriges strategiska förhållanden'.

33 Steckzén, *Personliga minnen*, 29, 'Som historisk forskare gick han ut från en förutbestämd tes och anpassade källorna därefter'; on the Gustavus Adolphus project, see Lars Ericson [Wolke], 'Clio i österled. Krigsarkivets, krigshistoriska avdelningens och Gustav Adolf-projektets arkivforskningar till stormaktstidens militärhistoria i Ostpreussen under 1920-talet', in Kent Zetterberg & Gunnar Åselius (eds.), *Historia, krig och statskonst. En vänbok till Klaus-Richard Böhme* (Stockholm: Probus, 2000); the evaluation of the general staff history of Gustavus Adolphus presented by Sven Lundquist in his article 'Slaget vid Breitenfeld', *Historisk tidskrift*, 83/1 (1963) remains relevant.

CHAPTER 10

Fighting for the Kaiser

The Danish minority
in the German army, 1914–18

Claus Bundgård Christensen

The Battle of Mons in August 1914 occupies an important place in military history because it was the first battle Britain fought in the Great War. A less well-known fact is that in the German regiments that were advancing against accurate rifle fire, many of the soldiers regarded themselves as Danes. In the First World War, around 26,000 Danish-speaking German citizens from Northern Schleswig fought in the German army, because of Denmark's defeat and the annexation of Schleswig-Holstein by Prussia in the Second War of Schleswig in 1864. As a result, a large group of Danes became German citizens, and were thus obliged to do military service in the German army. These soldiers called themselves 'Danes' or 'Danish Northern Schleswigers'. Their native tongue was Danish and the thousands of letters they sent back from the front were written in Danish. The written language is important in the present context because it reveals a great deal about the men's national orientation. From the 1880s German was the only language taught in public schools. When soldiers in the German army wrote home in Danish, they did so because they came from families who by private initiative and as a reaction against Germanization had taught their children to write in Danish.[1]

When Northern Schleswig was reunited with Denmark after a referendum in 1920 it had a population of around 163,000. The majority lived in rural communities and worked in agriculture in

267

a region dominated by medium-sized farms; the remainder in numerous, scattered villages and small market towns. The largest city in the region was Flensburg (which remained German after the referendum) with around 60,000 inhabitants. Since the majority of the Danish soldiers came from rural backgrounds, their experience of the war in many ways resembled that of men from other rural areas of Germany.

Although relations between the German authorities and the Danish-speaking population in Schleswig had worsened in the pre-war period due to the German hard-line policy towards the Danish minority, members of that minority could still express their political views relatively freely until the outbreak of war. For example, the Danes were represented by their own MPs in the Reichstag. The Danes, especially the soldiers at the front, often felt they were treated worse by the military authorities than the German soldiers because they belonged to the Danish minority. In some cases this was true. In general, however, there is no doubt that the Danes were treated considerably better than the soldiers from Alsace-Lorraine.[2]

This article investigates the Danish-speaking soldiers' war experiences, integration into the German army, and conduct as a minority fighting for a fatherland that was not their own. Because the German army archives were destroyed in a fire during the Second World War, this study draws not only on the limited surviving military sources in the military archives, but also on evidence from the German civilian authorities, letters from the front, and memoirs.

In an army of millions of men, 26,000 soldiers is not a significant number. Yet it is still possible to follow the Danes as a group because of the structure of the German army, where regiments and battalions where raised on a regional basis. Between 1914–18 the majority of Danes served in the three infantry regiments: the 84th Regiment, the 86th Regiment, and the 86th Reserve Regiment, with battalions drawn from cities with a dominant or considerable Danish population. Germany was divided into twenty-four army corps districts of which the IX Corps covered Schleswig. The 84th and 86th Regiments belonged to the 18th Infantry Division, the 86th Reserve Regiment to the 18th Reserve Division.[3]

The men were aged between 17 and 49.[4] Around 4,000 of their number were killed and more than 6,000 were wounded, the majority of the dead and wounded being in their early twenties since the older men were often to be found serving behind the front, as territorial reservists, or on the less dangerous Eastern Front. The Northern Schleswig regiments almost exclusively fought on the Western Front and participated in many of the major battles, including Verdun, Somme, Arras, and Cambrai.

At the outbreak of war, the reaction in Northern Schleswig was in many ways similar to that in other parts of the German countryside.[5] The Danish minority's reaction to mobilization and war was predominantly one of anxiety and sorrow, very different from the supposed *Augusterlebnis*, or Spirit of 1914, said to have gripped the country.[6] In his diary, the (Danish) MP H. P. Hanssen, described a typical response in the streets of the city of Aabenraa on 1 August 1914:

> I shall never forget the picture: pale, serious men, dully resigned; women in tears; young couples clinging to each other oblivious to their surroundings; sobbing children.[7]

When the battalions started to leave Northern Schleswig the sceptical attitude still dominated. When the 2nd Battalion, 84th Regiment marched out of the predominantly Danish city of Haderslev, the atmosphere was far from enthusiastic. One of the soldiers in the battalion, Peter Frank, remembered that when the commander held a speech the soldiers answered with a weak 'Hurrah'. The civilians watched in silence, the only exception being some young people from a largely German local school.[8] It is characteristic that the most enthusiastic reaction in Northern Schleswig was to be found in German-dominated Flensburg. Here a more excited crowd followed the 86th and 86th Reserve Regiments. Many had tears in their eyes, but the soldiers and civilians were singing German songs and hurrahing.[9]

There were several reasons for the widespread negative attitude toward the war and military service. One very important reason was the many practical problems the war raised in rural areas, where farmers and farm labourers had to leave their homes midharvest.

This was not a specifically Danish wartime experience, of course; on the contrary, it was shared by many other soldiers from rural backgrounds.[10]

Although the relations between the German- and Danish-minded populations were relatively calm in the years before the First World War, tensions between the German authorities and the Danish minority increased in the period. The German hard line towards the Danes manifested itself in a wide range of irritations, from economic restrictions on farmers to a series of bans targeting the Danish community.[11] In the spring and summer of 1914 the atmosphere was especially tense because of the large-scale German celebration of the fiftieth anniversary of the 1864 victory over Denmark in Northern Schleswig. These celebrations left the Danish minority in a rather gloomy mood. The relations between the local authorities and the Danes in Northern Schleswig deteriorated even further in the days following the mobilization. Almost immediately after the declaration of a state of siege, the military command—the General Command in Altona—ordered a wave of arrests of members of the Danish minority in Northern Schleswig, targeting prominent men in the community. The Germans regarded 118 of the prisoners as politically suspect. The remaining 172 were Danes who were arrested because of their knowledge of coastal waters; their arrest was seen as a security precaution, because it was feared that they might assist the British Navy or help deserters to cross the border to Denmark. The German action did nothing to improve the tense atmosphere or the Danes' mistrust of the authorities. To make things even worse, all Danish newspapers published in Germany were closed. The lack of trusted newspapers resulted in rumours about assaults and crimes carried out by the Germans.[12] The rumours were false, the newspapers were reopened, and the prisoners were released unharmed after a few weeks, but the distrustful German attitude followed the Danish Northern Schleswigers to the front and consequently marked these soldiers' wartime experiences.

Although the Danish minority in general had few positive expectations of the German state and the German army, it is never the less possible to find a mixed attitude among the Danish men.

The most outspokenly negative reaction to mobilization was to be found among the older group of soldiers who were married and often owned a farm. They were established members of society whose status rested on marriage and property.[13] The farmer Hans Petersen got the news about the mobilization when he was working in his cornfield and a neighbour shouted something to him. He could not hear him properly and only caught the word '*mobil*'. He immediately understood what had happened and explained later that the word had a choking effect as if something disgusting had just hit him.[14] Another typical reaction is to be found in a letter of 2 August 1914 in which Peter Kræmer described the situation in Northern Schleswig to his sister in Denmark a day before he himself had to join his regiment:

> This morning around 30 from our town left. Almost all married men like Mathias Mygind, Anders Højer, and so forth. You can well imagine the reaction among women and children. One should hardly think that something like this could be possible in our enlightened times. I do not understand how anyone can take responsibility for this.[15]

A thorough study of the reactions of Danish soldiers to the mobilization and military service shows a more ambiguous reaction than the sort seen in H. P. Hanssen's diary. The Danes' reactions to the war also depended on the soldiers' age and financial and social position. The younger soldiers often reacted more positively: the majority of the young men under 30 years did not have a wife, children, or a farm to care about. For this group the war and military service offered prestige and a chance to see something of the world. Although they regarded themselves as Danes, and certainly did not have any particularly negative conceptions about France or Great Britain, many of them looked forward to their service with a mixture of excitement and fear. Anders Jensen, who was wounded, wrote to his brother from hospital in Essen in November 1914 admitting that the summer had not been that bad 'because it was a bit adventurous and interesting'.[16] Others described a cheerful atmosphere, with many young Danish soldiers happy to be in the company of their

271

friends and to get away from work and home. This positive reaction was in many cases strengthened in the first days after joining their regiments because of the opportunity to drink beer and visit restaurants in bigger cities like Flensburg.[17]

One of the most important factors in shaping the soldiers' wartime experiences was the composition of their company and regiment. For Danes in the German army it was crucial to be together with other Danish-speaking soldiers. Although men from the Danish minority spoke German very well, the issue of Danish-speaking comrades dominates letters from the front, diaries, and memoirs. Just how important it was is evident from the sensitive moment when the men were placed in their different sections.[18] At this point the Danes often approached NCOs or junior officers to ask whether they could be put together with soldiers who spoke their own language. In many cases their request was accepted. In situations where the response was negative or where the soldiers found themselves in regiments where they were the only representative from the Danish minority, the men would often go to great lengths to make contact with other Danish-speaking soldiers. Thus it was not uncommon for men to leave their sections at the front, with or without permission, when they heard of neighbouring regiments where they knew there were Danes. In other cases they met Danish-speaking soldiers by chance: such random encounters were very often highlighted in both letters and memoirs. A typical example is to be found in Jacob Bergholdt's memoirs. He was in the 222nd Regiment and participating in the Battle of Verdun. During heavy fighting, a soldier from another regiment jumped down into his machine-gun nest. They started to talk in German, but Bergholdt could tell from his accent that the man came from Northern Schleswig, so he asked if he would prefer to speak Danish. The soldier's reaction is a good example of how much such encounters were appreciated. When the man realized that Bergholdt was a Dane he threw his arms around him:

> I can still see the man before me. He was not very big, skinny and almost livid in the face. His uniform after a tour in the trenches was filthy from top to bottom. He was in short a sorry sight and, to

use a German expression, '*abgekämpft*' [worn-out]. But the sound of his mother tongue had for a brief moment cheered him up.[19]

For soldiers in regiments raised in Northern Schleswig it was more or less a matter of course that many or even the majority of their comrades could speak Danish. Exactly how many of the soldiers in the 84th and 86th Regiments and the 86th Reserve Regiment would have regarded themselves as Danes varied according to the period. The highest concentration was to be found in the summer and autumn of 1914. The exact percentage of Danish-speaking soldiers in the three regiments is not known because of archival losses, but in letters and postcards the men very often list the names of Danish-speaking friends in their units. From such sources it is possible to give a fairly accurate estimate of the percentage of Danes in these regiments. In August 1914 the MP H. P. Hanssen estimated that around 50 per cent of the men in the 86th Regiment were Danes.[20] In the two other regiments for 1914–18 the percentages of Danes were between 10–60 per cent. The highest concentrations were to be found in sections raised in the Danish-dominated cities of Sønderborg, Haderslev and Flensburg. During 1914 the regiments were involved in the Battle of Mons in August and a few weeks later in the First Battle of the Marne. On the 6 September, the 86th Regiment lost around 700 men in the battle around Esternay, many of whom were Danish-speaking soldiers.[21] In the following year the 86th Reserve Regiment took heavy causalities in the Battle of Soissons and in trench fighting at Moulin-sous-Touvent.[22] The casualties in these early battles had to be replaced with reservists and volunteers who often came from other parts of Germany than Northern Schleswig. From late 1914 and onwards the declining number of Danish-speaking soldiers in the regiments is a returning issue in letters from the front. The lack of Danish-speaking comrades was often described as a problem. From 1916 onwards the German army in general tried to maintain the regional composition of its regiments, but the numbers of Danes in these three particular regiments were never as high as in the summer of 1914.

The Danes' national identity manifested itself in many situations. One of the most visible was the use of national symbols such as the Dannebrog, the red-and-white Danish national flag. Many soldiers carried a Dannebrog in the pocket of their uniform, and in group photographs the soldiers sometimes posed with it.[23] Pictures were in general an important medium in displaying national identity. In the regional archives in Southern Jutland there are numerous examples of group photographs where soldiers carry placards with messages written in Danish—the most common message simply read '*Nordens Sønner*' ('Sons of the North')—or held examples of the Danish minority's own newspapers. Holidays such as Christmas were also typical occasions when national identity was on display. Danish-speaking soldiers often chose to celebrate with other Danes if at all possible, and Christmas trees in trenches and barracks were often decorated with the Dannebrog.[24]

Despite the fact that many of these soldiers expressed a longing to be with other Danish-speaking men, they also established positive relations with ethnic German soldiers. To survive trench warfare on the Western Front, friendship was one of the most important coping strategies.[25] Especially for those men who transferred to units with few or no other Danish-speaking soldiers, it is obvious that the men established positive contacts with the ethnic Germans in their squad or section without any great problem.

Although the regiments with many Danes performed relatively well on the battlefield and the 18th and 18th Reserve Divisions were considered reliable, the Germans in many cases mistrusted the Danish soldiers' loyalty. Danes were eligible for promotion to NCO ranks, military law did not recognize ethnic distinctions, and the Danish-speaking soldiers received the same training and equipment as ethnic German soldiers, yet despite this German officers repeatedly demonstrated their mistrust of the Danes under their command—a mistrust that was rooted in the belief that men from the Danish minority were more unreliable than their German comrades. One such occasion unfolded in the aftermath of a French attack on the 86th Regiment at Moulin on 6 June 1915, a day known in the official regimental history as the 'Black Day at Moulin'.[26] In one day the French army managed to press 50–500 metres into the German trench system along a front almost a kilometre long. The Germans lost more than 1,000 men in the day's action. In the official regimental history, the author, the former company commander Wilhelm Jürgensen, explained the defeat as the result of Danish espionage. Although Jürgensen admitted that he had no real evidence of this, he claimed that information about the German trenches and positions had been given to spies in Denmark.[27] Naturally, this does not suffice as evidence of German mistrust since the regimental history was published many years after the war, but it was not an isolated example. The Black Day at Moulin also resulted in similar examples of German wariness in the summer of 1915. In July 1915, IX Corps contacted the local civilian authorities in Northern Schleswig with information about the conduct of Danish-speaking soldiers after the French attack. After a large group of soldiers had surrendered, men from the 86th Regiment removed national symbols from their uniforms and mocked the German nation. The French treated and welcomed these soldiers as their brothers, and some of the French officers even addressed them in Danish. The Deputy General Command of IX Corps launched an investigation, conducted by the civilian authorities in Northern Schleswig. Their investigations concluded that of the soldiers who had surrendered, only a minority were Danish-speaking: thus the response from the highest civil authority in Northern Schleswig, the Landrat, was plain, and it did not correspond with mistrust of the military authorities. The Landrat, Hugo Löw, stated that the investigation was an unfair attempt to blame the Danes for a military defeat and that the Danish-speaking population of Northern Schleswig never would commit such treason.[28] The investigation had no consequences for the Danish minority, but it is a clear example of how in some cases the military authorities were openly mistrustful of this group of soldiers.

It has been suggested that ethnic minorities fighting in the German army during the First World War were more inclined to go over to the enemy.[29] Certainly some 4,000 Danes in the German army became prisoners of war, and while because of archival losses it is impossible to determine the exact and general circumstances under which they surrendered, it seems those who did often displayed a positive attitude towards surrender, evident in their letters home. One reason was the camps established by the

French and later the British. In August 1914, the French professor and Schleswig expert Paul Verrier contacted the French minister of war and explained the situation of the Danish-speaking soldiers. He suggested that France ought to do something for this particular group. The minister agreed and in 1915 the French government established a special prisoner-of-war camp in Aurillac for the Danes from Schleswig. Here they received better treatment than in the normal camps and enjoyed a far greater degree of freedom. A year later a similar camp was established in Feltham in England. In both camps the soldiers had access to libraries and, especially in England, priests from Denmark, who were active in what is best described as Danish agitation and propaganda—admission to the camp was decided by the 'General Assembly', in which one of the priests and a group of POWs decided if the prisoner in question really belonged to the Danish minority in Germany.[30] The exact number of POWs in the two camps is not known, but it was around 1,100. The existence of the Feltham and Aurillac camps was known by many soldiers at the front. Kresten Andresen wrote in a letter of April 1916 that 'It might be fun to come home on one of Paul Verrier's boats'.[31] The German authorities were of course not best pleased about the camps, consistently calling them 'traitor camps', and threatened a variety of consequences such as withholding financial support for relatives of the POWs there.[32] In 1919 more than 2,000 Danish POWs were repatriated to Denmark with the help of the Danish government. Among them were former inmates of Aurillac and Feltham. That same year they returned from Denmark to Germany, where the German authorities treated them on equal terms with other veterans. The reason for this restrained German reaction probably had to do with the situation in Schleswig in 1919, where circumstances had changed considerably since the end of the war. In 1919 a referendum was on its way and the political situation very different from the wartime period.

The German army was always alert to desertions amongst the Danes. It was relatively easy to cross the border between Germany and neutral Denmark, and when a German soldier deserted and crossed the border the Danish authorities would not send him back.

However, in 1914–15 very few Danes from Northern Schleswig fled to safety in Denmark. The reasons were partly practical—many expected the war to be over quickly—and partly political. The politicians who represented the Danish minority in Germany sent an unmistakable message in August 1914 that the Danes from Northern Schleswig should stay and do their duty, a stance that was generally accepted by the Danish minority.[33]

In 1916 the Northern Schleswig regiments participated in the Battle of Verdun, where the 84th Regiment suffered heavy losses.[34] The same year the 86th and 86th Reserve Regiment took part in both the First and Second Battles of the Somme. In July the 86th Regiment alone lost more than 1,300 men; in August the regiment returned to the battlefield, where it sustained more than 1,900 casualties, many of whom were Danish-speaking.[35] The terrible battles, the losses, and the prospect of no end to the war eroded the loyalty towards the German army. From 1916, desertion became more common than before. During the First World War, some 2,500 men illegally crossed the border to Denmark as deserters, but not all of them were Danish-speaking men from Northern Schleswig a number that also included ethnic Germans. It was fairly easy to cross the border since a network of helpers existed on both sides, and it is clear that a more positive conception of desertion developed in the last three years of the war—a conception very different to the one common to ethnic German soldiers, for whom the subject was taboo.[36] Options and consequences regarding desertion were openly discussed between Danish-speaking soldiers at the front. There was never any consensus on the subject. Some thought they should stay since desertion could result in all leave being cancelled at the front.[37] Others were more positive, saying that they had already done more than their duty to the Kaiser and the Imperial German Army. Although there was no agreement on the subject, the soldiers in general regarded the choice to be a personal one, and thus deserters were by no means excluded from the Danish-speaking soldiers' community during or after the war. An example of this comes from the 86th Regiment. Just before going on leave, Peter Toft told his Danish-speaking comrades that when he was back in Northern Schleswig he intended to cross the border into Denmark. His lieutenant, who also belonged to the Danish minority, knew that Peter Toft would not return and just asked him to say hello 'over there'.[38] After the war it was not uncommon for members of the veterans associations to reminisce in yearbooks and the like about how they had tricked the German border patrols and escaped to safety in Denmark.[39]

An important reason for the problems between the German military authorities and the Danes was language. The army's single language of command was German and therefore many regiments forbade the use of Danish. The MP H. P. Hanssen investigated the treatment of the Danish-speaking soldiers on a tour of inspection in Germany in the summer of 1915, and his report to the Ministry of War showed that in twenty-two regiments in Germany the commandant had banned the use of Danish.[40] It is difficult to gauge whether such bans were the result of mistrust or of more practical considerations, given that most officers did not understand Danish. Language bans were frequent in the early years of the war, but were largely abandoned from 1916 on. The Danish-speaking soldiers responded very negatively to such bans, and complained on numerous occasions to their politicians or higher-ranking officers. Their reaction became even more negative when divisional or regimental commanders tried to forbid the writing of letters in Danish because of the difficulties in carrying out censorship since very few censors were able to read Danish. In general the Danes saw such measures as German harassment and discrimination. The reaction among the soldiers was almost always the same: they simply ignored orders and continued to write home in their own language. The soldier Thorvald Dau felt insulted, and stated in a letter—in Danish—from the front that he would ignore the order: 'It is enough that I am doing my duty as a soldier'.[41] How typical Thorvald Dau's reaction was is evident from the many thousands of letters from Danish-speaking soldiers: very few letters from this group were written in German.

When hostilities ceased in November 1918, most Danish-speaking soldiers in the German army were happy to go home. Although patriotic sentiment may well be important in generating good performances on the battlefield, the Danes still performed relatively well.[42] As already noted, the divisions that comprised troops from Northern Schleswig were generally rated highly: in 1918, US military intelligence undertook a study of the German divisions fighting on the Eastern and Western Fronts that showed that during the war the 18th Division had been rated as first class, and it 'has always passed as being a good division'.[43] The performance of the 18th Reserve Division was never rated as highly as its sister division, but 'The morale of the division may be considered as passable'.[44]

In many cases the Danish-speaking soldiers mistrusted the German army, and the army often mistrusted the Danes. Why, in spite of this, the Danish-speaking soldiers acquitted themselves well on the battlefield can perhaps best be explained by political and psychological factors. In the first years of the war most Danes in Northern Schleswig supported a political line of cooperation with Germany in which military service played an important part. Another reason why almost no Danish-speaking soldiers escaped to safety by crossing the border to Denmark was the widespread expectation that the war would be short. In the last years of the war it became more common, and acceptable, to desert to Denmark when on leave in Northern Schleswig. Although it was relatively safe to cross the border, the numbers who did so were still relatively modest. An important reason here was German threats of what would happen to deserters who fled to neutral countries such as Denmark: they would lose their right to return home after the war. To the very end of the war this threat meant that relatively few Danish-speaking soldiers illegally crossed the border, although the number of deserters were higher among the Danish-speaking soldiers than their German peers. In units with many Danes, factors such as patriotic loyalty to Germany did not play any significant role, as many were fighting with soldiers from Northern Schleswig in a territorially conscripted force. This deployment policy resulted in German units with strong primary groups that successfully integrated Danish-speaking soldiers into the army. Although from 1915 more Danes than before served in units with a German majority, many of the Danish-speaking soldiers were in squads and sections with other Danes or Germans from Schleswig, where they also were integrated into the primary groups. Although their wartime experiences were often conflict-ridden, the study of the Danish minority in the German army shows that patriotic commitment proved not to be essential in generating compliance during wartime.

Notes

1 Claus Bundgård Christensen, *Danskere på vestfronten 1914–1918* (Copenhagen: Gyldendal, 2009).

2 For the soldiers from Alsace Lorraine, see Alan Kramer, 'Wackes at war: Alsace-Lorraine and the failure of the German national mobilization, 1914–1918', in John Horne (ed.), *State, society and mobilization in Europe during the First World War* (Cambridge: CUP, 1997).

3 Hermann Cron, *Geschichte des Deutschen Heeres im Weltkriege 1914–1918* (Berlin: Militärverlag Karl Siegismund, 1937).

4 Christensen 2009, 12.

5 Jeffrey Verhey, *The Spirit of 1914—Militarism, Myth and Mobilization in Germany* (Cambridge: CUP, 2002); Benjamin Ziemann, *Front und Heimat: Ländliche Kriegserfahrungen im südlichen Bayern 1914–1923* (Essen: Klartext, 1997).

6 Christensen 2009, 24.

7 H. P. Hanssen, *Fra krigstiden – Dagbogsoptegnelser* (Copenhagen: Gyldendalske Boghandel, 1925), 9, 'Aldrig glemmer jeg billedet: Blege, alvorlige mænd, dumpt resignerende, kvinder opløst I gård, unge par, som uden at ænse omgivelserne holdt hinanden fast omslyngende, hulkende børn'.

8 *DSK Årbog* (1965), 98.

9 Stadtarchiv Flensburg, XII Hs-Handschriften, Flensburg als Garnison.

10 See Ziemann 1997.

11 Christensen 2009.

12 René Rasmussen, 'Sønderjylland ved krigens udbrud 1914', in Inge Adriansen & Hans Schulz Hansen (eds.), *Sønderjyderne og den store krig* (Historisk samfund for Sønderjylland, 2006), 59–76.

13 Christensen 2009, 27.

14 Hans Petersen, *Et Aar i krig* (Haderslev: Andelsbogtrykkeriet, 1920), 6.

15 Lokalhistorisk Forening for Øster Lindet Sogn, Rødding, Brd. Kræmers privatarkiv, d.2.8 1914. 'Dags morgen rejste allerede ca. 30 her fra byen. Det var næsten udelukkende gifte mænd som Mathias Mygind, Anders Højer og så fremdeles. Du kan vel omtrent tænke dig, hvordan kvinder og børn forholder sig. Man skulle næsten ikke holde sådan noget for muligt i vor oplyste tid. Jeg forstår ikke, at nogen kan påtage sig ansvaret derfor'.

16 Christensen 2009, 28. 'For der var jo dog sådan lidt eventyrligt og interessant ved det, som stod for'.

17 Ibid. 28.

18 Ibid. 140–2.

19 I. J. I. Bergholdt, *Pligtens vej. En sønderjyde i 1. Verdenskrig* (Haderslev: Historisk samfund for Sønderjylland, 1969), 76. 'Jeg kan se manden for mig endnu. Han var ikke ret stor, mager og nærmest gusten i ansigtet. Uniformen var efter en tur gennem løbegraven tilsølet fra øverst til nederst. Han var kort sagt et ynkeligt syn og for at bruge et tysk indtryk- "abgekämpft". Dog havde modersmålets toner for en kort tid kvikket ham op.'

20 Christensen 2009, 150.

21 Ibid. 81–91; Wilhelm Jürgensen, *Das Füsilier Regiment 'Königin' Nr.86 im Weltkriege* (Berlin: Verlag von Gerhard Stalling, 1925), 32–37.

22 Friderich Klähn, *Geschichte des Reserve Infanterie Regiments Nr. 86 im Weltkriege* (Berlin: Verlag von Gerhard Stalling, 1925), 53–66.

23 For examples, see Christensen 2009, 284 & 291.

24 Ibid. 146.

25 For coping, see Alexander Watson, *Enduring the Great War. Combat, Morale and Collapse in the German and British Armies, 1914–1918* (Cambridge: CUP, 2008), 85–108.

26 Jürgensen 1925, 64–75.

27 Ibid. 74.

28 Landesarchiv Schleswig-Holstein, Abt.303/1711, 1. Armee, Armee Oberkommando, v. Kuhl, d.21.7 1915.

29 Benjamin Ziemann, 'Fahnenflucht im deutschen Heer 1914–1918', *Militärgeschichtlichen Mitteillungen* (1996), 93–130.

30 Landsarkivet for Sønderjylland, Aabenraa, Feltham-arkivet, Breve fra A.Troensegaard-Hansen, November 1916; René Rasmussen, 'Sønderjyder i allieret krigsfangenskab', in Adriansen & Schulz Hansen 2006 (above, n. 12).

31 Claus Bundgård Christensen, '"Gud naade os der skal med". Kresten Andresen og Første Verdenskrig', in Claus Bundgård Christensen (ed.), *Krestens breve og dagbøger. En dansker på vestfronten i Første Verdenskrig* (Copenhagen: Gyldendal, 2012), 13, 'Det kunde være morsomt at skulle opleve at komme med Poul Verriers skib hjem'.

32 Landsarkivet for Sønderjylland, Sønderborg landråd, ks. 694, Korpsverordnungsblatt für das IX. Armekorps, 4.5. 1918.

33 Christensen 2009, 264–77.

34 Ibid. 235–47; Hülsemann, *Geschichte des Infanterie Regiments von Manstein (Schleswigsches) Nr. 84 1914–1918* (Berlin: Oldenburg, 1929), 21.

35 Christensen 2009, 257.

36 Christoph Jahr, *Gewöhnlichen Soldaten. Desertion und Deserture im deutschen und britischen Heer 1914–1918* (Göttingen: Vandenhoeck & Ruprecht, 1996).

37 Christensen 2009, 280.

38 Ibid. 268; for another example, see Landsarkivet for Sønderjylland, Hansen, Hans P., gårdmand, 1914–18.

39 *DSK Årbog* (1962), 106.

40 Hanssen 1925, 127.

41 Landsarkivet for Sønderjylland, Dau, Nicolai, RA0134, 1913–1918, breve, August 1914.

42 On patriotic commitment and performance on the battlefield, see Alexander Watson, 'Fighting for Another Fatherland: The Polish Minority in the German Army, 1914–1918', *English Historical Review*, 126/522 (2011), 1137–65.

43 *Histories of two hundred and fifty-one divisions of the German Army which participated in the war (1914–1918)* (London: London Stamp Exchange, 1989), 287.

44 Ibid. 291.

CHAPTER 11

The Scandinavian Diggers

Foreign-born soldiers
in the Australian Imperial Force, 1914–1918[1]

Eirik Brazier

Kolding, Denmark, 20 July, 1915. … It is with deep regret that we have received a message from [the] High Commissioner's Offices 72 Victoria Street Westminster London S.W. dated 29th June, that our son, E[dvard] J. M. Anderson, No.752 B. Company 4. Battalion AIF Egypt, is [sic] killed at the Dardanelles in the middle of June. I would respectfully request that all my son's belongings of which he was possessed at his death be forwarded me, <u>his watch and everything he had</u>. These articles will be our only memories of our oldest son. … I am, yours obediently, A. M. Andersen, Fabrikant, Bella-Vista, Kolding, Danmark.[2]

The quote is taken from one of several letters written to the Australian authorities by Edvard Andersen's father, as he searched for more information regarding the death of his son at Gallipoli in 1915.[3] The young Edvard had gone to Australia from America searching for work in 1899, having 'no clothing other than that which he stood in and his boots were of his feet', as a fellow Dane described him.[4] He soon found work as a labourer in New South Wales, but when war was declared in August 1914 he joined the Australian expeditionary force and was part of the Allied landings at Gallipoli on 25 April 1915. He was reported killed in action ten days later, but his final resting place remains unknown, as his body was never recovered from the battlefield. Today he is remembered on the Lone

Pine memorial at Gallipoli alongside 4,900 other missing soldiers from Australia and New Zealand.[5]

The story of Edvard Andersen is not unique and it exemplifies the war experiences of thousands of emigrated Scandinavians who fought in the armed forces of a newly adopted country during the First World War. A cursory search reveals the existence of large contingents of Scandinavian immigrants in the armies of Canada, the US, and the UK in addition to smaller groups in France, Germany, Australia, South Africa, and New Zealand.[6] Who were these men, why did they enlist, and what did they experience as foreign-born soldiers in a war that was so bound up with exclusive nationalism? This chapter intends to explore these questions using a case study of around 1,100 first-generation Scandinavian immigrants who served in the Australian Imperial Force (AIF) between 1914 and 1919.

In Scandinavia, migrants have traditionally been understood as people who left their homeland in order to settle permanently in another part of the world.[7] For thousands of families this story rings true and much research has been devoted to the subject. There was, however, another large group that emigrated from Denmark, Norway, and Sweden with no firm plan of settling permanently abroad. This group of young, single Scandinavian men who left their families to travel the world in search of employment throughout the nineteenth and early twentieth centuries often came from an impoverished background, having received little or no education, and their gateway to the world was a career as a sailor. The large merchant fleets of the three Scandinavian countries acted as an international superhighway, allowing crews to travel and reach almost any corner of the world. The places they visited offered many alluring opportunities, which encouraged them to leave their ship, legally or illegally, in order to explore. They became immigrants in a new country, finding temporary employment doing a variety of menial tasks in various industries. Their status as immigrants could often be of a temporary nature, however. A slump in the local economic climate, the prospect of other lucrative offers, or personal choice might easily make these single men move on and seek out a new country. At the outbreak of war in 1914, however, the choices for these transient Scandinavian men became severely restricted, as sea travel became both more limited and dangerous.

Foreigners in Australia at the outbreak of war

The Commonwealth of Australia entered the war on 4 August 1914, with Prime Minister Andrew Fisher affirming the dominion's determination to 'stand beside the mother country' and 'defend her to our last man and our last shilling'.[8] These were sentiments that resonated well in a society primarily consisting of British-Australians and dominated by a public discourse of loyalty to Great Britain and the Empire. 'A spirit of imperial enthusiasm' was sweeping through the Commonwealth, according to the *Sydney Morning Herald*, as Victoria Barracks in Sydney and other recruiting offices across the country were inundated with offers from Australians eager to enlist for military service.[9] These displays of enthusiasm and outbursts of jingoism, however, were counterbalanced by less noticeable expressions of concern, pessimism, scepticism, and down-right opposition to the war in some layers of Australian society.[10] Even *The Argus*, a conservative and pro-imperialist newspaper, observed that there was little enthusiasm and more 'strained expectancy' among the crowds that waited on news about the war outside its offices in Melbourne.[11]

The Australian society that entered the war in 1914 was not a united one, as labour troubles and racial and class conflicts had caused deep and bitter divisions in the only recently unified Commonwealth.[12] There were many and complex reasons for these confrontations, but a contributing factor was a sharp increase in non-British immigration to the continent. Australia had traditionally been the destination for migrants from the British Isles, and their descendants dominated all sectors of public life from politics, the military, and the Church to newspapers. This state of affairs was then challenged by an influx of non-British immigrants towards the latter half of the nineteenth century. Scandinavians belonged to this increased inflow, but comprised only a small fraction of the total number, as only 14,806 first-generation Scandinavians were registered in 1911.[13]

Australian immigration statistics reveal the transitory nature of the Scandinavians presence. While some 6,000 Scandinavians arrived in Australia between 1913 and 1917, more than 5,000 left the continent in the same period. In other words, it would seem that few Scandinavians were actually settling permanently, and that most stayed for a while before moving on to other parts of the world. The story of Jens Edvard Valdemar Karl Ingvarson, or Jack Ingvarson as he was to be known, typifies the arrival story of many Scandinavian immigrants. Ingvarson, a Danish sailor, came to Fremantle from Montevideo in 1913, working on a ship carrying sand and stone. Unable to sell their cargo in Australia and with dissatisfaction mounting among the crew, Ingvarson jumped ship at the first opportunity. He found work on a local farm where he lived until he enlisted in 1915.[14] Not everyone found employment as quickly as Ingvarson, and working conditions could be far from easy for immigrants. Western Australia, for example, had seen the arrival of many Scandinavian immigrants attempting to profit from the gold rushes at the end of the nineteenth century. By the early 1900s the slum quarters of Perth and Fremantle were growing rapidly.[15] Conditions were not much better in other states, a common feature of all frontier societies. In 1910, the Danish and Swedish authorities went so far as to publicly warn their citizens from travelling to Australia in search of work, as the risk of failure and impoverishment was overwhelming.[16]

The arrival of these new immigrant groups were causing the composition of Australian society to change, albeit slowly, and challenging, in the eyes of homogenous Anglo-Australians, the natural order. This perceived challenge by the 'foreigner', matched with expressions of imperialism and loyalty to Britain, strengthened the public discourse of insiders and outsiders. The traditionally close political, cultural, and economic ties with Britain became important to all layers of British-Australian society and resulted in an abiding suspicion of those non-British immigrants who failed to do the same. Times of crisis, such as the Second Boer War (1899–1901), and the Commonwealth's physical distance from the mother country contributed to increased suspicion of the 'foreigner', for Australians considered themselves an isolated outpost of the British Empire in danger of being invaded.[17] These fears were often turned into hostility towards specific ethnic groups, especially those of German, Russian, and Eastern European descent, and Scandinavians, who could be mistaken for belonging to such groups, were made to feel the rising level of distrust towards outsiders.

The outbreak of war only accentuated existing attitudes towards the 'foreigner'. First-generation German, Austrian, and Italian immigrants were forced to register with the authorities, and thousands of them were placed in internment camps for the duration of the war.[18] Other non-naturalized citizens had to register and were required to carry a certificate of registration to prove that they could legally stay in Australia. Being classified as a 'friendly alien' did not shield Scandinavians from harassment and suspicion, however. The 'spy mania' that gripped most European countries found its way to Australia, and the authorities in all six states received information from concerned citizens about suspect activity among 'foreigners'.[19] Scandinavians were frequently mistaken for Germans and did not escape persecution. A Dane by the name of Charles Duus complained to *The Argus* of having been accused of being 'a German spy' and threatened with 'immediate personal injury'.[20] The Scandinavian newspaper *Norden* was made to feel the rising hostility against anything non-British when copies of the paper had to be submitted to military censors, and there were demands for it to be printed in English only. It was not until the editor informed the authorities that he had two sons at the front that permission to continue to use the Scandinavian languages was granted.[21] Among the immigrants there was an increased reluctance to use their native tongues, and there was a significant shift towards the use of English among Scandinavians during the war years.[22] The distrust of 'foreigners' extended to employment, as immigrants found fewer opportunities in a deteriorating Australian economy.

Australia's dependence on trade with Britain and the rest of Europe was exposed as a colossal disadvantage at the outbreak of war in 1914, and caused a minor collapse in the colony's economy. National unemployment leapt from 5.7 per cent to 11.0 per cent in the last six months of 1914.[23] Many of the Scandinavians who had settled faced hardship, but this paled in comparison to the challenges confronting the transitory and unskilled immigrants. With no permanent residency, a lack of connections to immigrant communities, and deficient language skills, they were hit extra hard by the recession, as they were met with the added challenge of many businesses being less than eager to hire 'suspect foreigners'.

There are few clues to the motives for enlistment among the Scandinavians. There were certainly those who displayed an eagerness to defeat Germany, especially among the Danish immigrants who had historical reasons for wanting to join the fight. 'God Bless England' was the title of a letter published in one newspaper, written by a Dane who had been born in Holstein while it was still part of Denmark. 'The terrible atrocities' that were now being inflicted by Germany on the rest of Europe filled him with 'horror and loathing, and must be punished'.[24] Sentiments of this kind were, however, primarily confined to those Scandinavians who had settled permanently in Australia. For the transitory immigrants the evidence is sketchier, but it could be argued that in a society that was showing increasing hostility towards 'foreigners' and had rising unemployment and far fewer job opportunities for outsiders, enlistment might offer employment, adventure, and a way of proving one's loyalty. Thus, military service would appeal especially to transient Scandinavians who lacked sufficient language skills, personal contacts, and cultural understanding to navigate the challenges brought by war.

Enlisting for service in the AIF

The Australian military contribution to the war was to be organized as an expeditionary force called the Australian Imperial Force. It was entirely a volunteer force, and the authorities had few difficulties in recruiting in the early stages of the war, as thousands of Australians rushed to enlist. At the end of 1914, more than 50,000 thousand men had enlisted in the AIF and by war's end more than 400,000 soldiers had been recruited.[25] This was an extraordinary number when one considers that the Australian population numbered only 5 million people. In fact, it turned out to be the highest ratio of soldiers per head of population within the British Empire.[26] Among these volunteers were about 1,100 Scandinavian immigrants, a number that pales into insignificance next to the overall numbers. Yet it is still a significant number when seen from the perspective of the size of the Scandinavian immigrant population in Australia, which in 1911 was close to 15,000.[27] Scandinavians in Australia did not enlist en masse, nor were there, as in Canada, separate battalions in which Scandinavians could serve together.[28] Instead, they enlisted alone or in the company of a few friends.

The scene recounted in the *Sydney Morning Herald* at a local recruiting office in 1915 is probably representative of the way in which many Scandinavians joined the AIF.

> Three Scandinavians, big and blonde, wanted to join the forces. They were all sailors, and had their discharges with them. They were told that they would have to go and get naturalised before they could offer their services. This seemed to dampen their ardour for a moment, then, as soon as the recruiting sergeant told them that if they brought up their papers they would be taken on, they were immensely pleased, because the recruiting sergeant told them that they were just the class of men wanted.[29]

The paper could inform its readers the next day that 'these fine men were among the first batch … and proudly produced their papers to show that they had thrown in their lot with the Australians.'[30] It has not been possible to ascertain the motives of the Scandinavian recruits, but economic depression, unemployment, and stigmatization of the 'foreigner' were all factors that are likely to have played an important role in their choice to enlist. An effective propaganda campaign directed at encouraging specific groups in society to enlist must also be considered a prime reason for Scandinavian recruitment. Scandinavian men who were married and settled might have escaped these recruitment drives, but single men became a favourite target of several official and unofficial recruitment campaigns. Privately initiated 'patriotic groups', such as the All-British Association in Western Australia, exerted pressure through public meetings in order to shame single men into service.[31] On an official level, several

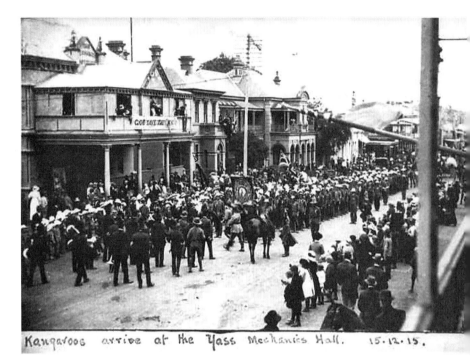

Kanqaroos arrive at the Yass Mechanics Hall. 15.12.15.

FIGURE 1: Kangaroo marchers on their way to Sydney, 1915. (Australian War Memorial)

spectacular recruitment marches were organized, receiving much attention in the press. One such march was the 'Kangaroo march' from Wagga Wagga to Sydney in December 1915.[32] An unknown young Norwegian joined the march during its stop in Binalong, where the Kangaroo marchers had paraded through town with school children forming an honour guard and 'singing patriotic songs'.[33] Single, 'foreign', civilian males were thus coming under increased pressure to enlist, and would have presented an obvious target for such marches.

While there were many motives for enlistment in the AIF, the act was in itself clearly construed as the ultimate test of loyalty to Australia, as seen in the case of the *Norden* editor. Enlistment, however, required British citizenship, and for many volunteers who had lived in Australia for any length of time it meant renouncing their Scandinavian citizenship. The outbreak of war and the wish to enlist seem to have forced many into becoming naturalized citizens, especially among the single Scandinavians, who might otherwise have preferred to retain their Danish, Norwegian, or Swedish citizenship. The rising demand for fresh troops during the recruitment crisis of 1916 and 1917 led the Australian authorities to relax their stand on the need for naturalization, which meant that friendly aliens such as Scandinavians were allowed to enlist before they had become British citizens.[34] This change in recruitment policy was reflected in the numerous declarations written by consulates of all three Scandinavian countries, which furnished volunteers with confirmation of their Danish, Norwegian, or Swedish citizenship and that there were no apparent reservations on the part of the Scandinavian authorities to their enlistment for military service in the AIF. This latter statement, at least in the case of Norwegian volunteers, echoed a similar official sanction for those volunteering for the French Foreign Legion, which had allowed several hundred Norwegians to serve in the French forces.[35]

Their service records reveals that most Scandinavian volunteers fell into a grey area when it came to their national identity, something mirrored in the various bonds retained with Scandinavia. The name of a parent or sibling still residing in Scandinavia was often listed as next of kin or as beneficiaries in wills, and gives further evidence to their status as temporary residents in Australia with no large personal network. While there were some recruits who clearly had settled in Australia, often giving the name of a wife, they were in the minority. The records also paint a detailed socioeconomic picture of the Scandinavian volunteers, and lends support to claims that the majority were unskilled, transitory workers, often with experience of the merchant fleet. 'Lumper', 'miner', 'sheet metalworker', 'railway packer' and 'labourer' are just a few of the occupations listed, and medical examinations give further evidence of the number of former sailors, as the documentation on 'Distinctive Marks' often was filled with detailed descriptions of numerous tattoos.[36]

Having been accepted for service there is little evidence of Scandinavians being ill-treated or harassed because of their origins. That said, there are a handful of examples of soldiers being

Figure 2: Former sailor Hans Peter Rasmussen, c. May 1915. He was killed at the Battle of the Somme in 1916. (Australian War Memorial)

discharged from duty due to language difficulties. A Norwegian, Hans Johnson, had lived for some time in Australia and was a naturalized citizen when he enlisted in 1915, but was treated with 'suspicion' and became the subject of a 'certain amount of persecution' by his fellow soldiers due to his foreign accent.[37] It can only be assumed that his Norwegian accent caused him to be suspected of being German. The officer in charge of the field hospital where he worked stated that the request for discharge came from Johnson himself and that he was 'the best worker in our unit.'[38] The majority of Scandinavian volunteers, however, were accepted and soon on their way to the front.

Service in the AIF

The Gallipoli peninsula in the Ottoman Empire was to be the first test of the newly established forces of Australia and New Zealand, which were brought together as the Australian and New Zealand Army Corps (ANZAC). The troops made up the larger proportion of an Allied landing force whose ultimate aim was to open up a decisive Mediterranean front.[39] The majority of Australian troops had been training and preparing in Egypt since the beginning of 1915, and in April that year about 21,000 ANZAC troops set sail for the peninsula.[40] On Sunday 25 April, the first Australian soldiers landed on the beaches of Gallipoli and were met with fierce resistance from the Turkish defenders. The promises of an easy victory proved to be false and intense fighting continued until January 1916, at which time the invasion attempt was abandoned and the troops were evacuated. The campaign was a bloody baptism of fire for the untried Australian troops, with more than 8,000 killed and close to 18,000 wounded.[41] In Australia, the news of the intense fighting and heavy casualties on the peninsula brought home the terrifying realities of modern warfare, leaving a lasting impression on the Australian society.[42]

The campaign saw the first casualties among the Scandinavian soldiers and the first death notifications were dispatched to Norway, Denmark, and Sweden. These telegrams offered bereaved relatives

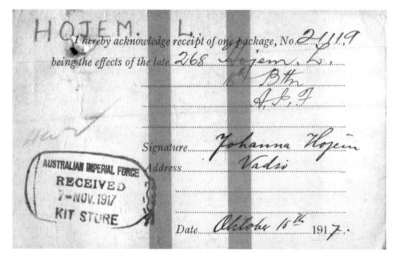

FIGURE 3: The advice of delivery slip that accompanied the package of Lauritz Hojem's personal effects, signed by his mother in Vadsø.

some details of the death of the soldier and were often followed by a package of his personal possessions, as was the case with Danish-born Edvard Andersen already mentioned. The process of locating the relatives of a fallen soldier was often a drawn-out process, especially in the case of immigrants. Poorly maintained records, language confusion, and the anglicization of Scandinavian names often left forms illegible, which resulted in delays. Charles Syversen, a former Norwegian master mariner, was reported as missing, presumed dead, during the fighting on Gallipoli in August 1915. A 'Charles Syversen of Horton, Norway' was listed as his next of kin and the Australian authorities sent several inquiries to different locations in Norway through official channels before they received a satisfactory reply. The answer came from a Syver Iversen in Horten who stated that he had a son by the name of Karl Andreas Syversen who had left his family 'for the sea' twenty years before.[43] He included the last letter the family had received from him and a picture in his reply to AIF Headquarters. The information was enough to confirm that Charles and Karl were one and the same, and a package containing a felt hat, a shaving brush, and a hairbrush could be returned to his family. At least another ten Scandinavian soldiers were killed and an unknown number injured during the campaign before the last troops were finally evacuated from Gallipoli in early January 1916, bringing to an end the first major military operation by Australian troops.

The Gallipoli Campaign had drained the AIF of soldiers, but fresh replacements were already being trained to join the rest of the Australian troops who had been sent to fight in France. The enlistment papers show that Scandinavians were joining the AIF at an ever-increasing rate after Gallipoli. These new recruits entered service in 1916 and 1917, as Australian forces took part in some of the bloodiest engagements of the war. All this constant action exacted a heavy toll on the Australian forces and led to concerns about Australia's ability to find enough fresh troops for service. The Imperial High Command threatened to amalgamate Australian units with existing British regiments if not enough recruits were found. The shortage of recruits led the Australian government to contemplate the introduction of conscription, and two plebiscites were held on the issue, one in 1916 and another in 1917.[44] The result in both was no, but the ferocious debates between the 'Yes' and 'No' campaigns strengthened the hostility and suspicion among Anglo-Australians towards the 'foreigner'.[45]

War exhaustion began to tell, putting a strain on the troops themselves, and casualty rates climbed at an alarming rate. Louise Drange, a Gallipoli veteran, was wounded a second time in August 1916, as Australian units attempted to gain an advantage at Pozières in the Somme valley. A letter was sent by the Australian authorities to his father in Bergen that he was 'lying seriously ill at the 13th Stationary Hospital, Boulogne'.[46] This letter was probably the last sign of life that his family received from him. Louise recovered from his wound and was discharged back to Australia in 1917. An inquiry sent by the Norwegian Consulate on behalf of his father in 1924 returned no answer as to his whereabouts, which indicates that they had lost touch in the meantime. The Scandinavian consulates in Australia were not the only ones to handle communications between the Australian authorities and soldiers' relatives, as similar services were provided by the consulates in London. Waldemar Eckell, a secretary at the Norwegian consulate, handled the death notifications of several Norwegian soldiers and attempted to help in locating relatives back in Norway.[47]

In the wake of the heavy fighting of 1916–17, packages similar to those of the soldiers killed at Gallipoli were delivered throughout Scandinavia and charted a horrific map of the many battles that the Scandinavian soldiers fought in. In early October 1917, the Australians were part of the attacks at Passchendaele, a battle that was made all the more difficult by the muddy fields through which the soldiers had to advance. Johannes Rostgaard Rasmussen had arrived in Belgium only a month before the attack. He was reported missing, presumed killed, on 13 October. In his will he stated that all his personal belongings were to go to his sister in Denmark, but the Australian authorities were unable to locate her. Two years later, the Danish Consulate in Melbourne was still making inquiries with regards to the state of his case.[48] These scenes were repeated throughout the years of 1916 and 1917, as Allied forces attempted to break the deadlock on the Western Front. Many Scandinavians took part in these attacks and a heavy toll was inflicted on those who survived the fighting, both physically and psychologically. Kristian Engstrom, from Uppsala, arrived in France in late November 1916 and was part of the Australian raids on German trenches during the harsh winter of 1916–17. In early January 1917, he was admitted to hospital 'suffering from shell shock, classed as Battle casualty' and later discharged back to Australia in November.[49]

The Scandinavians serving with Australian units continued to see heavy action in 1918 as Allied forces attempted to gain an advantage. While private anguish followed in the wake of this fighting, as a new wave of death notifications reached Scandinavia, the last year of the war also witnessed the first Scandinavian newspaper articles about the volunteers.[50] These stories were only a small part of a broader narrative of battlefield experiences articulated by the larger community of expatriate Scandinavians, finding its way home as information started to flow with greater ease between Scandinavian countries and the rest of the world towards the end of the war.[51] In Norway, the growing realization among government officials of the participation of its own citizens in the war prompted an official response, as the Norwegian Ministry of Foreign Affairs published guidelines on how widows and families could claim compensation from the Australian authorities.[52]

Going home

On the eleventh day of the eleventh month of 1918 an armistice came into effect between the Allies and Germany. The exact number of Scandinavians killed and wounded remains to be determined, but their casualty rates were probably little different from the rest of the AIF. The final tally for Australia was 215,585 killed or wounded—a casualty rate of 64.98 per cent, the highest of any Imperial contingent.[53] The surviving Australian troops, the majority stationed in Europe, were demobilized, but due to the large number of soldiers this process would take time and many of them remained stationed in Europe throughout 1918–19. Scandinavian soldiers who did not immediately return home to Australia were granted special dispensation to visit family and friends in their home countries. Hjalmar Nilsen, a former Norwegian sailor, was granted leave to visit his family in Fredrikshald in December 1919.[54] While some soldiers decided return to their home country, the majority of the Scandinavian soldiers, however, seem initially to have returned to Australia, although the transient nature of their lives was again to manifest itself after demobilization, as a number of them seem to have immigrated to other parts of the world in the years after 1919.

Australian society, like many others, struggled to give sufficient aid to returning soldiers. Many soldiers were still recovering from their wounds and deeply traumatized by their war experiences. Their war pensions were insufficient to live on, and work was difficult to find for those with permanent injuries, as even trade unions were reluctant to hire disabled ex-servicemen.[55] The psychological effects of the war were also emerging and different forms of substance abuse became a form of escape for many soldiers, including some Scandinavians. Jørgen Christian Jensen was one of them. He had led an attack on a sheltered German machine gun defended by forty-five enemy soldiers in 1917 and been awarded the Victoria Cross, promoted to sergeant, and become a celebrated hero.[56] Later the same year he was seriously wounded, receiving a gunshot to the head, and spent the remainder of the war in a series of hospitals.[57] The experiences of the war seem to have haunted him after his return home to Australia and he became an alcoholic.[58] He died a few years after his return in 1922, aged only 31.[59] Cases of 'shell-shock' and similar disorders were found among other returned Scandinavians, such as Sigurd Christoffersen who continued to suffer from his war experiences after 1918 and was admitted to Callan Park Mental Hospital, Sydney, which was known for its treatment of 'shell-shocked' soldiers.[60] Only a few months later he died, probably as a result of what would today be considered posttraumatic stress disorder. Arthur Butler concluded in his official history of the Australian Medical Services that the problem of a 'nervous breakdown … is only 20 per cent. a war problem and 80 per cent. a problem of war's aftermath'.[61] Recognition of these forms of casualty was only emerging at the end of the First World War and treatment was often rudimentary.

When the war was over, the search for missing Scandinavian soldiers continued throughout the 1920s and 1930s. In 1921, the Norwegian Ministry of Foreign Affairs published a list in *Aftenposten* of the names of several fallen AIF soldiers whose Norwegian relatives had not been traced.[62] One of the last requests for information regarding missing soldiers was lodged with the Australian Military Headquarters in Melbourne as late as 1939.[63] Requests made their way through a host of different channels ranging from the Salvation Army to incidental encounters. In 1933, an Australian timber merchant informed the authorities of his recent visit to Norway where he had met 'an old lady who was anxiously enquiring about her son, who had immigrated to Australia some years before the war'.[64] The woman's son had enlisted in the AIF in 1917, but a German gas attack in the closing months of the war had left him with serious injuries. He had visited his mother in Norway while convalescing in Britain, but there seems to have been no further contact between them after 1919.

The Scandinavian foreign ministries acted as hubs in most of these cases, relaying information between relatives and the Australian authorities in a number of different ways. These searches were often made difficult due to the fact that several returned soldiers had returned to their pre-war profession as sailors. Erling Pedersen lodged an inquiry with the Norwegian authorities with regards to the whereabouts of his brother, Alfred Pedersen, who was presumed to have served in the AIF. The Norwegian Consulate General was able to identify him as a returned soldier, but a permanent address was not forthcoming since 'he follows the occupation of a seaman [and] it would be very difficult to trace his whereabouts at the present time'.[65] While a number of enquiries were sent *to* Australia, there was also many sent *from* Australia, as the military authorities attempted to trace the next of kin of the fallen. Incomplete or out-of-date information made the task difficult, however, and cases accumulated in the archives of the Scandinavian foreign ministries as a testament to the challenges.

Conclusions

In this chapter it has only been possible to scratch the surface of the topic of Scandinavian immigrants who served in the First World War. However, by exploring the experiences of the Scandinavian AIF soldiers before, during, and after the war, it is possible to offer some reflections on who they were, why they enlisted, and what they experienced during the war.

From their attestation papers it seems clear the Scandinavian immigrants who served in the AIF can be divided into two groups: those who had chosen to settle permanently in Australia, and those for whom Australia was a port of call. The majority of AIF Scandinavians belonged to the latter group of transient immigrants—single men, with little or no education, who used the global reach of the merchant fleets to traverse the world in search of employment and adventure. Australia, with its frontier economy, provided these transitory, unskilled workers a temporary stay and a host of opportunities. The geographical isolation of Australia and her society's firm anchoring in British culture meant that loyalty to Britain and the Empire were important values and defined society's insiders and outsiders. Increased immigration at the turn of twentieth century, combined with the perceived risk of a foreign invasion, created an atmosphere in which non-British individuals often were considered a threat. Suspicion towards 'foreigners' only increased at the outbreak of war in 1914, and was aided by the subsequent economic downturn, which left many transient immigrants under ever-increasing pressure to prove their loyalty. Cut off from Europe, with few personal connections, growing hostility directed at suspect 'foreigners', and difficulty in finding employment, Scandinavians faced a series of problems that might have prompted many of them to enlist in the Australian war effort. Hardship and opportunism are offered here as the likely explanations for military service, rather than the traditional nationalistic motives.

The war experiences of the Scandinavian volunteers seem not to have differed much from those of other AIF soldiers. What the stories of dead and missing Scandinavian soldiers do reveal, though, are the previously unknown connections between Scandinavian society and the war. The death notifications delivered to next of kin in Denmark, Norway, and Sweden have made it possible to sketch a crude, incomplete map of the bonds between Scandinavian soldiers and the communities of their birth. The process of informing next of kin shows the degree of involvement by official institutions, newspapers, and private individuals in the Scandinavian countries, lending substance to the bare record and hinting at the impression they might have made. Further research should make it possible to trace more material in the form of private letters, diaries, and other personal documents to shed light on the soldiers' direct contacts with Scandinavian society. An investigation into the cases of those granted 'Scandinavian leave' might offer fruitful insights and provide more tangible evidence. In the end, the history of the Scandinavian soldiers in the AIF offers additional nuances to the current narrative of Scandinavia and the First World War, and raises the question of whether it is possible to fully understand the repercussions of the First World War on Scandinavia if the war experiences of Danish, Swedish, and Norwegian expatriates are missing from the story.

Notes

1 'Digger' is a generic term or nickname given to soldiers from Australia or New Zealand, similar to the British 'Tommy Atkins' or American 'Dough-boy'.

2 National Archives of Australia (NAA), B2455, Anderson, E. J. M., letter from A. M. Andersen to the Department of Defence, Melbourne, original translation from the Danish by the Australian military authorities: 'Med dyb Sorg har vi modtaget Efterretning fra High Commissionaer's Offices 72 Victoria Street Westminster, London S.W. den 29 Juni om at vor Søn E. J. Andersen, No 752 B. Compagni 4. Batalion AIF Egypt er Dræbt I Kampen ved Dardanellerne midt I Juni Maaned; jeg tillader mig høfligst at anmode Dem om at tilsende mig alt der har tilhørd min Søn jeg beder Dem spesielt hvis det er Dem muligt at sende mig alt han var i Bsidelse av ved hans Død, hans Uhr. samd alle hans Efterladenskaber, som for os er et kært Minde om vor kære ældste Søn ... Erbødigst A. M. Andersen, Fabrikant, Bella-Vista, Kolding, Danmark' (I have kept given names and surnames as they appear in the original material).

3 His father received two packages containing personal belongings, but the watch was never found.

4 NAA, B2455, Anderson, E. J. M., letter from Hans Martin Sørensen to Officer-in-Charge, Base Records, 17 May 1920; A1, 1914/10125, Edward Jorgen Martin Anderson, Naturalization.

5 NAA, B2455, Anderson, E. J. M., Casualty Form—Active Service.

6 For examples of Scandinavians in the Canadian services, see *Aftenposten*, 11 June 1917; for the American case, see *Aftenposten*, 7 July 1920.

7 On Scandinavian migration, see Leslie Moch, *Moving Europeans: migration in Western Europe since 1650*, Bloomington: Indiana University Press, 1992; Ingrid Semmingsen, *Norway to America: a history of the migration*, Minneapolis, University of Minnesota Press, 1978.

8 Charles W. E. Bean, *The Official history of Australia in the war of 1914–1918*, Sydney, Angus & Robertson, 1938, 16.

9 *Sydney Morning Herald*, 6 August 1914.

10 Bobbie Oliver, *War and peace in Western Australia : the social and political impact of the Great War, 1914–1926*, Nedlands, W.A., University of Western Australia Press, 1995; James Bennett, *Rats and revolutionaries: the labour movement in Australia and New Zealand 1890–1940*, Dunedin, University of Otago Press, 2003.

11 *The Argus*, 6 August 1914.

12 The Commonwealth of Australia was created in 1901 by federation of the six colonies of New South Wales, Queensland, South Australia, Western Australia, Victoria and Tasmania, see Stuart Macintyre, *The Oxford History*

SCANDINAVIA IN THE FIRST WORLD WAR

of *Australia: Vol. 4, 1902–1942 the Succeeding Age*, Oxford, Oxford University Press, 1986, 45.

13 Olavi Koivukangas and John Stanley Martin, *The Scandinavians in Australia*, Melbourne, AE Press, 1986, 110.

14 Koivukangas and Martin, 146–147.

15 Oliver, 39.

16 *The Brisbane Courier*, 10 February 1910.

17 John Williams, *German Anzacs and the First World War*, Sydney, University of New South Wales Press, 2003, 19; Neville Meaney, *A history of Australian defence and foreign policy, 1901-23,* Sydney, Sydney University Press, 2009.

18 Similar actions were taken in Canada and the US.

19 For 'spy mania', see Nik. Brandal & Ola Teige and Claes Ahlund in this volume.

20 *The Argus*, 21 January 1916.

21 Koivukangas and Martin, 138.

22 Koivukangas and Martin, 113.

23 Raymond Evans, *Loyalty and disloyalty: social conflict on the Queensland homefront, 1914-18*, Sydney, Allen & Unwin, 1987, 23.

24 *The Advertiser*, 20 May 1915.

25 Bean, 871–72.

26 Jeffrey Grey, *A military history of Australia*, Cambridge, Cambridge University Press, 1990, 120.

27 Koivukangas and Martin, 110.

28 In Canada, Endre J. Cleven, from Skudenes, organized the 197th battalion 'The Vikings of Canada' as part of the Canadian Expeditionary Force (CEF), but Scandinavians were found throughout the battalions of the CEF; for expressions of Danish identity within the German army, see Claus Bundgård Christensen in the present volume.

29 *Sydney Morning Herald*, 16 June 1915.

30 *Sydney Morning Herald*, 17 June 1915.

31 Oliver, 72.

32 Sherry Morris and Harold Fife, *The Kangaroo March: from Wagga Wagga to the Western Front*, Wagga Wagga N.S.W., S. Morris, 2006.

33 *Sydney Morning Herald*, 14 December 1915.

34 *Western Argus*, 26 June 1917; however, 'aboriginal natives' were still not allowed to serve in the AIF.

35 Newspaper reports of Norwegian volunteers serving with the French Foreign Legion had already begun to appear in August 1914 (see *Aftenposten*, 15 August 1914).

36 See for example, NAA, B2455, Berentsen, Anton Severin.

37 NAA, B2455, Johnson, Hans, letter from O.C. Field Hospital to Head Quarters, 29 September 1915.

38 NAA, B2455, Johnson, Hans.

39 The campaign is often considered, in the popular mind, to be a purely ANZAC endeavour, but some 40,000 troops from Britain and France also took part.

40 Michael McKernan, *Australia, two Centuries of war & peace*, Australian War Memorial, Canberra in association with Allen & Unwin, Australia, 1988, 160.

41 Great Britain, War Office, *Statistics of the military effort of the British Empire during the great war, 1914–1920*, London, H.M. Stationery Office, [1922].

42 25 April is a national day of remembrance in both Australia and New Zealand, akin to Remembrance Day in Europe.

43 NAA, B2455, Syversen, Charles.

44 Frederick Perry, *The Commonwealth armies: manpower and organisation in two world wars*, Manchester, Manchester University Press, 1988, 156; Grey, 112–114.

45 On the eve of the first referendum in 1916 a crowd of 2,000 civilians and soldiers destroyed several Greek-owned businesses in Perth, see Oliver, 103.

46 NAA, B2455, Drange, L., letter from Royal Norwegian Consulate to the Officer-in-charge, Base Records, Victoria Barracks, Melbourne, 6 March 1924.

47 See, for example, NAA B2455, Pedersen, Nils Christian.

48 NAA, B2455, Rasmussen, Johannes Rostgaard.

49 NAA, B2455, Engstrom, Kristian.

50 For Norwegian examples, see *Aftenposten,* 1 and 15 August 1918.

51 Eirik Brazier, 'The Search for a Norwegian Identity in the Trenches, in Conflict in Memory: Interpersonal and Intergenerational Remembering of War. Conflict and Transition', paper given at the Matchpoints Seminar, 10–12 May 2012, Aarhus University, Denmark.

52 *Aftenposten*, 6 June 1918.

53 Arthur G. Butler, *The Australian army medical services in the war of 1914–1918*, Melbourne, Australian War Memorial, 1938, 56.

54 NAA, B2455, Nilsen, Hjalmar.

55 Evans, 110.

56 NAA, B2455, Jensen, Jorgan Christian.

57 NAA, B2455, Jensen, Jorgan Christian.

58 Koivukangas and Martin, 112.

59 *The Advertiser*, 1 June 1922.

60 NAA, B2455, Christoffersen, Sigurd.

61 Butler, 142.

62 *Aftenposten*, 17 November 1921.

63 NAA, B2455, Johnsen, Peter.

64 NAA, B2455, Larsen, Bernhard Johan.
65 NAA, B2455, Pedersen, Alfred, letter from Officer-in-Charge of Base
   Records to The Norwegian Consul General, 25 July 1921.

CHAPTER 12

The horse field ambulance in Tampere in 1918

Swedish Red Star women and the Finnish Civil War

Anne Hedén

During the Finnish Civil War, a group of women volunteers from the Swedish Red Star animal relief organization helped set up and run a field ambulance—a mobile field hospital—for military horses in Tampere, behind White lines. Primary source material that shows women's participation in war is a rare occurrence. Even in modern times, when the issue of women's agency in armed conflict has been studied more thoroughly, sources that deal specifically with women in the theatre of war are not exactly abundant.[1] It is for this reason the journal kept by the Swedish veterinary orderly Stina Linderdahl during the Finnish Civil War, the records of the Swedish Red Star field ambulance in Tampere, and the articles written by Linderdahl's colleague Signe Fryberg for the conservative daily newspapers in Stockholm in the spring of 1918 are so important in fully understanding both Swedish support for the Whites in the Finnish Civil War and, more specifically, the contribution made by women. Both Linderdahl and Fryberg worked at the Tampere horse field ambulance from April to June 1918, and their own accounts and the hospital's records are the chief sources used here.[2]

In view of the fact that the red star even then was strongly connected to the imagery of the Russian Revolution, it is important to note that the name of the Swedish animal welfare organization was chosen in 1917 to echo that of the International Committee of the Red Cross, and also to demonstrate its affiliation with L'Étoile Rouge, the international organization that had been founded in 1914 to bring together the various national equine relief organizations. In 1941 the Swedish Red Star changed its name to the Swedish Blue Star.[3]

Finland in 1918

Finland's short and bloody civil war, which began by the end of January 1918 when Russia was still a combatant in the First World War, was a consequence of the continuing war. The Russian Revolution had been triggered by the chain reaction to the Russian losses against Germany, and the rising chaos of Tsarist Russia contributed to the escalation of the military conflict in the Grand Duchy of Finland, then part of the Russian Empire. Other contributing factors were the struggles between the workers' movement and the conservative Establishment during a period of soaring unemployment, poverty, and starvation.[4]

Once the Russian Revolution had begun, the Russian Empire effectively collapsed, while the troops that had belonged to the Tsarist army remained in Finland. Before the outbreak of Finnish Civil War, Finland's conservative 'Whites' had started recruiting volunteers for various local militia groups (the so-called Protection Corps, or White Guard), while the radical wing of the Social Democrats set about forming the 'Red Guards'. The Whites drew their support from trade, industry, and agriculture, the Reds from workers and crofters. During the strikes and unrest in Finland in the summer of 1917, an arms race developed between the Whites and the Reds, while the Finnish declaration of independence on 6 December 1917 was a result of bourgeois, right-wing fears that the Russian Revolution would spread into Finland. When the Bolshevik government agreed to Finnish independence in late 1917 it was indeed to speed up the revolution in the country. In the middle of January 1918, the Finnish Senate (the government) decided to reinforce law and order using the White Guard. The Reds interpreted this as an attempt to halt the revolution; even the reformist Social Democrats saw confrontation as the only solution, according to the Finnish historian Henrik Meinander, as it was known that the Whites could expect military support from Germany. At the beginning of April 1918, German troops arrived in the south of Finland and by the end of April it was clear that the Whites had won the Civil War. In May, the White Finnish general Gustaf Mannerheim held a victory parade in Helsinki.[5] Meinander has calculated that the total number of dead in the Civil War came to 38,500, of whom some 11,000 were killed in the actual fighting. Immediately after the war at least 11,800 people were killed by the Whites, while 80,000 were placed in camps where 13,500 died from hunger and disease.[6]

Compulsory military service, which was introduced by law in February, provided the White army with crucial reinforcements; by contrast, only a small number of Russian troops took part on the Red side (approximately 10,000 out of 75,000 soldiers, and of these 10,000 only a minor group actually took part in the fighting), a fact compounded by the separate peace negotiations between Germany and Russia in Brest-Litovsk in March 1918, when the Russians agreed to evacuate their troops from Finland and stop all propaganda against the Finnish government.[7]

Historians such as Heikki Ylikangas and Aapo Roselius have pointed out that the Finnish Civil War to a great degree was prompted by a determination to rout Finland's workers' movement.[8] Further, it had been embarked on in the expectation of a German expansion eastwards. After the expected collapse of the Russian Revolution, the victors of the Finnish Civil War were planning to expand the borders of Finland to include East Karelia. The understanding was that this would be under political subordination to Germany, including the election of a German prince as king of Finland. When Germany was defeated in the First World War, this plan was scrapped along with the Whites' loyalty to Germany. In the newly Entente-friendly Finland, now also a buffer zone against Communist Russia, general elections were held in 1919 and reforms passed: crofters were given some land rights, and compulsory school attendance was introduced, along with freedom of expression and religion. In 1919 the Social Democrats were the largest party in the Eduskunta (Parliament); however, the centre parties determined policy.[9]

For several decades, academic circles in Finland were heavily influenced by the Whites' view of the Civil War, which resulted in a research tradition that held it to be a struggle for liberty from Russia. Later research, mainly in the 1960s and onwards, tends to draw on other points of view, as Ylikangas has noted.[10]

Swedish support for the Whites in 1918

In January 1918, the Swedish organization Finlands vänner (Friends of Finland) was founded in Stockholm with the support of the Establishment and the business sector. Over a thousand Swedes, many of them career officers, NCOs, and other ranks, volunteered to fight for the white side in Finland, some in regular White units and most of them in the resultant Swedish Brigade as part of the White Guard.[11] Swedish businessmen raised money for the Swedish Brigade—and also to pay for a horse field ambulance.[12]

The Swedish supporters of the Whites in 1918 have been described as a relatively small group who enjoyed huge influence over the press.[13] Certainly, the horse field ambulance was followed with interest in the Swedish dailies. In her study of Swedish public opinion and representations of the First World War, Lina Sturfelt describes how depictions of horses as victims of war came to illustrate the war as a death machine in the Swedish press. In addition to dead soldiers, ruined churches, graveyards, and crucifixes, the images of 'massacred, rotting, blown-up horse carcasses on the battlefields' were used to illustrate civilian collapse.[14] From the Finnish Civil War came similar reports and images.

Horses in the First World War

Despite the motorization of the military and civilian society alike during the early 1900s, horses were still very important in warfare, and were used by cavalry forces as well as for transport. The military historian Martin van Creveld has pointed out that mechanization in itself led to an increase in the transport of materiel such as artillery, and consequently to a dramatic increase in the numbers of horses needed for draught and transportation, which in turn increased the amount of fodder needed to keep the army transports moving.[15] For the belligerent powers of the First World War, the conflict led to permanent shortages in the agricultural sector, compounded by the problem of finding enough horses for their armies.[16]

Although the Finnish Civil War was fought mainly along the railway lines, and even though the decisive battle was fought in and around the industrial city of Tampere, horses were used in large numbers, just as in the First World War in general.[17] During the Civil War, the Whites raised several cavalry units, from which developed the Nyland Dragoon Regiment and the Karelian Light Cavalry Regiment—and later the Tavastland Cavalry Regiment—commanded by Jäger officers, who had been trained in Germany. The units were included in the Finnish Cavalry Brigade from 1920.[18] Even in infantry regiments, horses were needed as mounts for the officers and for draught. In the Vasa Grenadier Regiment, raised by the Whites during the Civil War from Swedish-speaking volunteers from the Ostrobothnian region, a battalion of some 600 soldiers required at least 50 horses.[19]

Ylikangas describes a military organization where the officers rode horses and the majority of the soldiers marched on foot—and where the horses' training did not always keep pace with arms technology. He has a vivid account of a dashing White officer on a horse in the village of Länkipohja, an important objective for the White forces bent on taking Tampere. When the Red machine gun fire started, the officer was abruptly thrown off and the horse ran off to the nearby woods with the saddle hanging under its belly. Ylikangas confirms that the Red officers also liked fine horses: 'An impressive horse belonged to the equipment of every Red officer with any self-respect.'[20] He also gives a glimpse into the situation of the horses' civilian owners during the Civil War: as the conflict drew closer, the rural population hid their horses in barns in order to avoid them being seized by the warring parties.[21]

In this context, the organizing of a veterinary field hospital was important not only in order to keep military units operational through to the end of the Civil War, but also to build a functioning new army for an independent Finland. White Finland's political projects sat well with the Swedish armed forces' interest in military animal health care in a war situation. The Swedish Ministry of Defence and the Swedish Red Star were independently interested in collecting information about veterinary care of horses during war, and since the Swedish military did not have the capability to meet the full demand for veterinary care on the ground, volunteer organizations became a part of the Swedish mobilization plan for military veterinary services.[22]

Swedish patriotic women and Finland

The Swedish women volunteers and their understanding of the Finnish Civil War have been less researched than volunteers in the Swedish Brigade or Swedes in other Finnish White military units. The Swedish literature on the Finnish Civil War, consisting largely of memoirs written after the war, honours the Swedish Brigade and embraces the view that the military input of the Swedes in general was of great importance in the outcome of the conflict (a notion that has later been disputed).[23]

The Swedish officer corps, according to Gunnar Artéus, was at the time of the First World War noted for their conservatism, royalism, and keenness on re-armament against Russia. The military might of Germany was considered a role model to copy.[24] The song of the Swedish Brigade alluded to the grand ideals and memories of the past, looking back a couple of centuries to when Finland was still part of Sweden and Sweden was regarded as a great military nation. Some groupings among Finlands vänner (Friends of Finland) nursed hopes of a Swedish–Finnish reunification—or at least a reunification of Sweden and the Finnish Åland Islands.[25]

As Pia Olsson has pointed out, Finnish women who actively supported the Whites during the Civil War went on to become the core of the Lotta Svärd, the voluntary auxiliary force that was founded after the Civil War.[26] In 1928 the Lotta Svärd put together *Vita boken* ('The White Book'), a collection of stories of the Civil War from Finnish White women, with descriptions of the Whites' struggle for independence from Russia, firstly from the Tsarist Empire and later from the Bolsheviks. Relations with working-class and Red women were mostly cool.[27]

In comparison, the Swedish women who joined the volunteer organizations that served as auxiliaries to Swedish armed forces generally argued for the breaking down of boundaries between the classes and sexes, notwithstanding their conservatism as evident in their hawkishness, Russophobia, anti-liberalism, and elitism, combined with an admiration for Germany and a belief that war was inevitable and even purifying.[28] The historian Charlotte Tornbjer also points to the differences between the patriotic women's organizations such as the Red Cross, whose concerns were welfare and nursing, and the other, more ideological groups.[29]

The historian Madelene Lidestad has described the genesis of the Swedish Red Star in some detail. It was the voluntary association Kvinnlig Krigsberedskap (Women's War Preparedness) that took the initiative in 1917 in founding the Swedish Red Star: similar animal relief organizations already existed in France and the UK, and it was felt that Sweden needed a similar body that could work behind the lines in wartime. A number of other organizations with similar goals joined the Swedish Red Star when it was formed. The Swedish Red Star existed to care for military horses and to nurse animals wounded in battle, and to provide stand-ins for farmers or farmhands who had been called up for military service. The new organization was part of a public sphere where state appointments and voluntary activity interfaced. Women made up the majority of its members but only a minority of its governing body, which was composed of military officers, trade and industry representatives, the director of Veterinärhögskolan (the Veterinary College of Sweden), representatives from Djurskyddsföreningen (the Swedish Society for the Prevention of Cruelty to Animals), the director of Fältveterinärbyrån (the Army Veterinary Corps), as well as the women representatives.[30]

Research on women, gender, and war emphasizes the fact that war can both promote emancipation and reinforce traditional gender structures—the reason why the exercise of traditional gender roles in times of war can work as a strategy for women's organizations and activists intent on positioning themselves as advantageously as possible.[31] However, Lidestad points out that the process of integrating women into the war machinery could also serve to reinforce segregation, with women's gender roles again defined so that their work could be done separately, distinct from men's.[32]

Horse healthcare in Finland in 1918 was thus loaded with various meanings. One can study not only the course of the Civil War through the logistics of the Tampere horse field ambulance, but also the political (and possibly civilizing) significance of animal relief, as well as the emancipatory and gendered aspects of the Red Star movement's activities, where the process of defining what tasks and duties women should perform as veterinary orderlies was still a matter of some debate.

The horse field ambulance in Tampere

As soon as the Finnish Civil War began, the Swedish Red Star's central office looked into the possibilities of sending aid to Finland.[33] The resultant mobile field hospital—an ambulance in the original sense of the word—was financed by contributions from the business world, sanctioned by the Swedish armed forces and the Finnish government, and coordinated by the Swedish Red Star. The budget was 30,000 *kronor*, equating to 570,000 *kronor* in today's money, and ran to nursing equipment, stable kit, medical supplies, provisions, uniforms, and weapons and ammunition.[34] Ten members of the Red Star were recruited as veterinary orderlies. Some of them had been on preparatory courses in equine nursing run by the Red Star in 1917. A blacksmith and five grooms were also employed.[35] The decision regarding the field ambulance was taken on 20 March 1918, and the expedition arrived on 18 April in Tampere, which had been held by the Whites since 6 April.[36]

When the Whites had conquered Tampere the existing horse hospital had been destroyed, and equipment and surgical instruments were lacking. The new field ambulance was set up in an old sausage factory in the Karju area, not far from the centre of Tampere and in the vicinity of the Kalevankangas cemetery (where the Reds were buried in mass graves). At the time of arrival there were 64 horses waiting for immediate treatment and care. The Swedes had access to Red prisoners-of-war as extra hands, and work was led by two veterinary surgeons, Gerhard Forsell of the Swedish Veterinary College and Gustaf Danelius from Båstad.[37]

Quite apart from their wounds, the horses were generally in terrible shape when they arrived at the field ambulance.[38] The demand for draught horses and the overuse of horses seen during the Civil War was nothing unusual in wartime. The average life span of a horse used in artillery regiments was ten days in Germany and Serbia. In Tampere, horses went four days and nights without food and on the fifth day received a little fodder, after which they were used until they died, according to Stina Linderdahl in her diary.[39] And when the horses finally received veterinary attention, there was in particular one problem that was hard to address: starvation. It is clear from the records that even the field ambulance found it difficult to find enough fodder for its horses. The vets asked for more fodder for the horses that were completely emaciated; however, some were beyond saving, and had to be shot because of starvation, despite having spent several weeks at the ambulance.[40]

In an early article by a member in the Finnish Red Star (which was formed in 1918), the Russians' care of their animals is described as having been miserable to the point of cruelty even before the Revolution.[41] Yet conditions during the Finnish Civil War show that the mistreatment to army horses was not limited to any one side. A Swedish officer of the Vasa Grenadiers describes in his diary how on 18 April 1918 the Nyland Dragoons' horses had not received fodder for three days. He had also had to put his own horse to use as a draught horse during a forced march, during which several horses died. Roughly a week later he had to shoot the horse because it had been run into the ground. He considered the smaller *suomenhevonen* (Finnhorse) as having superior staying power, noting that the ones he had seen were 'wonders of strength and tenacity'.[42]

Apart from undernourishment, the common wounds and diseases amongst the field ambulance's patients were various types of tack injury, bullet wounds, blast and crushing injuries, colic, and equine distemper. Unusual bullet wounds were described in more detail—a horse with a bullet wound through the nasal bone, another where the bullet grazed a vertebra without damaging the horse's mobility—and the veterinary reports frequently note gunshot wounds to the horses' jaws or fragments of bullets embedded in the horses' muscles, while infected and open pressure wounds from saddles or harnesses were detailed at length.[43]

Between April and June 1918, 332 horses were treated, of which 220 were considered cured and 33 horses were put down. In May and June they faced an epidemic of glanders, a highly contagious disease, now rare, that attacks the respiratory mucous membranes.[44] All in all 157 operations were performed at the field ambulance, and about a third of them required anaesthesia.[45] For the more serious operations the staff had to lay the horses down on their sides before anaesthetizing them, a complicated procedure that demanded a high degree of cooperation and skill from the stable hands and veterinary orderlies.[46] Reading the material one finds a hierarchy among the diseases. The horses with scabies were treated by the Finnish vet. The scabies stable lay in the same camp where Red prisoners-of-war were held, in the former Russian barracks nearby.[47] On various occasions the Swedish vets said that they would not deal with horses with scabies at the field ambulance unless they also had war wounds. The fact that they continued to repeat this makes it clear that their priority was the treatment of horses wounded or damaged in the actual fighting. They even threatened that they would not treat any horses from units (the Nyland Dragoons and the Åbo battery) that had sent them horses with scabies, although in the event they never actually turned any away.[48]

Case records were kept of each horse that arrived at the ambulance, with a note of the sender, a description of the horse, the diagnosis, and sometimes even the horse's age and race. The source material from the ambulance is on the other hand very economical with information about where the horses came from. Many were brought in from White units, and some of these horses were logged as 'war loot' in the ambulance's records. It is striking just how old many of these looted horses were. On some occasions the vets pointed out to the units that brought in the horses that the documentation was unclear. Gustaf Danelius wrote in a report:

'At the time of discharge from the horse hospital a transfer chit is sent [with the horse], and, likewise, careful attention is paid to ensure that the unit concerned receives its horses back'. He also noted that horses without a known owner would be delivered to new Remontstyrelsen (the Remount Corps).[49] This did not seem to improve matters.

Some of the photographs of horses in Tampere included in Stina Linderdahl's diary look like workhorses—sturdy Finnhorses. Photographs from the Civil War often show Red guardsmen on horseback, usually more solid horses but also on slighter ones that had probably been Russian officers' horses previously.[50] The field ambulance's commissary, Dage Tenow, wrote in his account from 1919 that most of the horses were war loot from the Reds, who in turn had stolen them from rural farms.[51] A large proportion of the horses that were described more closely in the source material were branded in various ways, indicating that they came from stud farms. Presumably these were horses that had belonged to the Russian troops who in the spring of 1918 were on their way home. In the autumn of 1917 there had been a Russian force some 100,000 strong in Finland; at the turn of the year there were only 40,000 left.[52]

Ylikangas reckons that perhaps as few as a thousand Russian soldiers actually took part in the fighting on the Reds' side at the beginning of the Civil War—a tiny proportion of the Russian presence.[53] It is safe to infer that there must have been any amount of Russian materiel and horses going unused, and most likely easy to come by for either side—that much was confirmed by the Vasa Grenadier Regiment quartermaster, Mauritz Pettersson, who noted that vast numbers of horses were taken from the Reds.[54] He also remarked on the condition of the horses in the former Russian barracks outside Tampere, where the Whites found a couple of hundred horses when they entered the city.

> At the Russian stables, to the east of Tampere, there were several hundred horses. Most of them in pitiable state. Suffering from starvation and covered in scabies. It was common amongst the Russians for their horses to be badly treated and cared for.[55]

315

Pettersson's account reveals just how desirable horses were to both Whites and Reds during the Finnish Civil War, and that ownership constantly shifted depending on fortunes of war.[56] For example, he tells the story of an unfortunate White NCO who managed to make off with a beautiful horse from another military unit—only to discover that it was a White general's mount.[57] Pettersson also tells us who specifically were to become the new owners of the Russian horses found in the Tampere.

> Finland is rich in horses, but surely this war has depleted the country's herd. Saddle horses are rare. The horses that were taken from Russians were given to Nyland Dragoons. I myself had a former Russian officer's horse taken at Vasa.[58]

It is a plausible conclusion that the branded horses had previously belonged to the Russian army—and that both Reds and Whites used the Russian army horses alongside their own Finnhorses. As mentioned, the vets from time to time returned to the problem with ownership when in contact with different military units: the horses' identity papers were often incomplete, and the vets pointed out that it would be better if ownership were stated more clearly.[59] Similarly, Stina Linderdahl mentioned in her diary that people came to the field ambulance 'all the time looking for their stolen horses.'[60]

The vets and staff seem to have tried to share out the cured horses as fairly as possible between the military units. The horses were either handed over to the units that had brought them in in the first place, or were passed on to the White's Remount Corps, which farmed out any horses that were surplus to requirements to farmers who had none. In 1919 the field ambulance's commissary Dage Tenow was to write that 'the larger part of the horses went to serve peaceful ends and not the bloody deeds of war.'[61] The question of who benefited from the horses when they were finally discharged can be traced from the records in several instances. Horses that were well could not be given back to their previous owners unless they had been checked by the newly created Remount Corps as well as by the equally new security police, the Central Detective Police (then a military outfit under White army HQ, later to become the civilian State Police). About ten owners had their horses returned to them once they had been checked by the Central Detective Police, according to the field ambulance's records.[62]

One problem that had to be dealt with was the interest from White officers in obtaining functioning horses from the ambulance. One week before the military parade on 15 May, when Mannerheim and the White troops marched in triumph through Helsinki, it was noted that a Captain Lundkvist had been informed that his brown-black horse had already been given to the Remount Corps to be used in Helsinki. On another occasion a White officer, Artillery Captain Seth Grönhagen, tried to claim a horse and dogcart without having permission to do so, and was met by stiff resistance from the staff who thought the horse and wagon was for their needs first. When one of the female veterinary orderlies challenged him, saying he did not have permission, he nevertheless rode off without paying the slightest heed to their objections.[63] The vet wrote a letter of protest to the commander of Grönhagen's regiment and made the field ambulance's stance very clear: the captain had exceeded his authority. A day or so later it was noted that a Swedish officer, Colonel Hamilton, had duly reprimanded Grönhagen.[64]

This highlights the difficult position in which the women veterinary orderlies found themselves when it came to the chain of command: they were both part of the military hierarchy and outside it. This was mirrored in the almost dual judgement on the contributions made by the women of the field ambulance. The Red Star orderlies' womanly compassion, nursing skills, and sense of duty to their patients was essential for the horses' proper treatment and care, according to Major Otto Zethelius of the Swedish Red Star's board,[65] a view very much in line with the carefully expressed emancipatory ambitions to be found in later texts and articles concerning the Swedish Red Star's operations in Tampere in 1918.[66] Yet all the same, traditional military aspects of the women's work were also appreciated, albeit in a more confidential manner in the field ambulance's records. Apparently those nurses who were calm in stressful situations and had a good hand with the animals, and who could concentrate and work independently, were considered to have good leadership qualities. Those who did not possess these traits, in particular those who had no discipline, ended up at the bottom of the list.[67] The ability to handle horses with as little fuss as possible was occasionally more important than the division into strictly manly or womanly attributes that was a condition of the women's presence in Tampere. This point of view, however, was never mentioned in the Red Star's *printed* material.

Another perspective that became increasingly unimportant in the Swedish Red Star propaganda after 1918 was chauvinist patriotism, 'Grand Swedishness', of the old school. The Red Star orderly Signe Fryberg, who wrote articles about the Tampere field ambulance in *Svenska Dagbladet* and *Stockholms Dagblad* (both conservative dailies), liked to elaborate on the courage of the Swedish officers, and how 'slender and elegant' and so very gentlemanly to the Swedish female veterinary orderlies they were (one of the paragons was quoted as saying, 'If one could only be a horse').[68]

Fryberg's description of Finland in 1918 thus echoes the general political stance of the Swedish women who had volunteered for the auxiliary organizations. It could even be said she viewed the Finnish Civil War with a wishful hope that Sweden would regain its former position as a great military nation. Fryberg also reported gruesome propaganda stories, for example that it was forbidden to wear muffs in Tampere for fear of Reds using them to conceal weapons. She also told the story of the waitress who shot White soldiers by hiding a gun under her tray.[69]

Interestingly, Fryberg's interpretation of the Red Star's efforts in Finland did not really chime with the organization's self-understanding, even in 1918. Sturfelt and others have pointed out that the chaos of the world war elicited a new Swedish self-awareness about Swedish neutrality, one connected to modernity and progressive thinking,[70] and this is certainly something that can be traced in Red Star publications from the 1920s and 1930s. However, the notion that Sweden was a force to be reckoned with, leading the way in modernity and progress, had already become important for the Red Star's self-image back in 1918.[71]

Tenow, Zethelius, and the vets all leaned more towards a modernized version of 'Grand Swedishness', where neutral Sweden was understood as leading the way in modernization and humanitarianism, and an example to the belligerent countries, particularly when it came to organizing hospital care for the sick and wounded horses—where women could take part, using their motherly and feminine qualities to best advantage. Thus veterinary care and humane methods in treating animals were ways of instilling the modern virtues, and Sweden was the guiding light. As the modernization of Finland beckoned, Sweden stepped in to support the sensible, commendably civic elements in a not always so organized process. Tenow regarded the Swedish input as a way of educating the Finns in how to run their own country: 'The authorities were most obliging, but often their attempts were frustrated by their own and other governing bodies' loose organization and lack of ability.'[72]

Linderdahl's diary is more difficult to place. She was the only one at the horse field ambulance whose private thoughts on what she saw and heard about the persecution of the Reds have come down to us. However, she was mostly rather accepting of White propaganda. She recounted going with some of the other orderlies to visit the prisoner-of-war camp in the former Russian barracks in the vicinity when they heard gunfire and a little while later saw Red prisoners lying dead. She recorded a conversation with a Finnish White guard who explained how to execute prisoners. She saw the prisoners digging their own graves. She noticed that many coffins were too big for the dead; that later the bigger coffins were burned and smaller coffins were used; that a dead woman in one of the open coffins was dressed only in her underwear; that in another coffin a woman lay with her mouth open as if in the middle of a scream.[73]

The Swedes' immediate reaction was to deplore the Reds. But they were also considered responsible for the Civil War and the horrors it brought. Only with time did the veterinary orderlies begin to feel empathy for the prisoners and their situation in the camps, probably because they came into daily contact with a group of Red prisoners who worked as stable hands. The veterinary orderlies sometimes gave them extra food, and cut their hair on occasion. They also demanded to keep two stable hands who were about to be moved.[74] None of this did much to change the fact that the men and women of the field ambulance were convinced that the Whites had society's best interest at heart. Although, that said, during April and May 1918 Linderdahl became more and more irritated with the Swedish White officers who behaved violently, and even in some cases turned out to be crooks and opportunists.[75]

Conclusion

Within the framework of veterinary care during the Finnish Civil War, several causes can be said to have co-existed. A civilian insistence on viewing horses as animals to be protected was combined with antipathy towards the Reds (with horses as their victims), enthusiasm for female emancipation, and Swedish chauvinism of both the older, hawkish variety and the condescendingly humanitarian variety. Veterinary care for horses became important in the White propaganda produced by Finns and Swedes alike—the Reds mistreated their horses, which were subsequently saved by the Whites.

In Signe Fryberg's account of the mobile field hospital set up by the Swedish Red Star in Tampere, one can detect a romantic nostalgia for Sweden's past as a leading military power. Dage Tenow and Otto Zethelius placed the wounded horses in another context, and it was their view that came to dominate the Red Star's account of its own history. Tenow tended to what Sturfelt has called progressive and forward-thinking Swedish neutrality, which in this context can be labelled as a more modern form of 'Grand Swedishness', where the maintenance of peace, not war, is central. Tenow clearly saw a possibility for a more prominent Swedish role, especially when it came to veterinary care. Stina Linderdahl, meanwhile, wrote in far greater detail about the devastation of the city of Tampere, and her diary, with its acute observations, is more difficult to define in the context of Grand Swedish narratives. Possibly her account could be read as a counter-narrative on the destructiveness of war in general.

In its own historiography, the Swedish Red Star developed an understanding of its horse field ambulance expedition to Finland that set it firmly in the narrative of Sweden as the role model for the new Finland, while it proved women's ability to work as veterinary orderlies. In an article from 1929, Otto Zethelius concluded that when it came to the protection of animals, Sweden was a pioneering country, and a cultivated one to boot.[76] Thus it is interesting to note that this standpoint had already been spelled out as early as 1918.[77]

Notes

1 Maria Sjöberg, *Kvinnor i fält: 1550–1850* (Möklinta: Gidlunds, 2008), 11–12, 21-24.

2 The records of the activities of the Swedish Red Star (from 1941, the Swedish Blue Star) in Finland in April–June 1918 are held in Krigsarkivet (the Military Archives of Sweden) in Stockholm. The organization's archive also contains collections of press cuttings and various other sources concerning the horse ambulance and the Finnish Civil War in 1918. See Krigsarkivet (KrA), Svenska blå stjärnan (SBS), Centralstyrelsens förvaltningsberättelse för 1917, volym 1, serie B2; ibid., 'Svenska Röda Stjärnan, Finlandsambulansen 1918, Diarium, Konceptbok', volym 1, serie F1 (Finlandsambulansen 1918); ibid., serie Ö1 (press cuttings). See also Stina Linderdahl, *Stina Linderdahls dagbok från finska kriget 1918* (Sundborn: Linderdahlska stiftelsen, 1993); Dage Tenow, *Med Svenska Röda Stjärnan bland krigsskadade hästar i Finland* (Stockholm: Djurens rätt, 1919), *Djurens rätt* being the organ of Nordiska samfundet för bekämpande av det vetenskapliga djurplågeriet (the Nordic Association Against the Scientific Maltreatment of Animals); and KrA, Avdelningen för enskilda arkiv, Mauritz Petterssons.

3 Leif Törnquist, *Stjärna i förändring. SBS blå stjärna och dess historia* (Stockholm: Svenska blå stjärnan, 1997), 7–8, 10–11.

4 Heikki Ylikangas, *Vägen till Tammerfors* (Stockholm: Atlantis, 1995), 24–5, 30.

5 Henrik Meinander, *Finlands historia: linjer, strukturer, vändpunkter* (Stockholm: Atlantis, 2006), 151–5.

6 Meinander 2006, 151–5.

7 John W. Wheeler-Bennet, *Brest-Litovsk. The Forgotten Peace, March 1918* (London: Macmillan, 1938), 256, 407.

8 Ylikangas 1995, 477–8; Aapo Roselius, *I bödlarnas fotspår – massavrättningar och terror i finska inbördeskriget 1918* (Stockholm: Atlantis, 2009), 227, 40–3.

9 Meinander 2006, 155–7; Matti Klinge, *Blick på Finlands historia* (Stockholm: Atlantis, 2001), 119, 120–1, 126.

10 Ylikangas 1995, 11–12.

321

11 Ingvar Flink, 'Svenska krigsförluster i Finland år 1918', in Lars Westerlund (ed.), *Norden och krigen i Finland och Baltikum åren 1918–1919* (Helsinki: Statsrådets kansli, 2004), 41.

12 According to the anonymous author of the preface to the edition of Linderdahl's diary (Linderdahl 1993, 4).

13 Carl Göran Andrae, *Revolt eller reform. Sverige inför revolutionerna i Europa 1917–1918* (Stockholm: Carlssons, 1998), 166.

14 Lina Sturfelt, *Eldens återsken. Första världskriget i svensk föreställningsvärld* (diss.; Lund: Sekel, 2008), 154.

15 Martin van Creveld, *Supplying war: logistics from Wallenstein to Patton* (Cambridge: CUP, 2004), 111.

16 William Hardy McNeill, *The Pursuit of Power: Technology, Armed Force, and Society Since AD 1000* (Chicago: University of Chicago Press, 1982), 339–40.

17 See, for example, the Swedish transportation officer Mauritz Pettersson's notes from the Finnish Civil War (KrA, Avdelningen för enskilda arkiv, Mauritz Pettersons arkiv, volym 1, 'Dagboksanteckningar från mitt deltagande i Finlands frihetskrig mot ryssar och rödgardister 1918'.)

18 *Uppslagsverket Finland,* <www.uppslagsverket.fi>, s.v. 'Nylands dragoner' and 'Tavastlands ryttarregemente', accessed 13 November 2011; Ylikangas 1995, 111.

19 KrA, Avdelningen för enskilda arkiv, Mauritz Petterssons arkiv, volym 1, Sixten Öberg, 'Wasabataljonens tillkomst och insats i Finska frihetskriget 1918 i stora drag', 2, 11.

20 Ylikangas 1995, 114.

21 Ibid. 113.

22 Madelene Lidestad, *Uppbåd, uppgifter, undantag. Om genusarbetsdelning i Sverige under första världskriget* (diss.; Stockholm Studies in History, 79; Stockholm: Stockholms universitet, 2005), 167–72; Tenow 1919, 2.

23 Lars Westerlund, 'Norden och krigen i Finland och Baltikum åren 1918–19. Litteraturöversikt och forskningsläge', in Westerlund 2004, 14; Ylikangas 1995, 322; Rainer Andersson, *Vad gjorde du i Finland far*, Helsinki 1999, 110-112.

24 Gunnar Artéus, 'Den svenska officerskårens politiska uppfattning år 1914', in Johan Engström & Lars Ericson (eds.), *Mellan björnen och örnen. Sverige och Östersjön under det första världskriget 1914–1918* (Acta Visbyensia, 9; Visby: Gotlands fornsal, 1994), 81–85.

25 Flink 2004, 31; Andrae 1998, 157. For the words of the Swedish Brigade's march, see Riksarkivet, Stockholm (National Archives of Sweden), <www.ra.se>, s.v. 'Svenska brigaden i Finland 1918', accessed 13 March 2012.

26 Pia Olsson, *Eteen vapahan valkean Suomen: kansatieteellinen tutkimus lottatoiminnasta paikallisella tasolla vuoteen 1939* [For Finland—white and

free: an ethnological study of the Lotta Svärd women's auxiliaries at local level up to 1939] (diss.; Helsinki: University of Helsinki, 1999), with an English summary, 275–280.

27 Helmi Anneberg-Pentti, Jenny af Forselles & Fanni Luukkonen, 'Ofärds-åren', in Lotta Svärd (ed.), *Vita boken* (Helsinki: Lotta Svärd, centralstyrelsen, 1928), 3.

28 Sif Bokholm, *I otakt med tiden: om rösträttsmotstånd, antipacifism och nazism bland svenska kvinnor* (Stockholm: Atlantis, 2008), 141, 206.

29 Charlotte Tornbjer, *Den nationella modern: moderskap i konstruktioner av svensk nationell gemenskap under 1900-talets första hälft* (diss.; Lund: Nordic Academic Press, 2002), 203–204.

30 Lidestad 2005, 167–72.

31 Joyce P. Kaufman & Kristen P. Williams, *Women and war: gender identity and activism in times of conflict* (Sterling, Va.: Kumarian Press, 2010), 6; Susan R. Grayzel, *Women's identities at war: gender, motherhood, and politics in Britain and France during the First World War* (Chapel Hill, NC: University of North Carolina Press, 1999), 3. Grayzel also points out (ibid. 5) that women's increasing participation in the war effort created concern for the social order. Kronsell and Svedberg also emphazise that nation-building and militarization are closely connected and strongly gendered (Annica Kronsell & Erika Svedberg (eds.), *Making gender, making war: violence, military and peacekeeping practices* (New York: Routledge, 2012), 3, 7.

32 Lidestad 2005, 191.

33 KrA, SBS arkiv, F1, volym 1, 'Finlandsambulansen 1918', excerpt from *Svenska Röda Stjärnans jubileumsskrift 1937*.

34 According to the anonymous author of the preface to the edition of Linderdahl's diary (Linderdahl 1993, 4-5).

35 The Red Star veterinary assistants were Signe Fryberg, Greta Barthelson, Margit Beckman, Irène Fryberg, Selma Guldbrand, Margit Hellsten, Anna Kindahl, Stina Linderdahl, Margit Seth, and Ellen Wesström. The grooms were Johan Johansson, P. Petersson, G. Johansson, J. Andersson, Augusti Persson, and G. Berg (blacksmith) (see 'Finlandsambulansen 1918', *Svenska Röda Stjärnans jubileumsskrift 1937*, 54; KrA, SBS arkiv, Centralstyrelsen för Svenska Röda Stjärnan, Förvaltningsberättelse för 1918, bilaga 9, 86; KrA, SBS arkiv, F1, volym 1, Handlingar rörande Röda Stjärnans första år).

36 'Finlandsambulansen 1918', *Svenska Röda Stjärnans jubileumsskrift 1937*, 54.

37 According to the anonymous author of the preface to the edition of Linderdahl's diary (Linderdahl 1993, 4–5).

38 Ibid. 20.

39 Ibid. 8.

40 KrA, SBS arkiv, F1, volym 1, 'Svenska Röda Stjärnan, Finlandsambulansen 1918, Diarium, Konceptbok', Gustaf Danelius entries 16 & 22 May 1918.
41 KrA, SBS arkiv, serie Ö1, T. K. Frostén, 'Djuren i kriget. Några anmärkningar av T. K. Frostén, Helsingfors 1918' (Finska Röda stjärnans skriftserie, 1; Helsinki, 1918), 7–8, 23.
42 KrA, Avdelningen för enskilda arkiv, Mauritz Petterssons arkiv, 64, 72–73. The most common type of horse at the time in Finland was the so-called Finnhorse or Finnish horse: in the 1910s there were some 200,000 in Finland. They were used both for riding and for draught, by Finns and the Russian military alike. See Sällskapet Nordiskt Kallblod (Society for the Nordic work horse) 'Bekanta dig med finnhästen', available at <www.nordisktkallblod.se> and <http://www.suomenhevonen.info/hippos/sh2007/pdf/Shruotsi_nettiin.pdf>, accessed 15 August 2012; see *Lantmannens uppslagsbok* (Stockholm: Norstedt, 1923), available at <http://runeberg.org/lantuppsl/0276.html>, s.v. 'finsk häst', accessed 13 November 2011; see also KrA, Generalstaben, Utrikesavdelningen, serie E1a, volym 1, Meddelande från 1. byrån nr 14:51 till utrikesavdelningen 2. detaljen, 27 May 1914, an unsigned note, probably from the Swedish military attaché in Saint Petersburg.
43 KrA, SBS arkiv, F1, volym 1, 'Svenska Röda Stjärnan, Finlandsambulansen 1918, Diarium, Konceptbok', Gustaf Danelius, 'Rapport över Svenska Röda Stjärnans Finlandsambulans verksamhet under tiden 22/4–16/5 1918'.
44 Tenow 1919, 11.
45 Ibid. 12.
46 The horse that was going to be operated on was put next to the operating table and cords were secured around the joints just above the hooves. Cords were also placed around the horse's abdomen. Four people would then pull the horse up onto the table, while those who stood at the hooves would at the same time lift them up from the ground. One person stood at the head and another by the tail (Tenow 1919, 6–8).
47 According to the anonymous author of the preface to the edition of Linderdahl's diary (Linderdahl 1993, 5).
48 KrA, SBS arkiv, F1, volym 1, 'Svenska Röda Stjärnan, Finlandsambulansen 1918, Diarium, Konceptbok', Gustaf Danelius, rapport, 7–8 May 1918.
49 Ibid. 22 April–16 May.
50 Pertti Haapala & Tuomas Hoppu (eds.), *Tampere 1918: A town in the Civil War* (Tampere: Tampereen Museot, 2010), 64, 89.
51 Tenow 1919, 12
52 Lars Westerlund, *Massakern i Jakobstad: klubbliv, jägarprotest och privatjustis* (Helsinki: Åbo akademi & Folkkontraktet i Finland, 1993), 8–9.
53 Ylikangas 1995, 60.

54 KrA, Avdelningen för enskilda arkiv, Mauritz Pettersons arkiv, Pettersson 1918, volym 1, 59–60, 76.

55 Ibid. 59–60.

56 The Bolsheviks protested to Germany in the late spring of 1918 about German military landing parties and Finnish White Guards having seized Russian materiel in Northern Finland, thus violating the Treaty of Brest-Litovsk (see Wheeler-Bennet 1938, 330).

57 KrA, Avdelningen för enskilda arkiv, Mauritz Petterssons arkiv, Pettersson 1918, volym 1, 60.

58 Ibid.

59 KrA, SBS arkiv, F1, volym 1, 'Svenska Röda Stjärnan, Finlandsambulansen 1918, Diarium, Konceptbok', Danelius, rapport 22 April–16 May 1918, entries 7 & 21 May and 14 June 1918; Linderdahl 1993, 20.

60 Linderdahl 1993, 9, 21.

61 Tenow 1919, 12.

62 KrA, SBS arkiv, F1, volym 1, 'Svenska Röda Stjärnan, Finlandsambulansen 1918, Diarium, Konceptbok', Danelius, entries 11/5–12/5, 23/5 1918; see also Uppslagsverket Finland, 'Detektiva centralpolisen', http://www. uppslagsverket.fi/bin/view/Uppslagsverket/DetektivaCentralpolisen?templ ate=highlightsearch&search=detektiva%20polisen, accessed 20 September 2012.

63 Linderdahl 1993, 20.

64 KrA, SBS arkiv, F1, volym 1, 'Svenska Röda Stjärnan, Finlandsambulansen 1918, Diarium, Konceptbok', Danelius, notations 5/5–6/5 1918, including a copy of letter of protest.

65 Otto Zethelius, Svenska Röda stjärnan och dess fredsverksamhet: fredsarbetets bärande grundvalar och Röda stjärnans betydelse för den veterinära sjukvården (Stockholm: Svenska Röda stjärnans centralbyrå, 1919); see also KrA, SBS arkiv, Ö1, 'Till svenska Röda Stjärnans veterinärambulans' by O.Z., the poem read at the homecoming celebration of the Swedish Red Star group on their return to Stockholm on 30 June 1918.

66 KrA, SBS arkiv, F1, volym 1, 'Svenska Röda Stjärnan, Finlandsambulansen 1918, Diarium, Konceptbok', 'Finlandsambulansen 1918', excerpt from Svenska Röda Stjärnans jubileumsskrift 1937.

67 KrA, SBS arkiv, F1, volym 1, 'Svenska Röda Stjärnan, Finlandsambulansen 1918, Diarium, Konceptbok', Gustaf Danelius, 'Konfidentiellt. Personalkritik', 10/7 1918.

68 See, for example, Signe Fryberg, 'Röda stjärnsystrarna framme vid målet', Stockholms Dagblad, 21 April 1918; KrA, SBS arkiv, Ö1, 'Kungens död', n.d.

69 Fryberg 1918.

70 Sturfelt 2008, 253.

SCANDINAVIA IN THE FIRST WORLD WAR

71 Quelq'une, 'Svenska Röda stjärnans finska barmhärtighetsverk. Ledaren dr
   Forsell anser resultatet högst tillfreddställande', May 1918, 'Röda Stjärnans
   Finlandsambulans återkommen til Stockholm', *Stockholms Dagblad*, 1 July
   1918; Quelq'une, 'Hur det känns att vara sjuksköterska för krigshästar',
   Stockholms Dagblad, 11 June 1918; KrA, SBS arkiv, Ö1.
72 Tenow 1919, 1, 9–10.
73 Linderdahl 1993, 8.
74 Ibid. 11.
75 Ibid. 25–6.
76 Otto Zethelius, 'Några ord om Svenska Röda Stjärnans verksamhet', in
   Svenska Röda Stjärnan (Stockholm: Röda stjärnornas klubb, 1929).
77 Translations by Pamela Robertson-Pearce and Charlotte Merton.

CHAPTER 13

Neutral merchant seamen
at war

The experiences of Scandinavian seamen
during the First World War

Bjarne Søndergaard Bendtsen

Seaborne trade has always played a crucial role for the three Scandinavian countries. During the First World War, with the belligerents' escalating use of *Handelskrieg* as a weapon, the importance of this trade both in its own right and, no less importantly, for enabling the export of products and for supplying industry and the home markets as such, became even more significant. In spite of the increasing dependency on seaborne trade, and the fact that the Scandinavian merchant seamen suffered heavily during the war, their efforts have largely been overshadowed by *nouveau riche* war profiteers at home, when anything at all is remembered about the First World War in Scandinavia. The chapter offers a short survey of the neutral Scandinavian merchant seamen's war efforts as they were depicted in memoirs and literature and on monuments, with Denmark as the central case.[1]

When the monument to the seamen who lost their lives aboard Danish merchantmen during the First World War was dedicated 9 May 1928, it was an inter-Scandinavian event. The Norwegian, Swedish, Icelandic, and Finnish ministers to Copenhagen participated, along with the Danish king and other members of the royal family, shipowners, several present and former Danish ministers, politicians, and some 2,000–3,000 invited notables, not least including the bereaved families of the seamen to be commemorated.[2] The area around the monument was not only decorated with Danish flags but with the flags of the other Nordic countries as well—an approach to the event that was a logical consequence of the fact that of the 648 seamen commemorated by the monument, 531 were Danish, 7 Icelandic, 39 Swedish, 28 Norwegian, and 11 Finnish, while 32 came from other nations, as the chairman of Dansk Dampskibsrederiforening (Danish Steamship Owners' Association), A. O. Andersen, stated in his speech at the dedication.[3] Dansk Dampskibsrederiforening had initiated the plans for the monument and donated the funds for it; therefore, only ships owned by members of the association were included.

In addition to this inter-Scandinavian approach to the commemoration, the dedication interestingly enough did not take place on the tenth anniversary of the Armistice, but instead on the day for the Danish victory in the Battle of Helgoland in 1864, and thus connecting the loss of lives in the world war to one of the only successes in the traumatic war against Prussia and Austria, and thereby to the 1920 reunification of Northern Schleswig with Denmark, which was a direct consequence of the German defeat in the world war.

The newspapers generally described the monument and the dedication of it as a graceful and dignified memorial to the seamen's efforts during the war,[4] but there were also critical voices: in an otherwise positive article, *Ekstrabladet* mentioned *en passant* that it was strange that the Stock Exchange did not fly its flag—of course hinting at the enormous amounts of money earned from stocks and shares during the war, especially from shipping.[5] Neither were the seamen themselves wholly accepting. Their union's magazine, *Ny Tid*, had run critical articles since the latter part of the war regarding, among other things, the creation of a fund that could support the relatives of seamen who lost their lives or the ability to work, and take care of their families during and after a war. Now, caustic comments contrasted the spending of money on the monument with the unwillingness to compensate the seamen for risking their lives sailing in war zones: 'The thought of a monument can be very nice, but in the light of the distress among Danish seamen, it is stones over bread.'[6]

Whereas it seems to have been a matter of opinion how the monument was regarded, there was hardly any doubt as to who was the culprit when it came to endangering the lives of the neutral seamen, or to the negative effects of the German submarine warfare on the nation's image during the war, which meant that the Germans were regarded as cold-blooded murderers and barbarians even in the still neutral parts of the world. The interference in neutral trade was strongly criticized by the neutral world, initially led by the US, and German attacks on neutral, unarmed merchant vessels, as well as on neutral and enemy passenger liners (in particular, the sinking of the *Lusitania* on 7 May 1915, where 127 of the 1,198 people killed were US citizens)[7] and ultimately the German declaration of the *uneingeschränkter U-Boot-Krieg*—unrestricted submarine warfare—on 1 February 1917, would lead to the US declaring war on Germany on 4 April 1917. Unsurprisingly, these topics also played a central role in the judgement of Germany in the neutral Scandinavian countries, not least since seaborne trade and shipping were highly important for these countries' economies and the supply of their home markets. This was especially the case in Norway, whose commercial fleet was the world's fourth largest in 1914.

Losses of Scandinavian merchant ships and seamen during the war were immense. The Norwegian merchant navy suffered especially heavily: 829 ships were lost, totalling 1,239,283 gross register tons, 30 ships suffered damage, 67 ships disappeared, and 22 were condemned, adding up to a war loss of 49.3 per cent of its 1914 tonnage.[8] According to the Norwegian Shipping Board's statistics, 1,162 Norwegian seamen 'perished by acts of war, while "a large number" were wounded in the course of attacks', as the Norwegian economist and historian Wilhelm Keilhau writes: 'And to these figures must, undoubtedly, be added the greater part of the crews who manned the 67 ships which disappeared, crews who represented a loss of another 943 men.'[9] Or potentially 2,105 in all.[10] During the years 1914–18, Denmark lost 305 ships or 281,834 GRT, resulting in the deaths of 667 people,[11] and Sweden lost 280 ships or 291,549 GRT (1919–20 included), and 659 people were killed at sea.[12] Only the British ship losses were higher than the Norwegian,[13] and the Norwegian losses meant that her merchant navy fell from fourth to sixth place in world tonnage after the war.[14]

Even so, at least in Denmark, the seamen's efforts were not held in much regard—or so both contemporary and later sources claimed.

Neutrality, blockades, and contraband lists

As the war dragged on, pressure from the belligerent parties made life in the neutral countries, and the very idea of neutrality, increasingly difficult. Especially the constant addition of items to the contraband list and the expansions of the restricted zones directly influenced the conditions for neutral shipping and resulted in difficulties for the neutrals.

There were endless disputes among intellectuals in the belligerent states and neutral countries alike about who started not only the war, but also the *Handelskrieg*,[15] which principally consisted of blockading civilian society as a weapon against the enemy. The British naval blockade of supplies to the Central Powers would, in the course of events, include the neutral European states more and more, and the German submarine blockade of Great Britain directly involved neutral ships sailing to British ports. This was more than ever the case after the unrestricted submarine war was declared on 1 February 1917, which meant that every vessel entering the German war zone around the British Isles, the English Channel, the French Atlantic and the Mediterranean coasts was considered an enemy vessel and would be sunk without warning.

But, to be fair, it was the British who introduced the blockade by imposing restrictions on trade on 20 August 1914; restrictions which 'began the erosion of the maritime laws of war'.[16] In the early part of the war, Britain furthermore led the way in unilateral extensions to the list of absolute and conditional contraband—a clear breach of the London Declaration of 1909, which, of course, neither Britain nor Germany had ratified. Iron-ore was declared conditional contraband by the British on 21 September 1914, for example, which dealt a serious blow to Swedish exports. Sweden succeeded in getting iron-ore removed from the list,[17] though not for long: on 29 October iron-ore was added to the category of absolute contraband.[18]

The Germans would soon follow suit when it came to unilateral extensions to contraband lists, and in October 1914 they began seizing neutral ships in the Baltic and taking them to German ports to search. This flouting of maritime law led to the Scandinavian countries sending identical notes to the belligerents on 12 November 1914, 'protesting the closing of shipping routes by mines, the extensions of search, and the free interpretation of contraband.'[19] Nevertheless, the escalation of the blockades and other *Handelskrieg* measures did not stop, and the situation for the small neutrals became increasingly difficult, especially after the US entered the war.

Danish imports from and exports to Germany, which naturally did not only rely on seaborne cargo but could take place overland, were potential breaches of the Allied blockade of the Central Powers, and a key reason behind the Allied attempts to include the northern neutrals in the blockade. Neither could Swedish trade with Germany be efficiently controlled by the Allies since Germany had power over the Baltic. Geostrategic circumstances played a significant role in the way the different belligerent parties influenced the Scandinavian countries: Denmark was so undeniably within the German sphere of interest and influence that it had to take Berlin into account in any measure it took; Swedish trade interests—iron-ore and timber exports being the most important in this context—were controlled by Germany and connected to German interests; and Norway was positioned in the Allies' sphere of interest, not least due to its large merchant navy traditionally sailing to British Empire ports.

Thus, it soon became apparent that the geostrategic positions of the Scandinavian countries and the most important belligerent powers—Britain and Germany—combined with the way the world war almost instantly took on the character of total warfare in a way unknown before, would influence neutrality and not least neutral shipping down to the slightest detail.[20]

Scandinavian shipmasters remember the danger zones

These details, with their many horrors, were to involve forced time-charter voyages in the danger zones and the outright requisitioning of neutral ships, as the belligerents, and especially the Allies, became more and more short of tonnage. Neutral merchantmen had to sail for the Allies to obtain bunker coal or even to be granted permission to leave Allied ports; at some points the Allies demanded a certain amount of tonnage put to their disposal to allow neutral vessels to leave ports, or that another neutral vessel should arrive before permission to leave port was granted. In short, coal was a powerful tool with which to threaten the Scandinavians, as they were all reliant on especially British coal; not only for bunker use but also for their industries and for heating purposes at home.

Still, there does not seem to have been much appreciation for the seamen's work and the troubles they faced—at least according to the following sources. In one of the earliest articles about Danish commercial navigation during the war, State meteorologist C. I. H. Speerschneider complains about the Danish people's lost understanding of life at sea and particularly their lack of appreciation of the seamen's efforts:

> He [the seaman] never won much recognition, however, but it is not his fault that it is so. It is society's fault, our over-intelligent and aestheticizing society, oblivious to life's true values, which has not understood how it stands in debt to our seafarers, and which in its eternally flourishing social aspirations looks down its nose at the plain sailor, who has the advantage over most of the males on dry land, that he has seen the world and life and is a man.[21]

This positively homoerotic glorification of the seamen's manliness might not be what one would expect from a government official, but it clearly expresses his frustration at how to his mind the Danish public had disregarded the seamen's sufferings and important work for the country.

Much later, in 1938, the Danish sea captain N. Th. Brinch published his memoirs *En dansk Skibsførers Rejser i Farezonen under*

Verdenskrigen 1914–1918 ('A Danish shipmaster's voyages in the danger zone'), which contains a critique of the way the seamen's efforts were regarded by the country's non-seafaring population that largely chimes with Speerschneider's. Here, the neutral seamen's work during the war is explicitly equated to war work, along with bitter complaints about the lack of recognition:

> No honour awaited him [the seaman], no one or perhaps just a few understood him. Of course, the seaman had to do his duty, but only a few could see his effort during the World War clearly, maybe the greatest effort made. But when the war ended, the belligerents had forgotten him, and the population ashore hardly noticed him.[22]

And later in the book, when writing about the neutral seamen who were killed while on forced voyages for the Allies:

> Was it for the fatherland's sake that they fell? No, then they would have been honoured and praised. They did not even bring necessities to their country, for they were time-chartered, like we were and so many others … This was the effort of the Danish merchant seamen in the great World War, the only direct effort made by Danish trades.[23]

Furthermore, Brinch complains about the unfair situation of the neutral seamen, who were forced to sail for the Allies, with the same risk of being attacked by German submarines as the Allied merchantmen, but without the protection of armaments with which the Allied ships were issued during the war. When the neutral ships were requisitioned or time-chartered, they even had to paint over the neutral flags on the hulls.[24]

The same aspect is explicitly evident in the title of the Norwegian captain I. Øvreseth's memoirs about his voyages during the war: *Vi som var våbenløse: en skibsførers erindringer fra krigstiden 1914–18* ('We who were unarmed: a shipmaster's memoirs of the war, 1914–18') (1932). Like Brinch, Øvreseth sailed the different danger zones for almost the entire war. Øvreseth is definitely not anti-

FIGURE 1: I. Øvreseth *Vi som var våbenløse* (1932). The dramatic 1930s style cover illustration shows the moment a torpedo or mine strikes a neutral Norwegian ship, seemingly using the Norwegian flag on the side of the hull as a target.

British—even though he did rescue three escaped German prisoners of war, one of whom was from Northern Schleswig, in the autumn of 1914 while sailing for Arkhangelsk.[25] Throughout the war, he only sailed to Allied ports, which of course soon would be a consequence of the belligerents' attitude towards neutrals calling at enemy ports, regarding them as enemy vessels. And even though he complains about the harsh measures that were taken, especially at the east coast ports of England, where the crews were regarded with suspicion as potential spies and kept as prisoners on their own ships, he seems to understand these measures and support the Allies. The merciless brutality of the German submarines and the German mining of the seas at random would naturally evoke a strong aversion in neutral merchant sailors to the power responsible for such actions. However, the British requisitioning of Øvreseth's and many other Norwegian and neutral ships, and particularly the way they handled the requisitioning—suspending right of ownership and refusing him the assistance of a lawyer and permission to contact his company in Norway—does lead to critical remarks.

Even Speerschneider, in a rare moment, criticizes the British for endangering neutral seamen's lives by sailing under false neutral flags, logically leading to German repressions against real neutral ships.[26] The Allied use of false neutral flags and the use of the so-called Q-ships or 'mystery ships'—decoy vessels used against submarines that were 'disguised as unarmed merchantmen but carried concealed naval armament', luring the submarines into a surface attack instead of using their expensive torpedoes—clearly made sailing in the war zones even more dangerous for the neutrals.[27] In the English poet Alfred Noyes's propaganda book, *Mystery Ships (Trapping the 'U' Boat)* (1916), makes nary a mention of this unsporting approach to the game. On the other hand, a strong critique of the German lack of sportsmanship can be found in Noyes's book, which was published in Danish and Swedish translations along with his *Open Boats* (1917), about the cowardly behaviour of German submarines, leaving the crews of sunken ships to their fate in open boats on the high seas.[28]

Neutral seamen in literature

Brinch's bitter recollections of the way the seamen were almost completely ignored in Denmark during the war are not quite true. Despite the seamen's complaints about having been forgotten, there seems to have been a genuine appreciation of the importance of their efforts—not least financially—in the neutral countries during the war. An example is the cover of the Danish mainstream weekly *Verden og Vi* on 19 January 1917, which shows a photograph of the snow-covered bridge of the steamer *Oscar II* with four officers of the watch, solemnly steering the ship.[29] The photo is accompanied by the caption: 'One of the ships that brings the money home.'[30]

Perhaps the Danish newspapers did indeed not write much about the seamen's fate, but quite understandably so, bearing in mind Denmark's necessarily cautious approach to its southern neighbour, which was the primary reason for the Danish 1915 War Press Act, making it illegal to print certain criticisms of government actions. Prior to this, any mention of foreign and local warships and merchant vessels had been made illegal, not least to avoid supplying the many spies that worked in Denmark with such information, so the laconic paragraphs in Danish newspapers about torpedoed or mined ships were not only due to a lack of interest. Furthermore, some papers did criticize the situation less cautiously in longer articles. The independent conservative *Vort Land*, for instance, wrote about the sinking of the Danish steamer *Lars Kruse* in the English Channel on 4 February 1917, on a voyage from Buenos Aires to Rotterdam with provisions for the Belgian Relief Committee.[31] The sinking led to the deaths of 17 men, and much bitterness in neutral Denmark. *Vort Land* quotes exhaustively from the evidence given by the sole survivor, 1st Engineer Møller, at the inquiry, without, however, going so far as to be openly critical of the incident. Still, there can be no doubt as to the intention of the article, and to the paper's position on the sinking: the article's last words describe the cowardly behaviour of the German submarine captain, whom the day after the sinking of *Lars Kruse* had picked up Møller, but later put him in the lifeboat of another torpedoed steamer that the submarine had in tow, and promised to take ashore. Eventually, Møller and the crew of the other steamer were left to their fate at sea.[32]

Moreover, highly indignant poems were published—including in the newspapers—along with novels dealing with the topic. One example is journalist and author Aage Hermann (1888–1949) who worked for the pro-government yellow paper *Ekstrabladet*, and published numerous critical poems there about the war and the situation of the neutral seamen. His poems on this topic were later published in the collection *Krigens Digte* ('The poems of the war') (1915; 2nd rev. 1918). In a poem about the real steamer *Eos*, Hermann used part of a newspaper report about the wrecked ship as a kind of motto or introduction to make the indignant tone of the poem and the grieving wife of the seaman appear the more realistic, and probably also to express fairly open criticism of the war at sea—a technique that was used by other contemporary poets as well. Meanwhile, *Ekstrabladet* printed caustically satirical drawings by the socialist illustrator Anton Hansen about seamen paying the price for the ample and easy money the war profiteers and speculators were making.[33]

Still, the war at sea was only mentioned in minor Danish works,[34] and, to my knowledge, only indirectly in Swedish literature, as in Selma Lagerlöf's *Bannlyst* (1918; *The Outcast*, 1920). Here, the war sporadically appears as seen from the shores of neutral Sweden with uncanny descriptions of the many thousand dead from the Battle of Jutland on 31 May–1 June 1916, floating in their life vests towards Sweden's west coast, used as a symbol of the horror and madness of war. In Norwegian literature, however, the topic was treated more directly in a canonical work: *Vår ære og vår makt* ('Our honour and our power') (1935) by the socialist author and journalist Nordahl Grieg (1902–1943), a play that focus on the hardships suffered by Norwegian seamen and their families during the First World War, effectively contrasted to despicable war profiteers earning millions, not least from the seamen's sufferings. The cynical profiteers for instance greet the news that their ship *Blåeggen* has been torpedoed in the English Channel with the question, Has anybody been killed?—instantly followed by a discussion of the value of the ship and the lucrative insurance payout, meaning that they will earn two million *kroner* by the sinking.[35] At the same time, the profiteering shipowners bemoan the seamen's demands for higher wages and danger money. Grieg's play took its title from Bjørnstjerne Bjørnson's poem 'Norsk sjømandssang' of 1868 ('Norwegian sailor's song'), which declared that the country's honour and power had been brought to it by the white sails of the merchant navy.[36]

In a contemporary example of a critical attitude towards the war against neutral merchantmen, the Norwegian poet Nils Collett Vogt (1864–1937) published the poem 'Et Ord for Dagen' ('A word for the day') in the collection *Hjemkomst* ('Homecoming') (1917). The poem has the date 17 May 1917 as a parenthetical subtitle—Norwegian Constitution Day, which traditionally is celebrated by Norwegians high and low. For Collett, the celebration of his country in the year 1917 is bleak: 'Little do I know to celebrate | in this gory age. | A greeting to those at sea | who are fighting our fight!'[37] As he says in the last verse, he sees the seamen's efforts as a kind of neutral war effort, risking their lives to keep the lines of supply open.

Likewise, two Danish novels published during the war condemned German submarine warfare in angry terms: *Sporløst–!* ('Without a Trace')(1917) by the painter and writer Christian Bogø (1882–1945), and *Hvorfor–? Fortælling fra Undervandsbaads-Krigen* ('Why? A tale from the submarine war') (1918) by the socialist and suffragist Olga Eggers (1875–1945). Bogø, whose father was a sea captain, strongly sympathized with the seamen—in 1922 he wrote the jubilee publication for the Danish seamen's union, *Sømændenes Forbund i Danmark: 1897–1922*—and he continuously criticized the lack of security aboard the ships, not least during the war when the owners and shareholders earned vast profits from the increased freight rates. Hence, a major topic in *Sporløst* is that the ship's owners did not invest in the crew's safety by installing a wireless telegraph on board—a simple measure that would have warned the ship about the German declaration of unrestricted submarine warfare four days prior to its sinking. The same motif was used, though without the stinging critique, in the popular screen version of Bogø and J. Ravn-Jonsen's play *Barken Margrethe af Danmark* (1934), in which one of the seamen's home-made radio saves the ship and her crew in a storm. Furthermore, it was not only a literary theme, but also taken up in a later article by Speerschneider.[38]

In the film *Barken Margrethe af Danmark*, which figures on the Danish Film Institute's top 100,[39] the war is not mentioned despite the fact that it was based on the unpublished light melodrama of the same name; a play that seems to have had the submarine war as its focus. It was given its first performance at Aarhus Teater on 26 December 1918, and a review of the premiere describes the play's topic as 'the conditions of Danish seamen during the world war'.[40] The reviewer, with the appropriately chosen signature '*Tremasteren*' ('The three-master'), writes that he had feared it would be tasteless to take up this serious and tragic topic as the motif for an entertaining melodrama,[41] performed before an overfed Christmas audience, so soon after the tragedies took place. But it succeeded in this delicate balancing act

> if only that in spite of the Christmas goose and the roast pork and all the fun and ornaments, if only that the audience for a single moment would shudder with terror such as the one these sailors has endured, a sense of the honour and glory with which their conduct throughout the war has bedecked the flag and the nation, then the play was justified, and honour was satisfied.[42]

The reviewer seems to have felt a genuine respect for the seamen, which also is reflected by the title of the review: 'Folkekomedien om den danske Sømandshelt' (The melodrama about the Danish naval hero'). One of the songs in the play, Bogø's 'Sømandssang' ('Sea shanty'), uses the same motif as Øvreseth's title, along with the prevalent characterization of the neutral seamen as brave and conscientious, keeping supplies coming to the blockaded countries: 'who came unarmed under fire, so tarred and salty? ... It was the Danish sailors who go on ...'[43]

The 1935–6 serialized version of the story—four booklets illustrated with drawings by Bogø and stills from the film—is also set during the war, at least initially. There are descriptions of German submarine warfare as utterly reprehensible, but also explicit detestation of war profiteers and speculators. When the young hero, the future mate on the bark *Margrethe*, Paul Hansen, visits the stock exchange at Copenhagen, he thinks:

> While the Danish seaman entered the danger zone unarmed or went on duty voyages and risked his life, a crowd of speculators were getting rich here at the stock exchange by speculating in steamship rates. Paul had a vivid sense that in these people's eyes the seaman's blood was not worth any more than the blood that flows when the housewife cuts the head off a fish. A deep disgust seized him.[44]

The play was a big success: first it ran for 41 performances at Aarhus Teater, and then in September 1919 it was put on at Sønderbros Teater in Copenhagen, where it ran for at least 350 performances.[45] Thus, Brinch's complaints that the seamen's efforts during the war were soon forgotten cannot be said to be altogether true. But perhaps he would object to the kind of commemoration offered by sentimental and shallow works such as this play.

Bogø had already treated the war at sea in his début, the adventurous children's book *I Krigens Kølvand* ('In the wake of the war') (1916). In it, the seamen's situation is also treated in a light fashion, as the genre dictates, but the war is evident throughout the book, both because the ship the boy hero, Ole West, mistakenly boards then sails right through the Battle of Jutland, and because West sabotages an Austrian submarine, deviously based at an as yet neutral Greek island. The boy hero's actions against an Austrian vessel reflect the author's attitude towards the belligerents—he was clearly hostile to the Central Powers. This is even more evident in the serious novel *Sporløst*, which came out in November 1917, striking a mercilessly critical note on Germany's unrestricted submarine war even in the title, with its clear reference to the Luxburg affair.[46] The book tells the story of the real steamer *Lars Kruse*, mentioned above, lightly disguised as *Søren Kanne*, by focusing on the surviving engineer, renamed Henrik Mørk.

A review in *Ekstrabladet* said that 'His book is at once a eulogy to the Danish merchant navy and an accusation against those who exploit it to satisfy greedy shareholders,' and that Bogø's realistic art is moving, for instance in the description of the torpedoing of the ship.[47] The accusation against the speculators is evident throughout the book, but with the most chilly effect in the shorter, second part of it, in which Mørk, the sole survivor tells his eerie story to his wife: 'Your memories and my thoughts are going to be the flowers on the graves of those who are no more—!',[48] his wife says. Mørk's narration gets more and more fragmented as he tells his tale about sitting on an overturned lifeboat with 'two mates who had frozen to death by my side',[49] nearly freezing to death himself, thinking the bitterly paradoxical situation through:

> Danish seamen who did not want to go to war because they wanted to be neutral!
> Danish seamen who had been to war.
> But no medals for valour!
> No glory!
> No honour!
> Just duty!
> And thanks!
> From whom?
> From the shipowner?
> From the speculators in 'Tramp'!
> From the Danish people!
> From the Entente, which forced us to do duty voyages between mines and torpedoes, and taunted us for wanting to be neutral!
> From the Central Powers, which torpedo the ships with our mates and sink them ruthlessly!
> Without a trace—![50]

Mørk, his thoughts rambling from cold and horror on his lonely boat, eventually wishes to take an active part in the war: 'Oh, just once to be allowed to wring the neck of one of them, those boys—! But to be forced to sail straight into the arms of death—with two—two Danish flags on the sides and then being shot down like sparrows!'[51] He follows this outburst with the rhetorical question: 'Is that honour?' To suffer passively like they have done? And it is a Scandinavian matter:

> Was it Denmark's honour that was guarded!
> And Norway's!
> And Sweden's!
> Guarded by their seamen!
> And what did they do in return for their seamen?
> Why did they not provide us with jobs and rights, when they call attention to our duty?
> Why do you not protest?
> Aloud, at least a little louder![52]

But, he concludes, the answer to the northern neutrals' feeble protests is that might is right.

This fragmented prose style almost resembles modern poetry, with a tinge of German *O-Mensch* expressionism when Mørk is saved by the submarine that probably torpedoed his ship, and his German saviour says, with the deepest compassion: 'Mensch, wie siehst du aus!' Mørk takes his hand—the hand that possibly killed his crewmates, and thus the book ends on a note of forgiveness.[53]

Olga Eggers's book is even more indignant and strongly anti-German—in 1916 she wrote the book *De derhjemme* ('Those at home'), which is set in Paris and seen from a woman's perspective, and her sympathies are clearly with the Allies. *Hvorfor–?* is likewise written from the viewpoint of women, passively suffering at home while their men are at sea.

'Danes' in the Kaiserliche Marine

Perhaps because of the Danish use of privateers in the wars against Britain in the early 1800s,[54] Danish Schleswigers in the German navy who took part in this kind of warfare were not completely ignored or condemned during the interwar years. There was even some pride taken in their efforts. The journalist Christen P. Christensen (1898–1956) wrote a fairly popular series of fictionalized memoirs

FIGURE 2: Cover illustration of Olga Eggers's *Hvorfor–? Fortælling fra Under-vandsbaads-Krigen* (1918). The sky below the threatening clouds and the striking lightning is a bloody red, as is the drowned seaman—killed by the surfacing U-boat, the illustration seems to say.

of these seamen—*Kejserens sidste Kaperkrydser* ('The Kaiser's last privateer cruiser') (1934) and the sequel *Fire Aar paa Quiriquina* ('Four years at Quiriquina') (1935)—based on the experiences of blacksmith Christian Støckler from Tønder, who had already published his own version of his experiences in eight small books: *Mine Oplevelser* ('My experiences') (1932–3). Støckler sailed with the famous German light cruiser *SMS Dresden*, which took part in the battles at Coronel (1 November 1914) and Falkland (8 December 1914), and was eventually sunk by British cruisers in neutral waters off the Chilean Juan Fernandez Isles on 14 March 1915. Interestingly, Christensen focuses on German and Danish bravery during the battles, and 'the ambition and urge to bring order from chaos which dominates the Northern European' during the internment, as his preface to the second book says,[55] whereas Støckler himself was highly critical of war and militarism. An explanation can be sought in the fact that during the German occupation of Denmark, Christensen came into the open by writing for the Danish Nazi press.

His racist bias and admiration of Germany is also evident in the book *Sønderjyder forsvarer Østafrika 1914–18* (1937) (*Blockade and Jungle*, 1941) about Nis Kock from Sønderborg, who sailed with the German blockade runner *SS Kronborg* to East Africa. The book offers no condemnation of Danish-speaking soldiers being used to run the Allied blockade by sailing under false Danish colours—*SS Kronborg* was really the British cargo ship *SS Rubens*, which had been seized by Germany at the outbreak of war and turned into a 'Danish' ship.[56] The crew of this ship were handpicked, Danish-speaking soldiers from Northern Schleswig. It left Wilhelmshaven on 18 February 1915, going north of The Faroe Islands to run the blockade, with coal and ammunition for Lettow-Vorbeck's troops in East Africa and for the cruiser *SMS Königsberg*, blockaded by British men-of-war in Tanganyika. Here, *Kronborg* eventually was attacked and sunk by the British. Kock survived and took part in Lettow-Vorbeck's adventurous African campaign, until he wound up in a POW camp in Egypt.

Whereas Christensen's version of Kock's story sold fairly well even in the late 1930s—it was reissued five times—Danes who had served in the German submarines quite understandably did not publish their memoirs in post-war, reunited Denmark. Their war experiences were not included in the story about the Danes in the German army, fighting for a cause that was not their own, as the prevailing collective narrative about the Northern Schleswigers' participation in the war would have it.[57] Yet, at least one example does exist: Johannes Ingwersen's short description of his time with *UE19*: 'Admiralitetet melder *"UE 19" er ikke vendt tilbage!*' ('The Admiralty announces: *"UE 19" has not returned!*'), published in the 1956 yearbook of the Northern Schleswigers' veterans' organization.[58] Ingwersen does not, however, tell a story about sinking Allied or neutral vessels, but instead a rather innocent though highly dramatic story about an accident that happened to his submarine and led to its capture by the British. In the middle of June 1917, when *UE 19* was patrolling off the east coast of England, it hit and got stuck in the hull of a wreck while submerged. Ingwersen was ordered to crawl out of one of the torpedo tubes to find out why the boat cannot surface. Sitting on the wreck, stark naked, and enjoying the nice weather for a moment while he tries to find out how to rescue his comrades below, he notices a fishing boat and signals to it. When it arrives, it emerges that it is a camouflaged warship, and submarine and crew are taken prisoner—one of the crew of the British ship is actually Danish, for which the story does not offer explanation. The story ends with a sarcastic comment on German heroism, as represented by German newspapers' reports of the incident: 'After an heroic battle with the enemy, submarine E-19 has not returned!' Ingwersen's approach to his wartime experiences, of course, may be instances of rationalizing and of his need to distance himself from the submarines' poor reputation in neutral Denmark, especially as shown by his choice of telling this comparatively innocent story.

Commemoration and popular memory

The Danish monument for its seamen killed during the war was dedicated in May 1928, nearly a decade after the armistice. The critical voices—claiming that bread would have been preferred to stones, and that the survivors were still suffering in order to make a living—

could also have pointed to the rather belated commemoration. Still, the monument had been in preparation since 1923, but questions of its design postponed its realization. The Norwegian monument: *Minnehallen* at Stavern was dedicated nearly two years earlier on 1 August 1926.[59] The crypt of the memory hall contains eleven tablets with the names of 1,892 perished seamen, and later the names of the casualties in the Second World War were added: no fewer than 5,670 names. The crypt furthermore contains the poem Hermann Wildenvey (1885–1959) wrote to the seamen, written for the monument in 1926, which strikes a note similar to Øvreseth's later title: 'Without sword, without weapon, | without the edge of enmity | they kept open the road at sea | for the Norwegian flag.'[60] And in the last stanza of the poem, he calls the seamen 'warriors of peace', echoing the widespread Scandinavian self-perception of being of a more enlightened, rational, and peaceful breed than the belligerents.

The Swedish *Sjömanstornet*—the Seamen's Tower—in Gothenburg was dedicated on 14 July 1933, nearly seven years after *Minnehallen*, commemorating 684 Swedish seamen, 36 of whom were women, who lost their lives on Swedish ships during the war, and whose names are inscribed on the base of the tower;[61] 103 foreigners lost their lives, most of whom were Scandinavians, but also Russians, Germans, Americans, Greeks, and at least one Arab, yet these foreigners and the 434 Swedes who were killed aboard foreign ships are not commemorated by the monument.

As for the belatedness of the Danish monument, even the British *Mercantile Marine Memorial* on Tower Hill, London, was dedicated later—on 12 December 1928—so the amount of time spent on creating the monument was not unusual. And, as was the case with the official Danish monument for the soldiers who fought for Germany and the Allies, dedicated in 1934, local monuments had already been erected for the killed seamen at Fanø, Marstal, Hirtshals, and other seaports. Still, the dilapidated state of the monument at Copenhagen—at least until its restoration in 2011—in many ways reflects the commemoration of the seamen's efforts during the war.

One explanation for the neglect of the merchant seamen's efforts and sacrifices in the war might be their transnational character.

After all, the Danish monument to the seamen does not only commemorate Danes, but also seamen from many other nations. This, in the still highly nationalistic interwar era, probably did not sit well with the bias of collective memory. Another possible explanation is the very nature of sailing: the sea was an extremely dangerous place to work, even without the additional dangers of war. The British historian F. J. Lindop has calculated the death rate in the period 1901–10 as 1 in 76 for sailing ships and 1 in 163 for steam, making seafaring under sail 'roughly four times more dangerous than coalmining.'[62] Seamen were used to working under dangerous conditions, without necessarily being classified as heroes.

A further explanation is connected to the dishonourable and shameful aspects of earning money from other people's misery: the fact that, taken as a whole, the neutrals made a fortune out of the war without actively participating. This side of the war has left it predominantly remembered as the stalking-ground of the *nouveau riche* war profiteer: *gullaschbaronen*—the goulash baron—even became a popular topos in the Scandinavian light literature and cabaret of the day. In Norway, Johan Falkberget's bestseller *Bør Børson jr.* (1920), is not completely forgotten; the Swedish examples, which were the most numerous, included Henning Berger's *Gulaschbaronerna* ('The goulash barons') (1916) about wartime Copenhagen (where the author had lived for several years), which was serialized in the largest Danish newspaper at the time, *Politiken*; and in Denmark, the earliest example was Palle Rosenkrantz's *Gullasch-Hansens Rejse til Petrograd under Verdenskrigen* ('Goulash-Hansen's journey to Petrograd during the Great War') (1915), while the same year the cabaret singer Frederik Jensen's hit 'Gullask!'[63] gave a humorous recipe for the foul slop that gave the war profiteers their Scandinavia-wide sobriquet. Even in the late 1920s and early 1930s the topos continued to appear in Danish literature, from a canonical writer's work, Martin Andersen Nexø's *Midt i en Jærntid* (1929) (*In God's Country*, 1930), to one of the more popular entertaining examples, Niels Kjøngsdal's *Bankegaarden* (1931). The novel by this forgotten author has the subtitle 'A Novel from the Age of Goulash', indicating its evergreen status: even so soon after the war, the goulash baron had become its dominant memory in the Scandinavian countries, even giving the period its name, leaving little or no space for the seamen's sacrifices.

Wartime speculation was closely linked to the sea, of course, as the shares of steamship and other shipping companies were among the most profitable. Danish steamship shares peaked at an astonishing 632 in October 1916 (1 July 1914 = 100), whereas another usually profitable business, banking, only reached 186, in October 1918.[64] In satire and literature, speculation was often linked to the cynicism of profiteers more concerned with insurance payouts than the fate of the seamen on ships that foundered, of which especially Grieg's play is an example. However, there were also other views on this side to neutrality: take the shipowner, poet, and patron of the arts Hugo Marx Nielsen, complaining about the shipowners' reputation in Christian Bogø's magazine *Viking*:

> In literature and melodrama, the shipowner has almost always suffered the sorry fate of acting the villain;—God knows why,—but there is hardly a mean trick played on the poor man and the seaman that is not ascribed to him, and thus he has entered the public mind as a necessary appendage to a cold and calculating brain. No wonder then, that he was regarded as a bloodsucker during the war, latching onto the work of the poor without doing anything but count the gold that poured into his lap.[65]

By the end of 1924, the shipowners, profiteers, or goulash barons had already become the scapegoats for what happened during the war in the neutral countries, whereas, at least in Denmark, the role of passive sufferer had been filled by the many 'real' victims of war: the soldiers from Northern Schleswig who had been forced to fight for the old enemy, and now had become a rather paradoxical element in the reunited country. Still, despite the fact that the First World War has not played a significant role in Scandinavian historiography and literary history, and the war at sea even less so, there was still indignant literature being written about the treatment of the neutral seamen.

Notes

1 The article is principally based on my Ph.D. dissertation, 'Mellem Fronterne. Studier i Første Verdenskrigs virkning på og udtryk i dansk kultur, med særligt fokus på litterære skildringer, 1914–1939' (University of Southern Denmark, 2011).

2 The short article about the dedication in *Social-Demokraten*, 10 May 1928, 3, reverses this list and mentions the relatives of the victims first. For the history of the monument, see Jens Peter Munk, '"At gøre sin Pligt, om saa Døden træder i vejen": Søfartsmonumentet på Langelinie', in Årbog. Handels- og Søfartsmuseet på Kronborg, 70 (2011), 9–42.

3 See, for example, *Medlemsblad for den alm. danske Skibsførerforening*, 19/5 (May 1928), column 144. The reason that the Icelandic seamen are mentioned second, thus breaching the numeral logic of the list, was probably that they were Danish citizens at the time.

4 See, for example, *Nationaltidende*, 9 May 1928, evening issue, and 10 May 1928, morning issue, or *Politiken*, 10 May 1928.

5 *Ekstrabladet*, 9 May 1928, 1.

6 The magazine of the Danish Seamen's Union (Sømændenes Forbund i Danmark), *Ny Tid*, 22/4 (April 1928), n.p., 'Tanken om et Monument kan være meget pæn, men paa Baggrund af Nøden blandt danske Sømænd, er det dog Sten for Brød.'

7 The figures vary: 128 in most sources, 127 in Gerhard Hirschfeld, Gerd Krumeich & Irina Renz (eds.), *Enzyklopädie Erster Weltkrieg* (Paderborn: Ferdinand Schöningh, 2009), 689.

8 Wilhelm Keilhau, 'Norway and the World War', in James T. Shotwell (ed.), *Sweden, Norway, Denmark and Iceland in the World War* (New Haven: Yale University Press, 1930), 360. It is not quite clear if the disappeared and condemned ships are included in the 49.3 per cent. See also *Sjøforklaringer over norske skibes krigsforlis*, v (Oslo, 1918), preface & 96–7; and Atle Thowsen, *Bergen og sjøfarten*, iv (Bergen: Bergens Rederiforening og Bergens Sjøfartsmuseum, 1983), 560–1.

9 Ibid.

10 The Norwegian monument for the seamen gives the number 1,892, see below.

11 *Samling af Søforklaringer over krigsforliste danske Skibe i Aarene 1914–1918 med et Tillæg*, (Copenhagen, 1921), Tables A and B in the appendix; C. Bloch, 'Danmark under Verdenskrigen' in 'Verdenskrigen', *Salmonsens Konversationsleksikon* (2nd edn., Copenhagen: J. H. Schultz, 1928), xxiv, 873.

12 *Svenska handelsflottans krigsförluster åren 1914–1920* (Stockholm, 1921), 117; and A. Örnberg, 'Världskriget' ('Kriget till sjöss'), *Nordisk Familjebok*, ed. Yngve Lorents (3rd edn., Stockholm: Aktiebolaget Familjebokens Förlag,

1934), xx. column 911–2. C. Ernest Fayle, *Seaborne Trade* (London: John Murray, 1924), iii. 466 gives 1,180,316 GRT for the Norwegian losses, 243,707 for the Danish, and 201,366 GRT for the Swedish, figures also used by Franklin D. Scott, *The United States and Scandinavia* (Cambridge, Mass.: Harvard University Press, 1950), 218.

13 Substantially higher: 7,830,855 GRT; see Fayle 1924, 466.

14 Keilhau 1930, 360.

15 The use of a German phrase for this side of the war, even today—see, for example, Stephen Pope & Elizabeth-Anne Wheal, *The Macmillan Dictionary of The First World War* (London: Macmillan, 1995)—gives a clear hint at an answer to this question, at least regarding the Anglo-Saxon parts of the world and as seen from an Allied point of view.

16 Franklin D. Scott, *Sweden: The Nation's History* (Minneapolis: University of Minnesota Press, 1977), 471.

17 Ibid.

18 See Lance Edwin Davis & Stanley L. Engerman, *Naval Blockades in Peace and War: An Economic History since 1750* (Cambridge: CUP, 2006), 13.

19 Ibid.

20 See C. I. Speerschneider, 'Vor Handelsskibsfart under Verdenskrigen', *Tidsskrift for Søvæsen*, 91 (1920), 56.

21 Speerschneider 1920, 114, 'Stor Anerkendelse har han [sømanden] dog aldrig vundet, men det er ikke hans Skyld og Skam, at det er saa. Det er Samfundets Skyld, vort overintelligente, æstetiserende og for Livets virkelige Værdier slappede Samfund, der ikke har forstaaet i hvilken Taknemmelighedsgæld det staar til vor Sømandsstand, og som i sin stadig blomstrende honette Ambition rynker paa Næsen ad den jævne Sømand, der har det forud for det meste Hankøn paa Landjorden, at han har set Verden og Livet og er en Mand.'

22 N. Th. Brinch, *En dansk Skibsførers Rejser i Farezonen under Verdenskrigen Juli 1914—Oktober 1918* (Esbjerg: no publisher given, 1938), 4, 'Ingen Hæder ventede ham, ingen eller maaske kun faa forstod ham. Naturligvis maatte Sømanden gøre sin Pligt, men kun faa havde klart Syn for hans store Indsats under Verdenskrigen, maaske den vægtigste Indsats, som blev ydet. Men da Krigen sluttede, havde de krigsførende glemt ham, og Landbefolkningen havde næppe bemærket ham.'

23 Brinch 1938, 38, 'Var det for Fædrelandets Skyld de faldt? Nej, saa vilde de senere være blevet hædret og lovprist. De førte end ikke Fornødenheder til deres Fædreland, thi de var timechartret, ligesom vi og saa mange andre … Dette var den danske Sømandsstands Indsats i den store Verdenskrig, den eneste direkte Indsats, som blev ydet af danske Stænder.'

24 Ibid. 37.

25 I. Øvreseth, *Vi som var våbenløse: en skibsførers erindringer fra krigstiden 1914–18* (Oslo: Aschehoug, 1932), 16.
26 Speerschneider 1920, 108.
27 Cf. Pope & Wheal 1995, 381. Here, no mention of the use of neutral colours is made.
28 The war at sea predictably played a central part in the propaganda war in the neutral countries—see, for example, the translation of William Archer's *The Pirate's Progress* (1918): *Sørøverens Færd* (Copenhagen: Pio, 1918) and parts of his polemics against the Danish critic Georg Brandes; or, in a different genre, the German submarine captain von Spiegel's diary, which sold fairly well in the Norwegian translation, *'U 202' Krigsdagbok* (Kristiania: Aschehoug, 1917).
29 Even though there did exist a Danish steamer by the same name, owned by DFDS, the ship on the magazine's cover probably is the famous Norwegian steamer—Henry Ford's ill-fated peace ship. For the Danish steamer, see <http://www.maritime-museum.dk/videnscenter/documents/1917.pdf>, accessed 2 June 2012.
30 'En af dem, der sejler Pengene ind'.
31 See *Samling af Søforklaringer over krigsforliste danske Skibe i Aarene 1914–1918 med et Tillæg* (Copenhagen, 1921), 271–5.
32 *Vort Land*, 13 February 1917, 4; see Bendtsen 2011, 198.
33 See Anton Hansen's memoirs, *Ung kunstner* (Copenhagen: Fremad, 1954), 151–5.
34 One recent Danish bestseller, Carsten Jensen's *Vi, de druknede* (2006; *We, the Drowned*, 2010), treats the seamen's war experiences thoroughly.
35 Nordahl Grieg, *Samlede verker*, iv (Oslo: Gyldendal Norsk Forlag, 1947), 310.
36 'vor ære og vor magt | har hvide seil os bragt.'
37 'Litet jeg vet at feste for | i denne bloddryppende Tid. | En Hilsen til dem, som paa Havet | kjæmper vor Strid!'
38 C. I. H. Speerschneider, 'Den danske Skibsfart under Verdenskrigen', in P. A. Rosenberg (ed.), *Verdenskrigen 1914–1918 og Tiden der fulgte*, xi (Copenhagen: Forlaget Danmark, 1935), 142–3.
39 See <http://www.dfi.dk/faktaomfilm/nationalfilmografien/nffilm.aspx?id=14428>, accessed 1 April 2012. Unfortunately, there is no information as to an actual position on the list, or the number of tickets sold, etc.
40 *Aarhus Stiftstidende*, 27 December 1918, 'et Emne som danske Sømænds Kaar under Verdenskrigen.'
41 '*Folkekomedie*' has less tragic connotations than melodrama.
42 *Aarhus Stiftstidende*, 27 December 1918, 'naar blot der trods Julegaas og Flæskesteg og alle Løjerne og Staffagen, naar blot der et eneste Øjeblik

vilde gaa et Gys gennem Tilskuerne, en isnende Følelse af den Rædsel, disse Søgutter har gennemgaaet, en Fornemmelse af den Hæder og Ære, de ved deres Optræden hele Krigen igennem har dækket Flag og Folk med, saa fik Folkeskuespillet sin Berettigelse, og saa var Æren reddet.'

43 Christian Bogø & J. Ravn-Jonsen, *Sangene af Folkeskuespillet Barken Margrethe af Danmark* (Copenhagen: Wilhelm Hansen Musik Forlag, 1919), 6–7, 'hvem stod vaabenløs for Skud, saa tjærede og salte? ... Det var de danske Sømænd, som gaar paa.'

44 Christian Bogø & J. Ravn-Jonsen, *Barken Margrethe af Danmark* (Copenhagen: Vikingens Forlag, 1935–6), 16, 'Medens den danske Sømand vaabenløs gik i Farezone eller i Pligtrejse og vovede sit Liv, stod her paa Københavns Børs ... en Flok Spekulanter og tjente sig rige ved at jobbe med Skibskurserne. Paul havde en levende Følelse af, at Sømandens Blod i disse Menneskers Øjne ikke var mere værd end det, der flyder, naar Husmoderen skærer Hovedet af en Fisk. En dyb Væmmelse bemægtigede sig ham'.

45 According to Bogø's magazine *Vikingen*, 1/3 (1925), 50–51 announcing a new production, noting that it had run for about 1,000 performances in Denmark thus far. Supposedly, it had run for more than 2,000 performances in Denmark and Sweden (see <http://www.danskefilm.dk/index2.html>, accessed 31 March 2012).

46 The telegram about Argentinean steamers sunk without trace—an affair that threatened to drag Sweden into the war (see Steven Koblik, *Sweden: The Neutral Victor* (Lund: Läromedelsförlagen, 1972), 95–130).

47 *Ekstrabladet*, 30 November 1917, 3, 'Hans Bog er paa én Gang en Lovsang til den danske Handelsmarine og en Anklage imod dem, der udnytter den til graadige Aktionæreres Tilfredsstillelse, og han hæver sig f. Eks. i Skildringen af Torpederingen til en Højde af realistisk Kunst, som virker betagende.' Actually, there was no proof that the ship was torpedoed; it might also have struck a mine.

48 Christian Bogø, *Sporløst –!* (Copenhagen: P. H. Fergo, 1917), 160, 'Dine Minder og mine Tanker skal være Blomsterne paa deres Grave, som ikke er mere – !'

49 Bogø 1917, 196, 'To ihjelfrosne Kammerater ved Siden'.

50 'Tramp' was the shipping company he worked for; Bogø 1917, 196–7, 'Danske Sømænd, der ikke vilde i Krig, fordi de vilde være neutrale! | Danske Sømænd, der havde været i Krig. | Men ingen Tapperhedstegn! | Ingen Hæder! | Ingen Ære! | Kun Pligt! | Og Tak! | Fra hvem? | Fra Rhederne? | Fra Spekulanterne i 'Tramp' [rederiet, han sejlede for]! | Fra Danmarks Folk! | Fra Ententen, der tvang os til Pligtrejser mellem Miner og Torpedoer, og haanede os, fordi vi vilde være neutrale! | Fra Centralmagterne, som torpederer Skibene med Kammeraterne og sænker dem Skaanselsløst! | Sporløst –! – '

51 Bogø 1917, 197, 'Aah, bare een Gang at faa Lov til at dreje Halsen om paa een af dem, disse Drenge –! Men dette at skulle sejle lige lukt ind i Dødens Arme – med to – to Dannebrogsflag paa Siden og saa blive skudt ned som Graaspurve.'

52 Bogø 1917, 197, 'Var det Danmarks Ære, der værnedes? | Og Norges! | Og Sverrigs! | Værgedes af deres Søfolk! | Og hvad gjorde de til Gengæld for deres Søfolk? | Hvorfor skaffede man os ikke vor Plads og Ret, naar man paataler vor Pligt? | Hvorfor protesterer I ikke? | Højt, i hvert Fald højere!'

53 Bogø 1917, 200.

54 Parallels were drawn with the early 1800s by, for example, the stockbroker Alfred Horwitz, *Pengeoverflodens Udskejelser i Fortid og Nutid* (Copenhagen: Nyt Nordisk Forlag, 1917), 10–22.

55 Chr. P. Christensen, *Fire Aar paa Quiriquina* (Copenhagen: Martins Forlag, 1935), 6, 'den Opdrift og Trang til at bringe Orden i Kaos, der behersker Nordeuropæeren'.

56 The Germans also sailed under Norwegian flag, for example to disguise the auxiliary cruiser *Greif* that was sunk in battle with the British armoured ship *Alcantara* on 29 February 1916 (see Knut Utstein Kloster, *Krigsår og gullflom. Skibsfarten under verdenskrigen* (Oslo: Gyldendal Norsk Forlag, 1935), facing 112; and <http://www.history.com/this-day-in-history/two-ships-sink-in-north-sea-battle>, accessed 2 June 2012).

57 See, for example, the inscription at the entrance of the official Danish monument for the war dead, *Marselisborgmonumentet* in Aarhus; Bendtsen, 'Marselisborgmonumentets mytekonstruktion', *1066 Tidsskrift for Historie*, 38/2 (June 2008), 3–12.

58 Foreningen af Dansksindede sønderjydske Krigsdeltagere (Society of Danish-minded Northern Schleswig Veterans), *D.S.K. Aarbog* (1956), 38–47.

59 See the long article on 'Minnehallens indvielse', *Aftenposten*, 2 August 1926.

60 'Uten verge, uten våpen, | uten avinds agg | holdt de vei på bølgen åpen | for det norske flagg.'

61 <http://www.goteborg.se/wps/portal/sjofartsmuseet>, accessed 2 June 2012.

62 See Tony Lane, 'The British Merchant Seaman at War', in Hugh Cecil & Peter H. Liddle (eds.) *Facing Armageddon. The First World War Experienced* (London: Leo Cooper, 1996), 159.

63 The spelling was not yet agreed on.

64 Einar Cohn, 'Denmark in the Great War', in James T. Shotwell (ed.), *Sweden, Norway, Denmark and Iceland in the World War* (New Haven: Yale University Press, 1930), 557.

65 Hugo Marx Nielsen, 'Skibsfarten og Rederne', *Viking. Havets, Havnens, Handelens og Hjemmets illustrerede Magasin*, 1/2 (December 1924), 9, 'Skibsrederen har i Litteraturen og i Folkekomedierne næsten altid haft den kranke Skæbne at skulle spille Skurk; – Guderne maa vide hvorfor, – men der er næsten ikke den Nedrighed overfor Fattigmand og Sømand, der ikke er tillagt ham og derigennem er gaaet ind i Befolkningens Bevidsthed som et nødvendigt Appendix til en kold og beregnende Hjerne. Intet Under derfor, at han under Krigen blev betragtet som en Blodsuger, der mæskede sig ved Fattigmands Arbejde uden selv at bestille andet end at tælle det Guld, der regnede ned i hans Skød.'

About the authors

Claes Ahlund is Professor of Comparative Literature at Åbo Akademi University, Finland. His published work includes two monographs on Swedish literature and the First World War: *Diktare i krig* ('Poets at war', 2007), on political poetry; and *Underhållning och propaganda* ('Entertainment and propaganda', 2010), on popular war novels.

Gunnar Åselius is Professor of Military History at the National Defence College, Stockholm. He has written on the image of Russia among Swedish security elites before 1914, Soviet naval strategy in the Baltic Sea during the interwar years, and on various aspects of the Cold War and the Swedish army during the nineteenth and twentieth centuries, including the role of history in the education of military officers.

Bjarne Søndergaard Bendtsen is External Lecturer in History at Aarhus University. His Ph.D. thesis (University of Southern Denmark, 2011) deals with Denmark and the First World War: *Mellem fronterne. Studier i Første Verdenskrigs virkning på og udtryk i dansk kultur* ('Between the lines: the First World War and Danish culture').

Nik. Brandal is a postgraduate research student at the Department of Archaeology, Conservation and History at the University of Oslo, Norway. His main research interest is political extremism. He is currently working on a project comparing the radicalization of the student Left in West Germany and the US in the 1960s, as well as a history of Norwegian volunteers in the First World War.

Eirik Brazier is a Ph.D. Candidate at the European University Institute in Florence, Italy. His particular fields of interest include cultural aspects of military cooperation in the British Empire, intelligence history, and the legal purge in Norway after the Second World War. He is currently involved in a project that examines Norwegian participation in the First World War.

Claus Bundgård Christensen is Associate Professor of History at Roskilde University, Denmark. He has published three books on the First World War: *Danskere på vestfronten 1914–1918* ('Danes on the Western Front 1914–1918', 2009); *Krestens breve 1914–18* ('Kresten's letters 1914–18', 2012); and *Verdenskrigens danske billeder* ('Danish images of the Great War', 2012). He is currently working on a book about the Waffen-SS.

Anne Hedén is a historian and journalist, and is currently working as a lecturer in history at Stockholm University, Sweden. Her principal research interest is the development of political and social movements, and the prerequisites and conditions that create political activism.

Rolf Hobson is senior researcher at the Norwegian Institute for Defence Studies, Oslo. He has specialized in German history, and has also worked in the fields of European political history and the history of international law. His publications include a survey, in Norwegian, of the 'war and society' approach to international history, and *Imperialism at Sea. Naval Strategic Thought, the Ideology of Sea Power and the Tirpitz Plan, 1875–1914* (2004).

Tom Kristiansen is Professor of History at the Norwegian Institute for Defence Studies, Oslo. He has written extensively on Scandinavian diplomatic, naval, and military history in the first half of the twentieth century, with particular focus on the relations between Scandinavia and the great powers, and Anglo-Norwegian relations. His latest book is a history of the Norwegian navy in the period 1905–1960, *Sjøforsvaret i krig og fred. Langs kysten og på havet gjennom 200 år*, ii: S*elvstendig og alliert i krig og fred* (2010).

Ulrik Lehrmann is Associate Professor at the Institute for the Study of Culture at the University of Southern Denmark, Odense. His research has focussed on socially distributed reading cultures in the nineteenth century, the history of media and journalism 1860–1950, and crime journalism in the popular press. He has contributed to *Dansk mediehistorie* ('Danish Media History'), 1–3 (1996–7) and has published on literary and media topics in Danish periodicals.

Anna Nordlund is Associate Senior Lecturer at Uppsala University, Sweden. Following her Ph.D. in comparative literature, her research has primarily addressed the outward conditions and expression of the Swedish author Selma Lagerlöf's success in the emerging media market of the nineteenth and early twentieth centuries, combining sociological and materialistic viewpoints with analyses of style and narration.

Sofi Qvarnström is Associate Senior Lecturer in Rhetoric at Lund University, Sweden. She is currently working on a project entitled 'The forest as promise, sacrifice and memory. Representations of Norrland and the industrialization process in Swedish fiction 1880–1920'.

Per Jostein Ringsby has a Ph.D. in history at the Department of Archaeology, Conservation and History at the University of Oslo, Norway. He wrote his thesis on Scandinavian peace associations in the late nineteenth and early twentieth centuries.

Gjermund Forfang Rongved is a postgraduate research student at the Department of Archaeology, Conservation and History at the University of Oslo, Norway. His thesis will analyse Norway's monetary and financial policy during the First World War.

Lina Sturfelt is Associate Senior Lecturer in Human Rights Studies at Lund University, Sweden. Her research interests include the cultural history of war (especially the First World War), military history, media narratives, national identity formation, and human rights discourses in a historical perspective. She is currently working on a project about colonial, national, and racist discourses in Swedish peacekeeping during the Cold War.

Nils Arne Sørensen is Professor of Contemporary European History at the University of Southern Denmark, Odense. He has specialized in identity politics, and comparative and transnational history, and has published on such topics as fascism, memory culture, public history, Americanization, and the First World War. He is the author of *Den Store Krig: Europæernes første verdenskrig* ('The Great War: the First World War of the Europeans', 2005).

Ola Teige is postdoctoral research fellow at the Department of History at the University of Oslo, Norway. His main research interests are Scandinavian social, military and political history in the period 1660–1850, particularly the local elites and their social networks, and Norwegian participation in World War One. He is currently working on a project on corruption in Norway in the late eighteenth and early nineteenth centuries in a comparative perspective, and a history of Norwegian volunteers in World War One.

Index